# Foreword

The non-executive role is an increasingly challenging one. Having been an active board member for many years I have witnessed at first hand the increase in the scope of the job and the commitment required. The expectations of investors, the media and regulators, and the demands of code-writers, have risen sharply. As a consequence the need for those taking on the role to be fully informed as to best practice has never been greater.

As Chairman of 3i, Europe's leading venture capital company, I know how our business thrives on having high quality boards in the companies we back. To enhance these, we created 3i's Independent Directors Programme, which Patrick Dunne has done so much to develop. Today 3i has become a leader in the provision and development of chairmen and directors for high-growth businesses. Our approach has been based on two premises. First, that 'better boards will make us (and those we back) more money'; and second, that 'chairmen and independent directors who add real value attract more respect, and so are better able to ensure appropriate governance'.

I have had the pleasure to work with some excellent non-executives in a broad range of businesses, from fledgling start ups to FTSE-100 worldwide companies. It has become increasingly clear to me that the defining qualities of good independent directors relate to their knowledge, judgement and influencing skills.

This book, which captures current best practice, is a most welcome addition to the Non- executive director's bank of knowledge.

Baroness Hogg

Chairman 3i Group PLC

# About the Authors

## Glynis D Morris BA, FCA

After taking an Honours degree in German Language and Literature at the University of Manchester, Glynis Morris trained with KPMG in Leeds and qualified as a chartered accountant in 1979. She spent 20 years with the firm, working in their offices in Leeds, London and Cambridge and gaining wide experience of both listed companies and groups and smaller private businesses. She specialised in technical and research work for a number of years, developing technical material for internal use and also for distribution to clients, and speaking regularly at conferences on accounting and company law issues. She became a partner in the firm in 1991, with a particular expertise in work in the education and charity sectors.

She left KPMG to set up her own practice near Cambridge in January 1996 and now provides accounting, audit and tax services to range of local clients as well as writing and lecturing extensively on accounting, auditing, company law and corporate governance issues.

She is the author of Tolley's Manual of Accounting and Tolley's Finance Director's Handbook and a regular contributor to a number of other LexisNexis publications.

## Patrick Dunne, Director 3i plc

Patrick is responsible for 3i's marketing world wide as well as its Chief Executive and Independent Director Programmes. 3i is a FTSE100 company and a leading international venture capital company with 36 locations in Europe, Asia Pacific and the US.

It has a long record of successfully backing entrepreneurial teams to start ups, grow existing businesses undertake buyouts and buy ins. Patrick joined in 1985 and has had a wide and varied career in 3i, doing deals and building up their MBI activity in Europe and more recently as part of the senior team.

He is a regular speaker and commentator on boardroom issues including 'Managing Board Disharmony'. His first book 'Running Board Meetings', published in 1997, received wide acclaim and is now in its second edition. The second, 'Directors Dilemmas', has been described by Sir John Harvey Jones as 'a major contribution to the thinking Director's education'.

Before joining 3i he spent time in the chemical industry with Air Products and at Cranfield getting his MBA. He is a Visiting Fellow at Cranfield School of Management, a regular columnist for Management Today, a member of the professional standards and communications committee of the European

Venture Capital association and a Trustee of the charity LEAP – Confronting conflict.

# Disclaimer

Whilst every care has been taken to ensure the accuracy of the contents of this work, no responsibility for any loss occasioned to any person acting or refraining from action as a result of any statement or examples in it can be accepted by any of the authors or the publisher.

# Contents

# Contents

# Contents

# Contents

*Contents*

# Contents

Contents

# Introduction

As Baroness Hogg has said in her foreword, the role of the non-executive has become ever more demanding and a quick scan through our list of contents bears this out. To be an effective non-executive requires a high level of judgement and skill and an increasing amount of knowledge. The aim of this book is to provide a comprehensive reference point for non executives no matter how experienced they are.

Throughout the book we will refer to the simple model of board effectiveness below

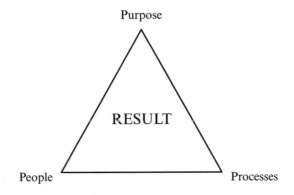

This model was developed by one of the authors as a process for increasing effectiveness in underperforming boards.

The premise of the model is that any board can increase its effectiveness by considering these three fundamental aspects. In high performing boards all members are clear on what the purpose of the board is, the membership of the board fits that purpose and the board has good processes in place to ensure it has the right strategy, the right resources and the right governance.

It is a good challenge for any prospective non-executive to question the current state of the board they are considering joining and also how they may be able to contribute in enhancing the performance of the Board as well as the company.

We have researched widely to discover latest best practice and drawn heavily on the leading surveys in the field, most notably in the UK, the Top Pay/3i Independent Chairman and Non-Executive director survey, and in the US, Korn/Ferry's Annual Board of Directors Study, as well as reviewing the many excellent guidance notes from organisations such as the Institute of Chartered Secretaries and Administrators and the National Association of Pension Funds.

The book was written at the same time as the Government's review of the role and effectiveness of non-executives was taking place. Publication was delayed to ensure that the guidance contained in the book was consistent and also to provide some views on the implications of the Higgs' review.

Whilst the book has been written with UK directors principally in mind we believe the principles covered are applicable internationally. However we have also included a brief summary of the major differences in the way that boards operate in different countries.

# 1. The Appointment Process for Non-Executives

## Introduction                                                            1.1

## At a glance                                                             1.2

> - The role of non-executive director must be clear and agreed before inviting candidates to apply.
> - The new non-executive needs to be prepared for the workload that awaits them, and should consider any training and development opportunities available.
> - The board should follow a standard process for recruiting a non-executive, and be rigorous in their assessment.
> - Hiring a non-executive should be followed up by a thorough induction and review process.

The appointment process of any new board member must be considered in the context of the board as a whole and take into account the specifics of the particular organisation involved. It also needs to be considered from the perspectives of the company, the non-executive, other board members and shareholders.

From the company's point of view the process is usually:

- agreement of the role;

- commitment to a selection and appointment process; and
- execution of that process up to and including the induction of the new board member.

From the prospective non-executive's perspective the process is:

- response to an approach from a company or a company's adviser;
- initial familiarisation and agreement to take part in the selection process;
- if selected, detailed due diligence;
- formal appointment; and
- induction.

For shareholders in public companies who aren't on the board the process has traditionally been very straightforward and limited to formally agreeing to the resolution to appoint the person.

In order to comply with the Combined Code the boards of listed companies must ensure that the process is 'formal and transparent'. However the reality has been that shareholders, other than those who are directors, have had little or no input to the appointment process, other than in situations of crisis. Indeed, research conducted for the Higgs Review (see **CHAPTER 6**) led to the view that 'a high degree of informality surrounds the process of appointing non-executive directors. Almost half of the non-executive directors surveyed for the Review were recruited to their role through personal contacts or friendships. Only four per cent had had a formal interview, and one per cent had obtained their job through answering an advertisement.'

Quite the opposite is true in venture capital backed private businesses where the VCs traditionally play an active role in the appointment of directors. In other private companies the key shareholders are normally involved as described above for the company.

At this stage matters will be kept simple by considering the issues with regard to a single appointment in a public company and going through the process comprehensively from the company's point of view.

Issues relating to multiple appointments at the same time are dealt with in **PARAGRAPH 1.9**. Private companies can easily adapt the process described omitting the obvious steps which a public company must take simply because it is listed. Looking at the process from the company's point of view is beneficial to the non-executive, especially if they also sit on a nominations committee, but some issues for prospective non-executives and candidates for specific appointments have also been added at the end.

If there is an effective nominations committee (see **CHAPTER 16 NOMINATIONS COMMITTEE**) then it is this group which is likely to be delegated to undertake or lead all of the above tasks. The remainder of the board then simply needs to endorse or refine their recommendations and support the process.

If there isn't a nominations committee of the board then it is well worth considering forming one on a temporary basis for the particular appointment. The principles of a good nominations committee are easily adapted to small companies.

## Agreeing the role                                              1.3

If the role of the board is clear then defining the role of the non-executive becomes a relatively straightforward task. A good place to start, if you the basic description of the role of the board is accepted as being:

- right strategy:
  to ensure that there is the right strategy for the ownership as well as the business, that it is being implemented and monitored and that there is a good process for formulating and adapting it;
- right resources:
  to ensure that the organisation has the right resources in place to meet the agreed strategy for the business and its ownership. The most important of these resources relate to people and money;
- right governance:
  to ensure appropriate corporate governance.

is to consider what role it is intended that the non-executive should play in each of the above. The Higgs Review came up with a broadly similar definition.

---

### The role of the board

The board is collectively responsible for promoting the success of the company by directing and supervising the company's affairs.

The board's role is to provide entrepreneurial leadership of the company within a framework of prudent and effective controls which enable risk to be assessed and managed.

The board should set the company's strategic aims, ensure that the necessary financial and human resources are in place for the company to meet its objectives, and review management performance.

The board should set the company's values and standards and ensure that its obligations to its shareholders and others are understood and met.

(Suggested Code principle A.1 and provision A.1.1).

---

They will need to fit the strategy for the business, the strategy for the ownership and of course with the board you have or are in the process of building.

They will also need to share or be able to work with the board's belief in whom they are working for. Reference is made in CHAPTER 3 BOARD

STRUCTURE AND PRACTICE to Professor Jay Lorsch's book *Pawns and Potentates* which has a very good description of the range of beliefs that directors have on this subject. For example some believe absolutely in shareholder primacy whilst others subscribe to the model which is very common in continental Europe, ie Co-Determination.

In practice the non-executive role is a complex one in which different aspects come to the fore at different times. The chart below is a summary of what one highly experienced non-executive believes he actually does.

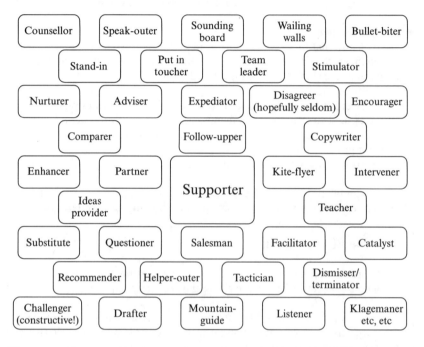

The reason *Supporter* is given such prominence is that the individual believed very strongly that unless he was seen as such by the CEO and executive directors of the company he would be unable to have sufficient influence when restraint was required.

What is clearly required is an approach which takes into account the generic qualities one might look for in a non-executive as well as the specific knowledge, skills, behaviours and potential pertaining to the particular circumstance.

## Defining the role and developing the candidate specification      1.4

Clarity about the role of the board makes it easier to clarify the role of the chairman or non-executive you are seeking. With this description it is then possible to develop a set of requisite competencies and experiences which candidates should have. All of which makes it easier to conduct a search and manage the process.

In **CHAPTER 3** the generic role of the chairman is defined as being to:

## Role of chairman                                                          1.5

- organise the composition, business and efficiency of the board;
- lead the board in the determination of its strategy and in the achievement of its objectives;
- ensure that the board has accurate and clear visibility of results and likely future trends;
- ensure that board committees are properly established, composed and operated;
- ensure effective relationships are maintained with all major stakeholders in the business i.e. customers, shareholders, employees, suppliers, government, local community, industry etc;
- enhance the company's public standing and reputation;
- develop a strong working relationship with the chief executive/managing director and ensure that there is a clear definition and agreement of the division of responsibilities.

All of which is underpinned with good judgement of people and commercial situations and the possession of strong influencing interpersonal skills. Again this description is consistent with that proposed by the Higgs Review for listed companies.

The importance of a clear definition and agreement of the division of responsibilities between the chairman and the chief executive can not be understated and this is dealt with in more detail in **CHAPTER 3**.

It is now uncommon in large plcs for the roles to be combined, with the exception of a temporary period where the chairman has fired the chief executive and is fulfilling the role on an interim basis.

The National Association of Pension Funds('NAPF') Review of the Corporate Governance of the top 400 UK plcs in 2001 contained the table below.

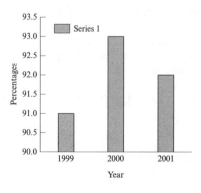

Research conducted for the Higgs Review found that only 5 FTSE100 companies, and 11 per cent of companies outside the FTSE350 have a joint chairman/chief executive.

## Role of non-executive                                    1.6

In chapter 3 the role has been split into two components 'Ensuring' and 'Adding Value'. It is believed that the non-executive who adds significant value has much greater influence with the other directors and is therefore much more likely to bring that influence to bear in ensuring that there is good governance.

The role of non-executive director includes ensuring that:

- there is a robust strategy for the ownership and development of the business, that it is regularly monitored and adapted as required;
- the company has the appropriate resources in place to meet its strategy. The two most important being human and financial; and
- there is appropriate corporate governance and a high standard of investor relations;

and adding value by:

- being a confidential sounding board to the directors;
- bringing an independent and broad view to the board; and
- helping the executive to achieve their business plans in whatever form is relevant given their experience and network.

It goes without saying that everything under 'Ensuring' adds value. This description is again consistent with that conceived in the Higgs Review.

A survey of 3i-backed CEOs across Europe in 2002 showed that what they wanted most from their non-executives was the following.

At this stage it is also helpful to consider the board team as a whole. An analysis of the current board members in terms of knowledge, skills and behaviours can be helpful in clarifying requirements. If you are going to do this it needs to be done in the context of matching the board against the intended strategy and the succession plans for existing members.

One approach to developing a candidate specification is to take the role and then consider what core competencies and experiences someone would have to have in order to fit this role in the specific situation concerned.

The core competencies can typically be grouped under the following headings:

- personal;
- professional and managerial; and
- entrepreneurial.

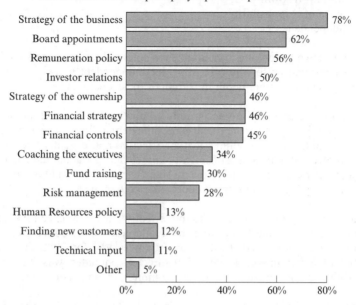

"In your company, in which of the following areas are non-executive directors principally expected to perform a role?"

Strategy of the business — 78%
Board appointments — 62%
Remuneration policy — 56%
Investor relations — 50%
Strategy of the ownership — 46%
Financial strategy — 46%
Financial controls — 45%
Coaching the executives — 34%
Fund raising — 30%
Risk management — 28%
Human Resources policy — 13%
Finding new customers — 12%
Technical input — 11%
Other — 5%

It should then be a fairly straightforward task to come up with a list of specific questions to ask at interview and in referencing to ascertain whether the candidates possess the requisite competencies. We make the assumption that the reader is a competent interviewer of senior business people but explore some of the differences between interviewing executives and non-executives in **PARAGRAPH 1.15**.

Some examples of competencies and characteristics which might be included within the three headings above are listed below.

## *Personal* 1.7

An interviewer will want to know that the candidates possess not just the personal qualities of a good non-executive director but that they will also work well with the team.

Here are some of the key qualities.

- Integrity
- Judgement
- Leadership
- Motivation
- Resilience
- Communicating and influencing style
- Interpersonal sensitivity
- Listening skills

- Intelligence
- Cultural flexibility
- Sense of responsibility
- Independence

If an interviewer is looking at candidates as potential future successors for the current chairman or for the role of senior independent non-executive then they may also seek more depth in certain of these qualities.

Motivation and capacity are not strictly competencies. Motivation has been included not just because the role has become demanding to execute well but also because the authors believe that an effective non-executive needs to be highly motivated to become sufficiently knowledgeable about the company's business and market place. Moreover a significant commitment is required to be sufficiently vigilant in terms of corporate governance.

Capacity is important because to be effective the non-executive has to commit sufficient time to the role, be available at short notice and not be distracted when involved. In the Top Pay/3i survey for 2002 the average number of appointments for the 419 directors included was 2.8 and the typical time commitment was two days a month for non-executives.

Independence has became a particularly hot topic in the post Enron, Worldcom and Marconi era. Why? Because of the sensitivities around remuneration, accuracy of financial disclosure and consequences of flawed strategic decisions. The challenges to US investment banks with regard to the way they managed conflicts of interest in the late nineties bull market added further fuel to fire.

How do people define independence? One widely used definition is

'Capable of exercising objective judgement'

This definition is used by a number of leading institutional investors including CALPERS. The UK's NAPF has a more detailed definition which we have included in the **APPENDICES** and according to their survey eighty two per cent of the top four hundred UK listed companies met this definition. It is based on describing what doesn't constitute independence, for example if the individual was formerly an executive or is paid by the company in any capacity other than as a non-executive director.

The Higgs report to the government in January 2003 defined independence as follows.

---

*Independence*

A non-executive director is considered independent when the board determines that the director is independent in character and judgement and

---

there are no relationships or circumstances which could affect, or appear to affect, the director's judgement.

Such relationships or circumstances would include where the director:

- is a former employee of the company or group until five years after employment (or any other material connection) has ended;
- has, or has had within the last three years, a material business relationship with the company either directly, or as a partner, shareholder, director or senior employee of a body that has such a relationship with the company;
- has received or receives additional remuneration from the company apart from a director's fee, participates in the company's share option or a performance-related pay scheme, or is a member of the company's pension scheme;
- has close family ties with any of the company's advisers, directors or senior employees;
- holds cross-directorships or has significant links with other directors through involvement in other companies or bodies;
- represents a significant shareholder; or
- has served on the board for more than ten years.

The board should identify in its annual report the non-executive directors it determines to be independent. The board should state its reasons if a director is considered to be independent notwithstanding the existence of relationships or circumstances which may appear relevant to its determination.

## *Professional and Managerial* 1.8

In order to fulfil the role well the candidate will need to be professionally competent, knowledgeable and experienced in a number of obvious areas, such as:

- strategy;
- technical;
- organisational;
- analytical;
- problem solving;
- chairing; and
- committee membership.

At 3i there is a strong preference for independent directors to be experienced chairmen, CEOs or finance directors so that they have encountered the professional and commercial situations that the executive are likely to encounter.

Technical knowledge means the knowledge of issues relating to being a director, for example, in the accounting and legal area, as well as a current knowledge of best business practice. In addition if the business is of a highly technical nature itself then the non-executive may require specific professional experience to be able to make informed judgements and communicate effectively with the rest of the board.

## *Entrepreneurial*     **1.9**

Entrepreneurialism is a much used word but seldom defined. For the purposes of this handbook it will be defined as being about 'capturing the value associated with a commercial opportunity'.

Entrepreneurialism is usually associated with people who enjoy making money and are strongly profit motivated. So what are entrepreneurial competencies?

●     Vision: Seeing the opportunity.

●     Judgement: Deciding whether the opportunity has significant value potential.

●     Conviction: Preparedness to listen, but also not to be swayed by every opinion.. To have a point of view and be prepared to stand up for it but also to take advice.

●     Decisiveness: Being prepared to seize opportunities, and prepared to recognise and act on mistakes.

●     Commercial acumen: Especially in terms of understanding value and timing.

In the authors' view these competencies or characteristics are relevant whatever the context of the business.

Interestingly a survey of the CEOs of 3i-backed businesses in the autumn of 2002 produced the following response to the question:

"What skills, knowledge and attributes do you principally
look for in a non-executive director?"

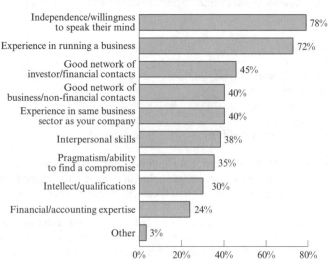

In summary, by going through the process of considering the context of the business and the core competencies and characteristics sought, a detailed candidate specification is straightforward to prepare.

## Issues for prospective non executives or candidates for appointments                                     1.10

Firstly, standing back from particular situation, it is worth anyone considering embarking upon a career as a non-executive addressing some basic questions such as these.

- Why do you want to take on these types of roles?
- Do you have the basic competencies to be effective?
- What will be your general approach and attitude to the role?
- What additional training do you require?
- Do you understand the risks involved?
- What sort of companies would be most appropriate?
- Can you organise the logistics and manage to fulfil other existing roles?
- Have you considered the financial and tax issues involved?
- If you are an executive in an existing business what will the likely reaction be amongst your existing colleagues, shareholders and press?
- How will you put yourself in the position to be considered for suitable positions?

Motivations vary but usually comprise one or all of the following.

- To learn through different roles or different types of business.
- For the retiring senior executive to keep involved in business.
- For those planning to retire in the medium term a non-executive role is a good step towards that transition.
- For the active executive, personal development.
- Prestige.
- Compensation.

With regard to competence to fulfil the role, the generic competencies and characteristics have been covered at **PARAGRAPHS 1.6–1.8**. There are however some specific issues relating to the active chief executive or other full time director embarking down the non-executive route for the first time, eg time commitment. The CEO role today especially in a public company is a very demanding one logistically. Degree of control is another issue. The chief executive's role carries with it a high degree of authority and status within a company. The non-executive's power is derived more from influence. Some CEOs find this transition difficult or frustrating. We cover some general observations on role transition below.

A number of factors will determine a candidate's approach and attitude to the role and these are:

- the experience they have had with non-executives in other situations;

- Their views on the role of the board and in particular who they think they are working for eg do they believe in shareholder primacy or co-determination? This is discussed in greater detail at the beginning of **CHAPTER 3 BOARD STRUCTURE AND PRACTICE**;
- the stance they adopt with the executive eg oversight, control or collaborator;
- the influence of external perception for example the press; and
- their personality.

For a particular appointment what due diligence should a candidate undertake before accepting an offer to join the board?

**PARAGRAPH 1.23** provides a good list of basic information candidates will need. Other things that need to be understood are:

- the owner's agenda;
- the strategy;
- how comfortable candidates are with the people;
- the financial position of the company and the key systems and controls; and
- the quality of board processes.
- The reality of joining a board and an awareness that not everything may be up to the expected standards.

Public company boards appear to have become less attractive to join than they used to be. Whilst the status associated with such appointments in all but the top companies has diminished the risks have become considerably greater. This was evidenced in this chart from an IDP survey conducted in 2002.

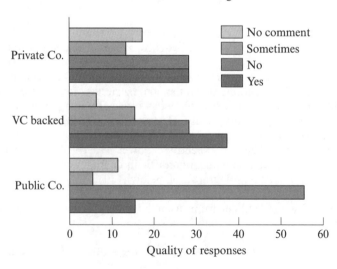

Is the risk/reward balance right?

Why was this case? In depth interviews revealed that the key reasons for the fall in attractiveness of PLC appointments were increased risk in relation to the rewards, increased formality/governance and finally the increased profile and attendant media intrusion.

Why were venture capital and private equity businesses so popular? Possibly because the VC and private equity firms are more realistic in their expectations, the rewards through having an equity interest are greater and the shareholders' objectives are clearer.

For those preparing for their first non-executive role it is well worth considering the chart below from a piece of work by Chris Parker and Ralph Lewis at Cranfield over twenty years ago. It was called '*Moving up... How to handle transitions to senior levels successfully*'. Although written clearly for executive transitions it is just as relevant for those moving into a non-executive role for the first time. Parker and Lewis came up with what they called the *transition curve* (see below). Interestingly whenever 3i has conducted research into what happens to managers involved in management buy outs through the buy out process it follows a similar pattern. This has been labelled *"the emotional roller coaster"*.

The transition rollercoaster

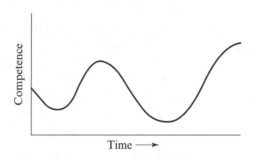

Parker and Lewis describe eight stages to the transition for those that get through it. We have adapted these for the non-executive.

| Rosy positive picture: | '*It's going to be fantastic.*'<br>This stage is usually before you start.<br>The position has been oversold.<br>You may have had less time for due diligence<br>than you would have ideally liked. |
| --- | --- |
| Immobilisation: | '*This isn't the job they told me it would be.*'<br>Natural feelings of Shock.<br>You become overwhelmed.<br>There has been a serious mismatch between<br>expectations and reality. |

| | |
|---|---|
| Disbelief: | *'I'm not having this, they'll have to sort it out'* Temporary retreat. It's someone else's responsibility to help me. False competence. I'll just carry on doing what I'm good at. Better explain why so 'In my last company we ....' |
| Incompetence: | *'Now everything is going wrong, It could be me.'* Awareness of the need to change. Frustration at not knowing what to do. Sink or swim time. |
| Accept reality: | *'Forget what's happened. I've got to sort this out.'* Let go of the past. I can see where I am going wrong. I need to find the solution. |
| Testing: | *'I think this might work.'* High energy. Determination to find the way out. Anger at the fact you have to and for all the false starts. Wonder if this is the way we should do it? |
| Search for meaning | *'Hey it's working.'* Understanding how it all fits together. Figuring out what works Post rationalising a little experimental success. |
| Integration | *'Everyone else thinks so as well.'* Getting your act together. Gaining credibility. Doing it naturally with people Understanding why. |

For situations where there are multiple new appointments simultaneously several people could be experiencing this at the same time. What happens if they all reach the valley of incompetence together? The rollercoaster doesn't fit everything but the basic principles are interesting. Just by thinking about this beforehand helps.

For executives taking on their first non-executive role this could be particularly appropriate. As could considering some of the training and development options described in CHAPTER 19.

Where there are multiple appointments being made at the same time a number of other factors need to be taken in to account. Namely that there will obviously be a bigger impact on the team dynamic. Care will be needed to ensure that the different candidate specifications are compatible and induction processes will need adapting.

## Commitment to a process                                                1.11

In order to gain commitment to a process from the board as a whole there needs to be agreement about what needs doing, who needs to do it and how they are going to do it. A rigorous process inevitably involves a significant time commitment from those involved.

## What needs doing?                                                       1.12

Normally, the following:

- developing the role and candidate specifications;
- agreeing a sourcing and selection process for candidates;
- if relevant selecting a search firm;
- sourcing, assessing and selecting candidates;
- offering and agreeing the terms of the appointment;
- formal approval of new board member; and
- induction and review.

Agreeing the role and developing a candidate specification has been covered above at **PARAGRAPHS 1.2–1.3**.

## Agreeing a sourcing and selection process for candidates               1.13

Once the board has a clear idea of the sort of person it is looking for, the next decision concerns the approach it is going to take to sourcing and selecting candidates. The basic approaches to sourcing are one or a mix of the following:

- using its own network;
- recommendations from its professional advisers or financial backers; and
- using a professional search firm.

PLCs will almost invariably use a search firm even if they intend using their own networks, advisers or advertising, for the following reasons:

- they need to be able to demonstrate to shareholders that the selection process has been carried out rigorously and objectively;
- a search firm will have access to a wider pool of candidates; and
- a search firm should be able to add value in terms of its selection processes.

The 2002 3i/Top Pay survey of 1200 directorships across a range of sizes of companies, public and private showed the following:

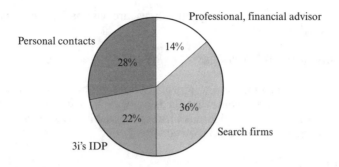

The trend has been for search firms to be used more frequently and dependence upon the personal networks of the board to fall. Around three quarters of this sample were public company appointments.

## Selecting a search firm, sourcing, assessing and selecting candidates                                                  1.14

If a search firm is used they will need to be carefully selected. It may be that the company has an established relationship with a firm who knows the board well and this can be an advantage. However this isn't always the case as the relationship may be too cosy, their skills are in recruiting executives rather than non-executives or they may not have access to the sorts of candidates the company are looking to attract. In any event it is always useful to benchmark them against an alternative.

Let us assume that a company is in the position where it also has to select a search firm, agree their role in the process and how they will be managed. If we're conducting a selection process we will need some criteria for selection and to conduct a beauty parade of potential suppliers.

These are the normal criteria for selection in these circumstances.

- Track record of the firm in the non-executive area relevant to your company.
- Track record of the individual leading the assignment and their research assistant.
- Quality of their processes.
- Ability to deliver within the timeframe you have agreed.
- International capability if relevant.
- Knowledge on compensation issues.
- Strength of their assessment and referencing techniques.
- Fit with your type of business.
- Cost.

The company will also need to know from them who their off limits clients are. This is usually less of an issue than it is in the executive area.

In terms of conducting a beauty parade there are a number of factors to consider.

- Who from the nominations committee will take part in the selection?
- The board will need to select a small number of appropriate firms, three is usually enough.
- Consideration needs to be given as to how they are going to be paid – fixed fee or success related. For non-executive appointments it is normal for the fee to be fixed and not linked to package as is customary for executive roles.
- Good search consultants will want to be sure that the specification is right so a company should be prepared to be challenged on it and worry about those who don't.

Some good beauty parade questions are:

- What experience do you have of similar appointments?
- Can you give me the names of company chairmen and the non-executives you have found for them and would you be happy for me to call them?
- How is your candidate database organised?
- Would it be possible for one of our staff to visit your offices and see your database?
- What core competencies do you think a non-executive for our business should have?
- What will your role in the process be?
- Can I interview the researcher who will be helping you with this assignment?
- Could you describe your candidate referencing process in detail?
- How attractive a role do you think this will be?
- How will you describe our company to potential candidates?
- How will you describe the role to potential candidates?
- Is this a role you think you will need to advertise for?
- If so what is your process for doing this and what will the associated costs be?
- With regard to cost will it be on a retained or contingent basis?
- Will the cost be linked to the successful candidate's package and if so which elements?
- Will there be compensation if the candidate proves unsuccessful within the first year?

The firm should also be referenced and not just with the referees they provide.

Careful consideration needs to be given to the issue of whether to undertake a discrete targeted search or a more open approach involving advertising for candidates. There has been an increase in the number of companies doing both. Traditionally if search firms where used at all it was for a discrete search and advertising was unusual. Here are some of the issues involved in considering using an advertised approach.

## Advertising                                                    1.15

> - May take longer because it involves a bigger processing job.
> - Is usually done in addition to search so may be more expensive.
> - Reaches a broader audience so may attract candidates you would never had access to.
> - Is another means of advertising your company and showing you recruit in a professional way.

Once a search firm has been selected for the assignment they will need careful management. The best way to ensure this occurs is to agree a timetable at the outset together with a process for approving expenses and then insist on weekly status reports. The first response from them should include the following:

- detailed candidate specification;
- summary of the process to be adopted for fulfilling the assignment; and
- terms and conditions of the search firm for this specific assignment.

An example of a letter from a leading search firm to a new client following a verbal briefing is contained in the **APPENDICES**.

## Interviewing candidates                                       1.16

In this section, comments will focus on the areas of main difference between interviewing executives and non-executives. The authors make the assumption that the reader is an experienced and competent interviewer of the former. The authors make the further assumption that the interviewing process will involve a number of candidates. In their view choice is essential.

The interviewing process is typically defined by:

- who is doing it;
- how they do it ; and
- how they interpret what they learn.

With regard to who is doing it for non-executive appointments, where a search firm is involved the process would normally be interviews with:

- the search consultant;
- the chairman of the nominations committee and/or someone delegated by them to undertake the first interview on behalf of the company;
- a series of second interviews with the chairman and chief executive; and
- meetings for the purposes of endorsement with as many of the other executives or non-executives as appropriate in the circumstances.

The balance of buying and selling between the company and the applicant may differ significantly in this context and it might well be the case that the candidate requires to meet all of the directors before he is prepared to accept a seat on the board. Clearly then there is a significant time commitment required from both sides. It is therefore important to communicate well with candidates throughout the process and for candidates not chosen to be told as quickly and sensitively as possible.

In terms of the approach taken to interviewing it is recommended that a competency based approach be adopted that takes into account the seniority of the candidate. The fundamental principles behind a competency based approach are that it involves structured interviews, significant preparation beforehand, and a focus on evaluating whether the candidate has the knowledge skills and behaviours to undertake the role.

In the authors' experience very senior people have few problems with a rigorous approach being adopted as long as it is respectful and handled in a non mechanistic way. At this stage in the relationship the approach taken to the interviewing process will be providing the candidate with a view of how seriously the company takes the role and the professionalism with which it approaches senior appointments. Moreover highly successful chief executives or senior executives don't always make good non-executives due to their dominant personalities and egos. If the candidate is not prepared to go through a more rigorous process it should be understood why.

The SAE method of interview is also relevant in this context. The objective of this approach is to find the evidence to demonstrate a competency. Put simply the interviewer asks the candidate to describe a **Situation** which they think may be appropriate, discovers the **Actions** taken by the candidate and then follow through by finding out what the **Effect** was. It makes the referencing process later much easier. Grateful thanks go to Carmel Siverosa from Oxford Consulting Group who first introduced this to one of the authors.

Using actual strategic issues that the company has to explore the likely contribution the prospective non-executive can make is a good way of gathering evidence as to their judgement and influencing style. It may not be appropriate at this stage of the discussions to share the most sensitive issues the company is facing so hypothetical situations may need to suffice.

It is also important to determine the relevance of a candidate's experience and skills to the company. In addition the board will want to test for a compatible belief system about what a board is about, test for potential conflicts of interest and ensure there are no logistical issues which might inhibit performance.

## Referencing                                                   1.17

Referencing is undertaken principally to calibrate the views derived from the interviewing process and confirm that there is a good fit in terms of competence and compatibility. At the same time it is to ensure that the individual's integrity and reputation meet the required standard.

A referencing process is defined by the following:

- when it is done;
- who is doing it;
- who they seek references from;
- what they ask;
- how they ask it; and;
- how they interpret what they learn?

With regard to who undertakes the referencing this is usually a mix of the chairman of the nominations committee, the company secretary and if relevant the search firm. The chairman of the board as a whole may also want to make his own enquiries.

Most candidates will have provided a list of people they would be willing for the board to contact. The obvious issue if the exercise is confined to these people is that they are inevitably likely to be positive. Most search firms have a database of contacts and the facility to select from that people who worked with, in, or served on the boards of, the same companies as the candidate.

In terms of what to ask, the following provides a useful framework for questions for establishing both competence to fulfil the role and fit with the team.

- Establish how well the referee really knows the candidate, in what context, how objective the referee is and how qualified the referee is to express a view on non-executive competence.
- Gain information relating to key competencies sought, motivation, capacity, style and weaknesses.
- Probe situational effectiveness of candidate.
- Confirm track record, integrity and reputation.
- Finally always ask the open 'is there anything else you feel I need to know about them' question.

The 'how?' is normally telephone or letter. The phone is much more powerful. Whatever the method good preparation is the key and it is always advisable to prepare a question plan and a sheet to record views under the key headings.

In addition to the above it is now normal for qualification and credit checks to be performed. The search firm will generally undertake this as part of their referencing process. One thing it is very important to remember when recording personal information is the requirements of the *Data Protection Act 1998*.

The decision as to when you undertake referencing in reality is down to the specific circumstances. Typically a degree of informal referencing will take place before candidates are met with the more formal and rigorous elements taking place later in the process.

Finally it is important to remember to get back properly to unsuccessful candidates, they could still be very useful contacts for the business or your next non-executive director.

## Who needs to do what? 1.18

The chairman of the nominations committee should be leading the process and ensuring that the board is well informed and appropriately involved. The operation of nominations committees is covered in CHAPTER **16** NOMINATIONS COMMITTEE. One interesting aspect is the role of the chairman of the board and the CEO. The quality of the chairman and CEO and their attitude to the appointment has a significant influence on its attractiveness to candidates.

## Offering and agreeing the terms of the appointment 1.19

An appointment will typically be offered subject to formal approval by the board (see below)

In the 3i/IRS Survey in 2003, 98 per cent of those surveyed had formal letters of appointment. 15 per cent of these were for one year, 32 per cent for two years and 51 per cent for three years or more.

CHAPTER **9** DIRECTORS' REMUNERATION AND BENEFITS covers remuneration and benefits in more detail but some summary comments are made here.

## Compensation 1.20

We will confine ourselves here simply to the process of determining what will be appropriate remuneration for the non-executive. CHAPTER **9** contains comprehensive data on current rates for particular profiles of situation.

The nominations committee and the remuneration committee should already have an agreed package for the non-executives with details on all the components of the package. These will normally include:

- a basic fee based on an assumed time commitment;
- an additional fee payable for membership of board committees;
- an agreed basis of payment for circumstances where the director's time commitment is significantly greater than originally envisaged e.g. During a takeover, Initial Public Offering etc;
- a description of allowable expenses and the process for claiming them;
- clarity over directors' and officers' liability insurance, ie whether it is paid for by the company or the individual and the details of the cover provided. See CHAPTER **13** INSURANCE for more information relating to directors' and officers' liability insurance.
- a proposal regarding obtaining equity in the company where relevant for example in venture capital or private equity backed businesses; and
- services provided by the company to enable the director to carry out his duties(eg access to legal advice).

If they do and this has been recently reviewed then this should be the starting point of a proposal to the candidate. If they don't then CHAPTER 9 covers how to develop a remuneration scheme for non-executives.

It is important to be clear and realistic about the time commitment expected of the non-executive and have arrangements in place for circumstances when there may well be significantly more input required.

| Turnover of company (£m) | <10 | 11–30 | 31–100 | 101–500 | 501–1000 | >1000 |
|---|---|---|---|---|---|---|
| **Independent Director** | | | | | | |
| Formal meeting days | 12 | 13 | 13 | 13 | 15 | 16 |
| Preparation & travel | 4 | 6 | 6 | 6 | 6 | 7 |
| Visits & other | 1 | 2 | 2 | 2 | 2 | 3 |
| **Total** | 17 | 21 | 21 | 21 | 21 | 26 |
| **Chairman** | | | | | | |
| Formal meeting days | 14 | 14 | 15 | 15 | 16 | 18 |
| Preparation & travel | 9 | 12 | 12 | 12 | 13 | 14 |
| Visits & other | 2 | 4 | 4 | 3 | 4 | 5 |
| Investor relations and Ambassadorial days | 8 | 10 | 12 | 21 | 18 | 16 |
| **Total** | 33 | 40 | 43 | 51 | 51 | 53 |

Once it has been decided what will be paid and how, the next thing to decide is whether this is discussed directly or through the search firm. Usually this will all have been agreed at the beginning of the process, the search firm will have clear parameters in which to operate and the package will have been communicated to candidates at the start of the process.

For most sizeable businesses remuneration consultants will have been consulted to ensure that executive and non-executive remuneration is comparable to similar organisations. For smaller organisations there are a number of surveys which can be used as reference points including the annual 3i Independent Remuneration Solutions Independent Chairman and Non-Executive Director Survey. The company's lawyers, accountants and, if it has them, venture backers should also be able to provide guidance.

## Formal approval of new board member                        1.21

If the board has a nomination committee, the process for the particular appointment is likely to have been approved at an earlier board meeting. It is also normal for the recruitment process to include interviews of the prospective new board member by the chairman, chief executive and other members of the board. Good non-executives often won't accept the offer to join the board until they have met the entire board. Therefore at the point the nominations committee is making its recommendation to the board as a whole, the candidate is likely to have been met by most or all of the board. Approval is therefore likely to be a formality.

Other issues to consider at this stage are notifications which it will be necessary to make for eg Stock Exchange, bank and the press. In venture capital and private equity backed situation the investors are normally actively involved in the process and, if on the board, likely to be a member of the nominations committee.

## Induction process                                          1.22

One of the major challenges any new non-executive faces is how to gain sufficient familiarity with the business and its markets to make informed judgements. The quality of the induction process will have a significant influence on their success in meeting this challenge. So what are the objectives of a good induction process, what should the non-executive gain familiarity with first and how should the process be organised?

### *Objectives of a good induction process*                   1.23

There are two key objectives and these are to:

- gain sufficient knowledge to make well informed judgements; and to
- build relationships with the key players to gain the influence to bring those judgements to bear.

In the authors' view the induction process should be planned and agreed before the appointment is formalised and then summarised in the appointment letter (see the APPENDICES). The following is an extract of the relevant section from such a letter. As can be seen this involves a considerable volume of material to read and absorb.

## *How the independent director will gain familiarity with the business*    **1.24**

Obviously you will have already been provided with extensive information in order for you to make an informed decision in accepting our offer to join the board. However for ease of reference and completeness we are delighted to include the enclosed pack which includes the following.

- Summary of key shareholders.
- Description of our key business activities with strategy and business model summaries for each.
- Board agendas, papers and minutes for the last twelve months.
- Schedule of Matters Reserved for the Board.
- Board calendar for the next twelve months together with a list of key dates.
- Copies of the last five years' audited accounts, together with the management letters from our auditors.
- Summary of our key profit recognition policies.
- Our budget document for the current year.
- Management accounts and commentary for the year to date.
- A selection of our latest promotional literature for the key parts of the business.
- Copies for the last year's staff magazines.
- Press cuttings for the last [relevant period].
- Our latest strategic plan document including the detailed plans for our major business units.
- A summary list of all of our subsidiary companies and a brief statement of their purpose and current financial and legal position.
- An organisational chart together with CVs and contact details for the members of the board.
- Investor relations strategy paper.
- A summary list of our key banking arrangements including the key covenants.
- Copies of the investment agreements between the company and our venture capital backers.
- [If public company] copies of our brokers' reports for the last two years.
- A list of the company's key advisors and their contact details. Incidentally we will write to them all notifying them of your appointment once it has been formalised.
- Memorandum and Articles of Association.
- Description of the review process for our non-executives.

We are delighted to let you know that we have now arranged the following induction schedule for you.

- Meetings with key business unit leaders.
- Meeting with chairman and chief executive to agree objectives for the year ahead.

- Meetings with Company's key advisors.
- Attendance at company's sales conference in Harrogate on 1 December.
- Attendance at board's strategy awayday on 15 December.

*Review process*                                                    **1.25**

The simplest way to review the performance of a new director is to ensure that they become part of the board's overall performance management system. The key elements of this for an individual director in most systems are:

- objectives set at appointment and reviewed annually with the chairman;
- a formal review after the first three months;
- feedback gathered by the chairman from the directors and other parties as relevant;
- that the non-executive is expected to give 360 degree feedback on other board members including the chairman; and
- an annual review meeting is held with the chairman. This is a two way meeting enabling the chairman to give feedback on performance, the non-executive and the chairman to set objectives for coming year and for the non-executive to give feedback to chairman.

The execution of this process is described in more detail in the APPENDICES.

The board also needs to set time aside each year to review its own operation.

# 2. Audit Matters

- Audit committees
- Appointment of external auditors
- Reporting by external auditors
- Remuneration of external auditors and their associates
- Internal audit

## Audit committees                                              2.1

## At a glance                                                   2.2

- A well-constituted and well-run audit committee can bring considerable benefits.
- The Smith Report includes a proposed revision of the Combined Code provisions on audit committees.
- The audit committee should be formally constituted and should have written terms of reference.
- The Combined Code includes specific provisions on the membership of the audit committee.
- Appointments to the audit committee should be by recommendation of the nomination committee and should be for a fixed term.
- Audit committee members must disclose any potential conflicts of interest.
- The company should provide an induction programme and ongoing training and support for audit committee members.

- Management must provide the audit committee with all the information that it needs to discharge its responsibilities.
- The precise role of the audit committee should be tailored to the circumstances of the company.
- The audit committee should review all financial reporting documents before publication.
- The audit committee should monitor the company's internal control and risk management systems, and the procedures for whistleblowing.
- The audit committee should monitor and review the activities of the internal audit function.
- The audit committee has primary responsibility for making a recommendation to the shareholders on the appointment, reappointment or removal of the external auditors.
- The audit committee should approve the terms of engagement and remuneration of the external auditor.
- The audit committee should assess the independence and objectivity of the external auditors each year.
- The audit committee should agree with the board the company's policy on:
  - the employment of former partners and employees of the audit firm; and
  - the provision of non-audit services by the auditors.
- The audit committee should agree the scope of external audit work each year.
- The audit committee should review the results of the external audit in conjunction with the annual report and accounts.
- The audit committee should consider the auditor's report to management, together with management's response to the points raised.
- At the end of the audit cycle, the audit committee should assess the effectiveness of the external audit process.
- The audit committee should meet sufficiently often to be able to review and monitor major issues, and at least three times each year.
- Only audit committee members are entitled to be present at meetings, but other individuals may attend by invitation.
- The audit committee chairman should report regularly to the main board.
- The directors' report should include a separate section each year describing the role and responsibilities of the audit committee and the actions taken to discharge those responsibilities.
- The effectiveness of the audit committee should be reviewed annually by both the committee and the main board.

## Benefits of an audit committee                          2.3

Audit committees have become an important aspect of corporate governance in recent years, partly as a result of the recommendations set out in the

Combined Code but also because companies have begun to appreciate the benefits that an effective audit committee can bring in terms of providing additional assurance on the adequacy of the company's system of internal control and on the quality of its financial information (for both internal and external use) and of its financial decision-making. Although the Combined Code applies primarily to listed companies, the principles underlying the recommendations apply to every company and all directors are therefore encouraged to follow them. The recommendations are equally relevant for not-for-profit organisations, particularly where there is a high degree of public interest in their activities, for instance charities and public sector bodies. The potential benefits of an audit committee include:

- improved quality of financial reporting and increased public confidence in the credibility and objectivity of financial statements;
- the creation of a climate of discipline and control, which can help to reduce the opportunity for fraud;
- the opportunity for non-executive directors to contribute their independent judgement and play a positive role within the company;
- the provision of a forum for the financial director to raise issues of concern;
- the provision of a strong channel of communication between the external auditors and the board, enabling the auditors to raise issues of concern and to assert their independence in the event of a dispute with management;
- the strengthening of the internal audit function, by increasing its independence from management.

The report issued in January 2003 by the DTI Co-ordinating Group on Audit and Accounting Issues (CGAAI) as part of the Post-Enron initiative emphasises that the work of the audit committee is seen as central to the restoration of confidence in the capital markets.

## Potential drawbacks                                      2.4

However, there are some potential difficulties that companies need to be aware of when establishing and operating audit committees:

- the existence of an audit committee can result in the main board abdicating its collective responsibilities in respect of the audit and the review and approval of the annual accounts;
- the audit committee can become a barrier between the external auditors and the executive directors of the company; and
- the audit committee will not function effectively if it lacks the necessary understanding to deal with the accounting and auditing issues that will be brought to its attention.

Careful planning can prevent these becoming real issues in practice.

## The Smith Report 2.5

As part of the UK Government's response to the collapse of Enron, a small working group was appointed by Financial Reporting Council, under the chairmanship of Sir Robert Smith, to develop further the initial guidance on audit committees already included in the Combined Code. The resulting report 'Audit Committees: Combined Code Guidance', commonly referred to as the Smith Report, was published in January 2003. The report notes that the audit committee has a particular role, acting independently from the executive, in ensuring that the interests of shareholders in relation to financial reporting and internal control are properly protected. However, this is in no way intended to create a departure from the UK principle of the unitary board – all directors continue to have the same legal responsibility for the company's affairs and any disagreements must be resolved at board level. The report includes the draft of a revised section of the Combined Code on audit committees, together with supplementary guidance that is intended to assist boards in establishing and operating an audit committee and also to assist directors who serve as members of an audit committee. Certain essential requirements for audit committees are set out in bold text in the guidance, and compliance with these is considered necessary in order to achieve compliance with the Combined Code. Listed companies that do not meet with any of these essential requirements should include an explanation in the compliance statements that are required by the UK Listing Rules (see CHAPTER 6 CORPORATE GOVERNANCE). For instance, it is acknowledged that smaller listed companies may find it difficult to achieve full compliance, although this should always remain the objective. A checklist of the new requirements is set out in Appendix 1 to this chapter at PARAGRAPH 2.99. The detailed guidance in the Smith Report and the new section of the Combined Code (subject to any drafting issues that may be raised in the exposure period) is intended to be effective for accounting periods beginning on or after 1 July 2003. Changes of substance to the Code recommendations will not be accepted. Relevant issues raised in the Smith Report are discussed in the following sections.

## Constitution and terms of reference 2.6

The Combined Code recommends that an audit committee is constituted formally as a sub-committee of the main board, to ensure that there is a clear relationship between the two. The audit committee should report regularly to the main board and be answerable to it. The Smith Report specifies that the board should provide written terms of reference for the audit committee and sets out an example under the following headings.

- constitution;
- membership;
- attendance at meetings;
- frequency of meetings;
- authority;
- responsibilities;
- reporting procedures.

A further example, based on that in the Smith Report, is given in Appendix 2 to this chapter at **PARAGRAPH 2.100**. However, neither example is intended to be prescriptive and companies are encouraged to develop and tailor them to suit their own circumstances. In particular, the examples are drafted from the perspective of an individual company and will need adapting to cover the specific circumstances of a group. Terms of reference should be realistic and should give the committee sufficient resources and authority to perform its role effectively. The new guidance in the Smith Report recommends that the audit committee should carry out an annual review of its terms of reference and recommend to the board any changes that are considered necessary.

## Membership of the audit committee                    2.7

Membership of the audit committee is a critical issue – any committee can only be as good as the people that serve on it. In particular, the effectiveness of the audit committee often depends on a strong, independent chairman who has the confidence of both the board and the external auditors, and on the quality of the non-executive directors. The size and complexity of the company, and the size of the board of directors, will usually have a direct bearing on the size and membership of the audit committee. The Combined Code recommends that:

- the audit committee should have at least three members, all of whom should be independent non-executive directors – independence is defined as proposed in the Higgs Report (see **CHAPTER 13**);
- at least one member of the audit committee should have significant recent and relevant financial experience (the guidance suggests that this might be as an auditor or a finance director of a listed company) and should preferably hold a professional accountancy qualification.

The chairman of the company should not be a member of the audit committee. The present Combined Code recommends that details of the membership of the audit committee should be given in the company's annual report and that the chairman of the audit committee should be available to answer any questions raised by members at the company's Annual General Meeting. Under the proposals in the Smith Report, the directors' report should include a separate section describing the role, responsibilities and activities of the audit committee during the year (see **2.33** below)

## Skills and attributes                                 2.8

There should normally be wide consultation before recommending that an individual is appointed as a member of the committee. The Smith Report proposes that appointments should be by recommendation of the nomination committee (where there is one), in consultation with the audit committee chairman. Qualities that will commonly be taken into account in assessing an individual's suitability for membership of the audit committee will include:

- breadth of general business experience;

- knowledge of the company's operations, finances and accounting;
- understanding of the roles of external and internal auditors and familiarity with the main concepts of Auditing Standards;
- knowledge and understanding of the key aspects of financial reporting;
- personal qualities;
- commitment (including the amount of time that the individual can make available).

The audit committee will usually function as a team and it may therefore be appropriate to consider the balance of experience and abilities across the membership as a whole. The nature of the audit committee's activities makes it particularly important for the committee as a whole to have an adequate understanding of the management of business risk, accounting and financial reporting and internal control. Additional relevant skills may be needed, depending on the nature of the company's activities - for instance, where it is involved in specialised financial activities. Members of the company's executive management team should not be appointed to the audit committee as their attendance at every meeting could inhibit others from raising sensitive issues. However, their input to audit committee discussions may be needed from time to time, and there should a facility for them to attend audit committee meetings by invitation (see **2.30** below).

## Appointing a chairman                                        2.9

As noted above, the Cadbury Committee emphasised the importance of the chairman in ensuring the effective operation of the audit committee and the Smith Report emphasises the need for a frank and open relationship, and a high level of mutual trust, between the audit committee chairman and the board chairman, chief executive and finance director. The chairman of the audit committee will usually be appointed by the board as a whole. Particular qualities that will need to be assessed in appointing a chairman include:

- strength of personality;
- experience of the role of chairman;
- attitude to business risk management and control, and related ethical issues;
- attitude towards the audit function (both external and internal); and
- commitment (including the amount of time that he/she can make available).

## Length of appointment to audit committee                    2.10

The long-term nature of the activities of the audit committee mean that a certain degree of continuity of membership is helpful. However, this needs to be balanced against the need for fresh input and a new outlook from time to time. The Smith Report recommends that appointments should be for a period of up to three years, extendable by no more than two additional periods of three years, provided that the individual continues to be sufficiently independent. From a practical point of view, it is often helpful for the appointment periods of the individual members to end in different years so that the company is not faced with a loss of significant audit committee experience by two or three members retiring at the same time.

## Avoiding conflicts of interest                                    2.11

Individuals recommended for appointment to the audit committee should be required to confirm their independence at the time of appointment. Once appointed they are responsible for ensuring that their entry in the register of directors' interests is kept up to date and for declaring any potential conflict of interest in respect of agenda items at meetings of the audit committee. They should not vote on any item in respect of which they have a potential conflict of interest.

## Training and support for audit committee members       2.12

The Smith Report recommends that an induction programme is provided for each new audit committee member, covering:

- the role of the audit committee and its terms of reference;
- the expected time commitment; and
- an overview of the company's business, including the main business and financial dynamics and risks.

It may also be helpful to provide new members with summaries of the issues raised in recent reports from both external and internal auditors. Ongoing training should be provided to all audit committee members to enable them to keep up to date with issues relevant to their role. This training might cover:

- principles and developments in financial reporting and related company law;
- understanding financial statements, applicable accounting standards and recommended accounting practice;
- the regulatory framework for the company's business;
- the role of external and internal audit; and
- risk management.

The Smith Report notes that both induction programmes and ongoing training might take a variety of forms, including attendance at formal courses and conferences, internal seminars and briefing sessions led by external advisers. The audit committee should also be given the facility, and the funding, to obtain independent legal, accounting or other advice where it considers this to be necessary.

## Information provided to audit committee                 2.13

The Smith Report emphasises that management has an obligation to ensure that the audit committee is kept properly informed and to provide the information that it needs to fulfil its role. Management is expected to take the initiative in providing information to the committee, rather than waiting to be asked for it, and to make clear to all directors and employees that they must co-operate with the audit committee and provide any information requested.

## Role and activities of the audit committee                    2.14

The role of audit committees has become increasingly diverse as they have become more common. The detailed role and activities of the audit committee must be tailored to the needs of the individual company, but the principal role of the audit committee is summarised as providing assurance that the board's collective responsibility for financial matters and internal control is rigourously discharged. The Smith Report summarises the role and responsibilities of the audit committee under the following headings:

- Financial reporting;
- Internal financial controls and risk management systems;
- Whistleblowing;
- The internal audit process; and
- The external audit process:
    - appointment;
    - terms and remuneration;
    - independence and the provision of non-audit services; and
    - the annual audit cycle.

In the case of a group of companies, the parent board should ensure that there is adequate co-operation within the group, and with the external and internal auditors of each company within the group, to enable the audit committee to discharge its responsibilities. The Smith Report also emphasises that the work of the audit committee is wide-ranging, time-consuming and sometimes intensive – it is therefore important that members of the committee are able to make the appropriate amount of time available for the task and that they receive appropriate recompense for this.

## Financial reporting                                          2.15

The audit committee's responsibilities in relation to financial reporting cover:

- the interim statement;
- the preliminary announcement;
- the company's financial statements;
- the operating and financial review (OFR);
- the company's corporate governance statements; and
- the summary financial statement (where one is prepared).

Wherever practical, the audit committee should also review other statements containing financial information which require board approval prior to publication – for instance, the release of price sensitive information, or financial reports to regulators. Management are responsible for preparing accounts which show a true and fair view, and for meeting relevant accounting and disclosure requirements, and the audit committee's review should focus in particular on:

- comparisons with the previous year and the explanations for any significant variances;
- any changes in accounting policies and their disclosure in the accounts;
- any significant issues involving a high degree of judgement;
- any adjustments necessary as a result of the work carried out by the external auditors;
- going concern;
- disclosure of any significant commitments or contingent liabilities;
- impact of any significant events since the balance sheet date;
- compliance with accounting standards and other reporting requirements (including, where appropriate, those laid down by the FSA); and
- the results of the external audit.

In particular, management should explain the accounting treatment of any significant or unusual transactions, particularly where the treatment is open to different approaches, and the committee should consider whether the approach adopted is appropriate. Following their review, the audit committee should submit the relevant financial statements to the board with their recommendations on approval. If it is not satisfied with any aspect of the company's financial reporting, the audit committee should report its views to the board.

## Internal financial controls and risk management systems                                                2.16

The audit committee should monitor the integrity of the company's internal financial controls and, in the absence of other arrangements (for instance, the establishment of a separate risk committee) should assess the scope and effectiveness of the company's systems for assessing, managing and monitoring financial and other risks. Management should report to the committee on the effectiveness of the systems that they have established and, in particular, the results of any testing carried out by the internal and external auditors. Following their assessment, the audit committee should review the directors' statements in the annual report in respect of internal control and the management of risk (see CHAPTER 14 INTERNAL CONTROL).

## Whistleblowing                                                                    2.17

The audit committee should also review the company's procedures to enable staff to raise issues of concern in confidence and consider whether these provide for proportionate, independent investigation and follow-up of the matters raised (see CHAPTER 11 FRAUD AND ILLEGAL ACTS).

## The internal audit process                                                      2.18

Where the company has an internal audit function, the audit committee should monitor and review internal audit activities. This should normally include:

- reviewing and approving the remit of the internal audit function;
- confirming that there is appropriate liaison between external and internal auditors, to prevent duplication of work and make the most effective use of the available resources.
- confirming that the head of internal audit has direct access to the board chairman and to the audit committee, and is accountable to the audit committee;
- ensuring that the internal audit function is adequately resourced, maintains a suitable degree of independence from other functions within the company, has appropriate standing within the company and is given access to the information that it needs in order to fulfil its remit;
- reviewing the proposed annual programme of internal audit work before this is submitted to the board for approval;
- monitoring progress against the plan during the year;
- reviewing the results of internal audit work, together with management's response to the points raised; and
- monitoring and assessing the role and effectiveness of the internal audit function in the context of the company's risk management system.

The guidance in the Smith Report also notes that the audit committee should approve the appointment, or termination of appointment, of the head of internal audit. Where the company does not have an internal audit function, the Combined Code recommends that the board should consider from time to time the need to establish one. The Smith Report proposes that the Code should be amended to require annual consideration of this issue. The document *Internal Control: Guidance for Directors on the Combined Code'* issued by the Institute of Chartered Accountants in England & Wales in 1999 (often referred to as the Turnbull Report) also recommends that this assessment is carried out annually (see **CHAPTER 14 INTERNAL CONTROL**).

## Appointment of external auditors                    2.19

Technically, the annual appointment of the external auditors is a matter for the shareholders, but the board of directors will usually put forward recommendations for the shareholders to consider. The Smith Report states that the audit committee should have primary responsibility for making a recommendation to the shareholders on the appointment, reappointment or removal of the external auditors. The recommendation should be made initially to the board, and then to the company's shareholders. If the board does not accept the recommendation of the audit committee, the directors' report must include a statement from the audit committee explaining its recommendation and why the board has taken a different view. The audit committee's recommendation each year should be based on an assessment of the qualifications, expertise, resources, effectiveness and independence of the external auditors. The assessment should cover all aspects of the audit service and, as part of their review, the audit committee should obtain a report on the audit firm's own internal quality control procedures. If the external auditor resigns, the audit committee should investigate any issues giving rise to the resignation and consider whether any further action is required.

## Terms and remuneration of external auditors 2.20

The audit committee is responsible for approving the terms of engagement and the remuneration to be paid to the external auditor in respect of audit services. The committee should review the audit engagement letter at the start of each audit and confirm that it has been updated to deal with any new issues or requirements and any other changes in circumstances since the previous year. The committee should also satisfy itself that:

- the remuneration payable is appropriate for the service provided; and
- an effective audit can be carried out for that fee.

## Independence 2.21

The audit committee should assess the independence and objectivity of the external auditors each year, taking into account relevant professional and regulatory requirements. The assessment should cover all relationships between the company and the audit firm, including the provision of non-audit services. In the case of listed companies, professional auditing standards require the auditors to make certain disclosures in respect of their independence each year (see **2.41** below) and the guidance in the Smith Report also recommends that the audit committee seek annual information from the audit firm on the policies and processes that it adopts to maintain independence and monitor compliance with relevant professional requirements, including the current UK requirement for the appointment of the audit engagement partner to be rotated at least every five years and that of other key audit partners to be rotated at least every seven years. Factors to consider when assessing independence are covered in more detail in **2.39** to **2.44** below.

## Employment of auditor's former employees 2.22

The Smith Report recommends that the audit committee should agree with the board the company's policy on the employment of former partners and employees of the audit firm, especially any who were part of the audit team. The committee should then monitor the application of the policy and should consider in particular the number of such individuals currently employed in senior positions within the company and whether this could impair, or be perceived to impair, the independence of the audit firm.

## Provision of non-audit services 2.23

The audit committee should develop and recommend to the board the company's policy on the provision of non-audit services by the audit firm, the objective being to ensure that the provision of such services does not impair the independence or objectivity of the auditor. Issues to be considered by the audit committee include:

- whether the audit firm is a suitable supplier of the services – for instance, as a result of its skills and experience;

- whether appropriate safeguards are in place to prevent any threat to independence or objectivity in the conduct of the external audit;
- the nature of the non-audit services and the related fee levels, individually and in aggregate, relative to the audit fee; and
- the criteria which govern the compensation of the individuals performing the audit.

Other issues to consider in the context of the provision of non-audit services are summarised in **2.43** to **2.44** below. The company's formal policy should specify the types of work for which the external auditors can be engaged without formal approval, those from which the external auditors should be excluded, and those which require formal referral to the audit committee for a decision. The committee may also wish to set fee limits in general or for specific classes of work. In principle, the audit committee should not agree to the auditors providing non-audit services which:

- result in the external auditor auditing the work of its own firm;
- result in the external auditor making management decisions for the company;
- create a mutuality of interest between the external auditor and the company; or
- put the external auditor into the position of advocate for the company.

The annual report to shareholders should explain how the company's policy provides appropriate protection of auditor independence.

## Agreeing the scope of the external audit 2.24

Before the detailed audit work commences each year, the audit committee should discuss and agree with the auditors the scope of their work and the overall work plan, including planned materiality levels and proposed resources to carry out the plan. In the case of a group with a complex structure or overseas interests, more than one firm of auditors may be involved, and the audit committee will need to be satisfied that proper co-ordination between the various auditors can be achieved. This meeting with the auditors will also provide a suitable opportunity to consider recent changes in accounting standards and reporting requirements and the potential impact for the company. Where additional information needs to be prepared or collated as a result of these changes, early consideration of the issues should help to ensure that the company has sufficient time to put the necessary procedures in place. It will also be important to consider any changes that have taken place within the business, or are planned for the near future, and their impact for the annual accounts and the audit (for instance, new business activities or potential closures). The aim should be to identify any likely problem areas at this stage, so that solutions can be identified in good time. If the company has an internal audit function, it will be important to ensure that there is good liaison between the internal and external auditors, to avoid any potential duplication of work and make the most effective use of all the available resources. In the case of listed companies, the auditors will often have additional reporting responsibilities in respect of the interim report and corporate governance issues, and the nature and scope of their work in these areas also needs to be considered and agreed.

## Reviewing the results of the external audit 2.25

The results of the external audit should be reviewed in conjunction with the annual report and accounts as the two are inextricably linked. In particular the audit committee should:

- discuss with the auditors any issues identified during the course of their work, distinguishing those that have been resolved and any that remain unresolved, and any reservations that the external auditors have in respect of the annual report and accounts;
- review the key accounting and audit judgements; and
- review the level of errors identified during the audit and obtain explanations from management and the auditors for any that remain unadjusted.

The audit committee should also review the audit representation letter before it is signed by management, and consider whether the information given is complete and appropriate, based on the committee's own knowledge. In particular, the committee should explore any non-standard issues raised in the representation letter. Other issues that may need to be considered at this stage include:

- adequacy of the company's accounting records and systems of internal control;
- any breakdowns in systems and controls identified during the audit;
- any other irregularities identified during the course of the audit; and
- where relevant, the auditors' opinion on the company's statement of compliance with the Combined Code and the consistency of the company's statements on going concern and internal control with the knowledge gained by the external auditors during the course of their work.

This will usually be an appropriate time for the audit committee to discuss the actual audit costs with the auditors and to begin thinking about any changes to the audit approach that may be needed for the following year – planning for the next year will usually be most effective when the successes and difficulties of the current year are fresh in the mind.

## Reviewing the auditors' report to management 2.26

At the conclusion of the audit, the auditors will usually issue a formal written report on:

- any significant weaknesses in the accounting or internal control systems that have come to their attention during the audit, together with their recommendations for improvements;

- any significant business issues that have come to their attention during the audit, together with their advice (for instance, potential economies or improvements in efficiency); and
- any significant errors identified during the audit and comments on any individual accounting policies or practices that they consider need to be drawn to the attention of the directors or senior management.

The audit committee should consider this report, together with management's response to the points raised. This is considered in more detail at **2.64** below.

## Assessing the effectiveness of external audit     2.27

At the end of the audit cycle, the audit committee should assess the effectiveness of the external audit process and review:

- any significant changes from the original audit plan and the reasons for these;
- the robustness and perceptiveness of the auditors in handling the key accounting and auditing judgements identified and in responding to questions from the audit committee;
- feedback from key individuals (eg finance director, head of internal audit) on the conduct of the external audit; and
- the content of the management letter and any commentary on the systems of internal control, to assess whether these demonstrate a good understanding of the business and whether any recommendations have been acted upon.

## Frequency and timing of audit committee meetings     2.28

In practice, most audit committees meet between two and four times a year, depending on the complexity of the company's activities. The Smith Report now recommends that there should be no fewer than three meetings each year, to coincide with key dates within the financial reporting cycle, although it also notes that most committees will need to meet more often than this. The important point is for the committee to meet sufficiently often to be able to review and monitor major issues. The terms of reference may provide for additional meetings to be held in emergencies (for instance, where a prompt decision is needed) or for specific purposes. It is also important to consider the timing of the audit committee's meetings in relation to:

- the scheduled meetings of the main board, so that the audit committee can report and put forward its recommendations in a timely manner; and
- the company's financial timetable – in the case of quoted companies, this will need to take into account the publication of the interim report, preliminary announcement and annual report and accounts so that the audit committee can make its input at the appropriate point.

Sufficient time should be allowed between audit committee and main board meetings to enable issues requiring further work to be properly followed up and reported to the board where appropriate. Meetings should be planned well in advance to encourage a good attendance by committee members and so that finance staff, external auditors and internal auditors have plenty of notice of when information will need to be presented. In larger organisations, it may be appropriate for the location of the meetings to be varied, to give audit committee members the opportunity to visit key operational sites. The Smith Report also notes that the audit committee chairman, and to a lesser extent, other committee members, will usually want to keep in touch on a continuing basis with key individuals within the company and with the external audit lead partner.

## Agendas                                                            2.29

The annual accounts production and audit schedules will often provide a useful starting point when scheduling meetings of the audit committee and agreeing agendas. A suitable schedule of meetings for a quoted company might be as follows:

| Timing | Main agenda items |
|---|---|
| Approximately 5 months into the financial year | (i) Consideration of the scope of the external auditors' work on the interim report;<br>(ii) Consideration of report from the Head of Internal Audit, covering:<br>• progress with planned work programme;<br>• issues arising since the last report;<br>• follow-up of significant points raised in previous report.<br>(iii) Self-assessment of the committee's effectiveness and review of terms of reference for the committee to confirm these are still appropriate or to identify changes to be put to the board for consideration. |
| Approximately 7 months into the financial year | (i) Consideration of recent or imminent developments in financial reporting and their impact for the company;<br>(ii) Review of the interim report prior to its release;<br>(iii) Consideration of the results of the external auditors' work on the interim report; |

| | | |
|---|---|---|
| | (iv) | Discussion with the external auditors on the proposed audit approach and the audit plan; |
| | (v) | Consideration of proposed external audit fee. |
| Approximately 10 months into the financial year | (i) | Consideration of report from the Head of Internal Audit, covering:<br>● progress with planned work programme;<br>● issues arising since the last report;<br>● follow-up of significant points raised in previous report. |
| | (ii) | Consideration of the scope of internal audit work for the next financial year. |
| Prior to the release of the preliminary announcement | (i) | Consideration of the annual report and accounts; |
| | (ii) | Review of the results and effectiveness of the external audit; |
| | (iii) | Review of external audit costs; |
| | (iv) | Review of the service provided by the external auditors and their independence, and recommendation on appointment (or reappointment) of auditors; |
| | (v) | Consideration of annual report from the Head of Internal Audit, covering:<br>● summary of work completed for the previous financial year and comparison with planned work programme;<br>● issues arising since the last report;<br>● follow-up of significant points raised in previous report.<br>● progress on work planned for the current financial year. |

Where the company has an internal audit function, the review of reports from this department may be dealt with as a separate agenda item at the meetings

Audit Matters

dealing with external audit issues (as suggested above), or may be covered in separate meetings. For instance, in the case of an unquoted company, there will not usually be an interim report and it may therefore be appropriate to schedule four audit committee meetings during the year to deal alternately with internal audit and external audit issues.

## Other attendees                                                        2.30

The Smith Report states categorically that no one other than the audit committee chairman and members is entitled to be present at a meeting of the audit committee. However, other individuals may attend by invitation of the committee and the finance director, the head of internal audit and the external auditors will usually be invited to attend. Depending on the circumstances, they may only need to attend for part of the meeting. It is recommended that the audit committee should meet at least once each year with the external and internal auditors without management present to ensure that the auditors have an opportunity to raise any issues of concern. In practice, this can usually be arranged to take place at the conclusion of one of the regular audit committee meetings.

## Attendance records                                                     2.31

It is good practice to keep detailed attendance records for audit committee meetings and for the board of directors to review these on an annual basis to confirm that each member is making an appropriate contribution to the work of the committee. Attendance information will also need to be retained in future for inclusion in the annual report on the committee's activities (see **2.33** below).

## Reporting to the main board                                            2.32

The agendas for meetings of the main board should include a report from the chairman of the audit committee as a regular item. This enables the audit committee to report to the board on the main points arising from its discussions with both external and internal auditors and also to put recommendations to the board when appropriate. The board has collective responsibility for the annual accounts and for internal control within the company, but will usually look to the audit committee for advice on issues relating to financial reporting, internal controls and the financial aspects of corporate governance. The audit committee will also have responsibility for making recommendations to the board on the appointment or reappointment of auditors and the agreement of the external audit fee. Minutes of the meetings of the audit committee will usually be circulated to all board members for information. The guidance in the Smith Report notes that, where there is disagreement between the audit committee and the board, adequate time should be made available for discussion, and hopefully resolution, of the issue. If the matter cannot be resolved, the audit committee should have the right to report the issue to the shareholders within the annual report on its activities.

## Reporting to shareholders                                          2.33

The Smith Report requires the directors' report to include a separate section each year describing the role and responsibilities of the audit committee and the actions taken to discharge those responsibilities. The recommended contents of the report include:

- a summary of the main responsibilities of the audit committee;
- the names of all members of the audit committee during the period (with appointment and resignation dates where appropriate) and details of the relevant qualifications, expertise and experience of each member;
- details of any dedicated resources available to the committee;
- the number of audit committee meetings and the attendance by each member;
- details of the remuneration policies for members of the audit committee (or a cross-reference to the Directors' Remuneration Report);
- the actions and procedures carried out to:
  - monitor the integrity of the financial statements;
  - review the integrity of the company's internal financial control and risk management systems;
  - review the independence of the external auditors, including disclosure of the company's policy on the provision of non-audit services and an explanation of how this protects auditor independence;
  - oversee the external audit process, including confirmation that its effectiveness has been assessed;
- an explanation of the recommendation to the board on the appointment of the external auditors and, where applicable, the process adopted to select a new auditor; and
- confirmation that the plans and work of the internal audit department have been reviewed or, if there is no internal audit function, an explanation of the committee's consideration of the need to establish one.

## Self-assessment and appraisal                                      2.34

The Smith Report recommends that the effectiveness of the audit committee should be reviewed annually by both the committee and the board. This might be done by considering developments generally in the role and activities of audit committees and discussing with the main board the extent to which the audit committee is considered to have fulfilled the various aspects of its terms of reference. Feedback might also be sought from the head of internal audit and the external auditors on these points. Specific issues to consider might include:

- are there appropriate procedures for appointing committee members?
- does the committee have the appropriate mix of knowledge and skills?
- is the amount and nature of training and administrative support appropriate?

- are the committee's terms of reference appropriate?
- does the committee adequately fulfil its role?
- is the frequency and timing of committee meetings appropriate?
- are agendas and appropriate supporting information circulated to committee members in good time?
- how effective are the committee's relationships with management, internal audit and the external auditors?
- does the committee's workload require a change of emphasis?
- does the committee need subsidiary committees to deal with significant or overseas business units?
- if subsidiary committees are already in place, are the arrangements working effectively?
- what significant issues does the committee need to address in the coming year?

The audit committee should report formally to the main board each year on the results of their self-assessment. It is also best practice for the chairman of the main board, together with the executive directors, to review the contribution of individual non-executives to the work of the board, including where appropriate their activities as members of the audit committee.

## Appointment of external auditors                          2.35

## At a glance                                               2.36

- Every company is required to appoint auditors, unless audit exemption applies.
- Only certain individuals and firms are eligible for appointment as a company auditor.
- The auditors must be, and must be seen to be, independent of the company.
- New guidance on independence is likely, following the UK post-Enron review
- In particular, the provision of non-audit services by the auditors may impact on their independence.
- The audit committee should consider periodically whether a change of auditor is required.
- Complex provisions apply under *CA 1985* on a change of auditor.
- Professional standards require any new auditor to communicate with the predecessor audit firm.
- Company law grants auditors specific rights to information, and imposes specific duties on them.

## Requirement to appoint auditors                           2.37

Under *section 384(1)* of the *Companies Act 1985* (*CA 1985*), every company must appoint an auditor or auditors. The only exceptions to this, set out in *section 388A* of *CA 1985*, are for dormant companies and certain small companies, which may be exempt from an annual audit under sections *249AA* and *249A* respectively. The legislation sets out specific procedures for the appointment process, and for the filling of any casual vacancies that arise. The auditors appointed generally hold office from the conclusion of the meeting at which they are appointed until the conclusion of the next general meeting at which accounts are laid. A separate process is set out for the appointment of the first auditors, and separate provisions also apply in the case of a private company which chooses to take advantage of the elective regime to reduce the need for regular formal meetings of the company.

## Eligibility for appointment as company auditor            2.38

Under *section 25* of the *Companies Act 1989* (*CA 1989*), either an individual or a firm may be appointed as a company auditor, but they will only be eligible for appointment if they are a member of a recognised supervisory body (as defined in *section 30* of *CA 1989*) and eligible for appointment under the rules of that supervisory body. Specific requirements on recognised supervisory bodies are set out in *Schedule 11* to *CA 1989*. The supervisory bodies currently recognised in relation to the appointment of company auditors are the:

- Institute of Chartered Accountants in England and Wales;
- Institute of Chartered Accountants of Scotland;
- Institute of Chartered Accountants in Ireland;
- Association of Chartered Certified Accountants; and
- Association of Authorised Public Accountants.

Special provisions apply to certain individuals who qualified for appointment as a company auditor prior to 1 January 1990 other than by membership of one of these bodies. An auditor who becomes ineligible for appointment during his term of office must vacate office immediately and give written notice to the company. The auditor is also required to make a formal statement of any circumstances connected with his ceasing to hold office (see **2.46** below). Where an auditor was ineligible for appointment for any part of the period during which the audit was conducted, the Secretary of State can require the company to engage the services of someone who is eligible for appointment to audit the relevant accounts again or to review the original audit and report on whether a second audit is required.

## Auditor independence                                       2.39

Under *section 27* of *CA 1989*, a person is ineligible for appointment as auditor of a company if he or she is:

- an officer or employee of the company; or
- a partner or employee of such a person, or in a partnership of which such a person is a partner; or
- ineligible by virtue of either of the above for appointment as auditor of

any associated undertaking of the company – in this context, an associated undertaking is defined as:

- a parent undertaking of the company;
- a subsidiary undertaking of the company; or
- a subsidiary undertaking of any parent undertaking of the company.

The rules therefore encompass the widest group of which the company is a member. *Section 744(1)* of *CA 1985* defines an officer of the company as including a director, manager or secretary – an individual or firm therefore cannot act as both auditor to and secretary of the same company. The report of the DTI Co-ordinating Group on Audit and Accounting Issues (CGAAI) published in January 2003 emphasises the importance of the external auditor being perceived to be independent as well as actually being independent in practice.

## Professional requirements on independence          2.40

The various recognised supervisory bodies and professional requirements also impose stringent requirements on auditor independence. These cover issues which may create a potential conflict of interest for the auditor and deal with situations such as:

- undue financial dependence on the audit client;
- actual or threatened litigation in respect of an audit client;
- personal or family relationships;
- beneficial interests in shares and other investments;
- involvement of the audit firm as trustee;
- provision of other services to an audit client;
- a partner or senior member of staff joining an audit client.

The guidance sets out suggested safeguards that may help to reduce threats to independence in these and similar situations. If appropriate safeguards against the impairment of objectivity and independence cannot be put in place, the audit firm should not accept the appointment, or should resign in the case of an existing appointment. The Institute of Chartered Accountants in England and Wales (ICAEW) has also recently introduced a two-year cooling off period for listed companies where an audit partner wishes to join an audit client as a director or senior employee.

## Annual disclosures on independence          2.41

The auditors of listed companies are required by Statement of Auditing Standards (SAS) 610 (Revised) 'Communication of audit matters to those charged with governance' to disclose at least annually in writing to the audit committee all relationships between the auditor firm (and its related entities) and the client (and its related entities) that may reasonably be thought to affect the independence of the audit firm and the objectivity of the audit team, together with the related safeguards that are in place. The auditors must also confirm in writing to the audit committee each year that, in their professional judgement, the audit firm is independent within the meaning of regulatory and professional requirements and that the objectivity of the audit team is not impaired.

## Post-Enron review 2.42

Auditor independence is also an issue that has been considered in detail by the DTI as part of the post-Enron review. The CGAAI report makes the following points:

- UK requirements should continue to be based on principles rather than detailed, prescriptive rules but there need to be tougher and clearer safeguards, particularly on the provision of non-audit services to an audit client;
- There is a need for improved qualitative guidance for audit firms on economic dependence on a single audit client (which can arise at the level of the firm as whole, an individual office or an individual partner).
- For periods starting on or after 1 January 2003, audit firms with listed and other public interest clients should voluntarily publish an annual report including whole firm financial information, details on their organisational structure and reward systems, information on how quality is achieved and monitored, and their policies and procedures for managing threats to their independence.
- Audit firms with listed and public interest clients should disclose in that annual report any fees representing more than 5% of total fees and should also ensure that the audit committee or board of the relevant audit client is aware of their potential economic dependency on the appointment.
- The responsibility for setting standards on independence should be transferred from the regulatory bodies to an independent body.
- The unit responsible for monitoring the performance of audit firms with listed clients should continue to develop inspection themes (such as auditor independence) and should publish annual information on how it monitors the independence requirements and aggregate information on the effectiveness of the management of such matters by the major audit firms.

The review decided against the mandatory rotation of audit firms on the grounds that this:

- may have a negative impact on audit quality and effectiveness, particularly in the early years of an audit appointment;
- would create significant additional costs, especially in terms of management time; and
- has had no strong positive impact in countries where it has been introduced.

The review group concluded that there were sensible and effective alternatives to mandatory rotation. These include giving the audit committee specific responsibility for periodic consideration of whether a change of external auditors is needed and the professional accountancy bodies' current requirement that the appointment of the audit engagement partner should be rotated at least every five years and that of other key audit partners at least every seven years.

## Provision of non-audit services                                      2.43

At present, there are only limited restrictions in the UK on the provision of non-audit services to the company by the auditors and their associates, although the amount paid for these services must be disclosed in the accounts each year (see **2.69** below). Recent changes have introduced more stringent requirements on the circumstances in which an audit firm can provide the following services to an audit client:

- valuation services;
- internal audit services;
- design and implementation of financial information systems;
- services connected with the recruitment of senior managers; and
- acting for the client in the resolution of litigation.

However, the potential impact of the present situation on the independence and integrity of auditors is an issue that has come under increasing scrutiny in recent years. The International Federation of Accountants (IFAC) has recently incorporated new rules on independence into its Code of Ethics, which is intended to serve as a model for the development of national ethical guidance and which has generally been adopted by the UK accountancy bodies. This highlights the fact that:

- auditors must necessarily develop a good understanding of their clients and the clients will benefit from this knowledge and skill being brought to bear in non-audit areas; and
- by becoming involved in other areas, the audit firm will obtain additional information of benefit to the audit role.

It therefore does not prohibit the provision of non-audit services to an audit client, provided that any potential threats to independence can be eliminated or reduced to an acceptable level by the introduction of appropriate safeguards. The IFAC Code includes detailed guidance on the identification of threats and the consideration of suitable safeguards.

## Results of CGAAI review                                              2.44

The CGAAI review (see **2.41** above) also considered this issue in some detail and made the following recommendations:

- UK requirements should continue to be based on principles rather than rules, but there should be tougher and clearer safeguards to ensure that

50

the joint provision of audit and non-audit services does not undermine, or appear to undermine, auditor independence.

- Each type of non-audit service should be assessed against a number of key principles and, in particular, auditors should not provide non-audit services which involve taking management decisions, auditing their own work or acting as advocate for the client in an adversarial situation.
- In the case of listed companies, there should be an enhanced role for the audit committee in approving the purchase of non-audit services from the audit firm and justifying this to the shareholders;
- There should be fuller disclosure on the nature and value of non-audit services provided to the company by the audit firm – the Institute of Chartered Accountants in England and Wales (ICAEW) has recently developed draft guidance on this (see **2.75** below).

In particular, the review concluded that additional guidance should be developed on the provision of litigation support, actuarial services and taxation services (other than the application of well tried and tested tax law). There should also be a strong presumption against the acceptability of the audit firm providing internal audit services, other than in exceptional circumstances. The provision of services relating to IT and financial information systems is only acceptable where specific safeguards are in place and certain conditions have been met. Under the recommendations in the Smith Report (see **2.5** above) the audit committee will be responsible for recommending to the board a company policy on the provision of non-audit services by the audit firm and for monitoring compliance with the agreed policy (see **2.23** above).

## Regular review of audit arrangements                                    2.45

Changes in audit appointments may come about when auditors resign, do not seek reappointment or are not reappointed by the company. Broadly similar rules apply under *CA 1985* whatever the reason for the change. It is normal practice for companies to review their audit arrangements on a regular basis. This may be particularly important as a business develops and expands and its overall needs change. In the case of a listed company, the audit committee is required to carry out an annual assessment of the independence, objectivity and effectiveness of the external audit (see **2.27** above), and should consider periodically whether any change of audit firm is needed. Issues to be considered might include:

- do the auditors have the appropriate degree of industry knowledge and experience?
- is the independence of the auditors still assured?
- can the auditors provide the necessary geographical coverage?
- how effective has the audit service been in recent years?
- how well do the auditors communicate with company management on significant business issues and any material weaknesses identified in the systems of internal control?
- does the audit provide value for money?

- are the auditors able to provide the full range of services that the company requires?

From time to time, the company may wish to invite other firms to submit a proposal and fee quote for undertaking the audit. This may result from a positive decision to appoint new auditors (for instance, if the company is not satisfied with the audit service it is currently receiving, or if expansion of the business means that the current auditors are no longer able to provide the level of service that the company requires) or it may be done simply to confirm that the company is receiving value for money under its present arrangements. The process can involve a considerable amount of management time and will therefore not usually be undertaken more regularly than once every three to five years.

## Resignation or removal of auditors                                   2.46

Complex provisions apply under *CA 1985* when auditors resign from office, do not seek reappointment or are removed during their term of office. These provisions give the the auditors certain rights to bring any information they consider necessary to the attention of the members or creditors of the company, and impose certain obligations on the company and its directors to ensure that the information is duly conveyed. Special notice must also be given for any resolution to remove auditors before their term of office has expired and for any resolution to appoint as auditors someone other than the retiring auditor, and there are detailed provisions in the legislation on sending copies to the auditors concerned. In particular, *CA 1985* requires any auditor who ceases to hold office, for whatever reason, to deposit at the company's registered office:

- a statement of any circumstances connected with their ceasing to hold office that they consider should be brought to the attention of the members or creditors of the company; or
- a statement that there are no such circumstances.

If the auditors' statement details circumstances that they consider should be brought to the attention of members and creditors, the company has 14 days in which to send a copy to every person who is entitled to be sent copies of the accounts or to apply to the court on the grounds that the auditors are using the statement to secure needless publicity.

## Professional requirements on a change of auditor          2.47

Where a company proposes to appoint new auditors, professional standards require the new auditor to communicate directly with the outgoing auditor before accepting appointment. The new audit firm will usually seek written permission from the company to communicate with the outgoing auditor and will ask the company to give written authority to the outgoing audit firm to discuss the matter freely with the proposed new auditor. If this permission is refused, the proposed new auditor will generally not be able to accept nomination or appointment. If an issue of conflicting viewpoints between the company and the existing auditor is raised in the response, the prospective audit firm is required to discuss the conflict with the company and satisfy themselves either that the company's view is one which they can accept as reasonable, or that the company accepts that the new auditor might have to express a contrary opinion (for instance, that the issue might result in a qualified audit report).

## Rights of external auditors 2.48

Company law grants external auditors various rights in relation to their appointment. In particular they are:

- entitled to receive all notices of, and other communications relating to, any general meeting of the company which a member of the company is entitled to receive;
- entitled to attend any general meeting of the company and to be heard at any meeting they attend on any part of the business which concerns them as auditors;
- given a right of access at all times to the company's books, accounts and vouchers and entitled to require from the officers of the company the information and explanations that they consider necessary in order to perform their duties as auditors; and
- in the case of a private company acting by means of a written resolution, entitled to be sent a copy of the resolution at or before the time that it is sent to the members for signature.

The DTI document 'Modern Company Law for a Competitive Economy: Final Report' issued in July 2001 recommends that this duty (and its criminal sanction) should be extended to all company employees, and that directors should have an additional duty to volunteer information to the auditors where, under the normal standards of skill and care, they recognise (or should recognise) that it is likely to be material to the audit. The Government White Paper 'Modernising Company Law' issued in July 2002 confirmed the intention to proceed on this basis. In a group situation, subsidiary companies and their auditors have a duty to provide any information and explanations reasonably required by the auditors of the parent company. In the case of overseas entities (ie those not subject to UK company law), the parent company should take all reasonable steps to ensure similar compliance.

## Duties of external auditors 2.49

The duties imposed on external auditors under *CA 1985* are:

- to report to the members on all annual accounts of the company that are to be laid before the company in general meeting during their term of office (see **2.51** below);
- to consider whether the information given in the directors' report is

consistent with the accounts for that financial year and to refer to any inconsistency in their report on the accounts;

- to carry out appropriate investigations to enable them to form an opinion on whether:
  - ■ proper accounting records have been kept by the company;
  - ■ proper returns adequate for audit purposes have been received from any branches not visited by them; and
  - ■ the company's individual accounts are in agreement with the accounting records and returns;
    – if the auditors are not satisfied on any of these issues, they must state this fact in their report on the annual accounts;
    if they have not received all the information and explanations they consider necessary in order to perform their audit, to state this fact in their audit report;

- if the accounts do not include all of the required disclosures in respect of directors' emoluments and other benefits, or transactions between the company and its directors or other officers, to include a statement of the missing details in their audit report, so far as they are reasonably able to do so (in the case of listed companies, the FSA has extended this responsibility to cover the additional disclosures in respect of directors' remuneration required under the Listing Rules); and

- if the directors have taken advantage of *section 248* of *CA 1985*, which relieves small and medium-sized companies from the requirement to prepare group accounts, but in the opinion of the auditors the company is not entitled to this exemption, to state this fact in their report on the company's accounts.

In highly regulated sectors, such as the banking and financial service sectors, auditors may be required to report directly to the regulator on certain matters specified in legislation or by the relevant regulator. They also have a duty to report directly to the regulator information which comes to their attention during the course of their work if there is reasonable cause for them to believe that this information may be of material significance to the regulator in carrying out his functions. Detailed guidance on this duty to report is provided in Statement of Auditing Standards 620 (SAS 620) 'The auditors' right and duty to report to regulators in the financial sector'.

## Reporting by external auditors                                          2.50

## At a glance                                                             2.51

- The auditors are required to report to the members on all annual accounts of the company.
- Auditing standards set out requirements on the form and content of audit reports.
- A separate audit opinion is required on summary financial statements prepared by a listed company.

- Auditors are also required to express an opinion on any revised accounts or reports issued by the company.
- If the audit report is qualified, the auditors must make a separate report in respect of any proposed distribution by the company.
- *CA 1985* requires a formal report from the auditors (or, in some cases, from independent accountants) in certain other circumstances.
- The auditors will usually also report to management on any issues arising from their work.
- In the case of a listed company, the auditors are required to review certain disclosures and statements made by the directors under the Combined Code.
- The auditors may also review and report on any interim report published by the company.

## Report on annual accounts                                    2.52

The auditors are required to report to the members on all annual accounts of the company that are to be laid before the company in general meeting during their term of office. If the company has elected to dispense with the laying of accounts, the auditors are required to report on all annual accounts sent to the members and others during the auditors' term of office. Their report must state:

- whether, in the opinion of the auditors, the accounts have been prepared in accordance with the requirements of *CA 1985*; and
- whether the accounts give a true and fair view:
  - in the case of an individual balance sheet, of the state of affairs of the company at the end of the financial period;
  - in the case of an individual profit and loss account, of the profit or loss of the company for the financial year; and
  - in the case of group accounts, of the state of affairs of the undertakings included in the consolidation as a whole, and of the profit or loss of those undertakings for the financial year, so far as concerns the members of the company.

Where the company is required to prepare a directors' remuneration report for accounting periods ending on or after 31 December 2002, the auditors are also required to report on certain aspects of these disclosures. The auditors must also review the directors' report and report on any inconsistencies between this and the financial statements.

## *Requirements of Auditing Standards*                         2.53

Statement of Auditing Standards 600 (SAS 600) 'Auditors' reports on financial statements' sets out detailed additional requirements, which must be followed whenever an auditors' opinion is expressed in terms of whether the financial statements give a true and fair view. Under this standard, the auditors' report must contain:

- a title identifying the person(s) to whom the report is addressed;
- an introductory paragraph identifying the financial statements that have been audited;
- separate sections dealing with:
  - the respective responsibilities of the directors and the auditors;
  - the basis of the auditors' opinion; and
  - the auditors' opinion;
- the signature of the auditors; and
- the date of the audit report.

These detailed requirements were introduced to improve the general understanding of the respective roles and responsibilities of the directors and the auditors, and the level of work undertaken during an audit. The example reports set out in SAS 600 have been updated by APB Bulletin 2001/2 'Revisions to the wording of auditors' reports on financial statements and the interim review report' and, for accounting periods ending on or after 31 December 2002, have been revised further by APB Bulletin 2002/2 'The United Kingdom Directors' Remuneration Report Regulations 2002'. The first changes were principally to take account of the increase in financial reporting on the internet and the consequent need to identify clearly which items are covered by the audit report and which accounting standards and auditing standards have been applied. The second change reflects the new requirement for the auditors to report on certain aspects of the Directors' Remuneration Report. SAS 600 also sets out detailed requirements on the dating and signature of the audit report. Auditors should not sign their report until the financial statements have been approved by the directors, and the date on the audit report should be the date on which the auditors physically sign to express their opinion on the financial statements.

## *Qualified opinions, adverse opinions and disclaimers* 2.54

Under SAS 600, auditors are required to express a qualified opinion when:

- they disagree with the treatment or disclosure of an item in the financial statements; or
- there has been a limitation on the scope of their work (for instance, where there is inadequate evidence to support a figure in the accounts); and
- in the auditors' opinion, the effect is, or may be, material to the financial statements.

An adverse opinion must be issued when the effect of a disagreement is so material that the auditors conclude that the financial statements are seriously misleading, and a disclaimer of opinion must be expressed when the possible effect of a limitation in scope is so material that the auditors are unable to express an opinion on the financial statements.

## *Fundamental uncertainty*                                    **2.55**

SAS 600 also considers the situation of a fundamental uncertainty which is adequately accounted for and disclosed in the financial statements (for instance where the outcome of a significant litigation issue is still unclear, or the negotiation of bank facilities is still in progress). In these circumstances the auditors are required to add an explanatory paragraph to their report, drawing attention to the fundamental uncertainty but making clear that their opinion is not qualified in this respect.

## Summary financial statements                              **2.56**

*CA 1985* permits listed companies to issue summary financial statements to their members, rather than copies of the full accounts, provided that certain conditions are properly observed (see **CHAPTER 10 FINANCIAL REPORTING**). Summary financial statements must be derived from the annual accounts and directors' report, and must comply with the requirements of *section 251* of *CA 1985* as regards their form and content. The summary financial statements are specifically required to include:

- an opinion from the auditors on whether the summary financial statements are consistent with the full accounts and directors' report;
- a statement on whether the auditors' report on the full accounts was qualified or unqualified – if it was qualified, the auditors' report on the full accounts must be set out in the summary financial statements, together with any additional information needed to understand the qualification (eg a particular note to the accounts); and
- a statement on whether the auditors' report on the full accounts contained a statement under *section 237(2)* of *CA 1985* (inadequate accounting records or returns, or accounts not in agreement with the accounting records or returns) or under *section 237(3)* of *CA 1985* (failure to obtain all information and explanations the auditors' considered necessary) – if such a statement was included, the auditors' report on the full accounts must be set out in the summary financial statements.

The latest example of an auditors' statement on the summary financial statement is given in APB Bulletin 2001/2 'The United Kingdom Directors' Remuneration Report Regulations 2002'.

## Revised accounts and/or directors' report                 **2.57**

Where the company issues revised annual accounts under *sections 245* or *245A* of *CA 1985* and the *Companies (Revision of Defective Accounts and Report) Regulations 1990 (SI 1990/2570 as amended by subsequent SIs)*, the auditors are required to state whether, in their opinion:

- the revised accounts have been properly prepared in accordance with the provisions of *CA 1985* as they have effect under the Regulations;

- a true and fair view, seen as at the date on which the original annual accounts were approved, is given by the revised accounts with respect to the matters set out in *section 235(2)* of *CA 1985*; and
- the original annual accounts failed to comply with the requirements of *CA 1985* in the respects identified by the directors.

Where a revised directors' report or directors' remuneration report is issued under same sections and regulations, the auditors are required to state whether, in their opinion, the information given in the revised report is consistent with the annual accounts for the relevant year (which must be stated). Example reports are given in APB Practice Note 8 'Reports by auditors under company legislation in the United Kingdom'. If there has been a change of auditors, the directors can resolve that the report be made by the auditors who reported on the original accounts and directors' report, provided that they are willing to do so and that they would still be eligible for appointment as auditors.

## Distribution where the audit report is qualified 2.58

Where a company intends to make a distribution and the auditors have issued a qualified audit report on the last annual accounts, *section 271(4)* of *CA 1985* requires the auditors to make a written statement on whether, in their opinion, the matter in respect of which their report is qualified is material for the purpose of determining whether the proposed distribution contravenes the requirements of *sections 263 to 265* and *270* of *CA 1985* on profits available for distribution. The auditors can make this written statement either simultaneously with their report on the annual accounts or at a later date, but it must be laid before the company in general meeting before the distribution is made. An example report is given in APB Practice Note 8 'Reports by auditors under company legislation in the United Kingdom'. The report can only be made by the auditors who qualified their report on the relevant accounts.

## Distribution by public company based on initial accounts 2.59

Where a company wishes to make a distribution during its first accounting reference period, or before the accounts for that period have been laid before the members or delivered to the registrar, initial accounts must be prepared to support the distribution. In the case of a public company, *section 273* of *CA 1985* requires initial accounts to be:

- properly prepared in accordance with the normal accounting requirements of *CA 1985*;
- approved and signed by the directors; and
- delivered to the registrar.

The auditors are required to report whether, in their opinion, the initial accounts have been properly prepared (which is specifically defined as showing a true and fair view of the state of the company's affairs at the balance sheet date and the profit or loss for the relevant period, and complying with the relevant accounting provisions of *CA 1985*). An example report is given in APB Practice Note 8 'Reports by auditors under company legislation in the United Kingdom'. If the report is qualified, the auditors must also state whether, in their opinion, the matter in respect of which their report is qualified is material for the purpose of determining whether the proposed distribution contravenes the requirements of *sections 263* to *265* and *270* of *CA 1985* on profits available for distribution. The auditors' report (and the statement, where relevant) must be delivered to the Registrar of Companies with the initial accounts before the distribution takes place.

## Re-registration of a private company as a public company                              2.60

A private company that wishes to reregister as public must deliver certain documents to the Registrar of Companies, including an audited balance sheet and related notes as at a date not more than seven months before the application to reregister. The auditors are required to make an unqualified written statement that, in their opinion, this balance sheet shows that the amount of the company's net assets (as defined in *section 264(2)* of *CA 1985*) at this balance sheet date was not less than the aggregate of its called up share capital and undistributable reserves. An example report is given in APB Practice Note 8 'Reports by auditors under company legislation in the United Kingdom'. If the company's last audited accounts covered a period ending more than seven months before the application, an updated balance sheet will need to be prepared by the company and audited by the auditors.

## Redemption or purchase of own shares out of capital      2.61

Where a private company redeems or purchases its own shares wholly or partly out of capital, the directors are required by *section 173* of *CA 1985* to make a statutory declaration specifying the amount of the permissible capital payment for the shares in question and setting out their opinion that:

- there are no grounds on which the company could be found unable to pay its debts immediately following the payment out of capital; and
- the company will be able to continue to carry on business as a going concern throughout the year immediately following the date of the payment and will be able to pay its debts as they fall due.

The form and content of this declaration, and the issues that the directors must take into account when making it, are specified in the legislation. When the declaration is delivered to the registrar, it must have attached to it a report by the auditors, addressed to the directors, stating that:

- they have enquired into the company's state of affairs;
- in their opinion, the amount specified in the declaration as the permissible capital payment has been properly determined in accordance with *section 171* and *172* of *CA 1985*; and

- they are not aware of anything to indicate that the opinion expressed by the directors in the declaration is unreasonable in all the circumstances.

An example report is given in APB Practice Note 8 'Reports by auditors under company legislation in the United Kingdom'. The legislation makes no provision for this report to be qualified, so if the auditors are unable to make these statements the redemption or purchase cannot proceed.

## Financial assistance for the purchase of own shares    2.62

Financial assistance for the purchase of own shares can only be given in very specific circumstances. Before the assistance is given, the directors must make a statutory declaration setting out details of the proposed financial assistance and expressing their opinion that:

- there are no grounds on which the company could be found unable to pay its debts immediately following the giving of the financial assistance; and either
- the company will be able to pay its debts as they fall due during the year immediately following the giving of the assistance; or,
- if it is intended to commence the winding-up of the company within 12 months, the company will be able to pay its debts in full within 12 months of the commencement of the winding-up.

The form and content of this declaration, and the issues that the directors must take into account when making it, are set out in *section 156* of *CA 1985*. When the declaration is delivered to the registrar, it must have attached to it a report by the auditors, addressed to the directors, stating that:

- they have enquired into the state of affairs of the company; and
- they are not aware of anything to indicate that the opinion expressed by the directors in the declaration is unreasonable in all the circumstances.

An example report is given in APB Practice Note 8 'Reports by auditors under company legislation in the United Kingdom'. Once again, the legislation makes no provision for this report to be qualified, so if the auditors are unable to make these statements, the directors cannot proceed with the proposed financial assistance.

## Allotment of shares by a public company other than for cash    2.63

Where a public company proposes to allot shares for consideration in a form other than cash, it is usually required by *section 103* of *CA 1985* to obtain a report on the value of the assets to be received as consideration for the shares. This report must be obtained in the six months before the date of allotment and must be made by independent accountants who may, but need not, be the auditors of the company. If they are not the auditors, they must be qualified to act as auditors (see **2.38** and **2.39** above). Under *section 108* of *CA 1985*:

- the independent accountants may rely on a valuation made by another specialist who appears to them to have the requisite knowledge and experience, and who is not associated with the company (eg as an officer or employee of the company or group) – in practice they will have to follow the detailed guidance in Statement of Auditing Standards 520 (SAS 520) 'Using the work of an expert' if they wish to adopt this approach;
- their report must state:
  - the nominal value of the relevant shares;
  - the amount of any premium payable on the shares;
  - a description of the consideration;
  - if they have valued part (or all) of the consideration themselves, a description of that part, the method of valuation and the date of valuation; and
  - where all or part of the consideration has been valued by another person, a statement of this fact, the valuer's name, knowledge and experience, a description of the consideration, and the method and date of valuation;
- the report must also contain, or be accompanied by, a note by the independent accountants that:
  - where a valuation has been carried out by another person, it appeared reasonable to them to arrange or accept this;
  - the method of valuation was reasonable in all the circumstances;
  - it appears to them that there has been no material change in the value of the consideration since the valuation; and
  - on the basis of the valuation, the value of the consideration together with any cash to be paid is not less than the aggregate of the nominal value of the shares and any premium to be treated as paid up.

An example report is given in APB Practice Note 8 'Reports by auditors under company legislation in the United Kingdom'. The legislation makes no provision for the independent accountants' report to be qualified. Additional requirements apply under *section 108(7)* of *CA 1985* where the consideration for the transfer of a non-cash asset is only partly satisfied by the allotment of shares.

## Transfer of non-cash assets to a public company by a member of the company 2.64

In the first two years following registration or re-registration as a public company, *section 104* of *CA 1985* requires a company to obtain approval by an ordinary resolution of the company if it wishes to purchase from a subscriber to the company's memorandum a non-cash asset for consideration worth one tenth or more of the nominal value of the company's issued share capital. In addition, a valuation report similar to that required on the allotment of share for non-cash consideration must have been made to the company in the six months immediately preceding the transfer. The report must be made by independent accountants qualified to act as auditors (although they need not be **the** auditors) and the same rules apply on accepting a valuation carried out by another person as for the allotment of shares by a public company other than for cash (see **2.62** above). In addition, under *section 109* of *CA 1985*, the independent accountants' report must:

- state the consideration to be received and given, describing the assets and specifying any amounts to be paid or received in cash;
- state the method and date of valuation;
- contain, or be accompanied by, a note by the independent accountants that:
  - where a valuation has been carried out by another person, it appeared reasonable to them to arrange or accept this;
  - the method of valuation was reasonable in all the circumstances;
  - it appears to them that there has been no material change in the value of the consideration since the valuation; and
  - on the basis of the valuation, the value of the consideration to be received by the company is not less than the value of the consideration to be given.

The legislation makes no provision for the independent accountants' report to be qualified. Additional requirements apply under *section 109(3)* of *CA 1985* where the consideration is given only partly for the transfer of a non-cash asset.

## Reporting to management                                    2.65

During the audit, or at the conclusion of their work, the auditors will usually report formally to the directors or senior management on:

- any significant weaknesses in the accounting or internal control systems that have come to their attention during the audit, together with their recommendations for improvements;
- any significant business issues that have come to their attention during the audit, together with their advice (for instance, potential economies or improvements in efficiency); and
- any significant errors identified during the audit and comments on any individual accounting policies or practices that they consider need to be drawn to the attention of the directors or senior management.

If the company has an audit committee, these issues may be reported to the directors through the audit committee (see **2.26** above). Auditing Standards require auditors to report significant weaknesses in accounting and internal control systems to the directors or senior management on a timely basis, unless the weakness has already been identified by the entity and appropriate corrective action taken. The auditors will usually ask directors or senior management to respond to the points raised in their report, indicating the actions to be taken. Less significant issues will usually be discussed at a meeting with the directors or senior management and the points raised documented for future reference, together with any action agreed. It is normal practice for auditors to follow up all the issues that have been reported, usually during their subsequent audit, to confirm that the action agreed in response to the points raised has actually been taken.

## *Scope of report* 2.66

The auditors' work is carried out on a test basis and will normally be concentrated on those areas that present the highest risk of material error or misstatement in the accounts. The nature of the work therefore means that the auditors' report to management cannot be a comprehensive statement of all weaknesses which may exist in the accounting and internal control systems, or of all improvements that could be made. The auditors' formal report will therefore usually emphasise that it covers only those issues that have come to their attention during the course of the audit, and may give an explanation of the audit approach to help the directors understand the scope of the work undertaken.

## *Confidentiality of reports* 2.67

The reports that auditors issue to the directors or senior management are confidential documents and the auditors will therefore usually include in the report a statement that it has been prepared solely for the use of the company's management and should not be disclosed or quoted to another party without the prior written consent of the auditors. Similarly, the auditors will not usually provide a copy of the report to another party without the prior written consent of the directors. However, in certain regulated industries (such as the banking and financial services sectors) and in the public sector, auditors will often have a duty to provide copies of their reports to the relevant regulatory body or funding council.

## Reporting under the Combined Code 2.68

The FSA Listing Rules require the directors of listed companies to make statements in the annual report on compliance with the best practice provisions of the Combined Code and on going concern. These requirements are considered in more detail in CHAPTER 6 CORPORATE GOVERNANCE. Where the FSA requires the directors to make such statements, the Listing Rules stipulate that they must also be reviewed by the auditors. In the case of the compliance statement, the auditors' review is only required to cover those aspects of the Code that can be verified objectively. There is no requirement under the Listing Rules for the auditors to prepare a formal report on the results of their review, or for such a report to be published. The latest APB guidance now requires the extent of the auditors' review of the corporate governance statements to be explained in the section of the audit report that explains the auditors' responsibilities. Examples can be found in APB Bulletin 2001/2 'Revisions to the Wording of Auditors' Reports on Financial Statements and the Interim Review Report' (updated by APB Bulletin 2002/2 'The United Kingdom Directors' Remuneration Report Regulations 2002' for accounting periods ending on or after 31 December 2002). If the auditors are not satisfied with the adequacy of the corporate governance disclosures and cannot resolve the problems through discussion with the directors, they are required to report their concerns in a separate paragraph as part of their opinion on the financial statements, but this will not constitute a qualification of their report on the annual accounts.

## Agreement of scope of review                                    2.69

It is important that the respective responsibilities of the directors and the auditors in relation to the corporate governance statements, and the scope of the auditors' work on the statements, are clarified at an early stage to prevent any potential misunderstandings. The intention of the present Listing Rules is to ensure that auditors provide some assurance on the directors' corporate governance disclosures, but to avoid substantial additional audit work and the consequent financial implications that this would have for companies. The scope of the auditors' work in respect of corporate governance statements should be set out in a formal engagement letter between the company and the auditors. This can be dealt with as a stand-alone document or as a separate section of the engagement letter for the statutory audit. APB Bulletin 1995/1 'The Combined Code: Requirements of Auditors under the Listing Rules of the London Stock Exchange' (now the FSA) sets out guidance on the detailed procedures that auditors should normally undertake when reviewing corporate governance statements.

## Reporting on interim reports                                     2.70

Listed companies are required by the FSA Listing Rules to issue an interim report each year, giving details of their results for the first half of the financial year. There is currently no formal requirement for auditors to review or report on interim reports before they are published. APB Bulletin 1999/4 'Review of Interim Financial Information' sets out guidance on the procedures that should be undertaken where auditors are asked to review an interim report, although it notes that the directors (or, where relevant, the audit committee) may ask the auditors to carry out specific agreed procedures as an alternative to this. Where an interim report is reviewed in accordance with the APB guidance, the FSA Listing Rules require the auditors' review report to be published as part of the interim report. The ASB Statement 'Interim reports' also recommends disclosure of the extent to which the information given in the interim report has been audited or reviewed. The latest guidance on the wording of the review report can be found in APB Bulletin 2001/2 'Revisions to the Wording of Auditors' Reports on Financial Statements and the Interim Review Report'. Because the recommended review work is limited in scope, and does not constitute an audit, the auditors will normally report in terms of 'negative assurance' – in other words, they report that nothing has come to their attention to indicate that material modification is required to the information presented in the report. APB Bulletin 1999/4 recommends that, where the scope of the work agreed between the directors and auditors is less than that set out in the Bulletin, the directors should describe the interim report as 'neither audited nor reviewed'.

# Remuneration of external auditors and their associates  2.71

## At a glance  2.72

- The directors are usually authorised to agree the remuneration of the external auditors.
- The remuneration paid to the auditors for their work as auditors must be disclosed in the notes to the accounts.
- The accounts must also disclose any remuneration paid to the auditors or their associates for non-audit services.
- The ICAEW has issued proposals for more extensive disclosures on non-audit services.

## Remuneration for services as auditors  2.73

*CA 1985* provides for the remuneration of the auditors to be fixed as follows:

- where the auditors have been appointed by the company, their remuneration should be fixed by the company in general meeting, or in any other way decided by the company in general meeting (in practice, most companies resolve to give the directors authority to agree the auditors' remuneration);
- where the auditors have been appointed by the directors, their remuneration should be fixed by the directors; and
- where the auditors have been appointed by the Secretary of State, their remuneration should be fixed by the Secretary of State.

The legislation defines remuneration as including amounts paid in respect of expenses and any benefits in kind, but in practice, professional and ethical guidelines will usually prevent auditors from accepting benefits in kind from the company. In the case of listed companies, the audit committee should be responsible for making recommendations to the board, and thence to the shareholders, on the remuneration of the external auditors (see **2.20** above).

## Disclosure of remuneration for services as auditors  2.74

Under *section 390A* of *CA 1985*, the remuneration paid to the auditors in respect of their work as auditors must be disclosed in the notes to the annual accounts. The amount to be disclosed should include the audit fee and any amounts payable in respect of expenses. The legislation also requires the disclosure to include the estimated money value of any benefits in kind received by the auditors in respect of their services as auditors and a description of the nature of these benefits. However, professional and ethical guidelines will usually prevent auditors from accepting benefits in kind from the company.

**Audit Matters**

## Remuneration for non-audit services 2.75

Disclosure requirements in respect of non-audit fees were originally introduced into UK companies' legislation by the *Companies Act 1985 (Disclosure of Remuneration for Non-Audit Work Regulations 1991 (SI 1991/2128)* and were updated by the *Companies Act 1985 (Disclosure of Remuneration for Non-Audit Work) (Amendment) Regulations 1995 (SI 1995/1520)*. *Regulation 4* of *SI 1991/2128* exempts companies that qualify as small or medium-sized from these disclosure requirements. The figure to be disclosed in respect of non-audit work is the aggregate amount of remuneration payable to the auditors and their associates in respect of work carried out during the financial year, regardless of whether this has actually been billed to the company during the period. Comparative figures must also be given. Non-audit work will usually comprise services such as accounting assistance, payroll services, tax compliance and advisory work, and consultancy. Once again, remuneration specifically includes expenses and the estimated money value of benefits in kind, and both the nature and the estimated money value of any benefits must be disclosed, although these are unlikely to arise in practice. Where the auditors or their associates are also the auditors of any UK subsidiary undertakings of the company, any amounts payable by the subsidiaries in respect of non-audit services must also be included. The regulations specifically require the auditors to provide the company with such information as it needs to be able to comply with the disclosure requirements. Where more than one auditor has held office during the year, separate disclosure is required in respect of each set of auditors and their associates.

## Associates of auditors 2.76

The definition of associates for this purpose is very complex but it broadly includes:

- any partnership in which the auditors are a partner or with which the auditors have a partner in common;
- any body corporate in the same group as the auditors;
- any directors of the auditors;
- any body corporate in which the auditor, a partner of the auditors or a director of the auditors controls the exercise of 20% or more of the voting rights, or any other body corporate in the same group as such a body corporate.

If such a relationship exists at any time during the financial year, the entity is regarded as an associate of the auditors for that year. Reference should be made to the detail in *SI 1991/2128* if there is any doubt over whether an entity should be treated as an associate of the auditors. Amendments to the regulations introduced during 1995 specifically exclude entities that might otherwise have been treated as associates of the auditors as a result of insolvency and receivership appointments.

# ICAEW proposals for change                           2.77

Draft guidance on more extensive disclosure of the nature and value of non-audit services provided by auditors was published by the ICAEW in December 2002. The draft is based on EC recommendations and recommends that full and transparent disclosure should be made of all fees due to the audit firm and its network firms in relation to work performed during the period for the audit client and all entities controlled by that client. In the case of joint audits, the same disclosures should be given for each audit firm. The disclosures should cover both the nature and extent of the services provided and the review and approval process followed, and should provide sufficient information to enable a user of the accounts to judge whether the potential for conflicts of interest has been satisfactorily addressed. The draft recommends that fees are analysed into the following categories:

- Statutory audit services:   Annual audit
                              Regulatory reporting
- Further assurance services  (eg interim statement review, advice
                              on accounting matters, non-regulatory
                              reporting on internal controls, due
                              diligence work on acquisitions,
                              environmental audits)
- Tax advisory services
- Other non-audit services:   Financial information technology
                              Internal audit
                              Valuation
                              Litigation
                              Recruitment
                              Other services

Amounts that are not material may be included under 'other services'. Further analysis should be given where the amounts in individual categories are material and differ substantially from one another and narrative explanations should be given where this would be helpful. The non-audit fees disclosure currently required by statute covers only UK entities and, where there are also overseas entities (which are included in the ICAEW disclosure recommendations), the UK element of non-audit fees will therefore need to be shown separately. Fees should be calculated on an accruals basis and should include fees for all services where the substance of the arrangement is that the service has been rendered to the client, even if the fee itself has been paid by another party (eg the client's solicitor in the case of litigation support). Comments on the ICAEW proposals have been requested by 20 March 2003.

**Internal audit** 2.78

---

**At a glance** 2.79

- The primary role of internal audit is to assist in the identification of risk and provide assurance that the internal control system is effective in reducing risk to an acceptable level.
- There are significant differences between the roles of external and internal auditors.
- A strong internal audit function can enable management to demonstrate that they are taking their responsibilities seriously.
- Internal auditors may also carry out special assignments to assist in the achievement of business objectives.
- An internal audit function can be established in-house or subcontracted to an appropriate external organisation.
- Formal terms of reference should be developed for internal audit.
- The head of internal audit should have appropriate professional expertise and carry the respect, confidence and support of senior management.
- The internal audit department must have adequate resources to carry out its work.
- Internal auditors must be genuinely independent of the company's systems and operations.
- The scope of internal audit work should generally be unrestricted.
- The first stage in planning internal audit work is to prepare an audit needs assessment and strategic and annual internal audit plans.
- Internal audit should issue individual reports on each system or operational area covered.
- The audit committee should review summary reports and an annual report.
- Good liaison between the internal and external audit can help both to operate more efficiently.

---

**Role of internal audit** 2.80

The role of internal audit has altered considerably over the years, reflecting the changing needs of business and management. This is especially true in recent years, as corporate governance issues have been given an increasingly high profile. Directors and senior management are much more aware of their responsibilities for the control of business risk and for the establishment of systems and controls to safeguard assets, prevent fraud and irregularity and enhance the efficient operation of the business. The primary role of an internal audit function is to assist management in identifying potential risk and to provide assurance that the company's system of internal control is effective in reducing business risk to an acceptable level. It also acts as a useful source of information for management on what is actually happening in practice within the business, and provides support and advice by identifying needs and recommending policies, procedures and controls to resolve potential problems as they are identified. In the case of a public company, the work of internal audit will usually be a significant factor in enabling the directors to report on internal control as required by the Combined Code. The Code also recommends that companies that do not have an internal audit function should from time to time review the need for one. Under the proposals in the Smith Report, this review will become an annual requirement.

## Distinction between external audit and internal audit    2.81

There are significant differences between the roles of external auditors and internal auditors. External auditors are appointed by the shareholders and report to them by expressing an independent opinion on whether the company's annual accounts show a true and fair view of the state of affairs of the company at the balance sheet date and of its profit or loss for the financial year. The work of the external auditors is therefore directed towards identifying any potentially material misstatement in the annual accounts, and confirming that the accounting treatments and disclosures required by the legislation and by accounting standards have been properly dealt with. Internal audit is a service function of the company, focusing its efforts on the effectiveness of the company's systems of internal control and reporting any weaknesses and concerns to management. Companies legislation generally requires every UK company to appoint external auditors (the only exceptions being dormant companies and certain small companies as explained in **2.37** above), but management can choose whether or not to establish an internal audit function.

The principal distinctions between external and internal audit can therefore be summarised as follows:

|  | External auditors | Internal auditors |
|---|---|---|
| Appointed by | Shareholders | Management |
| Report to | Shareholders | Management |
| Role defined by | Statute | Management |
| Primary function | Independent opinion on the annual accounts | Assisting management with the identification and control of business risk |

Although the roles of external auditors and internal auditors are quite distinct, good liaison between the two can help both to operate more efficiently.

## How not to use internal audit    2.82

Historically, there been a considerable degree of confusion over the precise role of internal audit. It is important to recognise that internal auditors are not responsible for designing and implementing systems and procedures, nor are they responsible for the prevention and detection of fraud and irregularity. These are, and must always remain, the responsibility of management. Internal auditors have an important role to play in assisting management to fulfil their responsibilities, and they will frequently recommend changes to systems and procedures, or new controls that should be introduced. However, if they were to become directly involved in designing and implementing systems and procedures, their independence from the operating functions could be seriously impaired. For the same reason, it is essential that internal auditors are not seen as a floating resource who can be used to cover for the unexpected departure or long-term absence of accounting and other staff.

## Benefits of internal audit 2.83

The heightened profile of corporate governance issues, and public reporting on aspects such as internal control under the Combined Code, has generally increased management's awareness of their responsibilities and encouraged them to reconsider how these responsibilities can best be fulfilled in practice. Internal audit has had a relatively high profile within the public sector for some years, but has generally been slower to develop within the private sector, except in the largest organisations. In the past, internal audit departments tended be given a low status within the organisation, but the benefits of an well-organised and high calibre internal audit function are now becoming clearer to companies of all sizes. Management always retains the responsibility for identifying business risk and introducing procedures and controls to reduce risk to an acceptable level. However, establishing a strong internal audit function to assist with this can enable management to demonstrate clearly that they have paid due attention to the relevant issues, and that the procedures and controls that have been put in place are being subjected to continual scrutiny. This is particularly important as the business develops – without regular independent scrutiny, the procedures and controls can easily become out of date and fail to provide adequate cover in new areas of operation.

## Areas usually covered by internal audit 2.84

Internal audit will usually provide assurance on:

- safeguarding of the company's assets;
- the completeness and accuracy of the company's accounting and other records;
- the adequacy and effectiveness of measures to prevent fraud and other irregularity;
- the overall efficiency of the operations.

The internal auditors should develop a strong, in-depth knowledge of the company's operating systems, coupled with their own professional expertise, and they are therefore in a good position to advise management on the assessment of risk and the implementation of procedures and controls. If there is no internal audit function, the external auditors will usually need to carry out some review and testing of the company's systems and controls, but as their focus is the material accuracy of the annual accounts, their work will concentrate on financial controls rather than the company's overall system of internal control. The level and extent of their review and testing will also be lower, as the level of assurance needed for external audit purposes will not be as extensive as that required for effective management of the business.

## Special assignments                                        2.85

As well as assisting with the assessment and control of business risk, internal auditors often carry out special assignments and investigations to assist management in the achievement of business objectives, such as value for money reviews and more extensive investigations of specific business areas (for instance, a review of the effectiveness and efficiency of an individual part of the business operation, or of a particular service function, such as catering or maintenance). The areas selected for review may have been identified by management as needing investigation, or may have been highlighted by the internal auditors during their other work, or by the external auditors.

## Establishing an internal audit function                    2.86

An internal audit function is a service department within the organisation, assisting management to fulfil its responsibilities. In larger entities, there will usually be a separate internal audit department, its staffing levels being dependent on the size and complexity of the organisation and the level of work required throughout the year. In the case of a group, one internal audit department will normally serve all locations and subsidiaries within the group. In a smaller organisation, there may be insufficient work to justify a fully staffed internal audit department, or it may be that the department would be so small (for instance, requiring only one or two members of staff) that it would be difficult for it command the necessary authority within the business. However, this does not mean that it is totally impractical for a small company to operate an internal audit function. It should be possible to sub-contract internal audit work to an external organisation with the necessary skills and experience (for instance, a firm of accountants with internal audit expertise). The fact that the function is an internal one does not prevent it being provided from an outside source, although particular care may be needed in defining the terms and scope of the work.

## Terms of reference                                         2.87

The purpose, authority and scope of work of the internal audit department should be set out in a formal document. This will help to give the internal auditors the high profile within the organisation that is necessary if they are to function effectively. It should also clarify the independence of the internal auditors from the other parts of the business and the remit of internal audit, ensuring in particular that this is not restricted in any way and covers all aspects of the business. Where internal audit work is sub-contracted,

71

these matters will normally be dealt with in an engagement letter between the parties. In all cases, the terms of reference for the internal audit function should be regularly reviewed and updated, usually through the audit committee.

## Head of internal audit                                        2.88

It is important that the internal audit function, however it is organised, is headed up by an individual who has the necessary professional expertise and carries the respect, confidence and support of other members of the senior management team. He or she should preferably have an appropriate professional qualification, relevant experience and the personal skills needed to deal with individuals throughout the organisation and to handle potentially difficult and sensitive issues. There needs to be a close working relationship between the head of internal audit and the executive directors and also, where relevant, good communication between the head of internal audit and the audit committee. If the internal audit function is a separate department within the organisation, the head of internal audit will be a management appointment. If internal audit work is sub-contracted, the person with overall responsibility for the work (for instance, a partner in a firm of accountants) is in effect the head of internal audit, and it will be important to ensure that the necessary relationships can be put into place quickly and effectively. Where the company has an audit committee, this committee should participate in the appointment. The head of internal audit should have a direct line of communication to the chairman of the audit committee, to enable sensitive issues to be raised and discussed without executive management being present where necessary, and to demonstrate and strengthen the independence of the internal audit function.

## Staffing                                                      2.89

If the internal audit department is to achieve the necessary degree of respect and confidence within the organisation, it is essential that it has adequate resources to carry out its work. Wherever possible, internal audit staff should be suitably trained and professionally qualified. This does not necessarily mean that everyone needs to hold the same qualifications. The department should be viewed as a team and the skills and expertise available should be appropriate for the range of work that the department is expected to cover. The skills needed will inevitably vary, depending on the nature and complexity of the business. As well as financial expertise, the internal audit function may need skills in areas such as computing, logistics or environmental issues. On occasions it may be appropriate to second high calibre staff with particular skills from elsewhere in the organisation to assist with specific internal audit projects. This can be valuable in increasing general awareness and understanding of the internal audit function within the company, and can help to raise the profile of internal audit. It is important to remember that internal audit staff will need to deal with individuals throughout the organisation, and that they may sometimes be required to handle potentially difficult and sensitive situations. All internal audit staff need to have strong interpersonal and communication skills and to be confident in dealing with senior management.

## Independence and objectivity                                    2.90

Internal auditors must be genuinely independent of the systems and operations that they review and report on. Without a high degree of professional independence and objectivity, the internal audit function will not achieve the status and level of authority necessary for it to become a strong and effective management resource, and it will not command the respect and confidence of management and staff. There is also a risk that internal audit staff will not be able to make genuinely unbiased and impartial judgements if they have a close involvement in the detailed operations. It is essential that the head of internal audit is not given additional executive responsibilities within the organisation and that audit staff are not involved in the day to day operations of other parts of the business. This does not preclude the secondment of staff from other departments to assist with specific internal audit assignments as explained above, but long-term internal audit staff should not have a regular involvement in other departments.

It is particularly important that internal auditors are not seen as a floating resource who can be used to cover for the unexpected departure or long-term absence of key members of staff. The ability of the head of internal audit to communicate directly with the chairman of the audit committee whenever he or she considers necessary helps to demonstrate the independence of the internal audit function from the executive management. The audit committee (or management where there is no audit committee) should satisfy themselves each year that appropriate procedures are operating to safeguard the independence and objectivity of the internal audit function.

## Scope of internal audit work                                    2.91

The scope of the internal auditors' work should generally be unrestricted and should cover the full spectrum of the company's system of internal control. The scope of the work undertaken by the internal auditors will vary depending on the circumstances of the company and should be discussed and agreed by the board. Where appropriate, this will be dealt with initially by the audit committee, who will then submit detailed proposals to the board for consideration and formal approval. The scope of internal audit work will usually include:

- understanding and assessing the key business risks and reviewing the procedures used to identify and manage these;
- reviewing the adequacy and effectiveness of controls over financial and other operational information;
- reviewing the adequacy and effectiveness of the procedures established by management to safeguard the company's assets and resources, and to prevent fraud and irregularity;
- reviewing the adequacy and effectiveness of procedures designed to

ensure compliance with law and regulations that are central to the business;

● reviewing the adequacy and effectiveness of procedures designed to ensure that the policies and plans agreed by management are brought into effect;

● reviewing the efficiency and effectiveness of particular aspects of the business.

## Internal audit needs assessment and strategic plan          2.92

The initial stage in planning internal audit work will usually be to develop an internal audit needs assessment. This will identify all the aspects of the company's operations that will be subject to review by the internal auditors. In most organisations it will not be practical for all areas to be covered by internal audit in one year. It is normal practice for internal auditors to operate on a three or four year cycle, ensuring that all systems and operations are covered during the three or four year period. In some cases, all the work on a particular system or operational area may be carried out in one year – in other cases, work on an individual system or operation may be spread over the full audit period, so that some aspects are covered in each year of the cycle. Where a system or operational area is considered to be particularly critical to the business, it may be deemed necessary for it to be covered by internal audit each year. The overall audit needs assessment must therefore be developed into a strategic audit plan to demonstrate how full coverage will be achieved over the audit cycle (ie the three or four year period). In order to prepare a strategic audit plan, there will need to be some prioritisation of internal audit work over the audit cycle. Areas that are identified as high risk will generally be covered earlier in the audit cycle, and may be covered on more than one occasion during the cycle; areas that are deemed medium or low risk will generally be covered later in the audit cycle. Both the internal audit needs assessment and the strategic audit plan should be developed by the internal auditors in discussion with management and should be formally approved by the board (through the audit committee where appropriate).

## Annual review                                              2.93

The internal audit needs assessment and strategic audit plan must be reviewed and updated annually. There are very few situations where the needs assessment and strategic plan developed at the beginning of an audit cycle will not need to be adapted during the course of the cycle. Changes may be needed to:

● incorporate new systems and operations as the business develops;
● amend priorities because changes in circumstance have increased or reduced the risk associated with a particular aspect of the business;
● amend priorities on the basis of the results of internal audit work already completed.

Both the internal auditors and management should be involved in the review and update of the internal audit needs assessment and the strategic audit plan, and the revised documents should be approved by the board (through the audit committee where appropriate).

## Detailed internal audit plan                    2.94

Once the internal audit needs assessment and strategic audit plan have been approved, the internal audit department must develop a detailed audit plan for the current year, setting out the areas to be covered, the proposed timing of the work and the proposed reporting timetable. The plan should include adequate time for following up points raised in the reports on previous audits to confirm that the agreed action has in fact been taken and that the problem originally identified has been resolved as far as is practicable. The detailed audit plan for the year should also be approved by the board (through the audit committee, where appropriate). The head of internal audit should report regularly to management and to the audit committee on the progress of audit work against the plan for the year and explain any significant variations.

## Reports on individual systems and operations areas    2.95

Internal audit will issue individual reports on each system or operational area that has been subject to audit. Their reports will normally draw an overall conclusion in respect of that system or area, and will concentrate on high-lighting any potentially serious weaknesses or concerns identified during the audit, along with the internal auditors' recommendations for changes and improvements. The recommendations will normally be discussed with management and the agreed action noted for each item. It is usually helpful to agree a standard structure for internal audit reports – for instance:

- executive summary;
- the overall conclusions drawn by the auditors; and
- the detailed findings and recommendations for improvement, divided into:
    - major weaknesses and concerns; and
    - other issues

It is important that weaknesses and concerns are rigorously followed up by internal audit later in the year (or, where appropriate, later in the audit cycle), to confirm that the agreed action has actually been taken and that the potential problem originally identified has been satisfactorily resolved.

## Summary reports                                2.96

Summary reports on the results of the detailed work carried out by internal audit should be presented formally to the audit committee by the head of internal audit on a regular basis during the year. This reporting will normally take place on two or three occasions each year and may be combined with reports on the progress of audit work against the annual audit plan. A specific timetable for this level of reporting should be agreed at the beginning of the year.

## Annual report 2.97

The head of internal audit may also be asked to prepare an annual report summarising the work completed during the financial year and the overall conclusions drawn on the operation of the company's system of internal control. This will be particularly relevant for directors of listed companies who are required under the Combined Code to state in the annual report that they have reviewed the effectiveness of the company's system of internal financial control. An annual report from the head of internal audit will be one source of supporting information that the audit committee and board of directors will usually wish to review when considering the various directors' statements relating to compliance with the Combined Code.

## Liaison with external auditors 2.98

Although the roles of external auditors and internal auditors are quite distinct, good liaison between the two can help both to operate more efficiently and prevent any unnecessary duplication of work. Liaison normally works best when there are regular meetings and continuous dialogue between the two groups of auditors, and each has a good understanding of the audit approach adopted by the other. The most crucial aspect is to ensure that there is good communication each year at the planning stages of both internal and external audit work. If the external auditors are consulted when internal audit work is being planned, this may help to increase the usefulness of the results for external audit purposes and enable the external auditors to reduce the extent of their detailed audit testing. This does not mean that the external auditors should in any way decide the scope or nature of the internal audit work – this must remain a management responsibility – but by discussing and agreeing issues such as the timing of the work, the methods of sample selection and the documentation of results, it should be possible to ensure that the work of the internal auditors is of maximum benefit to the external auditors as well as to management. Similarly, when the detailed external audit work is being planned, it will be important for the external auditors to take full account of the extent and results of internal audit work. Where appropriate, the audit committee will usually be responsible for the overall monitoring of liaison between the two groups of auditors.

## *Impact of internal audit work on external audit procedures* 2.99

The external auditors retain sole responsibility for the independent audit opinion on the annual accounts, for deciding the nature and extent of the audit procedures to be carried out in support of that opinion and for all matters of judgement in relation to the audit opinion. However, as part of their work, the external auditors will need to obtain assurance on the completeness and accuracy of the company's accounting records (which will form the basis for the annual accounts) and the adequacy and effectiveness of the company's internal financial controls. Where the company has an internal audit function, the external auditors may be able to place reliance on the work of the internal auditors to help them achieve the level of assurance they require for external audit purposes, and this in turn may enable them to reduce the extent of some of their detailed audit testing. The external auditors will usually need to be satisfied that the internal audit function is adequately resourced, appropriately staffed and independent of those on whom it is reporting, that the work of the internal auditors is properly planned, supervised and documented, and that the recommendations made by the internal auditors carry appropriate weight within the organisation. Their procedures to assess these issues will usually include reviewing the reports and working papers of the internal audit department.

## *Impact of external audit work on internal audit procedures* 2.100

There is generally less scope for internal auditors to make detailed use of the work of the external auditors. However, regular feedback on weaknesses and irregularities identified during external audit work can be helpful in directing the work of internal audit to areas of potential business risk. The external auditors may also highlight operational areas where value for money reviews, efficiency reviews or other special investigations may usefully be incorporated in the internal audit work programme.

## Appendix 2A 2.101

## Checklist of Essential Requirements for Audit Committees 2.102

This checklist summarises the essential requirements for audit committees as set out in 'Audit Committees: Combined Code Guidance' (the Smith Report – see **2.5** above). The report should be consulted for further guidance on each of these issues.

● The board should establish an audit committee, the main role and responsibilities of which should be:
   ■ to monitor the integrity of the financial statements of the company;
   ■ to review the company's internal financial control system and, unless addressed by a separate risk committee or by the board itself, risk management systems;
   ■ to monitor and review the effectiveness of the company's internal audit function;
   ■ to make recommendations to the board in relation to the appointment of the external auditor and to approve the remuneration and terms of engagement of the external auditor, following appointment by the shareholders in general meeting.
   ■ to monitor and review the external auditor's independence, objectivity and effectiveness;
   ■ to develop and implement policy on the engagement of the external auditor to supply non-audit services.

- Where the audit committee's monitoring and review activities reveal cause for concern or scope for improvement, it should make recommendations to the board on the action needed to address the issue or to make the improvements.
- The audit committee should include at least three members, who should all be independent non-executive directors (as defined in the Higgs Report).
- No one other than the audit committee chairman and members is entitled to be present at a meeting of the audit committee.
- At least one member of the audit committee should have significant, recent and relevant financial experience, for example as an auditor or a finance director of a listed company.
- The audit committee should be provided with sufficient resources to undertake its duties.
- The board should provide written terms of reference for the audit committee.
- The audit committee should review the significant financial reporting issues and judgements made in connection with the preparation of the company's financial statements, interim reports, preliminary announcements and related formal statements.
- The audit committee should also review the clarity of the disclosures in the financial statements.
- Where, following its review, the audit committee is not satisfied with any aspect of the proposed financial reporting by the company, it should report its views to the board.
- The audit committee should monitor the integrity of the company's internal financial controls.
- In the absence of other arrangements (eg a separate risk committee) the audit committee should assess the scope and effectiveness of the systems established by management to identify, assess, manage and monitor financial and non-financial risks.
- The audit committee should monitor and review the internal audit activities. Where there is no internal audit function, the audit committee should consider annually whether there is a need for one and make a recommendation to the board. The reasons for the absence of an internal audit function should be explained in the relevant section of the annual report.
- The audit committee is the body responsible for overseeing the company's relations with the external auditor.
- The audit committee should have primary responsibility for making a recommendation on the appointment, reappointment and removal of the external auditors. This recommendation should be made to the board and thence to the shareholders for their approval in general meeting. If the board does not accept the audit committee's recommendation, the directors' report should include a statement from the audit committee explaining its recommendation and the reasons why the board has taken a different position.
- The audit committee should assess the qualification, expertise, resources, effectiveness and independence of the external auditors annually.

- The audit committee should approve the terms of engagement and the remuneration to be paid to the external auditor in respect of audit services provided.
- The audit committee should have procedures to ensure the independence and objectivity of the external auditor annually, taking into consideration relevant UK professional and regulatory requirements.
- The audit committee should develop and recommend to the board the company's policy on the provision of non-audit services by the auditor. The audit committee's objective should be to ensure that the provision of such services does not impair the external auditor's independence or objectivity.
- In determining the above policy, the audit committee should take into account relevant ethical guidance on the provision of non-audit services by the external audit firm, and in principle should not agree to the auditor providing a service if, having regard to the ethical guidance, the result is that:
  - the audit firm audits its own firm's work;
  - the external auditor makes management decisions for the company;
  - a mutuality of interest is created; or
  - the external auditor is put in the role of advocate for the company.
- Where non-audit services are provided by the external audit firm, the audit committee should satisfy itself that any safeguards required by ethical guidance are implemented.
- The annual report should explain to shareholders how the company's policy on the provision of non-audit services provides adequate protection of auditor independence.
- At the start of each annual audit cycle, the audit committee should ensure that appropriate plans are in place for the external audit.
- The audit committee should review with the external auditors the findings of their work.
- At the end of the annual audit cycle, the audit committee should assess the effectiveness of the audit process.
- The directors' report should contain a separate section that describes the role and responsibilities of the audit committee and the actions taken by the committee to discharge those responsibilities.
- The chairman of the audit committee should be present at the AGM to answer questions, through the chairman of the board, on the report on the audit committee's activities and matters within the scope of the audit committee's responsibilities.

## Appendix 2B      2.103

## Specimen Terms of Reference for an Audit Committee   2.104

These specimen terms of reference are for guidance only and are based on the example published in the Smith Report (see **2.5** above). Terms of reference should be developed and adapted to suit the specific circumstances of the company or group.

# 1 Constitution

1.1 The Board hereby resolves to establish a committee of the board, to be known as the Audit Committee ('the committee').

# 2 Membership

2.1 The committee shall be appointed by the board. All members of the committee shall be independent non-executive directors of the company. The committee shall consist of not less than three members. Two members shall comprise a quorum at any meeting of the committee.

2.2 The chairman of the committee shall be appointed by the Board from amongst the independent non-executive directors.

# 3 Attendance at meetings

3.1 The finance director, the head of internal audit and a representative of the external auditors shall attend meetings at the invitation of the committee.

3.2 The chairman of the board and other board members shall attend meetings if invited by the committee.

3.3 There should be at least one committee meeting, or part of a meeting, each year where the external auditors and internal auditors attend without management present.

3.4 The company secretary shall be the secretary to the committee.

# 4 Frequency of meetings

4.1 Meetings shall be held not less than three times each year and, where appropriate shall coincide with key dates in the company's financial reporting cycle.

4.2 Additional meetings shall be held as required, and the external auditors or internal auditors may request a meeting if they consider that one is necessary.

# 5 Authority

5.1 The committee is authorised by the board to:
- investigate any activity within its terms of reference;
- seek any information that it requires from any employee (and all employees are directed to co-operate with any request made by the committee); and
- obtain external legal or other independent professional advice and request advisers to attend meetings as necessary.

# 6 Responsibilities

6.1 The responsibilities of the committee shall be:
- to consider the appointment of the external auditor and assess the

independence of the external auditor, ensuring that key partners are rotated at appropriate intervals;

- to oversee the process for selecting the external auditor and make appropriate recommendations, through the board, to the shareholders for consideration at the AGM;
- to recommend the audit fee to the board and preapprove any fees in respect of non-audit service provided by the external auditor, and to ensure that the provision of non-audit services does not impair the independence or objectivity of the external auditor;
- to discuss with the external auditor, before the audit commences, the nature and scope of the audit, and any additional assurance or reporting that may be required, and to review the auditor's quality control procedures and the steps taken to respond to changes in regulatory and other requirements;
- to consider whether there is appropriate liaison and co-ordination between the internal and external auditors;
- to review the external auditor's management letter and management's response;
- to review the internal audit programme and ensure that the internal audit function is adequately resourced and has appropriate standing within the company;
- to consider management's response to any major internal audit or external audit recommendations;
- to approve the appointment or dismissal of the head of internal audit;
- to review the company's procedures for handling allegations from whistleblowers;
- to review reports from management and the internal auditors on the effectiveness of the systems for internal financial control, financial reporting and risk management.
- to review, and challenge where necessary, the actions and judgements of management in relation to the interim and annual financial statements before submission to the Board, paying particular attention to:
  - critical accounting policies and practices and any changes in them;
  - decisions requiring a major element of judgement;
  - the extent to which the financial statements are affected by any unusual transactions in the year, and how they are disclosed;
  - the clarity of disclosures;
  - significant adjustments resulting from the audit;
  - the going concern assumption;
  - compliance with accounting standards; and
  - compliance with stock exchange and other legal requirements;
- to review the company's statements on compliance with the Combined Code, going concern and the review of the effectiveness of the company's system of internal control prior to endorsement by the board, and in particular to review:
  - the policies and processes for identifying and assessing business risks and the management of those risks by the company;
  - the company's policies for ensuring compliance with relevant legal and regulatory requirements;

- ■ the company's policies for the prevention and detection of fraud;
- ■ the effectiveness of such policies and procedures in practice;
- to discuss any problems and reservations arising from the external audit and any matters that the external and internal auditors may wish to discuss (in the absence of management where necessary);
- to consider other topics and issues, as defined by the board.

# 7 Reporting procedures

7.1 The secretary shall circulate the minutes of meetings of the committee to all members of the board.

7.2 The chairman of the committee, or as a minimum another member of the committee, shall attend the board meeting at which the annual accounts and reports are approved.

7.3 The committee's responsibilities and activities during the year shall be disclosed in the annual reports and accounts.

7.4 The chairman of the committee shall attend the AGM and answer questions, through the chairman of the board, on the committee's responsibilities and activities.

# 8 Self-assessment and appraisal

8.1 The committee shall conduct an annual review of its work and terms of reference, and an annual assessment of its own effectiveness, and make recommendations to the board.

# 3. Board Structure and Practice

This chapter will start with role of the board and then look at the general principles around structuring an effective board. In this attention will be given to the purpose and the people rather than process and consider the importance of the context in which the board is operating.

## Role of the board                                          3.1

## At a glance                                               3.2

---

- The board is responsible for ensuring that the business has the necessary framework within which to function.
- The chairman has the responsibility for co-ordinating the board, it has been advised that this role not be combined with that of CEO.
- A clear majority of large UK firms have a Senior Independent non-Executive (SINE), but there are dangers that the holder of this role could compete with the Chairman.
- It is important to be clear which matters are reserved for the board and which are to be delegated to board committees.

---

It is absolutely critical that the role of the board is not only clear but well understood and agreed by all of its members. What follows is what the authors feel is a good general description of the role of the board.

- Right strategy:
  to ensure that there is the right strategy for the ownership as well as the

business, it is being implemented and monitored and that there is a good process for formulating and adapting it.
- Right resources:
to ensure that the organisation has the right resources in place to meet the agreed strategy for the business and its ownership. The most important of these resources relate to people and money.
- Right governance:
to ensure appropriate corporate governance.

This description is entirely consistent with that described in the Higgs Review (see **PARAGRAPH 1.2**)

But who is the board working for and to whom does it owe its responsibilities? A useful discussion of the issues around this topic is contained in Professor Jay Lorsch's *Pawns and Potentates* (see **BIBLIOGRAPHY**). Professor Lorsch has been Harvard Business School's board guru for some time and the book is clearly written for a US audience. Nevertheless it is a thought provoking publication for directors in any country.

Professor Lorsch puts forward three basic beliefs that boards or individual directors have. He labels directors as 'Traditionalists', 'Rationalizers' or 'Broad Constructionalists'.

To quote:

### The Traditionalists

'These Directors adhere to the strict belief in the primacy of the shareholder and decline to recognise that conflicts exist between their traditional legal perspective and that of other constituencies. They are in our experience, a true minority, and if we question the narrowness of their perspective, we question neither the integrity nor the competence they bring to the boardrooms. They have no doubts in the land of the corporation, the shareholder is king.'

### The Rationalizers

'These Directors see the conflicts and feel the tensions inherent in their responsibilities in an increasingly complex world. However they rationalise them away, implicitly following the view of the Delaware Courts that what's good for the shareholder will be good for the other constituencies, and for the corporation.'

### The Broad Constructionalists

'In contrast to the rationalisers, a larger, perhaps more thoughtful, group of directors openly recognises that their responsibilities encompass more than shareholders. If this attitude produces

> conflicts, they recognise and deal with them, without assuming that every decision must be in the shareholders' interests.'
>
> If we liken directors to Africa's magnificent ostriches, the broad constructionalists would be actively constructing the dangers of life on the sandy plains, while the rationalisers might gaze enviously at the buried heads of the traditionalists.

No secrets for which group of birds Professor Lorsch prefers. From the author's point of view it would seem that the success of a 'broad constructionalist' board or individual director will be down to the quality of their judgement.

In the United Kingdom, the United States and many other countries the unitary board is the prevailing system supported by the recognition of corporate social responsibility.

In France, Germany, Holland and other countries a two-tier system is in operation. This book is designed principally for the directors of UK companies. However these companies may have subsidiaries in other countries and indeed the directors themselves may be members of boards operating in a two-tier environment. For these reasons it is worth considering the issues involved.

The most useful book the authors found on the two-tier system is Gregory Francesco Maasen's *An International Comparison of Corporate Governance* first published in 1999 by Spencer Stuart.

In it he includes the following chart based on some work done by Gedajlovic at Concordia University Montreal in 1993. It is designed to show the spectrum of perspectives towards corporate governance.

| Shareholder ⟵ ⟶ Stakeholder | |
|---|---|
| Execs and non-execs<br>Fiduciaries of shareholders | Execs and non-execs are<br>fiduciaries of a variety of<br>claimants |
| Execs and non-execs should<br>adopt principles consistent<br>with maximisation of<br>shareholder value; | Execs and non-execs should<br>balance pluralistic claims; |
| Profitability and economic<br>efficiency are the standards of<br>efficacy; | Profitability and economic<br>efficiency are important in<br>addition to survival, long term<br>growth and stability; |
| The corporation is subordinate<br>to the interests of shareholders. | The corporation is seen as a<br>superordinate entity. |

It is exactly because of these different perspectives that the unitary or two-tier approach is taken. The dominance of the principle of co-determination in Germany and Holland results in a two-tier approach.

## What are two-tier boards?                                    3.3

The two tiers are usually a supervisory board and a management board. The supervisory board controls broad issues of policy and appoints the management board. The management board is responsible for the day to day control of the organisation. One of the main functions of two-tier boards is to give employees and other stakeholders who may not be shareholders some control over a company.

The principle difference between the unitary and two-tier approach to boards is therefore to do with decision making. The operation, names and composition of boards operating under the two-tier system varies from country to country.

## Board context                                               3.4

There are several factors, which will determine the context in which the board operates, namely:

- nature of ownership;
- type of business;
- size of organisation;
- international reach;
- financial position of the company;
- market position of the company;
- reputation of the company;
- ambition/vision;
- stability of the company; and
- legal and regulatory environment.

Each of these factors has an impact on the ideal composition of the board, the specific nature of the board's role and on the key processes which will ensure that the board is effective.

A clear analysis and statement of the above is also a very useful input to board performance reviews and also to the recruitment process for new directors.

## The key board roles and board composition                   3.5

We see six key board roles and these are:

- chairman;
- chief executive officer;
- chief financial officer;

- non-executive;
- executive; and
- company secretary.

The authors have also commented on the role of the Senior Independent Director, which came to prominence through the Hampel Committee's work. The focus of this book is on the non-executive, consequently every chapter contains significant detail on the non-executive's role in the relevant subject area. For this reason the authors have kept the description of the non-executive's role at a high level here and focussed on the other roles of chairman, chief executive and finance director.

The detailed roles of each are discussed later. The company secretary is normally differentiated from the others described above in that he or she is not usually a formal member of the board.

With regard to composition and balance the model adopted by most UK plcs is for the chairman and the non-executives to be in the majority. The US model is quite different as demonstrated by Korn/Ferry survey in 2001. Here the average size of a US board was eleven directors nine of whom were outside directors (ie non-executive). In the US it is also normal for the roles of chairman and chief executive to combined in the role of President of the corporation. The wisdom of this approach has seldom been challenged, that is until the collapse of Enron.

For private companies in the UK there is often a majority of executive and just two active non-executives.

The majority of UK plcs have opted to separate the roles of chairman and CEO. This was not the case prior to the seminal Cadbury Report on the Financial Aspects of Corporate Governance in 1992.

In his report Sir Adrian said

> 'Given the importance and particular nature of the Chairman's role, it should in principle be separate from that of the Chief Executive. If the two roles are combined in one person, it represents a considerable concentration of power. We recommend, therefore that there should be a clearly accepted division of responsibilities at the head of a company, which will ensure a balance of power and authority, such that no one individual has unfettered powers of decision. Where the chairman is also the chief executive, it is essential that there should be a strong and independent element on the board.'

In private companies for the roles to be combined. However it is normal in companies with significant venture capital or private equity backing for there to be a separation of roles.

The diversity of the background of board members has become a growing issue in many countries. In Korn/Ferry's 2001 US survey, three-quarters of the 902 companies polled had at least one female director, whilst only 4 per cent planned to add a foreign national. Interestingly they commented that the trend towards having non-residents on board was in reverse because of logistical challenges and cultural assimilation.

As part of Derek Higgs' review into the role and effectiveness of non-executive directors in the UK, a census of plc directors was made. This showed the following with respect to the diversity of UK plc boards.

- Only one FTSE 100 had a female chairman (3i Group plc)
- Only 2 had female Chief executives.
- 4% of executive directors are women and 6% non-execs.

As board composition is the responsibility of the chairman it is up to the chairman to ensure that the board is comprised of people from sufficiently diverse backgrounds to meet its objectives.

## Role of chairman                                                                 3.6

We see the role of the chairman as being to:

---

- organise the composition, business and efficiency of the board;
- lead the board in the determination of its strategy and in the achievement of its objectives;
- ensure that the board has accurate and clear visibility of results and likely future trends;
- ensure that board committees are properly established, composed and operated;
- ensure effective relationships are maintained with all major stakeholders in the business i.e. customers, shareholders, employees, suppliers, government, local community, industry etc;
- enhance the company's public standing and reputation;
- develop a strong working relationship with the chief executive/ managing director and ensure that there is a clear definition and agreement of the division of responsibilities.

---

In summary the chairman is the leader of the board. As such they should be prepared to step into the CEO role for short periods until a successor is appointed if necessary.

We also believe that it is essential for there to be a written description of the role of the chairman and for all directors of the company to be familiar with its contents. The chairman should also be subject to the board's performance review. In larger quoted companies the review of the performance of the chairman is normally led by the senior independent non-executive (SINE) who gathers the views of the other directors and provides the chairman with feedback. In smaller companies or where there isn't a SINE then this often done by the chief executive.

Organising the composition of the board includes dealing with the succession of the chief executive. This is covered in the next section on the role of the CEO. With respect to organising the composition of the board, clearly the chairman needs to ensure that there is an effective nominations process which the board supports.

There has been some debate as to whether the title 'non-executive chairman' has any validity. Many including the authors subscribe to the view that 'A chairman is a chairman' and believe that the role as described above is quite distinct from that of the non-executive. The responsibilities are exactly the same if there is the word chairman in the title.

Some including Hugh Parker, author of *Letters from a Chairman* hold strong views on this point.

> 'Any Chairman who calls himself- or allows himself to be called- a 'non-executive Chairman' comes perilously close to being a non Chairman!'

The insertion of 'non-executive' into the chairman's title is often simply to indicate that he or she is part-time. On this subject the chairman's time commitment can be significantly greater than that of a non-executive. The 3i/IRS survey for 2003 showed demonstrates this.

| Turnover £m | <10 | 11-30 | 31-100 | 101-500 | 501-1000 | £1bn plus |
|---|---|---|---|---|---|---|
| Median days | 33 | 40 | 43 | 51 | 51 | 53 |

These median figures hide the fact that significant numbers of chairmen are spending over two days per week on their roles. The circumstances of the company, their tenure in the role and the nature of their appointment will impact on this.

So what are the core competencies of a chairman? On **PARAGRAPH 1.5** in chapter one on the appointment processes for non-executives the core competencies and characteristics for non-executives were discussed. These were grouped under three headings:

- personal;
- professional and managerial; and
- entrepreneurial.

Whilst we believe that the lists are just as valid for chairmen as non-executives we would emphasise three things as being especially important for a chairman:

- integrity;
- judgement; and
- leadership.

A chairman is the leader of the board and should take responsibility for the team dynamic and ensuring that the potential of all board members is fulfilled whether they are executive or non-executive. To do this requires strong communication skills as well as significant commitment to the role.

Who organises the succession – the chairman? If the chairman is effective he or she will have considered succession, agreed a process with the board and an orderly succession will take place. Additionally the board will have a contingency plan to cope with the need to suddenly replace the chairman as a result of illness etc. There may or may not be a clearly identified successor appointed as Deputy chairman.

The situation that is most difficult is where the chairman is underperforming and there is no agreed process for replacing them. The approach to this difficult situation obviously depends upon the shareholding structure of the company, whether it is a listed company and so on.

Let's look at the larger quoted company situation first. If there is a senior independent director as described below then this person is the focal point for shareholders and other board members to make their views known on the performance of the chairman and their desire for change. If no one has been formally identified as a senior independent director and there is a deputy chairman then he or she will fulfil the role. If there is neither a SINE nor Deputy chairman then either one of the non-executives or the chief executive will have to lead the process.

Whoever takes on the role of resolving the situation if they have the unanimous or overwhelming majority support of the rest of the board and the key institutional Shareholders then the situation can be resolved fairly straightforwardly. The person simply informs the chairman that he has lost the confidence of his board and the company's key shareholders and gives him the opportunity to resign.

So why are so many situations unlike that described above? Often because:

- there isn't a clearly identified person to resolve the situation;
- the views of the other board members are not unanimous;
- even if they are some may not be prepared to support the chairman's removal;
- the chairman may not share the view that he is underperforming;
- personal interests may be placed ahead of those of the company; or
- the chairman may recognise reality but be reluctant to make it easy for his colleagues.

In smaller companies and especially private businesses where the chairman is also the major shareholder it can be much more difficult. An excellent book by Manfred Kets De Vries and Eric van der Loo on family companies, *Family Business*, covers this subject in great detail. In venture capital and private equity-backed businesses where the chairman is appointed by the lead investor, there is usually a mechanism for replacing them, whether the circumstances are a natural succession or removal for underperformance. For many smaller businesses there is no succession but instead a sale of the company. The important thing for any chairman is to have someone they trust and respect who will be able to hold up the mirror and help them decide when the time is right to go. They need not be in the business or on the board to do this. Indeed this is a role many a trusted adviser has fulfilled.

A number of real life situations and some guidance on effecting the removal of directors are contained one of the author's other publications *Directors Dilemmas* published by Kogan Page.

## Role of chief executive officer                                            3.7

A huge volume of literature is available on the subject of the role of the chief executive. There is even more if you count the autobiographical works of the more prominent CEOs in the US. This book will limit itself here to a fairly straightforward definition of the role, consider the competencies required of a CEO and then discuss some of the issues for non-executives working with CEOs.

The role of the chief executive officer can be described simply as

'To execute the plans and policies established by the board.'

In order to do this they will need to possess a wide range of knowledge and skills and the behavioural characteristics required to lead the rest of the company. They must also not just be a good CEO but one relevant to the circumstances of the company.

So what are the core competencies required of a CEO? There is as has been said much already written on this subject. What follows is a distillation of that and the conclusions of some work conducted by the 3i CEO programme to identify the competencies of successful CEOs in venture capital backed situations. Clearly the competencies required of any CEO are situation-dependent but we feel that the following provide a good generic basis from which to start.

The competencies are grouped under four categories.

- Leadership.
- Strategic capability.
- Enterprising and commercial.
- Problem solving and analytical capability.

We would define these as follows.

A CEO who is a competent leader:

- initiates action and takes responsibility;
- sets objectives for others gains their commitment;
- motivates and empowers others;
- introduces and leads change;
- recruits and develops high calibre people;
- builds a team spirit and inspires loyalty;
- instils a high degree of integrity in the organisation; and
- is conscious of the organisation's social responsibilities.

A CEO who has strong strategic competence:

- provides a compelling vision of the organisation's future potential;
- develops and communicates strategies and organisational goals;
- evaluates business options, anticipates trends and consequences;
- demonstrates a broad-based, long-term view of issues, events and activities;
- produces new ideas, approaches or insights; and
- is conscious of the overall strategic aims when discussing operational issues.

A CEO who is enterprising and commercial:

- thinks in terms of driving growth and adding value;
- enjoys making money and is strongly profit-oriented;
- demonstrates financial awareness, generating cash and controlling costs;
- understands the commercial drivers of a business;
- identifies new business opportunities for the organisation; and
- keeps up-to-date with competitor activity and market trends.

A CEO who has good problem solving and analytical capability:

- gathers comprehensive information to support decisions;
- probes for greater understanding and challenges assumptions;
- identifies and focuses on key issues;
- makes rational judgements from available information and analysis;
- thinks laterally and considers problems from different perspectives; and
- produces workable solutions.

It is hard for a CEO to possess all of the above without the underpinning of a fine sense of judgement, strong interpersonal skills and good antennae to sense issues ahead.

Evaluation of CEO performance is normally led by the chairman within the context of the evaluation of the board's performance as a whole. As with any other position the chairman has to judge whether the board has the right CEO and this may not be as simple as looking at current performance. Potential to implement the plans for the future is just as important.

The power and influence of the CEO changes in different settings. The CEO of a FTSE100 company is a powerful person but may have less power over his board than the CEO of the company who owns 100% of its equity. A description of the sources of power that non-executives have is contained in **PARAGRAPH 3.14**.

The style of CEOs varies as much as the attitude that they have towards their board. For some the rest of the board is a necessary inconvenience; for others, a powerful supporter in achieving their objectives. It is important for the non-executive to ascertain what this attitude is before taking the appointment and if the CEO's stance is not the most constructive to influence them to change.

A CEO needs people to calibrate views and keep their feet firmly on the ground. Even for the most wise and sensible chief executive the feelings of invincibility that can emerge following a period of prolonged success can prove highly damaging to them and their companies. The chairman should provide this type of support but non-executive directors can also be helpful.

Jack Welch the legendary former chief executive of General Electric gives a graphic example of the dangers of a chief executive who gets too full of himself and dominates the board in a delightfully named chapter 'Too full of myself' in his autobiography *Jack:Straight from the gut*:

---

'For chrissakes, Jack what are you going to do next? Buy McDonalds?'

The remark came from a foursome of guys across the seventh fairway at Augusta as I was teeing off from the third hole in April 1986. Four months after announcing the deal to buy RCA, I had just acquired Kidder, Peabody, one of Wall Street's oldest investment banking firms.

While the guys were only kidding, there were others who really didn't think much of our latest decision. At least three GE board members weren't too keen on it, including two of the most experienced directors in the financial services business Citibank Chairman Walt Wriston and J.P. Morgan President Lew Preston. Along with Andy Sigler, then Chairman of Champion International, they warned that the business was a lot different from our others.

'The talent goes up and down the elevators every day and can go in a heartbeat,' said Wriston. 'All you're buying is the furniture.'

At an April 1986 board meeting in Kansas City, I had argued for it – and unanimously swung the board my way.

It was a classic case of hubris. Flush with the success of our acquisitions of RCA in 1985 and Employers Reinsurance in 1984,

---

> I was on a roll. Frankly, I was just too full of myself. While internally I was still searching for the right feel for the company, on the acquisition front I thought I could make anything work.
>
> Soon I'd realise that I had taken it one step too far.

The best way for the non-executive towards developing a relationship with a CEO, regardless of whether they are taking a constructive attitude or not, is to provide significant added value on issues of importance to the CEO.

We now come to the challenging issue of CEO succession.

## CEO succession                                              3.8

The selection of a new Chief executive is definitely a defining moment in a company's history. Making the right choice is one of the board's most important responsibilities. Getting it wrong risks de-stabilising the board or worse could be disastrous for the company. If the typical period for a non-executive to serve is two three-year terms then CEO succession is something you are likely to encounter.

The situation where a board may find the need to select a new CEO is usually where the current CEO:

- is retiring, leaving a well-resourced and managed business with a clear strategy;
- is retiring, leaving significant issues in terms of strategy, resourcing or governance;
- becomes ill or dies and needs replacing urgently; or
- is fired for poor performance, poor conduct or some other reason.

Some research from 3i/Cranfield and Sanders and Sidney conducted in 1999 showed the following:

## Length of tenure of the CEOs of unquoted and quoted companies                                              3.9

|  | Average Tenure | 2 years or less | 2–5 years | 5–10years | 10 years or more |
|---|---|---|---|---|---|
| **Top 350 Quoted** | 5.25 | 25% | 36% | 26% | 13% |
| **Top 100** | 4.1 | 30% | 42% | 21% | 7% |
| **Next 250** | 5.75 | 23% | 34% | 28% | 15% |
| **Top 100 unquoted** | 9.75 | 18% | 28% | 24% | 30% |

The main factor influencing tenure was performance.

Another piece of research regularly conducted by PR agency Burson Marsteller shows the impact of the chief executive's reputation on the reputation of the company. Here is an extract from the latest report. A fuller version is contained in the **APPENDICES**.

> 'NEW YORK, October 25, 2001 – Today's CEOs have little time to prove themselves, according to a new national study released by international communications consulting firm Burson-Marsteller. **Building CEO Capital™**, the 3rd study of influential business stakeholders since 1997, reveals that today's CEO has only five earnings quarters on average to prove him or herself...
>
> In addition, the Burson-Marsteller study of 1,155 US chief executives, senior managers, financial analysts, institutional investors, business media and government officials confirms that the reputation of the CEO contributes heavily to how companies are perceived today. Nearly half (48%) of a company's reputation is attributed to a CEO's reputation. This is a dramatic rise of 20% from 40% in 1997. This trend is not isolated to the United States. The companion survey among influential stakeholders in the United Kingdom confirms the US findings with 49% attributed to the CEO.'

Whether the succession is deemed to be planned and orderly or abrupt due to a crisis the change always generates a high degree of anxiety both within and outside the company. Reactions to the choice the board makes will not only influence the success of chosen CEO but also influence the reputation of the board as a whole.

So how does the board give itself the maximum chance of making the right judgement, managing the process in the most effective way and coming out with a result that is defensible?

The starting point is to consider what approach the board would like to adopt both generally and for specific circumstances. There are a variety of ways. Not all of them will meet the objectives of the Combined Code that the process be 'formal and transparent'.

At one end of the spectrum there is what we would call the 'Relaxed' approach. Essentially the board waits until the need arises and picks the best available candidate internally or externally. The relaxed approach is clearly less effort in the short term but carries a greater degree of risk than the approach at the other end of the spectrum, which we would label the 'Ultimate Control' approach. Here the company has an overall succession plan and progressive management development programmes. There are a number of internal successors benchmarked against the best available outside. A good example of this recently was the very well publicised transition at General Electric from Jack Welch to Jeffrey Immelt in the US.

The reality for most boards is an approach somewhere between 'relaxed' and 'ultimate control' and somewhere between 'having a choice' or 'one well groomed heir apparent'. The important thing is to be clear what approach you are taking and why. If the company is a public one then the approach will need to be justified to shareholders and possibly the media. The risk, time and cost involved are different for each approach.

Before deciding the board should set some objectives, for example you may want to:

- have a formal and transparent process;
- obtain the best successor available internally or externally;
- make the appointment within a certain timeframe and cost;
- minimise the risk of an interregnum; or
- achieve maximum buy in from executive directors.

Does the board have an overall succession plan for other key roles? If not, a non-executive should be suggesting that there is one in place.

Having decided on an approach for the CEO succession, the board needs to decide how it wants to communicate on the issue. Some boards ensure that the process is well understood internally and externally. Others prefer a more discreet approach. If the succession is taking place as a result of an abrupt departure then it is far harder to manage the process behind closed doors.

If it is a retirement then the attitude of the current CEO will have an influence on the process. What should a retiring CEO's role be? At one level they should have had a major influence by producing a number of strong internal candidates. Inevitably they may have a preferred choice and this may be known to the board as a whole or just the chairman. A formal and transparent process may or may not endorse this choice and the chairman who is likely to be leading the process needs to ensure that the CEO doesn't steer the board inappropriately to choosing his preferred candidate. Many CEOs have the envelope in the safe for 'just in case' situations.

Historically CEOs used to pick their own successors, especially in the days of combined chairman and CEO.

When should the succession process start for an orderly transition where the CEO is leaving positively? It is easier if the chairman has a clear understanding of the CEO's intentions and ambitions. In these circumstances many chairmen have a preference for announcing who the new CEO will be at the time of the announcement of the current CEO's plans to retire. Where this is the case the board usually anticipates making an internal appointment.

The alternative is to announce the retirement and declare that a process to find a suitable successor is underway. The board may or may not disclose whether consideration is being given to external candidates.

Here are some of the views people have on whether the internal or external approach is better. Clearly they are not mutually exclusive and an internal candidate who genuinely wins over the best external candidates will have a stronger mandate.

- 'The board will have been seen to have failed in its duty if it hasn't been able to develop a successor who knows the business and is well respected externally.'
- 'External candidates tend to be favoured where the previous CEO appointment has failed and the company has significant issues.'
- 'There may be less turbulence and risk with an internal candidate.'
- 'You should avoid destructive competitions – businesses need depth of talent. A competition will just result in the disappointed candidates leaving.'
- 'It's so much easier to make an informed choice with internal candidates if you know them well already.'
- 'Don't narrow down to a single choice too soon, the best guys feel better for having won a competition.'
- 'If you've got an interregnum situation and you promote someone into the caretaker role and set an external process going, you'll almost certainly lose your caretaker.'

If the board ends up selecting a candidate who is going to be in the Group CEO role for the first time it is important that they understand the differences in the new role and receive appropriate development. The transition roller-coaster referred to in **PARAGRAPH 1.9** is relevant again.

Interregnum situations are often the most difficult, although the UK system of having separate chairmen and Chief executives makes it easier than in the USA where the roles are combined.

If the chairman has stepped into the CEO role and the board has granted additional powers to executive directors for a temporary period they need to recognise that it is easier for the chairman to step back once the successor is in place than it is for the executives to give up their recently gained powers.

The final thing to say on CEO succession is that getting it right makes the whole board's job a lot easier so it is well worth the effort in making the right choice.

## Role of Finance Director                                            3.10

Every non-executive is fundamentally dependent upon the quality of their finance director. Yet how do you ascertain before you join the board whether the FD is appropriate? This is an especially relevant question for non-executives on nominations committees who get involved in the selection of finance directors.

The simple model below is one way of thinking about the key elements of a finance director's capabilities. As you will see at the very base, underpinning everything else is integrity. Integrity means different things to different people. So it is critical for the non-executive to ensure that the FD has the shared sense of integrity.

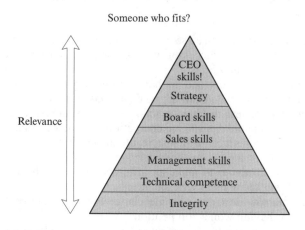

Someone who fits?

This was developed for a very popular 3i event for Independent Directors entitled *'How do you know a good FD when you see one?'* The event was run in the UK, France, Germany and Italy with attendees coming from a broad range of sectors and sizes of companies. The surprising thing was the level of consistency across the different countries and company contexts in what independent directors considered to be critical. There was a great deal of consensus around the above heirachy and the importance of ensuring relevance of fit between the finance director and the company.

There was also consensus on what a finance director is there to do which was split between 'ensuring' and 'adding value'.

Ensuring that:

- financial controls and systems are effective;
- financial resources are appropriate to meet the company's long and short-term requirements;
- the board is made fully aware of the company's financial position and has good visibility of future financial performance;
- the company has good relationships with providers of finance; and
- the finance team is appropriate and highly motivated.

Adding value by:

- being an active and contributing member of the board on issues other than finance;
- communicating well internally on financial matters so that staff have a

good appreciation of the company's financial position and the impact on the company's finance's of their actions;
- having a high reputation externally; and
- providing the board with insightful analysis from which to make key decisions.

The above seems a fairly simplistic description of the enormous range of duties a finance director has. However, a glimpse at the contents list of Tolley's *Finance Director's Handbook* reveals the true depth of the role.

One issue however where there was a lot of debate was over whether you really wanted to have a finance director who was capable of assuming the role of CEO. If the finance director has the capability to take on the duties of a CEO then they probably have a comparatively broad skill set and range of abilities which can be highly beneficial to the company, and they are often seen as an insurance policy if the CEO leaves or fails. The alternative view is that if they have the capability and ambition to become CEO then this may impair their relationship with the current CEO and make them less focussed on their key role. The obvious point to make is that it is important to understand both the capability and ambition of the finance director and whether this is appropriate to the circumstances of the company.

One considerable challenge for finance directors relates to them performing their function as a board member. The nature of their job is that they provide a key service to the board in terms of the provision of information and enablement of compliance with the legal and regulatory framework within which the board operates. It is probably harder for the Finance director to escape his functional silo than any other board member. The wise finance Director uses his team well to present information to the board saving his own air time for input as a member of the board as opposed to the head of the finance function.

One way for the finance director to gain experience as a fully contributing board member is by taking a non-executive position elsewhere.

In summary given the criticality of the finance director's role it is important for the non-executive to develop a good working relationship with the finance director.

## Role of senior independent non-executive                3.11

The term senior independent non-executive(SINE) first really came to prominence in the Hampel Report in 1998 and was intended to apply principally to listed companies.

In his report Sir Ronnie said the following:

'Cadbury also recommended that where the roles of chairman and chief executive officer were combined there should be a strong and independent element on the board, with a recognised senior member (code 1.2). But even where the roles of chairman and CEO are separated, we see a need for vigorously independent non-executive directors. There can in particular, be occasions when there is a need to convey concerns to the board other than through the chairman or CEO. To cover this eventuality we recommend that a senior independent non-executive director – eg a deputy chairman or the chairman of the remuneration committee – should have been identified in the annual report. We do not envisage that this individual would for this purpose need special responsibilities or an independent leadership role, nor do we think that to identify him or her should be divisive.'

In his recommendations therefore he concluded that:

'Whether or not the roles of chairman and chief executive officer are combined, a senior non-executive director should be identified in the annual report, to whom concerns can be conveyed.'

(Combined Code says SINE should be identified in the annual report.)

According to the Higgs Review over eighty per cent of the UK's top four hundred companies had identified a SINE in their annual reports.

But what is the role of a SINE and how does this relate to the role of the deputy chairman?

Hampel's intention was simply that one of the directors accepted the responsibility for acting as a focal point if there was subsequently a lack of confidence in the chairman amongst shareholders or the board. He had no intention of this position driving a wedge between the shareholders and the chairman. To avoid the danger of this many companies select a non-executive who is not a possible candidate to succeed the chairman.

In practice the senior independent non-executive also tends to be chairman of one or a number of the key board sub-committees eg Remuneration or Audit.

The two important words in the title are 'Senior' and 'Independent'. Independence is discussed in **PARAGRAPH 1.7**. Given that the SINE position is primarily intended for listed companies the definition of most importance is that of the key shareholders, ie the institutions. The NAPF criteria for independence are contained in the **APPENDICES**. Hermes, which has been a leading investor in terms of recognising the importance of good governance and investing resource into research and the development of best practice, produced a job description for the SINE.

The term 'senior' simply means that this is the nominated director to whom any unresolved concerns can be addressed, about the way in which the board operates, the implication being that they will do something about it. In practice it is normal for the institutional shareholders to express concerns they have about the chairman himself. Experience is developing of this role but to date it does seem to have been reserved for these situations.

Of all the issues raised by the Higgs Review the one which generated the most controversy was to do with the role of the senior independent non-executive, which is ironic given it is one of the briefest sections of his report. By way of introduction he recognises the sensitive area up front:

> 'Responses to consultation contained a range of views on the identification of a senior independent director. Some saw the role as unnecessary or divisive. It was pointed out that shareholders may make use of their own connections with non-executive directors, or contact the chairmen of board committees if they have concerns',

and

> 'Most respondents, however, supported the concept of a senior independent director, noting the importance of sensitivity in the conduct of the role. I agree with them.'

So naturally he then says the following:

> '*I therefore endorse the Code provision that a senior independent director be identified.* They should of course meet the test of independence set out in this report (Paragraph xx). Unless it is anticipated that they will become Chairman, and provided they meet the test of independence, the role could be assumed by the Deputy Chairman if there is one.'

So far so good. It was the final paragraph in this section which caused some very strong reactions from chairmen, company secretaries, chief executives and finance directors who thought that he had simply gone too far, was undermining their authority and creating a considerable extra burden.

> 'I see the role of the senior independent director as important in the relationship between major shareholders and the board as set out in 15.15 and 15.16 (see below). *The senior independent director should be available to shareholders, if they have reason for concern that contact through the normal channels of chairman of chief executive has failed to resolve. The senior independent director should also chair meetings between non-executive directors where the chairman does not attend.*'

Sections 15.15 and 15.16 were as follows:

> 'In addition, I propose that the senior independent director should attend sufficient of the regular meetings of management with a

range of major shareholders to develop a balanced understanding of the themes, issues and concerns of shareholders. The senior independent director should communicate these views to the non-executive directors and, as appropriate, to the board as a whole.

'Boards should also recognise that non-executive directors may also find it instructive to attend meetings with major investors from time to time and should be able to do so if they choose. Moreover, non-executive directors should expect to attend such meetings if requested by major investors in the company. They should, however, rely on the Chairman and the senior independent director to ensure a balanced view is taken of the range of shareholder views.'

There was also strong feedback from some institutional investors that, notwithstanding their feedback in the consultation process that they wanted more contact with non-executives, Higgs proposals if accepted would produce too great a time burden on them.

Such was the strength of feelings on this issue that it is likely that these proposals will be adapted before gaining the approval of the Financial Reporting Council.

The role of Deputy chairman in UK companies appears to be quite varied. In some they play an active role in promoting the company, are clearly identified as the chairman's successor and are someone who frequently represents the views of the company. At the other end of the spectrum they are respected elder statesman who have the role by dint of their past contribution but have minimal input.

The important thing is for the board and of course the individual to have clarity about what role they are expected to play and for shareholders to be comfortable with what that role is.

## Role of non-executives                                      3.12

The focus of this book is on the non-executive; consequently every chapter contains significant detail on the non-executive's role in the relevant subject area. For this reason we have kept the description of the non-executives role at a high level here. Paragraphs 1.5–1.8contain details on what core competencies non-executives are expected to have.

The title non-executive is a rather odd one in that it says what the role is not i.e. not an executive of the company, but it gives no clue as to what it is. There has been some debate as to whether a more constructive title would be of benefit. A survey conducted by 3i of non-executives in 2002 showed that many people didn't like the title 'non-executive' but that there was a great diversity of view over what would be better. The most popular choice was independent but 'only if there is a workable definition of what Independent means'. The Independent Review of Non-Executive Directors came to the same conclusion and so it seems unlikely that there will be any change in the forseeable future.

What the non-executives are expected to do is probably more important than what they are called. In chapter one we split the role into two components 'ensuring' and 'adding value'. We believe that Non-executives who add significant value have much greater influence with the other directors and are therefore much more likely to bring that influence to bear in ensuring that there is good governance.

Ensuring that:

● there is a robust strategy for the ownership and development of the business, that it is regularly monitored and adapted as required;
● the company has the appropriate resources in place to meet its strategy. The two most important being human and financial; and that
● there is appropriate corporate governance and a high standard of investor relations.

Adding value by:

● being a confidential sounding board to the directors;
● bringing an independent and broad view to the board; and
● helping the executive to achieve their business plans in whatever form is relevant given their experience and network.

It goes without saying that everything under 'Ensuring' adds value.

## Role of executive directors                                3.13

What is the role of executive directors as board members as distinct from their roles as functional or business unit heads? Firstly it is important that they consider issues from the perspective of the company as a whole and avoid becoming too representative of the interests of their own particular area of activity. The reality is that this is hard to do but that also other board members will take account of this. The good chairman develops the executive in this area and ensures that they are not confined to their functional silos.

Another issue relates to the degree of preparation the executive undertakes before board meetings. Striking the balance between an unhealthy level of rigorous preparation and ensuring that board meetings are not just a show for the non-executives is important.

The best board will involve good constructive contributions from executives and non-executives. It can happen that a chief executive of a major company would put a proposal of significance to the board without having the support the support of his executive although it is unlikely. Skilful chairmen and non-executives will sense whether this is the case and draw out the concerns if they haven't already been expressed.

The non-executive director needs to develop a good degree of knowledge of the executive and a significantly strong relationship with them so that they are prepared to trust and confide in them. This is especially so for those executive directors who are candidates to succeed the chief executive. Equally it is important for executive directors to take the initiative and make the same effort.

Most major companies will have an executive committee. This will sometimes be a straightforward subset of the board ie all of the executive directors but more typically it will include the executive directors and a small number of other senior personnel. The company secretary is also likely to be a member.

## Role of company secretary                                    3.14

All companies are legally required to appoint a company secretary. There has been much debate over the years as to what the role of a company secretary should be. The debate centreing around whether the role should be confined to the administrative matters relating to the smooth operation of the board and compliance or whether it should be much broader encompassing insurance and other functions. The current view of the ICSA is that the role comprises the following responsibilities:

- Ensuring compliance with law, regulation, the organisation's constitution and codes of practice.
- Raising matters which may warrant the attention of the board/trustees, especially legal and governance matters.
- Advising the board/trustees/directors as to their responsibilities to uphold good corporate governance and on constitutional and legal issues.
- Maintaining Statutory Records and submitting records to relevant regulators/registrars such as Companies House.
- Communicating with shareholders or external stakeholders in the organisation.
- Taking minutes of meetings, preparing agendas and ensuring that the necessary action is taken.
- Managing Pensions, Contracts, Employee Benefits, Insurance, Property, Risk or Health and Safety

Whatever falls within the company secretary's remit, as decided by the board, the company secretary must know what is going on within the company to be effective. For this reason the relationship the company secretary has with the chairman, the chief executive and the other executive directors and the attitude that they take towards him or her is critical. It is much easier in our view for the company secretary to be effective if they are a member of the executive committee of the board.

As the company secretary plays an important role in servicing the non-executives it is wise for any non-executive to establish good relationship with them. This can be done in all sorts of ways starting with straightforward acknowledgement and demonstration of thanks for the support the company Secretary provides.

Another role most company secretaries have is in helping the chairman and chief executive prepare board agendas. The topic of board agendas is covered in more detail on **PARAGRAPH 4.8**. Good ones canvass the non-executives for their views on what they would like on the agenda. This not only saves the chairman time but also can be a useful source of feedback for the chairman on what is really concerning the non-executives.

Company secretaries will normally report to the chief executive with a strong dotted line to the chairman and possibly some aspects of their role reporting through the finance director. For this reason ICSA have produced a useful guide called Reporting Lines for the Company Secretary (ref number 011101 available on their website www.icsa.org.uk).

## *Sources of power and influence for non-executives*    3.15

For a non-executive to be effective they have to have influence with their fellow board members and especially the chairman and chief executive. Without influence it is hard to make a genuine contribution no matter how good your judgement or relevant the knowledge that you possess. A well intentioned non-executive who takes the role seriously will become frustrated if their views are not respected or listened to. Respect is a very important word for non-executives.

Management guru Warren Bennis is reported to have said that

'Power is the ability to convert vision into reality.'

This is a very relevant quote for non-executives, whose power may be more ambiguous than executives.

So where do non-executives derive their power to influence their fellow directors? There are various sources.

One of the most straightforward descriptions of the sources power that people can use in business is contained in a 1995 Harvard Business School paper by Linda Hill entitled *Power Dynamics in Organisations*. Again this is another piece aimed at executives and probably those looking to become executive directors and leaders of businesses but the principles are just as relevant to non-executives.

The thesis is that there are principally two sources of power for managers 'positional' and 'personal'. The components of each are listed below.

| Positional power | Personal power |
|---|---|
| Formal authority | Expertise |
| Relevance | Track record |
| Centrality | Attractiveness |
| Autonomy Effort | Visibility |

Some are more obvious than others. *Formal Authority* is simply the rights, responsibilities and sanctions you possess by virtue of holding the position. For example the chairman of the Remuneration, Audit or nominations committee may feel more powerful than a non-executive who doesn't hold a chairmanship.

*Relevance* relates to how relevant your contribution is to the current priorities of the organisation or in our case board. Following our earlier case at various times the chairman of the different committees will be more or less influential.

*Centrality* relates to the position the person has in networks, which are important to the committee. A good example of this would be where the non-executive is a highly respected city or industry figure. They are in the position of bestowing patronage or access to resources.

*Autonomy* This is a difficult one for non-executives as on the one hand they have few delegated powers from the board other than those associated with their roles on the various sub committees. On the other hand they arguably they have more freedom to act in the sense of expressing views than their executive colleagues on the board.

'Visibility' is a relevant one for non-executives. The principle here is that the more visible your performance is, the more widely dispersed and recognised your power will be. Whilst their value to the chairman or chief executive is high, the fact that they are invisible to other executives means that the non-executive's real contribution is frequently underestimated by those other than the chairman and chief executive.

These are the positional power sources. In Hills paper she contends that the less you rely on the formal powers the more power you have. The authors believe this is a very relevant point for non-executives.

So, looking at the personal power sources:

*Expertise* – possibly the most obvious source of power as long as the expertise has relevance to the situation. It is often through using their expertise to support the executives that non-executives increase their influence.

*Track record* – This is another more obvious source of power. The non-executive who has successfully done what the executive directors are setting out to achieve and is in at least the same peer group as the other non-executives has an obvious advantage. 3i has found it much easier to introduce second time entrepreneurs ie those who have already completed a successful start up, buy out or buy-in as non-executives or chairman than those without this experience.

*Attractiveness* – This relates to physical and behavioural characteristics that others find attractive. A non-executive relying on physical attractiveness as a source of power would be unusual. Though there is one physical characteristic which, looking at the annual reports of US companies might anecdotally reinforce Hill's point that height has been shown to help in the US.

Although some would argue that physical attractiveness helps, we suspect that attractive behavioural characteristics count for more in the non-executive context. The charismatic and likeable find gaining support for their ideas easier than the grumpy or solemn.

*Effort* – Individuals who work hard are perceived as being more committed. Since the quality of the non-executive's relationships with other board members are important, effort needs to be put in to build and maintain them. In the post-Enron environment all non-executives are aware of the effort required to ensure that they have sufficient knowledge of the company and the directors.

In another Harvard Business School paper on the same subject, *Exercising Influence* Hill argues that in order to use your power to exercise influence on a subject you need to consider the following questions:

- Whose co-operation do you need?
- Whose compliance do you need? and
- Whose opposition would keep you form accomplishing your objective?

These are very helpful questions.

One other source of power relates to the power received by threatening resignation. This obviously should be reserved for special occasions and carefully used. There are a number of difficulties for a non-executive contemplating resignation and these relate to:

- reputational issues for them and the company;
- leaving the company with a weakened board;
- legal issues; and
- financial loss.

A non-executive with a reputation for threatening to resign every time he or she doesn't agree with something will find it hard to gain influence or additional appointments. A non-executive who does resign needs to do so in a very careful way to avoid reputational risk. Shareholders may be sympathetic as to the reasons why but disappointed that the non-executive has left them with a weakened board.

What other sanctions do non-executives have? As has been mentioned earlier, considerably more if they are involved in the audit, nominations or remuneration committees. However withdrawing consent or withholding signature may prove only a temporary source of power.

Finally, the authors believe that there is one other source of power for the non-executive that provides considerable influence and that is the moral high ground which is reached by always acting in the best interests of the company rather than one's own.

## Powers and responsibilities of the board and committees                                                    3.16

Confusion between the powers and responsibilities of the board, the committees of the board and individual board members reduces the effectiveness of the board and increases the risk of weak governance. Achieving clarity on the role of the board and the individual directors is the foundation stone of good governance and board effectiveness. However it is also important to be absolutely clear and precise about what decisions should only be decided by the board as a whole ('Matters reserved for the Board'), what decisions should only be decided by nominated committees of the board ('Matters delegated to the sub committees of the Board') and those to be decided by the executive ('Matters delegated to the executive').

The context of the board should drive the specifics but we have attempted below to look at the key areas to be considered in arriving at a detailed description for a specific business.

## Matters reserved for the Board                                           3.17

The Institute of Chartered Secretaries and Administrators has produced an excellent Guidance note (Ref 011104) which is also available on their website www.icsa.org.uk on Matters reserved for the Board. Although this has been produced for public companies it is easy to adapt for the purposes of private ones. A copy is contained in the APPENDICES.

The key items it covers are:

- Companies Act requirements;
- Stock Exchange/ Financial Services Authority;
- board membership and board committees;
- management; and
- Combined Code recommendations;

as well as a whole series of other items including:

- internal controls;
- health and safety;
- environmental;
- litigation; and
- dealing with urgent matters

The most challenging areas for many boards are included under the ICSA's management heading. Why? Because this covers:

- approval of the long term objectives and strategy;
- approval of budgets;
- key management appointments; and
- changes to the companies management and control structure.

The board's role in strategy is dealt with in CHAPTER 7 CORPORATE STRATEGY.

With respect to urgent matters the ICSA guidance note states that

> 'In all cases however the procedures should balance the need for urgency with the overriding principle that each director should be given as much information as possible and have an opportunity to requisition an emergency meeting of the board to discuss the matter prior to commitment of the Company.'

## Matters delegated to the sub committees of the board 3.18

The first issue is to determine what sub committees of the board it is appropriate to have.

If the company is a listed one then in order to satisfy the Combined Code there will be the following as a matter of course.

- Audit.
- Nominations.
- Remuneration.

The nature of business and other contextual factors will then determine the need for additional committees eg environmental, regulatory, risk management.

Sample terms of reference for each of the Audit and Compliance, Nominations and Remuneration committees are contained in the APPENDICES.

## Board balance 3.19

The Combined Code for listed companies states:

'that the board should include a balance of executive and non-executive directors (including independent non-executives) such that no individual or small group of individuals can dominate the board's decision taking.'

## Board away days                                          3.20

As was shown above(**PARAGRAPH 1.23**) nine out of ten boards hold away days principally to discuss strategy or the annual budget. **CHAPTER 7 CORPORATE STRATEGY** covers the board's role in strategy in detail. In this section we provide the following guidance for making away days effective.

- Be clear on the purpose of the away day and what your desired outcomes are eg selection from a number of strategic options.
- Decide whether to use an external facilitator.
- Decide whom to involve who isn't a member of the board(internal or external)
- The chairman or CEO should brief the facilitator about the team dynamics, 'politics' or taboo subjects.
- Hold the away day offsite.
- Don't allow interruptions except in an emergency.
- Don't start with an operational board meeting.
- Participants should be prepared to challenge each other, in particular to surface differences – a key to success is the quality of debate, both content and challenge.
- No one should be allowed to dominate the debate.
- Action points should have an individual(s) assigned to them with delivery deadlines and reporting criteria.
- Consideration should be given during the away day to the personal implications of any decisions taken.
- Ensure critical outputs from the away day get put on the agenda for subsequent board meetings.
- Follow up and review the output of the away day.

Using an external facilitator for such days has a number of advantages. However if you use one they need to be:

- credible with the participants and experienced at the appropriate level;
- prepared and able to challenge participants (collectively and individually);
- able to maintain an objective and neutral approach;
- able to generate an appropriate atmosphere; and
- have a clearly defined process for running the day, which is flexible enough to deviate from it when the participants require to do so.

Creating the right atmosphere is essential. A good chairman will ensure that there is the right blend of formality and informality. The social aspect is also important in building relationships, trust and respect between the board members.

We are especially grateful to Murray Steele at Cranfield School of Management for his support in compiling the above.

## Professional advice for non-executives 3.21

It has become the norm for non-executives to want to have access to independent (from the company) legal and technical advice. However this is an area not without its difficulties. Some of the issues involved are as follows.

- What type of advice is it appropriate and reasonable for a non-executive to request?
- What is the process for agreeing this?
- Which advisers should be used?

Take each point in turn and discuss.

ICSA have again produced a very helpful guidance note(number 011102) which is available on their website www.icsa.org.uk which contains a model board resolution which covers the key issues.

# 4. Meetings

---

- A company's Articles of Association often govern many aspects of board meetings, including convening meetings, quora of meetings and delegation of duties to individual directors.
- While most boards have sub-committees, too much delegation of authority to them is sometimes seen as an abdication of responsibility.
- A company's accounts, and the directors' interests, shall be laid before the members at an Annual General Meeting.
- An alternate director is not an agent, and is not obliged to vote the same way as the absent director.
- Minutes and post-meeting notification should be checked to ensure that they are accurate and that they fit with directors' recollections of what happened.

---

This chapter focuses on the formal aspects of the formal meetings that non-executive directors become involved in. These formal meetings are an important opportunity for non-executive directors to fulfil their role through adding value and ensuring good governance. They are not the only opportunity. The informal meetings and telephone conversations that non-executive directors hold with other directors are just as important in building the relationships and knowledge required to influence key decisions.

112

Two other books by one of the authors, *Running Board Meetings* and *Directors Dilemmas* (see **BIBLIOGRAPHY**) cover the informal aspects in considerable detail.

The main types of formal meetings non-executive directors become involved in are:

- board meetings;
- board sub-committee meetings;
- Annual General Meetings;
- Extraordinary General Meetings; and
- meetings for specific classes of shareholder ('Class Meetings').

The first two being 'meetings of directors' and the others being 'meetings of members' at which the directors attend. Before going into the formalities of each in detail we think that a non-executive should consider the following questions before any meeting.

- What is the purpose of the meeting?
- Who should be there?
- What role should each of the participants play?
- What should be on the agenda?
- What preparatory information is required to make the meeting effective?
- When should this information be circulated?
- How should the meeting be managed?
- What should be their own contribution to the meeting?
- How will decisions taken at the meeting be communicated and then brought into effect?
- Finally what formalities need to be observed?

## Meetings of directors 4.3

There are some general points to be made with regard to meetings of directors and these are as follows.

- The convening and holding of board meetings will normally be governed by the company's Articles of Association.
- Any director and the secretary at the director's request are usually empowered to call a meeting.
- The quorum for a board meeting will normally be fixed by the Articles. The *Companies (Tables A to F) Regulations 1985 (SI 1985/805)* Table A allows a quorum to be fixed by the directors and unless so fixed, shall be two. (More detail on Quorum issues are provided below at **PARAGRAPH 4.23**).
- It is usual for the Articles to require that a quorum be maintained throughout proceedings.
- A director interested in business to be conducted at a meeting must declare his interest. A quorum must be disinterested.

- Decisions of the directors may be recorded by Resolution in writing, signed by all the directors.
- The Articles of a company normally permit the delegation of certain powers of the directors to a committee.
- We have ignored sole director and single member situations on the grounds that there won't be a non-executive director involved!

## Board meetings                                                    4.4

Board meetings are the most frequent and generally the most important meetings that a non-executive director attends. These meetings of the executive and non-executive members of the board are where the key decisions are taken with regard to the strategy, resourcing and governance of the company. The chairman has the primary responsibility for managing these meetings and maximising their effectiveness.

## *Notice*                                                          4.5

The Articles of Association will normally set out the procedure for convening and holding board meetings. The *Companies (Tables A to F) Regulations 1985 (SI 1985/805)* Table A states that:

> 'A Director may, and the secretary at the request of a director shall, call a meeting of the directors.' (*regulation 88, Table A*).

It also provides that directors may regulate their proceedings as they think fit. There are no statutory provisions relating to the length of notice to be given for a board meeting and so 'reasonable' notice should be given to all directors. For most companies, board meetings are held at regular, predetermined intervals of which due notice is given, but from time to time meetings are called as and when necessary. As mentioned above it is good practice for the company (usually the company secretary) to produce a board calendar for the year ahead.

The notice reasonable for a particular meeting will depend, amongst other things, on the urgency and importance of the business to be discussed and the availability of the directors.

Notice of a board meeting may be given verbally, although it would be usual for written notice to be given. It is now common for companies to have made provision in their articles to give notice electronically (i.e. by email). Notice of a board meeting need not specify the business to be transacted, although it is good practice to do so.

As well as the agenda, a notice of a meeting will usually include the place, date and time for the meeting and unless directed in the Articles this can be circulated in any manner appropriate to a company, either by letter, fax, email or verbally.

## *Meetings by telephone* **4.6**

The Articles may permit directors to hold or participate in meetings by telephone. They require directors to be deemed present to be able to speak and be heard by the other directors at the 'meeting'. Consequently, unless the Articles specifically provide, a series of telephone calls on a one-to-one basis is unlikely to be permitted. Where a meeting is held by telephone/video conference the place of the meeting is taken as the place where the chairman participated from.

## *Frequency* **4.7**

There are differing views as to how frequently board meetings should be held. Some argue that to be sufficiently well informed, build the board's 'team spirit' and get through the increasing volume of work they should be monthly. Others argue that a monthly frequency tends to make them too operational in content and it is better to have fewer. A survey conducted by Top Pay Research Group and 3i in 2002 of over 400 directors who sat on over 1200 boards from start-ups to multi-billion pound companies showed the pattern below.

*How many times a year does the board meet?*

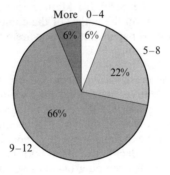

The average was eleven.

*Source Top Pay Research Group/ 3i survey 2002*

Eighty-nine per cent also met for separate budget or strategy sessions.

## *Length* **4.8**

With regard to the time a board meeting should take, again there are differences of view. The distribution in the 2002 TPRG survey was as follows.

## Average time of full board meeting(hours)

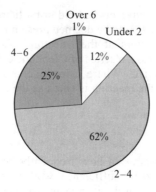

The average was 4 hours.

*Source Top Pay Research Group/ 3i survey 2002*

## Agendas 4.9

Unlike shareholder meetings, which are strictly governed by both the Articles and the Companies Act, directors are free, within fairly broad perimeters, to regulate their affairs as they feel fit. Matters to be discussed at a board meeting will be dependent on the nature of the company's business and the number of directors. Board papers and reports are either circulated with the agenda or tabled at the meeting.

Board meeting agendas are usually developed by the chairman, company secretary and chief executive. It is good practice to plan out the board's time for the year ahead given that there will be certain matters which need to be covered at certain times of the year, for example budgets, accounts, dividends and so on. In the authors view most boards only have five or six really important matters to decide each year and the board should therefore plan these items into the forthcoming agendas so that the proper preparation time is allowed. The company secretary will normally focus on the legal and compliance issues and ensure that the board is spending enough time on these.

### How many agenda items?

All routine items, for example; approval and signature of minutes of the last board meeting, any general meetings held after the last board meeting and financial statements, should be included in the agenda.

It is good practice, following a board meeting, for the chairman and/or company secretary to gather feedback from those attending and to ask them what items they would like to see on forthcoming agendas.

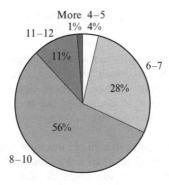

Reviewing agendas for the previous year is a healthy discipline and one normally performed by the company secretary. It can be fascinating to reflect on what the board actually spends its time on.

In researching *Running Board Meetings*, one of the authors noted that many directors complained that the following relationship occurred all too often.

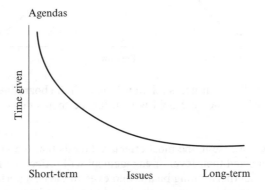

Cutting the number of board meetings is one way of solving this problem. Fewer meetings should lead to more focus on priorities, however this shouldn't be done at the expense of the board's knowledge of the company.

Quorum issues are dealt with below at **PARAGRAPH 4.23.**

## *Conduct of meetings* 4.10

There is no requirement of Company Law for a company to appoint a chairman. It is not a statutory position. However, the articles of association of most companies permit and sometimes require the directors to appoint one of their number to be chairman of the board.

In practice the chairman has the primary responsibility for ensuring the success of a board meeting. Engendering an atmosphere of energy, purpose, seriousness, rigour and trust will be the natural objective for any thoughtful chairman.

They will also work hard to harness the collective knowledge, skills and behaviours of those present to obtain not only the best decisions for the company but the maximum chance of those decisions being brought into effect. A good chairman is in control of the meeting and works hard but doesn't allow himself or anyone else to dominate proceedings.

The skilful chairman manages to achieve the right amount of pressure on the board. Using the analogy of the chart below, too little pressure in the board-room leads to sloppiness, and too often to hasty and ill-thought through decisions.

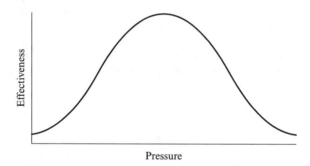

The strength of the chairman's relationships with the board members and the respect with which they are held will influence their ability to achieve the right balance.

It is probably the case in the most effective boards that the views expressed by the directors and their level of engagement will reflect their true position. However, in underperforming boards and even in the best performing boards there may be times when some of the board become 'silent seethers', who are unhappy with the conduct of the meeting yet for some reason not prepared, in the meeting at least, to say what they really think. The good chairman is alive to this and will either draw the person out in the meeting or make sure he follows up after the meeting has closed.

It is said that the best chairmen really do seem to know what is in the thought bubbles above their colleagues' heads. The chairman has a duty to ensure that all directors who wish to speak on a particular topic are given a reasonable opportunity to put forward the point of view. If matters become too heated, the chairman can, at his discretion, adjourn the meeting to enable tempers to cool. Adjournment may be for a few minutes or could, in some circum-stances, be until the next board meeting.

The Combined Code for listed companies also says that 'each director should receive the same information concerning the matters to be considered and each director should be given sufficient time in which to consider such information.'

Table A *(SI 1985/805)* confers the following specific powers upon the chairman of a board meeting and of general meetings:

- In the case of an equality of votes, the chairman shall have a second or casting vote (*Reg 88* for board meetings), and for general meetings. This casting vote is in addition to any other votes that the chairman may have. It is normal practice for the chairman to use this casting vote to maintain the status quo on the grounds that there is no majority in favour of change. However, it is entirely the chairman's discretion how he uses this vote, if at all.
- At a meeting of the directors or of a committee of the directors if a question arises as to the right of a director to vote, the question may, before the conclusion of the meeting, be referred to the chairman and his ruling shall be final and conclusive (*Reg 98*).

When a director considers that a course of action to be taken by the board is potentially damaging, depending on the nature of the action, he may feel it necessary to make a formal objection to the board. This being the case the formal objection should be minuted. It may also be appropriate for the dissenting director to resign, although this is unlikely to be considered an adequate discharge of his duties where the company is insolvent. The dissenting director must select the appropriate course of action based upon the nature and scale of his dissatisfaction with the affairs of the company.

Managing the contribution from the executive is another important ingredient of success. The artful chairman avoids the situation where the board meeting is simply a show for the non-executives or where the only executive who has a chance to speak is the chief executive. He also brings out the Finance Director as a fully functioning board member and doesn't confine them simply to the role of provider of information.

What should the non-executive director's contribution to board meetings be? In summary, to be very well prepared and to contribute to the discussions in a way that meets the objectives of their role. In order to do this they will recognise that there is limited airtime in which to make their contributions.

Consequently they are unlikely to squander it on minor points of detail or issues where others may make a stronger contribution. Asking good questions rather than giving good speeches is more likely to achieve this. They will also see themselves as a member of the board team and actively contribute to the team spirit of the board. This does not mean that they have to lose their objectivity.

The best non-executives spend some time after every board meeting reflecting on their performance and are conscious of where they have contributed to

Meetings

most effect and where they did the opposite. The best chairmen will also be providing them with regular and constructive feedback.

If the non-executive director feels that board meetings are not as effective as they should be he should raise this in a constructive manner with the chairman. Ultimately poorly managed board meetings will lead to deterioration in performance. If the chairman isn't able to enhance the effectiveness of board meetings then there is clearly an issue with the chairman. See PARAGRAPH 1.4 ROLE OF THE CHAIRMAN OF THE BOARD for more information.

## Standing committee meetings                                   4.11

The board may delegate certain powers to a standing committee. However they cannot do so unless the Articles of Association so provide. The Articles will normally also regulate the proceedings of such committees.

The directors must ensure that the board resolution establishing a committee is carefully drafted so that the committee's status and functions are clearly defined in terms of reference. Also, any limitation of the powers delegated by the board needs to be stated in the terms of reference.

It is useful from time to time to establish *ad hoc* committees of the board to deal with specific matters that cannot be dealt with practicably by the full board or which may require urgent attention between regular board meetings, ie progressing the acquisition or sale of certain assets, final sign off of accounts etc.

The Combined Code for listed companies recommends the establishment of standing audit, remuneration and nomination committees.

The most common board sub-committees are:

- audit;
- remuneration; and
- nominations and appointments,

and these are covered in detail in chapters X,Y and Z accordingly. There may be others depending on the nature of the business, for example an environmental committee.

Board sub-committees if managed well can save the board as a whole a considerable amount of time by delegating the detailed discussion of technical, time consuming or less strategic complex but vital issues. They also allow for more considered discussion with external advisers. The balance of what is discussed at board meetings and what is discussed in committee meetings needs to be carefully considered. Some directors see the proliferation of committees and the increasing scope of their work as a potentially dangerous abdication of responsibility.

In smaller companies with smaller boards it may seem difficult to adopt this approach. However many smaller companies have adopted and adapted the principles of delegation, specialisation and planning to suit their own requirements and situation.

Non-executive directors should know and understand the:

- terms of reference of all board sub-committees whether they are on them or not;
- specific powers delegated to that committee by the board as a whole;
- way in which the work of each sub-committee is to be communicated to the board; and should
- expect especially in public companies to be a member of at least one of the board sub-committees.

The selection of people to serve on sub-committees should be done on a rational basis. Whilst it is important that any member of a particular committee needs to be motivated to take part, just occasionally those most keen may not be the best choice.

## Annual General Meetings                                   4.12

An annual general meeting must be held once a year and not more than 15 months after the date of the last such meeting (*CA 1985, s 366*). The first annual general meeting, however, must be held within 18 months of incorporation.

There are divided views on the benefits of AGMs. Some share the view of the following company secretary:

'I do not believe that there is much, if any upside in the way a company conducts an AGM, but there is almost unlimited downside if it is not handled properly.'

Others share the view of a highly experienced chairman who preferred not to be named:

'We all know that the people who turn up won't be able to change the decisions at the meeting given the dominance of institutional shareholders these days. So you may say what's the point? What a waste of money and so on. The point is that the process we go through as a board to make sure that we can account well for ourselves on any point is a wonderful discipline.'

The ICSA best practice guide to AGMs (See bibliography) has the following to say:

'Although all companies are required to hold an AGM of their shareholders, the event is not merely a matter of legal form. It provides the principal forum in which directors account to the shareholders for their stewardship of the company. It also gives shareholders an opportunity to raise issues before voting on matters which require approval.'

The directors of a company will normally convene an annual general meeting but if the directors default in convening such a meeting within the statutory period, the Department of Trade and Industry may call or direct the calling of a general meeting upon the application of any member (*CA 1985, s 367*). The usual business of an AGM comprises the following:

- consideration of the annual report and accounts;
- declaration of a dividend (if any);
- election or re-election of directors;
- appointment or reappointment of auditors; and
- giving of authority to the directors to determine the auditors' remuneration.

This business is often referred to as 'ordinary' business although it is unusual for Articles of Association to now draw a distinction between ordinary and special business (Table A *(SI 1985/805)* does not).

The following points of practice should be noted with regard to the business of an annual general meeting.

- An annual general meeting must be held within the statutory time limits even if audited accounts are not available for consideration by the meeting at that time. Unless there is other business to transact it is normal for such meetings to be immediately adjourned, to be reconvened when accounts become available.
- Any business that may be transacted at an extraordinary general meeting of the company may also be transacted at an annual general meeting (sometimes referred to as 'special' business).
- Except where the members of a private company have approved an elective resolution to dispense with an AGM, directors are obliged to lay audited accounts before the company in a general meeting within ten months of the end of an accounting period for a private company, and within seven months for a public company (*CA 1985, s 244*). These time limits may be shorter in the case of a first accounting period.
- There is no statutory requirement for the notice convening the meeting or the auditors' report to the accounts to be read at the meeting. It is now common practice for members to be invited to take both as read.
- Attendance sheets should be made available at the meeting for completion by all persons (members and others) attending the meeting.
- The register of directors' interests must be available for inspection at the meeting.
- The members do not approve the audited accounts. The statutory requirement is merely that the accounts be laid before the company (*CA 1985, s 241(1)*). The accounts are therefore 'received' or 'adopted'.

- The quorum required for an annual general meeting will be set out in the Articles of Association.
- There is no statutory requirement for resolutions to be seconded at meetings of members. It is also unusual for the Articles to require resolutions to be seconded but nevertheless this remains a procedural custom for many companies.
- Resolutions have traditionally been decided on a show of hands. This does not take account of the number of shares held by each member present, nor does it include proxy votes received. Consequently most major public companies will also present to the meeting the proxies cast in favour of each motion. The chairman or a specified number of members are normally authorised to demand a poll and the Articles should be consulted to ascertain the exact requirements for the calling and conduct of a poll.
- Resolutions for the appointment or reappointment of directors to a public company should be voted upon separately; a single resolution to appoint two or more directors will be void (*CA 1985, s 292*). Although permitted, it is not good practice to present such a composite resolution at the AGM of a private company.

A private company may elect, by elective resolution, to dispense with the holding of annual general meetings (*CA 1985, s 366A*). An elective resolution is one approved by all the members entitled to attend and vote at a general meeting (*CA 1985, s 379A*).

An election has effect for the year in which it is made and subsequent years. An election cannot be used, however, to correct a default that has already taken place in failing to hold an AGM.

Where an election is in force and no AGM has been held for a particular year, any member may give notice to a company not later than three months before the end of the year, requiring the holding of an annual general meeting in that year. Such notice may be in writing or, with agreement, by electronic communication.

Where an election ceases to have effect (as a result, for example, of the company in general meeting approving an ordinary resolution to that effect), the company is not obliged to hold an AGM in that year if less than three months of the year remain when the election ceases to have effect.

It is usual for an election to dispense with the holding of AGMs to be coupled with elections to dispense with the laying of accounts and reports before a general meeting and to dispense with the obligation to appoint auditors annually.

The Institute of Company Secretaries and Administrators (ICSA) has produced an excellent guide on the subject entitled *A best practice guide to annual general Meetings*.

Meetings

## Extraordinary General Meetings                           4.13

There are three important things to note before we consider Extraordinary General Meetings in more detail and these are that:

- all general meetings other than Annual General Meetings are termed Extraordinary General Meetings;
- notice required for an EGM depends upon the resolution or resolutions to be considered, the Companies Acts and the Articles of Association; and
- all the business of an AGM may be considered at an EGM except that the Articles of Association may require directors to stand for re-election only at an AGM.

It normally falls to the directors to convene an Extraordinary General Meeting but *CA 1985, s 368* provides that on a member's requisition the directors of a company shall forthwith proceed to convene an extraordinary general meeting (See PARAGRAPH 4.22 REQUISITIONS BY MEMBERS).

The following points should also be considered regarding EGMs.

- The period of notice necessary for an Extraordinary General Meeting depends upon the resolution or resolutions to be proposed, the provisions of the Companies Acts and the Articles of Association (see PARAGRAPH 4.15 NOTICE OF GENERAL MEETINGS).
- Agreement to short notice of an Extraordinary General Meeting requires the approval of those members, who, being entitled to attend and vote at the meeting, hold not less than 95% in nominal value of the shares giving a right to attend and vote at such meeting. In the case of a company not having a share capital, the approval of the members exercising not less than 95% of the total voting rights is required (the members may elect to reduce this percentage in the case of a private company limited by share or by guarantee).
- It is possible for all the business of an Annual General Meeting to be conducted at an Extraordinary General Meeting (with the possible exception of the re-election of directors which may be reserved for an AGM by the Articles of Association (see the *Companies (Tables A to F) Regulations 1985 (SI 1985/805)* Table A)). Accordingly, if two sets of audited accounts are to be laid before the shareholders in one year (because, for example, an accounting period has been shortened), it is possible for the second set of accounts to be received by an Extraordinary General Meeting.

## Class meetings                                            4.14

The rights attaching to a particular class of share, or the provisions of *CA 1985*, may require a separate class meeting of shareholders to be held from time to time to approve a particular matter. Generally, the statutory provisions relating to the holding of general meetings apply equally to class meetings. However, particular provisions relate to a quorum and the giving of short notice (*CA 1985, ss 125(6)* and *369(4)*). All resolutions proposed at a class meeting are extraordinary resolutions.

The statutory provisions for the convening and holding of general meetings and the provisions in the Articles of Association relating to such meetings apply to class meetings with any necessary modifications. However, the quorum at a class meeting shall be two persons holding or representing by proxy at least one-third in nominal value of the issued shares of the particular class, and at an adjourned meeting one person holding shares of the class in question or his proxy (*CA 1985, s 125(6)*). Fourteen days' clear notice of a class meeting must be given to those entitled to receive notice. Agreement to short notice may, however, be given by a majority in number of the holders of the particular class of shares holding not less than 95% in nominal value of the shares (*CA 1985, s 369(4)*).

Resolutions to be proposed at a class meeting are extraordinary resolutions. Such resolutions require approval of three-quarters of the holders of the particular class attending, and entitled to attend and vote, in person or, where proxies are allowed, by proxy at a separate class meeting (see *CA 1985, s 378(1)* and hereafter). A copy of every extraordinary resolution must be filed at Companies House within 15 days of its date.

## Written resolutions of private companies          4.15

There are five key points with regard to written resolutions for private companies and these are as follows:

- Any company may approve members' resolutions by Resolution in writing. The Articles of Association will normally set out a procedure to be followed and, in the case of a private company, a statutory procedure is also available (*CA 1985, s 381*).
- Any resolution, whether Special, Extraordinary or Elective, may be approved by written resolution, *except* resolutions for the removal of the director or auditor.
- A written resolution may consist of one document or several documents signed by all the members.
- A copy of every written resolution must be sent to the auditors.
- In the case of certain resolutions, particular documents must be circulated to shareholders at or before the time a resolution is supplied to the member for signature.

It has been generally accepted that where all members demonstrate their consent to a particular matter which a general meeting of the shareholders has authority to approve, the consent will be as binding as a resolution of the shareholders at a general meeting properly convened and held.

Which resolutions can be written? Any resolution whether ordinary, special, extraordinary or elective (for private companies) may be approved by written resolutions, except resolutions for the removal of a director or auditor. In these cases the resolutions must be proposed at a general meeting duly convened and held.

The signatures may appear either on the same document or on several documents in like form. The resolution is dated when the resolution is signed by or on behalf of the last member to sign.

All written resolutions must be entered in a book, in the same way as minutes of proceedings of a general meeting of a company. Any such record, if purporting to be signed by a director of the company or by the secretary, would be evidence of the proceedings in agreeing to the resolution (*CA 1985, s 382A*).

The acceptance of written resolutions has necessitated the introduction of various procedural changes relating to the circulation of documents to shareholders. The company secretary will normally arrange this and will confirm that it has taken place. They principally relate to resolutions concerning:

- pre-emption waivers;
- purchase of own shares either on or off market; and
- directors' contracts or expenditure.

Non-executives should consult their company secretary if they have any doubts about whether the correct procedure is being followed with regard to a written resolution.

## Notice of general meetings                                  4.16

Generally, the length of notice to be given for general meetings is as follows.

- AGM: not less than 21 days (*CA 1985, s 369(1)*).
- Special resolution being proposed at a meeting: not less than 21 days' notice must be given, whether or not the meeting is an AGM or other general meeting of the company (*CA 1985, s 378(2)*).
- EGM: not less than 14 days' notice (*CA 1985, s 369(1)*). In the case of an unlimited company, not less than seven days' notice shall be given of a general meeting.

These will be understood to be 'Clear days' notice ie to exclude the day the notice is served and the day of the meeting itself. The ICSA guideline is that notice of an AGM and accompanying documents should be circulated to members not less than 20 working days (excluding weekends and bank holidays) in advance of a meeting. This recommendation is echoed by the Combined Code on Corporate Governance for listed companies.

Meetings of members may be called upon less than the statutory notice if approved by specified majorities of members. *All* members are generally entitled to receive notice of the meeting. The Articles should be consulted. In addition, the auditors and directors of the company should be given notice.

Certain details must be set out in a Notice of a meeting, either as a matter of practice or of law. A listed public company must also have regard to Stock Exchange requirements.

The Articles of a company may not provide for shorter notice periods to be given to members without consent. However, meetings may be called at shorter notice upon the agreement of members as follows.

- AGM: by all members entitled to attend and vote.
- Other general meetings: by a majority in number of the members having a right to attend and vote at the meeting and holding not less than 95% in nominal value of the shares giving a right to attend and vote at the meeting (*CA 1985, s 369(3)* and *CA 1985, s 378(3)*). The same majority must also consent to short notice of a meeting at which at which a special resolution is to be proposed (*CA 1985, s 378(3)*).
  This 95% in nominal value required for agreement to short notice may, in the case of a private company, be reduced to not less than 90% by elective resolution of the members (*CA 1985, s 369(4)* and *CA 1985, s 378(3)*).
- Separate class meetings: the provisions in relation to 'other general meetings' above also apply to separate class meetings.
- Elective resolutions at general meetings: agreement to short notice may not be given to any general meeting (or that part of a meeting) at which an elective resolution is to be proposed. An elective resolution may, however, be approved by written resolution, if practicable, thereby circumventing the notice requirements.

As has been said above the articles will almost invariably provide that 'clear days' notice is required i.e. excluding both the day of service of the notice and the day of the meeting. The position may be further complicated by a provision in the Articles stating that notice will be deemed to be given at the expiration of a certain period. For example, *regulation 115* of *Table A (SI 1985/805)* provides that a notice shall, unless the contrary is proved, be deemed to be given at the expiration of 48 hours after the envelope containing it was posted. It is common for other Articles to provide that service shall be deemed to be given at the expiration of 24 hours.

Great care must, therefore, be taken to ensure that the correct period of notice is given and, in this regard, it is essential that reference be made to the articles. For example, a company adopting *Companies (Tables A to F) Regulations 1985 (SI 1985/805)* Table A might give notice of an AGM as follows:

| | |
|---|---|
| Date of notice | 1 October |
| Deemed date of service | 3 October |
| 21 days run from | 4 October |
| Expiry of 21 days | 24 October |
| Earliest date for meeting | 25 October |

Notice of a general meeting may be given to a person electronically either to an address notified by the person to the company for that purpose or where the company and the person have agreed by access to a website (*CA 1985, s 369(4A)(4B)*). Where a notice is displayed on a website the person must be notified, in a manner for the time being agreed for the purpose between him and the company of:

- the publication of the notice on a website;
- the address of that website; and
- the place on the website where the notice may be accessed and how it may be accessed.

The notice must be published on the website throughout the period, beginning with the giving of the notification and ending with the conclusion of the meeting (*CA 1985, s 369(4C)*).

The notice displayed on a website must state that it concerns a notice of a company meeting served in accordance with *CA 1985*, must specify the place, date and time of the meeting and state whether the meeting is to be an annual or extraordinary meeting (*CA 1985, s 369(4C)*).

The provisions in *CA 1985* relating to the giving of notice by electronic communication override any provision in a company's Articles of Association to the contrary (*CA 1985, s 369(4E)*). In as far as the Articles of a company do not provide for notices and notifications to be served using electronic communications, the provisions of *Companies (Tables A to F) Regulations 1985 (SI 1985/805)* Table A shall apply (*CA 1985, s 369(4F)*).

The proceedings of a meeting shall not be invalidated if a notice is published on a website for a part but not all of the period mentioned in *CA 1985, s 369(4C)* and this is wholly due to circumstances which it would not be reasonable to have expected the company to prevent or avoid (*CA 1985, s 369(4D)*).

Notice of a meeting must be given to all those persons entitled to receive notice. This includes the following:

- every member of the company or every member of a particular class in the case of a separate class meeting, except:
  - a holder of shares of a particular class which does not enjoy the right to receive notice of or to attend or vote at general meetings e.g. non-voting preference shares;
  - a member who has no right to receive notice in terms of the Articles of Association e.g. a member resident overseas who has not provided an address within the United Kingdom for service of notice (*regulation 112, Companies (Tables A to F) Regulations 1985 (SI 1985/805)*);
  - in the case of joint holders, where the Articles provide that notice need only be given to the joint holder whose name first appears in

the register of members in respect of the joint holding (*regulation 111, Companies (Tables A to F) Regulations 1985 (SI 1985/805)*).
- the auditors of the company;
- the directors of the company; and
- all persons entitled to a share where a member has died or is bankrupt.

An omission to give due notice to any person entitled to receive it invalidates the meeting. However, the Articles normally provide that an accidental omission to give notice, or the non-receipt of notice by a person, should not invalidate the proceedings (*regulation 39, Table A (SI 1985/805)*).

A notice convening a general meeting must show the following:

- the name of the company;
- the date, place and hour of the meeting and the general nature of the business to be transacted;
- if appropriate, the fact that the meeting is the annual general meeting;
- the text of the resolutions to be proposed at the meeting and their type (i.e. ordinary, special, extraordinary or elective);
- a statement that a member entitled to attend and vote may appoint a proxy;
- the name of the director or secretary authorised to sign the notice and their office of director or secretary;
- date of the notice; and
- registered office address.

A public company must also have regard to stock exchange requirements. In addition, further ICSA guidelines for best practice for AGMs includes a recommendation that where the meeting includes special business, the notice should be accompanied by a letter or circular giving a full explanation of the resolution(s) to be considered.

An example of a notice of an Extraordinary General Meeting is given in appendix X.

## Appendix 4A 4.17

## Notice of Extraordinary General Meeting 4.18

### *Resolutions* 4.19

PLC

**NOTICE IS HEREBY GIVEN THAT** an Extraordinary General Meeting of the Company will be held at................on.........at.......to consider and if deemed fit to approve the following resolutions namely:

Meetings

## Ordinary Resolutions                                    4.20

1.  **THAT** the board be and is hereby generally and unconditionally autho-rised to exercise all powers of the company to allot relevant securities (within the meaning of *Section 80* of the *Companies Act 1985*) up to an aggregate nominal amount of £10,000,000 provided that this authority shall expire on the date of the next annual general meeting after the passing of this resolution save that the company may before such expiry make an offer or agreement which would or might require relevant securities to be allotted after such expiry and the board may allot rele-vant securities in pursuance of such an offer or agreement as if the authority conferred hereby had not expired. The authority conferred upon the directors by resolution approved on is hereby revoked.

2.  **THAT** the employee share option scheme ('the scheme') set out in the draft rules produced to the meeting and signed by the chairman for the purposes of identification be and is hereby approved and that the direc-tors be and are hereby authorised to:

    (a)  do all acts and things which they consider necessary or expedient to establish and carry the scheme into effect; and

    (b)  vote as directors on any matter connected with the scheme, notwithstanding that they may be interested in the same and any prohibition on interested directors voting contained in the Articles of Association of the Company be suspended to that extent, except that no director shall vote on any resolution concerning his own participation in the scheme or be counted in the quorum required for the consideration of any such resolution; and

    (c)  to issue to participants in the scheme such ordinary shares of each in the Company up to the limit contained in the rules of the scheme in satisfaction of the options exercised in accordance therewith.

3.  **THAT** the directors and the company be and hereby are authorised to enter into the contract with..............PLC (the "Bank") for the subscrip-tion by...............the Bank for.........ordinary shares of.....................each at a subscription price of pence per share and for the subscription by the Bank for £..............unsecured loan...........stock, further particulars of which are contained in Part I of the document of which this notice forms Part 2.

## Special Resolutions                                     4.21

4.  **THAT** subject to the passing of the previous resolution the board be and is hereby empowered pursuant to *Section 95* of the *Companies Act 1985* to allot equity securities (within the meaning of *Section 94* of the said Act) for cash pursuant to the authority conferred by the previous resolution as if *subsection (1)* of *Section 89* of the said Act did not apply to any such allotment provided that this power shall be limited:

    (a)  to the allotment of equity securities in connection with a rights issue in favour of ordinary shareholders where the equity securities respectively attributable to the interests of all ordinary share-holders are proportionate (as nearly as may be) to the respective numbers of ordinary shares held by them; and

(b)   to the allotment (otherwise than pursuant to subparagraph (a) above) of equity securities up to an aggregate nominal value of £

5.   **THAT** the draft regulations produced to the meeting and initialled by the chairman for the purposes of identification be adopted as the Articles of Association of the company in substitution for and to the exclusion of all the existing Articles of Association.

Date:.....................        BY ORDER OF THE BOARD
Registered Office        **Secretary**

A member entitled to attend and vote at the meeting is entitled to appoint a proxy to attend and vote in his place. A proxy need not be a member.

*Notes*                                                        **4.22**

**Resolution 1** – Directors cannot allot shares in the company (other than the shares allotted pursuant to an employee share scheme) unless they are autho-rised to do so by the company in general meeting. This resolution which replaces the previous authority given to directors at the AGM on.......................will permit the directors to allot shares up to a maximum nominal value of £10,000,000. This will allow the directors to make the proposed issue of................. Ordinary Shares of...............pence each.

**Resolution 2** – This resolution seeks approval to the proposed new employee share option scheme. The scheme is intended to be an 'approved' scheme ie approved by the Inland Revenue in terms of the *Income and Corporation Taxes Act 1988* (as amended) and enjoying the favourable tax treatment conferred upon such schemes. Application has been made to the Inland Revenue for formal approval of the scheme. A copy of the draft rules of the scheme and of the draft option agreement are available for inspection by any member at the Registered Office from the date of this notice until the date of the Extraordinary General Meeting on any weekday. (Saturdays, Sundays and public holidays excepted) during normal business hours and at the meeting itself.

**Resolution 3** – This resolution is included to give shareholders an opportu-nity to consider the Transaction.

**Resolution 4** – Under *Section 89* of the *Companies Act 1985*, if the directors wish to allot any of the unissued shares for cash (other than pursuant to an employee share scheme) they must in the first instance offer them to existing shareholders in proportion to their holdings. To enable the directors to make the specific allotment of shares to.............., the provisions of *Section 89(1)* of the Act must be waived by resolution of the shareholders. Except in the case of a rights issue, the waiver is limited to shares with an aggregate nominal value of £...............(the aggregate nominal value of the proposed share issue to...............). The reasons for recommending this application, the amount to be paid by..................and the directors' justification of that amount are set out in the chairman's letter to shareholders accompanying this notice.

**Resolution 5** – The agreement with...............necessitates changes to the Articles of Association. Details of the main changes are set out in the chairman's letter to shareholders accompanying this notice. A copy of the proposed new Articles of Association is available for inspection by any member from the date of this notice until the date of the Extraordinary General Meeting at the Registered Office on any weekday (Saturdays, Sundays and public holidays excepted) during normal business hours at the meeting itself.

## Requisitions by members                                  4.23

Members of a Company are empowered by *CA 1985* to requisition the directors to convene an Extraordinary Meeting. However:

- The requisitionists must hold not less than one tenth of the paid-up voting share capital of the company or if the company does not have a share capital to be able to exercise not less than one tenth of the total voting rights.
- On receipt of the requisition, the directors must convene an EGM within 21 days of the requisition date for a date not more than 28 days from the date of the notice of meeting. If they do not do so, the meeting may be convened by the requisitionists themselves for a date not more than three months after the date of the deposit of the requisition.
- Members have the right to requisition directors to include a resolution in the notice of an AGM.

On receipt of the requisition, the directors must proceed to convene an extraordinary general meeting within 21 days from the date of the requisition or, if they do not do so, the meeting may be convened by the requisitionists or any of them representing more than one-half of the total voting rights of them all. A meeting convened by the requisitionists shall be convened, as nearly as possible, in the same manner as that in which meetings are convened by the directors but no such meeting may be held more than three months after the date of the deposit of the requisition. Directors are deemed not to have duly convened the meeting if they convene a meeting for a date more than 28 days after the date of a notice convening the meeting (*CA 1985, s 368(8)*).

The company is obliged to reimburse the requisitionists for any reasonable expenses incurred by them by reason of the company's failure to convene a meeting, such amount to be retained by the company out of any fees or remuneration due or to become due to the directors in default.

Members also have the right to requisition the directors of a company to include in the notice of the next annual general meeting any resolution which may be properly moved and is intended to be moved at that meeting (*CA 1985, s 376* and *CA 1985, s 376(1)(a)*). Such requisitionists must be members representing not less than one-twentieth of the total voting rights of all the members, having, at the date of the requisition, a right to vote at the meeting to which the requisition relates, or not less than 100 members holding shares in the company on which there has been paid up an average sum, per member, not less than £100.

The requisitionists may also require the company to circulate to members any statement of not more than 1,000 words with respect to the matter referred to in any proposed resolution or the business to be dealt with at that meeting (*CA 1985, s 376(1)(a)*). Any requisition to include a resolution and to circulate a statement must be carried out at the expense of the requisitionists. Any requisition must be signed by the requisitionists, deposited at the registered office of the company and, in the case of a requisition requiring notice of a resolution, must be given to the company not less than six weeks before the meeting and, in the case of the statement, not less than one week before the meeting (*CA 1985, s 377*). There must be deposited or tendered with the requisition a sum reasonably sufficient to meet the company's expenses in giving effect to it.

## Quorums – Some points to note                     4.24

A quorum is defined as:

> 'The minimum number of persons whose presence is required, and who are entitled to vote, at a duly convened meeting.'

In general, no business may be transacted at a meeting at which a quorum is not present or maintained and any resolution passed at a meeting at which there is no quorum will be invalid. However, *regulation 90* of *Companies (Tables A to F) Regulations 1985 (SI 1985/805)* Table A provides that if the number of directors in office falls below the number necessary for a quorum, those directors may act, but only for the purpose of filling vacancies or for calling a general meeting.

Other points to note are that:

- The quorum for a directors' meeting is usually fixed by the Articles. Table A provides for a quorum of two and it is usual, in the case of a private company, for the Articles to permit a quorum of one.
- *CA 1985* provides that unless the Articles make specific provision, two persons present in person or by proxy will be a quorum at a general meeting.
- It is usual for the Articles to require that a quorum be maintained throughout proceedings.
- The quorum for an adjourned general meeting may differ from that required for the original meeting.
- Where a quorum cannot be raised for a particular reason it may be possible to make application to the court for a declaration that a

Meetings

- meeting of the members comprising less than the prescribed quorum may nevertheless conduct the valid business.
- It is normal for a company's Articles of Association to allow for proxies to be counted in the quorum of a meeting.
- A member who is disenfranchised for any reason may not be counted in a quorum.
- *CA 1985, s 125(6)* sets out the quorum necessary for any separate meeting of a particular class of shareholder as two persons holding or representing by proxy at least one-third in nominal value of the issued shares of the class in question and at an adjourned meeting one person holding shares of the class in question or his proxy.
- A quorum must be disinterested. *Regulations 94* and 95 of *Companies (Tables A to F) Regulations 1985 (SI 1985/805)*, for example, provide that, except for certain specified transactions, a director interested in business to be conducted at a meeting may not be counted in the quorum for the particular business to be transacted nor may he vote upon such a matter. Where a quorum cannot be raised for a particular item of business, it may be necessary for the matter to be placed before the company in a general meeting.
- Provision is now made in the articles of many companies for members to attend electronically (i.e. videoconferencing). For this to be effective the chairman and other board members need to be very mindful of the remote attendee and ensure they have the same opportunity to engage as those physically present.
- It is common in small private companies for the articles to relax the provisions of *regulations 94* and *95* of *Companies (Tables A to F) Regulations 1985 (SI 1985/805)* so that any director who declares an interest in a contract or arrangement made, or proposed to be made, with the company may, having declared such interest, be counted in the quorum of the meeting and be entitled to vote in respect thereof.

## Declarations of interest    4.25

A general notice of interest can be given by a director declaring the nature of his interest. For example a statement that he is a member of another specified company or connected person which is seeking to do business with the Company of which he is a director.

*Section 346* of the *Companies Act 1985* should be checked to ascertain who is connected with the director. However, such a notice must be given at a meeting of the directors, or the director must ensure that it is read at the next meeting of the directors after it is given.

Should the interest fall within the remit of *section 320* of *CA 1985* as a substantial property transaction involving a director acquiring from or transferring to the company a non-cash asset, the approval of members to the transaction by means of an ordinary resolution will be required, unless the value of the transaction is less than £1,000, or less than the lower of £100,000 or 10% of the company's net asset value.

In practice interests are often well known and this is a formality. However failure to notify the board of an interest risks seriously undermining trust and respect within the board and can damage reputations very easily. It is important therefore for directors to be diligent in notifying interests.

## Alternate directors attending board meetings          4.26

There may well be occasions when due either to prior commitments or unforeseen circumstances a director is unable to attend a board meeting. Should a director wish his opinion on a particular matter to be heard at a meeting and is unable to attend by telephonic or electronic means, the traditional option available to them is to appoint an alternate director. The *Companies Act 1985* does not contain provisions regarding alternate directors. The Articles of Association will need to be consulted to ensure that the director has the power to appoint an alternate director. If the company has adopted Table A, the provisions concerning alternate directors are contained in *regulations 65–69 Companies (Tables A to F) Regulations 1985 (SI 1985/805)*.

The appointment of an alternate director will often require the consent of the remaining directors.

The alternate director has the right to receive notice of all meetings of directors and all meetings of committees where the appointor is a member and to attend and vote at such meetings in his appointor's absence.

An alternate director is responsible for his own actions and his mistakes. He is not the agent of the director appointing him.

Under the provisions of *regulation 88 Companies (Tables A to F) Regulations 1985 (SI 1985/805)*, a director who is also an alternate at a board meeting can be entitled to two votes, one in his own right and the other on behalf of his appointor if they are absent.

If the appointment of the alternate director is only made for one meeting the appointment and the termination of that appointment should be notified at Companies House within the 14-day limit. If the company is fully listed, trading on AIM or has an OFEX dealing facility the appointment of an alternate director should be notified within the time period described under the continuing obligations for each.

## Observers and advisers          4.27

Independent advice and support are increasingly seen as an essential element of an effective board.

A board will often require their professional advisers to make presentations to the directors on specific issues when necessary. These advisers may, if permitted by the meeting, attend the entire meeting or just that part they are concerned with.

The auditors of a company have the statutory right to attend general meetings at which audited accounts are considered. If auditors attend board meetings regularly and advise on non-accounting matters they could be deemed to be a shadow director and thereby a director of the company for all purposes.

If a company has securities quoted on the stock exchange, AIM or on OFEX with a large shareholder base, the company's register of members will be maintained by a share registration agent. Share registration agents deal with all types of share transactions enquiries from shareholders, brokers and members of the public. They will also administer the distribution, receipt, scrutiny and recording of proxies and assist with the running of general meetings, which they would usually attend to process attendees and assist with voting if required.

## Minutes and post meeting notifications                      4.28

*Section 382* of the *Companies Act 1985* requires the directors to maintain minutes of all board meetings. This includes meetings held by telephone or via other electronic media. The statutory requirement is reinforced by *regulation 100* of *Companies (Tables A to F) Regulations 1985 (SI 1985/805)* (where applicable), which requires a record to be kept of all appointments of officers by the directors and all meetings of members, directors, committees of directors and holders of any class of shares.

The director should ensure that minutes kept are concise, accurate, impartial and unambiguous. All formal resolutions and decisions should be recorded with a short narrative where necessary. All matters of records should also be minuted. This would include declarations of interest, the tabling and consideration of reports and accounts and other documents, and more generally, such matters as members of the board wish to be recorded formally.

It is usual, and best practice, for the secretary to send draft minutes to the chairman for initial comment. The draft agreed by the chairman should then be circulated to those also present at the meeting for their consideration prior to the next meeting. It is important for a non-executive director to read these carefully and ensure that if his recollection differs from what has been recorded he raises it immediately with the company secretary. This is especially important for companies in difficulty or in danger of becoming insolvent.

There is sometimes a debate over whether the minutes should contain a summary of the discussion or just the decisions on a particular point. Views vary over the depth of detail required. In the US there was a trend (pre Enron and Worldcom!) to adopt a somewhat sterile and minimalist approach leaving less for lawyers to pick over and find fault with. The danger of this approach though is that it may be hard for the board to subsequently prove that it exercised due care on a particular issue. A variety of approaches are taken in the UK with a consensus on recording the key discussion points or matters taken into account.

Minutes of general meetings and board meetings should be kept separately. Shareholders do not have a right to inspect minutes of meetings of the directors and for this reason such minutes should be maintained separately.

Decisions by the board of a company on dividends, profits and other matters requiring announcement must be notified to the Company Announcement Office without delay and no later than 7.30am on the next following business day (Listing Rules 9.35).

Meetings

# 5. Corporate Ethics

## What are corporate ethics? 5.1

## At a glance 5.2

- Corporate ethical behaviour is becoming an increasingly high profile issue.
- A business that operates in an ethical way will be directly and indirectly sensitive and responsive to the reasonable needs of its various stakeholders.
- Corporate ethics should focus on internal issues that are within the company's control and over which it can exercise real influence.
- The specific ethical matters needing consideration, and the potential problem areas, will vary depending on the nature and scale of the company's operations.
- Ethical behaviour can only be achieved in a corporate culture where honesty and integrity are considered to be paramount.
- The benefits of ethical conduct may be difficult to measure, especially in the short-term, but high ethical standards are increasingly seen as an asset and unethical behaviour as a liability.
- Increased bureaucracy and controls are likely to be imposed if companies are not prepared to act voluntarily and demonstrate their commitment to corporate ethics.

## Increase in ethical awareness 5.3

The issue of corporate ethics has received an increasingly high profile in recent months, especially in the light of the problems at businesses such as Enron and Worldcom. In the past, it may have been tempting for directors to regard business ethics as well-intentioned but as of little practical value in the real world. However, ethical perspectives are coming more and more to the forefront of social thought, and the public - and in particular potential employees, investors and customers - are generally better informed and more ethically conscious than they were even ten years ago. There is currently a general degree of unease and scepticism about large, multinational corporations in particular. Many people have concluded that a company cannot consistently maintain both high profits and high principles, and that company executives are frequently engaged in the unscrupulous pursuit of profits at considerable cost to the environment and to the health and well-being of their employees and of consumers in general.

## Responsible action 5.4

A business that operates in an ethical way will be directly and indirectly sensitive and responsive to the reasonable needs of its various stakeholders – for instance, employees, customers, suppliers, the local community, the environment and society in general. Even company law recognises that the fiduciary duties and responsibilities of directors extend beyond their responsibility to the shareholders. Under the draft statement of directors' duties set out in the Government White Paper 'Modernising Company Law', published in July 2002, a director must act honestly and in good faith, and in the way that will be most likely to promote the success of the company for the benefit of its members as a whole. In reaching decisions, he/she must also take account of all the material factors that it is practicable to identify, including:

- the likely consequences in both the short and the long term, so far as a person of care and skill would consider them relevant; and
- all other factors that a person of care and skill would consider relevant, including the need for the company to:
  - foster business relationships with its employees, suppliers and customers;
  - consider the impact of its operations on the community and the environment;
  - maintain a reputation for high standards of business conduct; and
  - achieve outcomes that are fair between members.

A business that operates in an ethical manner will devote time and attention to meeting customer requirements, acting in a socially and environmentally responsible way, and making wise use of energy and non-renewable resources.

## Internal or external focus? 5.5

Corporate ethics and corporate social responsibility are sometimes seen as involving an outward-focused social vision for improvement – for instance, broad ideals set out in corporate codes and mission statements. In fact, they are much more about internal issues that are within the company's control and over which it can exercise real influence. The general public is becoming increasingly sceptical about codes and statements which do not appear to have any noticeable impact on the company's day to day activities and which perhaps represent good intentions rather than an actual commitment to change. Corporate ethics should be based on the broad principles of integrity and fairness, and should focus on issues such as product and service quality, customer satisfaction, fair business dealing, sound employment practices, transparency and accountability, and the responsibilities of the business to the local community and the environment. Acting in an ethically responsibly manner means acting thoughtfully and weighing up the benefits and harm that each particular course of action might bring in the longer-term. Unethical conduct is often focused on short-term advantages without considering the mid- and long-term consequences.

## Complex issues                                                          5.6

Corporate ethics is not a straightforward subject and many of the the surrounding issues can be complex. The specific ethical matters needing consideration in any business will vary depending on the nature and scale of its operations, but they might include:

- the sourcing of goods from low-wage countries;
- the use of child labour in developing countries;
- equity in pay and conditions;
- protecting the environment;
- ethical trading, and in particular the acceptability of making 'commission' payments.

Many of these issues will need to be considered in context of local conditions in the country concerned and the impact on the lifestyle of the individuals involved.

## Corporate culture                                                       5.7

Ethical behaviour can only be achieved in a corporate culture where honesty and integrity are considered to be paramount. Recent accounting scandals have raised numerous questions about the adoption of aggressive accounting techniques, the manipulation of profits and the use of off balance sheet financing and other financial engineering techniques to create a more favourable impression of the business. Directors need to give serious consideration to the following questions:

- What kind of organisation do we want this to be?
- Which values really matter to us?
- How do the directors articulate and reinforce these to other managers and staff?

- How do the directors react to the pressures arising from market expectations?
- How does this impact on other managers and staff?

Trust cannot be manufactured, but it is possible to create a climate where people feel that they can trust each other. This will only happen if the individuals at the top of the organisation set the appropriate ethos, targets and expectations and demonstrate these in their own actions, as well as communicating them clearly throughout the workforce and monitoring progress against the objectives.

## Potential problem areas                                           5.8

Potential problem areas will also vary depending on the nature and scale of the company's operations, but some of the more common issues include the following.

- *Incentive schemes*: Whilst incentive schemes can be a useful motivation tool, they also bring inherent dangers – it is now well-recognised that the payment of large executive bonuses, especially in the form of share options or based on profits, can encourage managers to take whatever action they deem necessary to maintain profit levels or keep the share price up. They can also encourage individuals to focus on short-term results rather than longer term issues such as the company's credibility and reputation. Reward schemes need to be designed around the company's longer term aims and to reward genuine performance (which may be more difficult to measure) rather than short-term achievements.
- *Market pressures*: Financial analysts tend to be preoccupied with immediate results and steadily rising earnings, but there are very few businesses that can achieve these over an extended period of time. Many executives feel compelled to feed the market's hunger for rapid growth and this can divert their energies away from managing the actual business towards managing the market's expectations of the company. Market demands can also result in over-optimistic predictions of growth and a reluctance to make a public acknowledgement of problems and weaknesses, although it is inevitable that difficulties will be encountered in any business from time to time.
- *Business survival*: Executives will sometimes feel compelled to adopt practices that they would otherwise consider unacceptable because it seems necessary to ensure the survival of the business and/or to protect their own careers – commercial demands therefore prevail over the guidance of their own consciences.
- *Commission payments*: The payment of a bribe is a legal offence in some countries, whilst others permit its deduction as an expense for tax purposes. Demands for 'commission' payments for favours done in business dealings can be a particular problem when dealing with officials and individuals in developing countries. Gaining an unlawful advantage by means of corruption is never legitimate under any circum-

Corporate Ethics

stances and businesses are generally advised to publicise the fact that they do not tolerate this, even when it might be commercially advantageous and would probably go undetected. However, there may be circumstances where a business sees less of a moral dilemma in making a payment in order to speed up a process that is legal and will be carried out in due course – although this undoubtedly puts those who can afford to pay at an advantage, and could therefore be considered contrary to fair trading. It is for each business to decide what is acceptable and what is not, but once this decision has been made, no compromise of the company's agreed standards should be permitted.

- *Gifts*: Gifts and hospitality from customers, suppliers and other business contacts may also give rise to problems. It is advisable to develop guidelines for both the giving and receiving of such items, usually with a requirement for disclosure of any significant gifts or hospitality offered.

It is also important that mechanisms are in place to allow appropriate consultation and discussion within the company on particular situations where it may be difficult to reach a judgement on whether a particular course of action is ethical or not.

## Investor confidence                                    5.9

Investor confidence is critical to the successful operation of the economic market. Clarity, transparency, accountability and fairness, supported by a sound system of financial reporting, are all essential if the public as a whole, and investors in particular, are to be able to evaluate risk, establish a market value for shares and generally participate in the equity culture.

## Benefits of ethical conduct                            5.10

The benefits of ethical conduct may be difficult to measure, especially in the short-term. The disadvantages, in terms of lost business and additional costs, are likely to be more readily apparent, especially in the early stages. It should also be recognised that a strict ethical policy will invariably lead to loss of market share in some countries. However, commercial success is usually interpreted these days as more than financial results and corporate reputation is now regarded as a valuable asset, albeit one which takes time to build. High ethical standards are increasingly recognised as an asset and unethical behaviour is seen as a liability. A strong corporate image can also bring competitive advantage and can help to attract investors, customers and potential employees. The benefits of high ethical standards include:

- attracting high quality employees – an ethically sound business is generally seen as a more attractive employer, especially as many employees today look at more than just remuneration when applying for a position;
- greater job satisfaction for employees – research has shown that there is a direct correlation between ethical conduct and job satisfaction and

that employees generally have a greater sense of belonging, and are more committed and innovative, in an environment in which ethical conduct has strong support from senior management;

- reduced likelihood of friction with campaigners and protest groups – such activities can divert a considerable amount of management time;
- reduced internal friction – employee morale tends to fall if the company becomes the focus of public criticism or if colleagues are seen, or thought, to be advancing their own careers in an unethical way;
- good relationships with the local community improve company credibility and reputation and can help to generate valuable public support for company expansion programmes.

Whilst some may have felt in the past that businesses acting in a socially responsible manner would not survive in a cut-throat, competitive, profit-focused market, research has in fact shown that such companies are usually more profitable in the long-term. Although financial costs may be incurred in developing and maintaining ethical awareness programmes, these appear to be significantly outweighed by the subsequent benefits gained.

## Avoiding further regulation                                   5.11

Businesses frequently complain about the extent and complexity of laws and regulations and the administrative overload that this can create. However, commercial freedom goes hand in hand with responsibility and the increased public awareness of, and demand for, ethical behaviour is likely to lead to increased bureaucracy and controls unless companies are prepared to act voluntarily and demonstrate their commitment to corporate ethics. Company directors need to accept the rapidly changing environment and be proactive in championing ethical standards rather than trying to defend positions that may have been acceptable in the past but are no longer considered to be so. Whilst individual corporate action may seem to have only a marginal affect, a positive example set and made plain for all to see may encourage others to follow suit and begin an upward trend. Positive change has to begin some-where.

## Action points for directors                                   5.12

- Set a good example and avoid involvement in anything that could lead employees to conclude that corrupt practices are encouraged or tolerated by the company.
- Develop an ethical code and require employees to confirm in writing each year that they have read, understood and applied these guidelines in their work (see **5.14** below).
- Make clear whether (and to what upper limits) gifts, hospitality and other favours may be accepted from business contacts, and when internal reporting of these is required.
- Require full disclosure from employees in strategic positions of their financial or other connections with suppliers, creditors and other business contacts.

Corporate Ethics

- Develop a regular training programme for employees on ethical issues (see **5.20** below).
- Appoint at least one senior individual to whom employees can turn for advice on ethical issues.
- Appoint one or more senior individuals to whom suspicions of unethical conduct can be reported in confidence (making it clear that such action will have no negative consequences for the reporting employee).
- Where appropriate, introduce procedures and controls that segregate duties and require at least two individuals to be involved in potentially sensitive decisions, and consider adopting a system of job rotation. (See also CHAPTER 14 INTERNAL CONTROL)
- Inform all business partners of the company's rules and encourage them to introduce corresponding safeguards if these are not already in place.
- Monitor compliance with the company's ethics code and be prepared to act on any violation that is identified (see **5.22** below)

## Developing and operating an ethical code          5.13

## At a glance          5.14

---

- An ethical code should establish the corporate culture that the board wishes to create and set down the standards of behaviour that the company expects.
- Every company should examine its corporate culture from time to time and consider whether any change is needed.
- A company's ethical code should reflect its specific circumstances and should not attempt to set standards which cannot reasonably be expected to be applied in practice.
- An independent review can help to ensure that the code takes account of all relevant interests and opinions.
- Ethical issues should incorporated into the company's ongoing training programme.
- Many companies find it helpful to require employees to sign an annual declaration that they have read, understood and applied the company's ethical code in their work.
- Regular checks should be made on compliance with the company's ethical code and stringent action taken in respect of any violations.

---

## What is an ethical code?          5.15

An ethical code should be more than a list of rules or instructions that must be followed – it should establish the corporate culture that the board wishes to create, and set down the standards of behaviour that the company expects when commercial decisions have to be taken under time or financial constraints. In particular, it should make clear that management is not indifferent to the way in which business goals are achieved. Directors might begin by considering the following questions:

- Does every employee understand what is expected of him/her?
- Is every employee encouraged to behave responsibly?
- Does the business have values that should never be sacrificed in pursuit of profit, and are these communicated effectively across the organisation?
- Is there a well-understood framework for making decisions on ethical issues – and does this apply to all levels within the business?
- Are employees encouraged to discuss any ethical dilemmas that they encounter – and is it clear who they should approach in these circumstances?
- How does the company respond in such a situation?
- Is it evident that the company expects and rewards ethical behaviour?

An ethical code can be established and operated in any size of organisation and, once developed and communicated, it should be regarded as binding on all directors and employees.

## Examining and changing corporate culture          5.16

Every company has a corporate culture – the unwritten rules that are understood, accepted and followed by everyone and which establish how the company is run on a day to day basis. In some companies, a specific corporate culture will have been created by management, whilst in others the culture may simply have evolved over time, without much attention being paid to whether or not it is right for the business. Every company should therefore examine its corporate culture from time to time and should consider whether any aspects have become outdated. More traditional, long-established companies may find it more difficult to accept that their corporate culture has become out of step with the views of today's society and that change is needed.

## Contents of an ethical code          5.17

Ethical codes can cover a broad range of issues, which generally include:

- the legal obligations of employees;
- employee conduct;
- insider dealing;
- honesty and integrity – including the transparency of company policy and actions;
- equity and fairness – including the treatment of stakeholders such as customers, suppliers, employees and their families, the local community and shareholders (especially any minority shareholders);
- stakeholder rights – including the confidentiality of information;
- product or service standards; and
- the exercise of corporate and managerial power.

To be effective, the code must reflect the specific circumstances of the company and should not attempt to set standards which cannot reasonably be expected to be applied in practice. It is important that a company's ethical code addresses any issues that are particularly sensitive, or that imply particular vulnerability, in the context of its activities. For instance, a company that has an extensive business involvement in developing countries may be more susceptible to requests for bribes or 'commission' payments and its ethical code must make clear what is and is not considered to be acceptable behaviour. Similarly, the approach to research and experimentation will be highly relevant to some businesses, but of no relevance whatsoever in others. It should also be remembered that a commitment to comply with legal requirements may not be sufficient to achieve ethical conduct when dealing with countries that offer little in the way of legislation on issues such as child labour, child protection, product safety and environmental protection. What is legal will not necessarily be ethical.

## Developing an ethical code                                           5.18

The key steps in developing an ethical code are as follows.

- Identify the company's stakeholders and how they are affected by the company's actions.
- Summarise the company's goals and how each employee can make an ethical contribution to achieving them.
- Decide on the company's ethical expectations and present these in the form of easily understandable, measurable and actionable statements.
- Design a training programme to ensure everyone understands how to implement the agreed principles on a daily basis and provide an ongoing facility for dealing with any queries that may arise.
- Incorporate the achievement of ethical goals into the employee appraisal process and reward programme.

Once finalised, the code is usually made available to the public as well as internally. An example of the ethics policy published by Maersk Line Limited is set out in the APPENDIX AT **5.30** to this chapter.

## Independent review                                                    5.19

Commissioning an independent review of the company's proposed ethical code can help to ensure that it deals with the underlying issues on a broad basis and takes into account all relevant interests and opinions, particularly where complex issues are involved. Whilst the final decision on the content of the code rests with management, an independent review can also help to ensure that any differences of opinion have been fully explored and resolved through sound argument rather than through the use of executive and managerial power.

## Implementation and training                                           5.20

Effective training and good internal communication are key elements in the process of implementing an ethical code. Encouraging ethical conduct involves developing good habits and it is important that ethical issues are incorporated into the company's ongoing training programme and not considered to be a one-off training matter. This also makes it easier to implement changes to the company's code where necessary. Case studies can be a valuable tool in encouraging a debate on specific ethical problems and can help to emphasise the fact that the underlying issues will often be complex and require careful consideration. Such discussions can also help to develop greater understanding between colleagues and to dispel the attitude that 'everybody does it' – employees might otherwise be tempted to use this to justify potentially unacceptable behaviour, especially if they consider it necessary for their own career development. It is important that the internal communication programme covers all directors and employees, and that at least one individual is identified who can be approached in confidence with queries on ethical issues.

## Annual employee sign-off                                       5.21

Many companies find it helpful to require employees to sign an annual declaration that they have read, understood and applied the company's ethical code in their work. This highlights the importance of the code and helps to keep ethical goals and standards at the forefront of the mind. Similarly, incorporating compliance with the code into the employee appraisal process and reward programme helps to demonstrate management's commitment to the underlying principles, although it is not always easy to find appropriate criteria by which to measure or evaluate ethical conduct.

## Violation of the code                                          5.22

Regular checks should be made on compliance with the company's ethical code. For instance, this might be incorporated into internal audit work or might be dealt with as a separate exercise by the officer with overall responsibility for ethical issues. Any potential violation of the ethical code must be investigated and stringent action taken where appropriate, so that all employees are given the clear message that management considers this to be a serious matter. Directors may also wish to implement whistle-blowing or similar confidential procedures to ensure that potential violations are highlighted at an early stage.

## Reporting on business ethics                                   5.23

### At a glance                                                   5.24

- There is an increasing interest in the approach of individual companies to business ethics and to corporate social responsibility in particular.
- Companies should consider developing a formal policy on corporate social responsibility issues.
- The ABI has issued disclosure guidelines to encourage companies to discuss corporate social responsibility matters in the annual report.

**Corporate Ethics**

- The DTI has set up a website to highlight the benefits of good practice in this area.
- Corporate social responsibility is also on the agenda of the European Commission.

## Increasing demand for information                                    5.25

There is an increasing interest in the approach of individual companies to ethical matters and to corporate social responsibility in particular. Boards must therefore be concerned with the effects that the company and its activities are having on society as a whole. These can extend from the way it treats its employees, suppliers and customers to issues such as protecting the environment, child labour, health and safety, and ethical conduct. Society has generally moved from a willingness to take good corporate behaviour on trust to wanting to see it demonstrated and explained. The recent revision of the ASB's *Statement Operating and Financial Review* recognises that company performance is now defined in much broader terms than financial performance and, in particular, that performance reporting might incorporate non-financial measures such as those relating to corporate social responsibility issues (see **10.58** ASB OPERATING AND FINANCIAL REVIEW).

## Developing a policy on corporate social responsibility    5.26

Companies should therefore be thinking about developing a policy on corporate social responsibility issues, as well as developing and publishing an ethical code. Points to consider include:

- does the company's corporate governance framework include accountability for managing corporate social responsibility issues?;
- do the company's performance reporting processes cover corporate social responsibility issues?;
- is there a formal mechanism for identifying stakeholder concerns and for providing them with feedback on progress?; and
- are the company's expectations on corporate social responsibility issues communicated to suppliers and other business partners?

## Disclosures on business ethics and corporate social responsibility                                              5.27

Ethical conduct is difficult to measure and at present analysts generally look for:

- confirmation that the company has a process for establishing ethical goals;
- a statement of business conduct or a published ethical code;
- procedures to assist the achievement of ethical goals (eg reward systems); and
- a feedback process to measure the achievement of ethical goals and

assist with the development and enhancement of the company's performance where necessary.

The Association of British Insurers (ABI) has produced disclosure guidelines to help institutional investors discuss these issues with the companies in which they invest. The guidelines note that investors are anxious to avoid unnecessary prescriptive requirements or the imposition of costly measures, but hope that shareholder value will be enhanced by the early identification and management of risks arising from social, environmental and ethical matters. Shareholders with a specific interest in ethical investment may look for more extensive disclosures and some companies may wish to give additional information to attract investment from specific investors. The guidelines recommend the following disclosures:

- The annual report should include a statement on whether the board:
  - takes regular account of the significance of social, environmental and ethical (SEE) matters to the business of the company;
  - takes account of SEE matters in the training of directors;
  - has identified and assessed the significant risks to the company's short and long term value arising from SEE matters, as well as the opportunities to enhance value that may arise from an appropriate response;
  - has received adequate information to make this assessment; and
  - has ensured that the company has in place effective systems for managing significant risks, including, where relevant, performance management systems and appropriate remuneration incentives.
- With regard to policies, procedures and verification, the annual report should:
  - include information on SEE-related risks and opportunities that may significantly affect the company's short- and long-term value, and how they might impact on the business;
  - describe the company's policies and procedures for managing risks to short- and long-term value arising from SEE matters – if the company has no such policies and procedures, the board should give reasons;
  - include information about the extent to which the company has complied with its policies and procedures for managing risks arising from SEE matters;
  - describe the procedures for verification of SEE disclosures.

It is hoped that the guidelines will help to develop best practice in the area of managing and reporting on corporate social responsibility issues. They are intended to be relevant to all companies, regardless of size, although it is acknowledged that smaller companies in particular may need time to achieve full compliance. Where appropriate, the ABI notes that a statement in the annual report on the intent to comply would be helpful.

Corporate Ethics

149

## DTI guidance 5.28

The DTI has set up a website to support its policy of assisting the development of greater contacts between business and society. The site contains a number of case studies showing the benefits that can be obtained by adhering to good practice in the area of corporate social responsibility. There is also information on the action being taken by the Government to facilitate the development of corporate social responsibility. The site can be found at www.societyandbusiness.gov.uk

## European perspective 5.29

Corporate social responsibility is also on the agenda of the European Commission. The EU's consultation paper *Promoting a European Framework for Corporate Social Responsibility* and the responses that it generated can be found on the Commission's website at http://europa.eu.int/comm/employment_social/soc-dial/csr/csr_index.htm.

## Appendix 5A 5.30

## Ethics Policy published by Maersk Line Limited 5.31

### *General Guidelines* 5.32

- We will not seek or take advantage of proprietary, confidential, or inside information that would give an unfair advantage in gaining business.
- We shall not give information to any one potential supplier that would provide any unfair advantage.
- We shall not offer nor solicit or accept gratuities, bribes, kickbacks, or promises for personal benefit in seeking or granting business from or to others.
- We shall not use corporate assets or business relationships for personal use or gain.
- We shall be truthful in our communications with customers, suppliers, shareholders, and each other.

### *Criteria for Individual Judgement* 5.33

- Is anyone's life, health, or safety endangered by this act?
- Is my action legal? If legal, is it also ethical?
- Does my action comply with Company policy and practice?
- Will this act be handled honestly in every respect?
- Would I be compromised or embarrassed if this act were known by my supervisor, fellow employees, subordinates, or friends?
- Does my intended action have the appearance of an inappropriate act or course of behaviour?
- Does this act meet my own personal code of behaviour?

- Am I uncomfortable doing this?
- Would my supervisors or peers act in this way?
- Should I ask my supervisor about this matter before I act?

If uncertainty persists after reviewing the above, then **ask** your supervisor, Director of Contracts, or the President.

These guidelines and criteria are purposely broad and further detail on the law, policies, procedures and standard practices are contained in appropriate specific procedures. Employees wishing further information should ask their supervisor. Additionally, the Director of Contracting can be asked for ethics guidance at any time.

# 6.  Corporate Governance

- Evolution of corporate governance since 1990 (including the Higgs Review)
- The Combined Code
- Directors
- Directors' remuneration
- Relations with shareholders
- Accountability and audit
- Institutional investors
- Reporting requirements

## The evolution of corporate governance since 1990    6.1

## At a glance    6.2

- The first detailed guidance on corporate governance was set out in the *Cadbury Code of Best Practice* in 1992.
- Corporate governance was defined in the Cadbury Report as the system by which companies are directed and controlled.
- Good corporate governance is based on the principles of openness, integrity and accountability
- Additional guidance was set out in the Greenbury(1995) and Hampel(1998) Codes of Best Practice and all existing guidance was then drawn together in the Combined Code.

- The Combined Code sets out the Principles of Good Governance and also best practice provisions for the adoption of those principles.
- Listed companies must disclose each year the extent to which they have applied the principles set out in the Combined Code, by means of a 'Comply or Explain' approach.
- A major review, initiated by the DTI and the Treasury, the Higgs review, was published in 2003.
- The recommendations of the Higgs review include a substantial revision to the combined code for reporting years starting on or after 1 July 2003.

## The Cadbury Code of Best Practice          6.3

Corporate governance became a high profile issue in December 1992, with the publication of the *Cadbury Code of Best Practice* and the *Report of the Committee on the Financial Aspects of Corporate Governance* (the 'Cadbury Report'). This Committee, chaired by Sir Adrian Cadbury, had been formed in 1991 at a time of general concern over standards of financial reporting and accountability, particularly in the light of the BCCI and Maxwell cases, and when controversy was beginning to develop over levels of directors' remuneration. The Committee's report was based on the premise that company directors should have the freedom to develop their companies and drive them forward, but that they should do so within an effective framework of accountability. The Committee's recommendations therefore focused primarily on the structure of the board, its control and reporting functions, and the role of the external auditors, and drew on principles that were already being widely followed. Although the recommendations were aimed mainly at listed companies, the Committee's objective was to raise the overall standards of corporate governance and the general level of public confidence in financial reporting. All entities were therefore encouraged to follow the recommendations in the *Cadbury Code of Best Practice*.

## Definition of corporate governance          6.4

Corporate governance was defined in the Cadbury Report as

'the system by which companies are directed and controlled'.

The role of the shareholders is to appoint the directors and the external auditors, and to satisfy themselves that an appropriate governance structure is in place. The directors are responsible for setting the company's strategic aims, providing the leadership to put these into effect, supervising the management of the business and reporting to shareholders on their stewardship. The financial aspects of corporate governance are identified as the way in which the board sets financial policy and oversees its implementation (including the use of financial controls) and the process of reporting to the shareholders on the activities and development of the company.

## Openness, integrity and accountability 6.5

The *Cadbury Code of Best Practice* was based on the principles of openness, integrity and accountability, which were described as follows in the Cadbury Report:

- openness is the basis for the confidence that must exist between a business and those who have a stake in its success – an open approach to the disclosure of information contributes to the efficient working of the market economy, prompts boards to take effective action and allows shareholders and other interested parties to scrutinise companies more closely;
- integrity means straightforward dealing and completeness – financial reporting should be honest and should present a balanced view of the company's affairs;
- the board of directors is accountable to the shareholders and effective accountability is achieved through the quality of information provided by the board to the shareholders and by the willingness of the shareholders to exercise their responsibilities as owners of the business.

## Subsequent developments preceding the 2003 Higgs Review 6.6

The Cadbury Committee addressed those aspects of corporate governance that it considered were most in need of immediate attention. However, they noted in their report that the situation was continually evolving, through the Accounting Standards Board's programme of new accounting standards, the development of best boardroom practice and the possibility of increased regulation through European Community initiatives. The Committee therefore emphasised the importance of keeping corporate governance guidance up to date and recommended that a further committee should be appointed within the following two to three years to examine progress on compliance with the *Cadbury Code* and consider the need to revise and update the recommendations in the light of emerging issues. The successor committee, under the chairmanship of Sir Richard Greenbury, developed new recommendations on the setting and disclosure of directors' remuneration in the *Greenbury Code of Best Practice* and a further committee, under the chairmanship of Sir Ronald Hampel, developed a new Combined Code which built on (and superseded) the recommendations set out in the Cadbury and the Greenbury Codes. The Combined Code is to be updated again with effect from 1 July 2003, following the Higgs Review. The likely changes are considered below.

## The Hampel Report 6.7

The main remit of the Hampel Committee was to review the implementation of, and levels of compliance with, the two Codes that had resulted from the work of the Cadbury and Greenbury Committees. The Hampel review resulted in the development of a new Combined Code, which drew together elements of the existing Codes and set out the broad principles of corporate governance, together with detailed guidance on the application of these principles in practice. The Hampel Report advocated a flexible approach to reporting on compliance with the Code, leaving directors free to choose how to explain their corporate governance policies in the light of the specific circumstances of the company or group. The new Combined Code was published in June 1998 and became fully effective for accounting periods ending on or after 22 December 2000 (although earlier implementation was required for aspects other than reporting on internal control).

## Structure of the Combined Code                                 6.8

The Combined Code is divided into two sections:

- Part 1 sets out the Principles of Good Governance under the following headings:
  A    Directors
  B    Directors' Remuneration
  C    Relations with Shareholders
  D    Accountability and Audit
  E    Institutional Investors
- Part 2 sets out the Code of Best Practice for the adoption of each of the principles set out in Part 1.

This chapter provides an overview of the detailed contents of the Combined Code. Practical guidance on the application of the Code principles and the best practice provisions can be found in other chapters. The Higgs review also recommended an additional schedule to be annexed to the code entitled 'Guidance on liability of non-executive directors: care, skill and diligence.'

## Disclosure of compliance with the Code                         6.9

For accounting periods ending on or after 31 December 1998, the Financial Services Authority (FSA) Listing Rules require each listed company to include in its accounts:

- a narrative statement of how it has applied the principles set out in Part 1 of the Combined Code, with explanations to enable the shareholders to evaluate how the principles have been applied; and
- a statement on whether or not it has complied throughout the accounting period with the best practice provisions set out under headings A to D of Part 2 of the Combined Code, with details of, and the reasons for, any areas or periods of non-compliance.

Other specific disclosures are required by certain sections of the Code. Further details on reporting under the Combined Code are given in **6.55** to **6.71** below

The additional disclosures recommended by the Higgs review are for reporting years starting on or after 1 July 2003.

## The Higgs Report on the Role and Effectiveness of Non-Executive Directors     6.10

In April 2002 in the wake of the Enron, Marconi and other high profile corporate collapses the UK government asked Derek Higgs, chairman of Partnerships UK plc and holder of directorships in companies as diverse as Egg plc and Coventry City Football Club, to conduct a review of the role and effectiveness of non-executive directors. His report went to two cabinet ministers Patricia Hewitt (Secretary of State for Trade and Industry) and Gordon Brown (Chancellor of the Exchequer).

Whilst the review was to focus on larger corporate businesses it was to consider the implications of any proposed changes for smaller companies. The review was published on 20 January 2003. After a very positive initial reaction the review generated considerable and heated debate especially with regard to the role of the senior independent director. There was also some challenge to the principle adopted first by Cadbury, but strongly endorsed by Higgs, of 'Comply or explain'. Some felt that the conditions of capital markets and the approach of institutional shareholders and their advisers would lead to 'Comply or breach' in practice.

At time of writing the recommendations of the review (available on website www.dti.gov.uk/cld/non_exec_review and summarised below) are under consideration but it is expected that the suggested new Combined Code for listed companies (also on the website) will be substantially adopted with a small number of modifications. It is also expected that new disclosure requirements will apply to companies reporting for years starting after 1 July 2003.

## Why did the review take place?     6.11

The government wanted to ensure that the UK system was sound and that the risk of another major corporate collapse through weak governance was minimised. They were also keen to consider the issue of the diversity of membership of public company boards.

## How did Higgs conduct the review?     6.12

In line with other recent government reviews no formal committee was put in place. Higgs was simply given the responsibility to get the job done. He then came up with a proposal for the way in which he was going to conduct the review which was approved. A small team from the DTI and Treasury was then formed for the duration of the review to support him.

The key stages of the review were as follows:

●     extensive research;

- a formal consultation process from which 200 responses were received;
- informal consultation;
- analysis of results;
- formulation of proposals;
- testing of proposals with a small group of friends and advisers of the Review;
- presentation to the Government;
- publication; and
- making change happen.

The website for the review (www.dti.gov.uk/cld/non_exec_review) contains a lot of detail including a selection of the research, the consultation document, over two hundred of the formal responses to it and the report itself.

The research undertaken by the review team was impressive, consisting of a census of listed company non-executives, a MORI poll of six hundred and fifty executive directors, non-executive directors and chairmen, in depth interviews with more than forty inputs. We have made reference to this research in several of the other chapters. The census of non-executive directors of UK listed companies was an especially welcome addition to the base of knowledge on this subject. By way of example here is the selection from this quantitative data which was contained in the published report itself.

---

## The current population of non-executive directors      6.13

As part of the Review, research was undertaken to build a factual picture of the current population of non-executive directors. The data (1) presented below is a summary of this research. The full analysis is on the Review's website (www.dti.gov.uk/cld/non_exec_review). It should be noted that the data was drawn on 17th July 2002 and so reflects the situation at that time.

There are 5,172 executive, 4,610 non-executive and 1,689 chairmen posts held by directors in UK listed companies (2).

Of the 3,908 individuals who hold non-executive directorships in UK listed companies, 80 per cent hold only one non-executive director post in a UK listed company, 10 per cent hold two non-executive posts in UK listed companies and 7 per cent also hold an executive directorship. 13 per cent of chairmen hold more than one chairmanship. 282 individuals hold both executive and non-executive director posts in UK listed companies.

Five FTSE 100 companies and 11 per cent of companies outside the FTSE 350 companies have a joint chairman/chief executive. 24 FTSE 100 chairmen were formerly the chief executive of the same company. Four per cent of executive director posts and six per cent of non-executive director posts

---

Corporate Governance

Average size and composition of boards

are held by women. Less than one per cent of chairmen are female. In the telephone survey, which was a representative sample of directors in UK listed companies, seven per cent of non-executive directors were not British and one per cent were from black and ethnic minority groups.

The average age of a non-executive director in the FTSE 100 is 59, with over three-quarters 55 or over. The average age of a FTSE 100 chairman is 62. Almost 40 per cent are 65 or over.

The average remuneration of a FTSE 100 non-executive director is £44,000 pa and £23,000 pa for a non-executive director of a company outside the FTSE 350. The average remuneration of a FTSE 100 chairman is £426,000 pa (compared to an average of £78,000 pa for a chairman of a company outside the FTSE 350).

The average time in post was 4.3 years for a FTSE 100 non-executive director and 4.5 years for a non-executive director in a company outside the FTSE 350. This implies that the average tenure of non-executive directors of UK listed companies is significantly longer than four years. The average time on the board for a FTSE 100 chairman was about eight years. For a chairman of a company outside the FTSE 350, the average time was about seven years.

Most listed companies have an audit committee and a remuneration committee. One FTSE 100 company does not have an audit or a remuneration committee and 15 per cent of companies outside the FTSE 350 do not have an audit committee.

The majority (71 per cent) of companies outside the FTSE 350 do not have a nomination committee. Six FTSE 100 companies do not have a nomination committee.

Investment companies (3) have a different structure as their boards typically consist of a manager together with non-executive directors. On average their boards have five members. They have therefore not been included in the main analysis.

Further data on them can be found on the website.

1    *The data was supplied by Hemscott and analysed by the Review Team. Further and fuller details are available on the Review website.*

2    *There are 1,702 listed companies in the UK, excluding investment companies (other than 3i).*

3    *There are 480 investment companies listed in the UK (excluding 3i).*

With regard to qualitative research Higgs also sought the views of those who have been most active in this area over the last decade and also spent some time looking at the international comparisons.

The US comparison was particularly interesting as throughout the period of the review the US was undergoing something of a crisis of confidence in governance and the capital markets were in turmoil. The US response was swift and legal focussing on accountability. The resulting Sarbanes Oxley legislation received a mixed reaction especially from chief executives.

The consultation process elicited over two hundred formal responses. A summary of the consultation document is contained in the **APPENDICES**. As with any consultation process views provided ranged from the blatantly self-serving to the original, well balanced and helpful.

## What did he conclude?                                           6.14

Essentially that the UK model of corporate governance is sound but there is an opportunity to improve through greater consistency of best practice. To quote directly:

> 'In the current global discussion about corporate governance the UK is relatively advantaged. Our approach has been evolving for more than a decade and the habits and instincts which breathe life into the system have also matured. Transparency and accountability are more developed than in some other markets.'

However he adopts a far from complacent tone in his report. For example:

> 'But there is much more that can be done. Costly boardroom failures, resulting in great loss of value and jobs, provide ready grounds for humility. Moreover whatever lead the UK may have had in this area it has not been used to full advantage.'

In his view the failures in the UK have been of a different nature to some of those in the US.

> 'Whereas in the US most governance discussion has focussed on corporate malpractice, in the UK sharp loss of shareholder value is more common than fraud or corporate collapse.'

He therefore concludes that a different approach is required in the UK than the one taken in the US:

> 'This review therefore focuses as much on enhancing the competence and effectiveness of boards in promoting business prosperity as on issues of accountability. My view of the role of the non-executive director in this process differs from that of US regulators who have tended to emphasise the monitoring role of the non-executive director at the possible expense of the contribution the non-executive can make to wealth creation. These two roles are complementary and should be seen as such.'

With regard to the rest of Europe:

> 'there has been much activity to strengthen corporate governance and company law standards, for example the Cromme Code in Germany and the Bouton code in France. Their recommendations are broadly consistent with the changes I suggest be made to the code.'

He found a high degree of consensus in the UK, especially over the principle of the unitary board. To quote:

> '... the majority view which I share sees considerable benefits continuing to flow from the unitary approach.'

and

> 'The research concludes that it is important to establish a spirit of partnership and mutual respect on the unitary board. This requires the non-executive director to build recognition by executives of their contribution in order to promote openness and trust. Only then can non-executive directors contribute effectively. The key to non-executive effectiveness lies more in behaviours and relationships than structures and processes.'

He found the same consensus with regard to the benefit of the separation of the chairman and chief executive's roles. Interestingly a comment made elsewhere in the report states:

> 'At the heart of the US corporate governance is a concentration of decision making autonomy in one individual, the Chairman and

Chief Executive Officer. Only around one fifth of US listed companies separate these roles. In contrast separation is more common practice in the UK which I believe is one of the core strengths of the UK corporate governance framework.'

Unsurprisingly Higgs found widespread recognition that the role of the non-executive had become more challenging, that in principle they should be paid more as time commitment and risk had grown, and that the expectations of investors have risen. One reason he gives for this is that institutions have found it hard to hold management to account directly themselves.

Interestingly he also found that

'Evidence diverged on the extent to which there is a shortage of good people to take on non-executive roles. Part of the problem seems to be that the supply of talent is not being sufficiently drawn upon.'

We would agree with this but feel as he hinted at in his report that there may be a shortage of people willing and able to take on the role of chairman.

On selection he made the following point:

'People are key. Critical to improving the effectiveness of non-executive directors is raising the quality of appointees. The evidence collected for this Review shows that the current population of non-executive directors is narrowly drawn. I make recommendations to promote an open, fair and rigorous appointment process which fosters a relentless meritocracy in appointments.'

The research supporting his review found that:

'A high level of informality surrounds the process of appointing non-executive directors. Half of the non-executive directors surveyed for the review were recruited to the role through friends and personal contacts. Only four per cent had a formal interview.'

Higgs however challenged the popular perception that there are a large number of people holding multiple non-executive directorships. He found that a only a quarter of non-executives in the census had more than one post in a listed company. They may of course have appointments in private companies and the public sector.

So to the no doubt disappointment of many and relief of others he concluded:

'The variety of different appointments and individual circumstances means that it is difficult and unrealistic to set a limit for the number of non-executive appointments that anyone not in full time employment should hold.'

He did, however, as noted below, make recommendations with regard to executive directors and chairman.

He also found the same degree of informality with regard to evaluating performance.

> 'Over three quarters of non-executive directors and over half of Chairmen never have a formal personal performance review.'

With regard to **diversity** his research found that:

- 'non-executives are typically white males nearing retirement age with previous PLC director experience.'
- 'There are less than twenty non-executives under the age of 45 in the FTSE100.'
- 'Of the 276 non-executives directors surveyed for this report, seven per cent were not British and one per cent not white.'
- 'Only six per cent of non-executive posts were held by women.'
- 'There was only one female chairman in the FTSE100 (3i Group PLC).'
- 'There was only one in the rest of the FTSE350.'

He found that diversity in the public sector was much greater, with thirty eight per cent of the 3,856 appointments and re-appointments to public bodies being female and nine per cent from ethnic minorities.

> 'Most FTSE one hundred companies have a nominations committee, compared to only thirty per cent of small and mid-cap companies. However interviews conducted for the review suggested that where the nominations committee does exist it is the least developed of the board's committees, usually meeting irregularly and often without a clear understanding of the extent of its role in the appointment process.'

Readers should therefore find the detail on selection processes contained in CHAPTER 1 helpful.

Higgs draws some comparisons with the public sector where much progress has been made in this area.

He found that that demand for training is very low particularly in larger companies. This view was endorsed by his research which found that two thirds of those in his telephone poll had had no specific training or development. However he also states that another factor might be that current provision may not match the needs of non-executives.

Interestingly, with regard to one of the main proposals coming out of the Hampel committee, that there should be a clearly designated Senior Independent Non-executive:

'Responses to the consultation contained a range of views...Some saw the role as unnecessary and divisive. It was pointed out that shareholders may make use of their own connections with non-executive directors, or contact the chairmen of board committees if they have concerns.'

The authors' view is that given that the SINE has most effect, or not, when there is an issue with the chairman, it is no surprise that views are divided.

There was no consensus on the need to change the name 'non-executive' and those that did suggest change had a variety of suggestions. Unsurprisingly therefore he recommends no change to the title.

Higgs recognised that remuneration has become an issue, as time commitment and risk have risen, by saying that:

'remuneration needs to be sufficient to attract and retain high calibre candidates but no more than is necessary for this purpose.'

and suggesting that companies use the per diem rates of their key advisers as a way of bringing balance to the debate. In this way fees would be commensurate with the size and complexity of the company.

A great deal of thought was given to the subject of liability of non-executive directors. He sums up the dilemma well in our view.

'A concern often put to me during the course of the review was about the potential liability attaching to non-executive director roles... Some argued that consideration should be given to proportional liability and capping liability by way of contract, or some form of business judgement defence. There was however, also some very strong support for the concept of the unitary board and for the legal duties of executive and non-executive directors to be the same. Moreover, some were concerned that if liability were reduced, non-executives would not take their responsibilities so seriously, and this could undermine the unitary board.'

He didn't believe that, at this stage, concerns about potential liability were having a significant effect in deterring people from putting themselves forward but acknowledged the risk that it could. The authors' view is that he may be right with respect to the larger, more prestigious companies but that it is already having an effect below this group (see chart on **PARAGRAPH 1.9**).

All of his recommendations are consistent with those proposed in the Company Law Review.

Although the review focussed on larger companies he also considered the issues with respect to smaller listed companies and concluded that

'There should be no differentiation in the Code's provisions between larger and smaller companies.'

He did, however

'recognise that it may take some time for smaller listed companies to comply with the new provisions and in the interim they will need to explain why they cannot do so and what steps they are taking.'

The consequence of these views is that he has taken an evolutionary rather than revolutionary approach with his recommendations:

'I do not believe that legislation is the way forward. Instead this review builds on the "comply or explain" approach established by Sir Adrian Cadbury a decade ago.'

With regard to his recommendations he concluded also that

'I do not presume a "one size fits all" approach to governance is appropriate. There will always be exceptions, but this does not negate the need to establish the expected norm, and putting the onus on companies who consider themselves exceptions to explain why. *It is not a blue-print for box tickers, but a counsel of best practice which must be intelligently implemented with discretion.*' (italics added).

## What were his recommendations for change? 6.15

A summary of the recommendations is contained on pages 5–10 of the report. (Available on the website www.dti.gov.uk/cld/non_exec_review) They are principally under the following headings.

- Roles of the board, chairman, non-executive and senior independent non-executive directors.
- The effective board.
- A definition of independence.
- Recruitment and appointment of non-executives and widening the pool.
- Induction and professional development of executive and non-executive directors and chairmen.
- Tenure and time commitment of non-executive directors.
- Remuneration of non-executive directors.
- Resignation of directors.
- Audit and Remuneration committees.
- Liability of non-executive directors.
- Relationships between non-executive directors and shareholders.
- Way in which change should be made.

All of these are covered in detail below. There are however a number of overall comments to be made.

Firstly we were delighted to see that the starting point for Higgs was the role of the board itself and that it is entirely consistent with the views expressed in chapters one and three. The proposal to include this description of the board's role in the Combined Code we think is very helpful.

Having put the chairman's and non-executive's roles in the context of the board, Higgs also provides a description of these roles and again these are proposed to be included in the Combined Code. Happily these are also consistent with the views we have expressed elsewhere in this book.

There are a number of suggested additions for disclosure in company's annual reports (for years starting on or after 1 July 2003) again all of these are covered in detail below:

Clearly one of the more challenging aspects of his brief related to the issue of diversity and widening the pool. Whilst not stated it seems clear that this was something that both he and the Review team and the government found easy in theory but hard in practice.

He indicates that it is hard to gain an appointment on a UK plc if you haven't had plc experience before and

> 'It has been suggested that search consultants have a tendency to identify candidates from a narrow pool of candidates.'

He suggests that one of the reasons why there might be so few female non-executive directors is that the areas where women are more strongly represented are not traditional routes to the board.

He encourages chairmen and chief executives to let their executive directors and suitable senior management just below board level take one non-executive position elsewhere.

He also says that all companies operating in international markets would benefit from having at least one international non-executive. It is hard to think of too many major companies that aren't international.

One of the areas where he does make a tangible proposal on diversity is to do with the crossover of the public and private sectors. He recommends the formation of a small group to identify the top people in the public sector who would be suitable for appointments in listed companies. Because women are represented to a much greater extent in the public sector he hopes that this will also improve the gender balance.

# Directors                                                  6.16

# At a glance                                                6.17

> - Section A of the Combined Code sets out governance principles in respect of directors
> - The Higgs Report proposes substantial revision of the existing principles.
> - The best practice provisions cover the following issues:
>   - the board;
>   - roles of the chairman and chief executive;
>   - board balance;
>   - supply of information to the board;
>   - appointments to the board;
>   - re-election of directors; and
>   - evaluating board performance.

# Combined Code principles                                   6.18

Section A of Part 1 of the Combined Code currently sets out the following principles in relation to directors.

- **The board**: Every listed company should be headed by an effective board which should lead and control the company.
- **Chairman and CEO**: There should be a clear division between the responsibilities at the head of the company to ensure a balance of power and authority, so that no one individual has unfettered powers of decision.
- **Board balance**: The board should include a balance of executive and non-executive directors (including independent non-executives) so that no individual or small group of individuals can dominate the board's decision-taking.
- **Supply of information**: The board should be supplied with information that is timely, in an appropriate form and of an appropriate quality to enable it to discharge its duties.
- **Appointments to the board**: There should be a formal and transparent procedure for the appointment of new directors.
- **Re-election**: All directors should be required to submit themselves for re-election at regular intervals and at least every three years.

# Proposed changes in respect of directors                   6.19

The Higgs Report recommends that this section of the Code should be updated as follows:

- **The board**: Every listed company should be headed by an effective board, The board is collectively responsible for promoting the success of the company by directing and supervising the company's affairs;

- **Chairman and CEO**: There are two key tasks at the top of every company – the running of the board and the executive responsibility for the running of the company's business. There should be a clear division of responsibilities at the head of the company which will ensure a balance of power and authority such that no one individual has unfettered powers of decision.
- **Board balance**: The board should include a balance of executive and non-executive directors (including independent non-executives) such that no individual or small group of individuals can dominate the board's decision-taking.
- **Appointments to the board**: There should be a formal, rigorous and transparent process for the appointment of new directors to the board.
- **Information and professional development**: The board should be supplied in a timely manner with information in an appropriate form and of an appropriate quality to enable it to discharge its duties. All new directors should receive induction on joining the board and should continually update and refresh their skills and knowledge.
- **Performance evaluation:** Boards should evaluate their performance.
- **Re-election:** All directors should be required to submit themselves for re-election at regular intervals and at least every three years subject to continued satisfactory performance.

The proposed changes therefore strengthen the previous recommendations on the separation of the roles of chairman and chief executive, emphasise the need for all directors to keep their skills and knowledge up to date, and incorporate a formal requirement for the board as a whole to evaluate its performance.

## The board                                                                6.20

The best practice guidance in Part 2 of the Combined Code, makes the following points in relation to the board:

- the board should meet regularly;
- there should be a formal schedule of matters specifically reserved for board decision;
- the board should agree a procedure for directors to take independent professional advice where necessary (at the company's expense) in furthering their duties;
- all directors should have access to the advice and services of the company secretary and any question of the removal of the company secretary should be a matter for the board as a whole;
- all directors should exercise independent judgement on issues of strategy, performance, resources (including key appointments) and standards of conduct; and
- every director should receive appropriate training when first appointed to the board of a listed company, and as necessary thereafter.

## Proposed changes in relation to the board     6.21

The Higgs Report proposes comprehensive changes by replacing the current provisions with the following:

- the board's role is to provide entrepreneurial leadership of the company, within a framework of prudent and effective controls which enable risk to be assessed and managed;
- the board should set the company's strategic aims, ensure that the necessary financial and human resources are in place for the company to meet its objectives, and review management performance;
- the board should set the company's values and standards and ensure that obligations to shareholders and others are fully understood and met;
- the board should meet regularly and there should be a formal schedule of matters reserved specifically for its decision;
- the number of meetings of the board and its main committees, together with details of individual attendance, should be disclosed in the annual report;
- the board should publish a high level statement of which decisions are to be taken by the board and which by management;
- non-executive directors should:
  - constructively challenge and contribute to the development of strategy;
  - scrutinise the performance of management in meeting agreed goals and objectives;
  - monitor the reporting of performance;
  - satisfy themselves that financial information is accurate and that financial controls and systems of risk management are robust and defensible;
  - be responsible for determining appropriate levels of executive remuneration;
  - have a prime role in appointing, and where necessary removing, senior management and in succession planning;
- the non-executive directors should meet regularly as a group without the executives present and at least once a year without the chairman present and the annual report should include a statement on whether such meetings have taken place – these meetings should be led by the senior independent director;
- where they have concerns about the way in which the company is being run or about a course of action being proposed by the board, directors should ensure that their concerns are recorded in the minutes if they cannot be resolved;
- where a non-executive director resigns, a written statement setting out the reasons should be provided to the chairman for circulation to the board; and
- companies should arrange appropriate insurance cover in respect of legal action against its directors.

There is consequently much more emphasis on the role of the non-executive directors and a new requirement for the non-executives to meet without executive management present.

## Roles of the chairman and CEO                                    6.22

The best practice guidance in Part 2 of the Combined Code currently makes three points in respect of the roles of the chairman and chief executive officer (CEO):

- a decision to combine the posts of chairman and CEO should be publicly justified;
- whatever approach is taken to these roles, the board should always include a strong and independent non-executive element, with a recognised senior member (other than the chairman) to whom any concerns can be conveyed; and
- the chairman, CEO and senior independent director should be identified in the annual report.

## Proposed changes in respect of chairman and CEO          6.23

Once again, the Higgs Report proposes some significant changes to this section of the Combined Code, suggesting that the current best practice provisions are replaced with the following:

- the roles of chairman and chief executive should not be exercised by the same individual;
- the division of responsibilities between the two should be clearly established, set out in writing and agreed by the board;
- the chairman and chief executive should be identified in the annual report;
- a chief executive should not go on to become chairman of the same company;
- on appointment, the chairman should meet the independence criteria set out in paragraph A.3.4 of the Combined Code (see **6.25** below);
- the chairman is responsible for:
  - leadership of the board;
  - ensuring the board's effectiveness on all aspects of its role;
  - setting the board's agenda;
  - ensuring that the directors receive accurate, timely and clear information;
  - facilitating the effective contribution of the non-executive directors;
  - ensuring constructive relations between executive and non-executive directors; and
  - ensuring effective communication with shareholders.

Although there is a strong encouragement in the present Code for the roles of chairman and CEO to be separated, there is an implied acceptance that combination of these roles may be justified in certain circumstances. The proposed revision sets out much more stringent requirements and provides more detailed guidance on the specific responsibilities of the chairman.

## Board balance 6.24

Legally, all directors are equally responsible for the decisions and actions of the board, regardless of whether their appointment is as an executive or non-executive. Whilst certain individuals may have particular responsibilities within the business, the board as a whole is responsible for ensuring that the company meets its obligations. The effectiveness of the board depends on how well the individual members work together as a team under the leadership of the chairman. The best practice guidance in Part 2 of the Combined Code currently includes two provisions on board balance:

- the board should include non-executive directors of sufficient calibre and number for their views to carry significant weight in board decisions – non-executive directors should comprise not less than one third of the board; and
- the majority of non-executive directors should be independent of management and free from any business or other relationship which could materially interfere with the exercise of their independent judgement.

The non-executive directors who are independent (as defined in the guidance) should be identified in the annual report.

## Proposed changes in respect of board balance 6.25

The Higgs Report recommends a substantial expansion of the best practice provisions on board balance, replacing the current provisions with the following:

- boards should not be so large as to be unwieldy, but should be of sufficient size to achieve a balance of skills and experience appropriate for the requirements of the business and to enable changes in the board's composition to be managed without undue disruption;
- there should a strong executive representation on the board to ensure that power and information are not concentrated in one or two individuals;
- all directors must take decisions objectively in the interests of the company;
- a non-executive director is considered to be independent when the board determines that he/she is independent in character and judgement and there are no relationships or circumstances which could affect, or appear to affect the director's judgement – in particular, such relationships or circumstances arise where the director:
    - is a former employee of the company or group, unless five years have elapsed since employment or any other material connection;

- has, or has had within the last three years, a material business relationship with the company either directly or as a partner, shareholder, director or senior employee of a body that has such a relationship with the company;
- receives (or has received) additional remuneration from the company apart from a director's fee, participates in the company's share option or performance-related pay scheme, or is a member of the company's pension scheme;
- has close family ties with any of the company's advisers, directors or senior employees;
- holds cross-directorships or has significant links with other directors through involvement in other companies or bodies;
- represents a significant shareholder; or
- has served on the board for more than ten years;

- the board should identify in the annual report the non-executive directors that it considers to be independent and should state its reasons if a director is considered to be independent in spite of the existence of relationships and circumstances that may appear relevant to such a decision;
- at least half of the board, excluding the chairman, should comprise non-executive directors determined by the board to be independent;
- a senior independent director should be identified in the annual report and should be available to shareholders if they have reason for concern which has failed to be resolved through contact through the normal channels of chairman or chief executive, or where such contact is inappropriate;
- unless the company is small, no individual should sit on all three principal board committees (ie audit, remuneration, nomination) at the same time.

The definition of independence in the context of non-executive directors is considerably more detailed than in the current Code, although it is based on similar factors to those included in related guidance currently issued by bodies such as Pensions Investment Research Consultants (PIRC) and the National Association of Pension Funds (NAPF). There is much greater emphasis on the board's collective responsibility for determining which directors are considered to be independent and for justifying their decision to the shareholders where there appears to be cause for doubt. The senior independent director is also given a wider role in the proposed new guidance and there is additional guidance on the size of the board and the need to achieve a good balance of skills and experience.

The implication of the above is that not all non-executives need to be independent. This is helpful as, in the authors' view, it would have been a retrograde step and presented significant difficulties for smaller listed companies if the review had recommended that all non-executives need to be independent.

## Supply of information to the board                              6.26

There are two elements to the current best practice guidance in Part 2 of the Combined Code on the supply of information to the board:

- management has an obligation to provide appropriate and timely information to the board – however, the details volunteered by management are unlikely to be sufficient in all circumstances and the directors should, therefore, make further enquiries where necessary; and

- the chairman is responsible for ensuring that all directors are properly briefed on issues arising at board meetings.

## Proposed changes on information and professional development                                                        6.27

The Higgs Report proposes that this section of the Combined Code be expanded to cover the professional development of directors as well as the supply of information. At present, professional development is covered only briefly under the provisions relating to the board (see **6.20** above). The following provisions are now proposed in this section:

- information volunteered by management may not be sufficient in all circumstances and directors should make further enquiries where necessary;

- the company secretary should be accountable to the board through the chairman on all governance matters;

- the board should agree a procedure for the directors, in the furtherance of their duties, to take independent professional advice at the company's expense.

- all directors should have access to the impartial advice and services of the company secretary, who is responsible to the board for ensuring that board procedures are followed and that applicable rules and regulations are complied with;

- under the direction of the chairman, the company secretary's responsibilities include:
  - facilitating induction and professional development;
  - ensuring good information flows within the board and its committees; and
  - ensuring good information flows between non-executive directors and senior management;

- both the appointment and the removal of the company secretary should be a matter for the board as a whole;

- the chairman is responsible for ensuring that new directors receive comprehensive, formal and tailored induction on joining the board – this should include meeting major investors;

- the chairman should ensure that the directors continually update the skills and knowledge required to fulfil their role on both the board and board committees, and the company should acknowledge that time and money need to be provided for this, as part of the cost of running an effective board.

The present Code provides only for directors to receive appropriate training when first appointed to the board of a listed company. The proposed new guidance is much more specific on the need for formal induction to be provided by the company at the time of appointment and for directors to keep up to date with issues relevant to their role on the board and its committees.

## Appointments to the board                                     6.28

The best practice guidance in Part 2 of the Combined Code currently includes only one provision on appointments to the board, but this includes three separate elements:

- unless the board is small, a nomination committee should be established to make recommendations to the board as a whole on the appointment of directors;
- a majority of the members of the nomination committee should be non-executive directors and the committee should be chaired either by the company chairman or by a non-executive director; and
- the members of the nomination committee, and the committee chairman, should be identified in the annual report.

Although the nomination committee will deal with the detailed aspects of the selection process and then make a recommendation to the board, the actual appointment of a new director should be a matter for the main board. Any director appointed by the board should also be subject to election by the shareholders at the first opportunity. The same appointment process should apply for both executive and non-executive directors.

## Proposed changes in respect of appointments         6.29

The Higgs Report proposes the following detailed provisions in respect of appointments to the board:

- all listed companies should have a nomination committee, with a majority of independent non-executive directors, to lead the process for board appointments and make recommendations to the board;
- the nomination committee may include the chairman of the board, but should be chaired by an independent non-executive director;
- the chairman and members of the nomination committee should be identified in the annual report;
- the nomination committee should make publicly available terms of reference explaining its role and the authority delegated to it by the board;
- before recommending an appointment, the nomination committee should evaluate the balance of skills, knowledge and experience on the board and in the light of this, prepare a description of the role and capabilities required for a particular appointment;

- the nomination committee should set out in the letter of appointment the time and responsibility envisaged in the appointment of a non-executive director, including those relating to chairmanship or membership of board committees or as the senior independent director;
- the board should set out to shareholders why they believe an individual should be appointed in a non-executive role and how he/she meets the requirements of the role;
- the non-executive director should confirm that he/she will have sufficient time to fulfil the role expected, taking into account other commitments – these commitments, and an indication of the time they require, should be disclosed to the company before appointment;
- the nomination committee should review annually the time required of a non-executive director and performance evaluation should be used to assess whether each non-executive director is spending enough time to fulfil his/her duties;
- if a non-executive director is offered an appointment elsewhere, he/she should inform the chairman before accepting any new appointment and the board should subsequently be informed;
- a full time executive director should not take on more than one non-executive directorship or become chairman of a major (FTSE 100) company and no individual should chair the board of more than one such company;
- the nomination committee should satisfy itself that appropriate succession plans are in place for appointments to the board and to senior management, and that an appropriate balance of skills on the board will be maintained;
- the annual report should include a statement from the nomination committee on its activities and the processes used in making appointments, and an explanation should be given if external advice or open advertising has not been used;
- the terms and conditions of appointment of non-executive directors should be published.

The new provisions are therefore much more comprehensive and are aimed at ensuring that the appointment of new directors is the result of a transparent, objective process. There are also new restrictions on the number of appointments that an individual can hold at any one time.

There was a strong reaction to the suggestion that an Independent Director should chair the nominations committee from many leading Chairmen. The authors have sympathy with their view that as leader of the board team the Chairman should also be Chairman of the nominations committee. We would expect that this might be one of the Higgs recommendations which does not make its way into a revised combined code.

One interesting new step in the formal appointment process suggested by Higgs is that

> '[w]hen an appointment of a non-executive director is put

forward for approval to shareholders, the board should explain why the appointee meets the requirements of the role.'

The authors believe that this apparently minor and somewhat detailed suggestion may have considerable impact. If companies are forced to say why someone is appropriate they will presumably have to have defined the role and conducted a rigorous process.

Higgs suggests that there are three principles that should be observed when a board is appointing a new chairman. These are that:

- the Senior Independent Director should lead the process (ie not the existing chairman) and anyone putting themselves forward shouldn't be involved in the appointment process;
- a systematic approach should be taken; and
- a range of candidates should be considered, ie don't pick from a choice of one.

## Re-election of directors                                        6.30

The best practice guidance in Part 2 of the Combined Code currently has two detailed provisions on the re-election of directors:

- non-executive directors should be appointed for a specified term (subject to re-election and the provisions of *CA 1985* on the removal of a director) and reappointment should not be automatic; and
- all directors should be subject to election by the shareholders at the first opportunity after their appointment, with re-election thereafter at intervals of not more than three years – sufficient biographical details should be given for all directors submitted for re-election, so that shareholders are able to make an informed decision.

## Proposed changes on re-election                            6.31

Once again, the Higgs Report proposes expanding on these recommendations by replacing the present guidance with the following provisions:

- non-executive directors should be appointed for specified terms, subject to re-election and to *CA 1985* provisions relating to the removal of a director, and reappointment should not be automatic;
- all directors should be subject to election by the shareholders at the first opportunity after their appointment, and to re-election thereafter at intervals of no more than three years;
- non-executive directors will normally be expected to serve two terms of three years, subject to continued satisfactory performance, but may exceptionally serve longer where this would be in the interests of the company and provided that the reasons are explained to shareholders;
- non-executive directors serving nine years or more should be subject to annual re-election;

- before proposing re-election, the chairman should confirm through performance evaluation that he/she is satisfied that the non-executive director continues to contribute effectively and demonstrate commitment to the role.

Although based on the existing provisions, the new proposals are much more stringent, particularly on the overall period that an individual serves as a non-executive director. Higgs recommends two terms of three years. He has however tried not to be too prescriptive here and it is welcome that he recognised the dangers inherent in an annual vote on all directors. It is interesting to note that his research showed that the average time served by FTSE 100 non-executives was 4.3 years (at July 17 2002) and that the research indicated an average tenure of non-executives was over eight years.

For chairmen the situation is slightly different. Higgs says that his research suggested that the average tenure of a listed company chairman is fifteen years. He also doesn't believe that there should be a standard term for tenure of the chairman.

## Evaluating board performance                                   6.32

The Higgs Report recommends the introduction of a new principle on evaluating board performance and also proposes the following best practice provisions:

- performance evaluation of the board, its committees and its individual directors should be undertaken at least once a year;
- the chairman should act on the results of this evaluation by recognising the strengths and addressing the weaknesses of the board and, where appropriate, appointing new board members or seeking the resignation of directors; and
- the board should state in the annual report whether such performance evaluation is taking place and how it is conducted.

## Directors' remuneration                                        6.33

## At a glance                                                     6.34

- Section B of the Combined Code sets out governance principles in respect of directors' remuneration.
- The best practice provisions cover the following issues:
  - level and make-up of remuneration;
  - performance-related pay;
  - service contracts and compensation;
  - procedure for developing remuneration policy;
  - disclosure of remuneration and the directors' remuneration report.

# Combined Code principles                                           6.35

Section B of Part 1 of the Combined Code sets out the following principles in relation to directors' remuneration:

- **Level and make-up of remuneration**: Levels of remuneration should be sufficient to attract and retain the directors needed to run the company successfully, but companies should avoid paying more than is necessary for this purpose; a proportion of executive directors' remuneration should be structured to link rewards to corporate and individual performance;
- **Procedure**: There should be a formal and transparent procedure for developing policy on executive remuneration and for fixing the remuneration packages of individual directors – no director should be involved in setting his/her own remuneration; and
- **Disclosure**: The company's annual report should include a statement of the company's remuneration policy and details of the remuneration of each individual director.

Apart from some minor wording changes, the Higgs Report does not propose any revision of these principles.

# Level and make-up of remuneration                                  6.36

The best practice guidance in Part 2 of Combined Code is divided two sections – remuneration policy, and service contracts and compensation. There are currently six provisions on remuneration policy:

- the remuneration committee should provide the packages necessary to attract, retain and motivate executive directors of the required quality, but should avoid paying more than is necessary;
- the remuneration committee should judge where to position the company relative to other companies, and should be aware of the remuneration packages and relative performance of other companies, but should use such comparisons with caution in view of the risk of increasing remuneration levels without a corresponding improvement in performance;
- the remuneration committee should be sensitive to the wider scene, including pay and conditions elsewhere in the group, especially when determining annual salary increases;
- performance-related elements should form a significant proportion of the total remuneration package for executive directors and should be designed to align their interests with those of the shareholder, and to give the directors a keen incentive to perform at the highest levels;
- executive share options should not be issued at a discount, except as permitted by Chapters 13.30 and 13.31 of the FSA Listing Rules; and
- in designing schemes of performance-related remuneration, the committee should follow the provisions set out in Schedule A to the *Combined Code* (see **6.37** below).

Corporate Governance

The Higgs Report proposes retaining these provisions, with minor amendments to the wording, and adding the following additional provision in respect of non-executive directors:

- levels of remuneration for non-executive directors should reflect the time and responsibilities of the role, but the remuneration of non-executive directors in share options should be avoided.

## Performance-related pay                                   6.37

Schedule A to the Combined Code comprises the guidance originally set out in the Greenbury Code of Best Practice on directors' remuneration, with a number of minor wording changes. It recommends that:

- the remuneration committee should consider whether directors should be eligible for annual bonuses and, if so, performance conditions should be relevant, stretching and designed to enhance the business – upper limits should always be considered and there may be a case for part payment in shares to be held for a significant period;
- the remuneration committee should consider whether the directors should be eligible for benefits under long-term incentive schemes, and in establishing such schemes should:
  - weigh traditional share option schemes against other kinds of long-term incentive schemes;
  - generally ensure that shares granted and other forms of deferred remuneration do not vest, and options are not exercisable, in less than three years;
  - encourage directors to hold their shares for a further period after vesting or exercise, subject to the need to finance any costs of acquisition or associated tax liabilities;
- where new long-term incentive schemes are proposed, these should be approved by the shareholders and should generally replace existing schemes, or at least form part of a well-considered overall plan incorporating existing schemes – the total rewards potentially available should not be excessive;
- payouts or grants under all incentive schemes (including new grants under existing share option schemes) should be subject to challenging performance criteria reflecting the company's objectives, and consideration should be given to criteria which reflect the company's performance relative to a group of comparator companies in certain key variables such as total shareholder return;
- grants under executive share option and other long-term incentive schemes should normally be phased rather than awarded in one large block;
- the remuneration committee should consider the pension consequences and associated costs to the company of increases in basic salary and other changes in remuneration, especially for directors close to retirement; and

- in general, neither annual bonuses nor benefits in kind should be pensionable.

No changes to these provisions are proposed in the Higgs Report.

## Service contracts and compensation                                   6.38

The best practice guidance dealing with directors' service contacts and compensation currently includes four provisions:

- there is a strong case for setting notice or contract periods at, or reducing them to, one year or less – the board should set this as an objective, even though it may not be possible to achieve immediately;
- if it is necessary to offer longer notice or contract periods to directors recruited externally, these should reduce after the initial period;
- the remuneration committee should consider what compensation commitments (including pension contributions) directors' service contracts would entail in the event of early termination – in particular, the committee should consider the advantages of providing explicitly in the initial contract for such compensation commitments other than in the case of removal for misconduct; and
- where the initial contract does not provide explicitly for compensation commitments the remuneration committee should, within legal constraints, tailor their approach in the case of early termination to the wide variety of circumstances – the broad aim should be to avoid rewarding poor performance while dealing fairly with departure in other circumstances, and to take a robust line on reducing compensation to reflect the departing director's obligations to mitigate loss.

The proposals in the Higgs Report retain these provisions without significant change, although the first one is more definite that notice or contract periods should be set at one year or less, and the third one also refers to the need to ensure that the arrangements do not have the effect of rewarding poor performance.

## Procedure for developing remuneration policy                          6.39

The best practice guidance in Part 2 of the Combined Code includes six provisions on procedures for developing remuneration policy:

- to avoid potential conflicts of interest, the board should establish a remuneration committee of independent non-executive directors to make recommendations to the board on the company's framework for executive remuneration and its cost, and to determine on behalf of the board specific remuneration packages (including pension rights and compensation payments) for each executive director;
- the remuneration committee should consist exclusively of non-executive directors who are independent of management and free from any business or other relationship which could materially affect the exercise of their independent judgement.

- the members of the remuneration committee should be listed in the annual report to shareholders; and
- the board (or the shareholders where the company's articles require this) should determine the remuneration of the non-executive directors (including the members of the remuneration committee) – where the company's articles permit, the responsibility may be delegated to a small sub-committee, which might include the chief executive;
- the remuneration committee should consult the chairman and/or chief executive about the proposals on the remuneration of other executive directors, and should have access to internal and external professional advice; and
- the chairman of the board should ensure that the company maintains appropriate contact with its principal shareholders on remuneration issues in the same way as for other matters.

Once again, the proposals in the Higgs Report retain these provisions without substantial amendment, except that:

- it is recommended that the remuneration committee should have at least three members;
- the new wording makes clear that the remuneration committee should have delegated responsibility for setting the remuneration of all executive directors and of the chairman, including pension rights and compensation payments, and for setting the level and structure of remuneration for senior executives;
- the remuneration committee is required to make publicly available its terms of reference, and to explain its role and the authority delegated to it by the board; and
- if executive directors or senior management are involved in advising or supporting the remuneration committee, this role should be clearly separated from their role within the business.

## Disclosure of remuneration 6.40

The best practice guidance in Part 2 of the Combined Code currently includes five provisions relating to the disclosure of directors' remuneration in the annual report:

- the board should report to the shareholders on remuneration each year – this report should form part of, or be annexed to, the company's annual report and accounts and should be the main vehicle through which the company accounts to the shareholders for directors' remuneration;
- the report should set out company policy on executive directors' remuneration and should draw attention to factors specific to the company;
- in preparing the report, the board should follow the provisions in Schedule B to the Combined Code (see **6.41** below);
- shareholders should be specifically invited to approve all new long-term incentive schemes (including share option schemes) in which

directors and senior executives will participate and which potentially commit shareholders' funds over more than one year or dilute the equity; and

- the board's annual report on remuneration should not be a standard item on the agenda for the AGM, but the board should consider each year whether the shareholders should be invited to approve the policy set out in the report, and should minute their conclusions on this.

The Higgs Report proposes retaining these provisions, although the wording of the second item is amended to clarify that the report should also set out the company policy on the remuneration of non-executive directors, and there are minor wording changes to some of the other provisions.

## Remuneration report                                      6.41

Schedule B to the Combined Code sets out the following recommendations on the preparation of the annual remuneration report:

- the report should include full details of all elements of the remuneration package of each individual director (by name), such as basic salary, benefits in kind, annual bonuses and long-term incentive schemes (including share options);
- information on share options (including SAYE options) should be given in accordance with the recommendations set out in UITF Abstract 10 *Disclosure of directors' share options* (this Abstract has been withdrawn for accounting periods ending on or after 31 December 2002 on the basis that equivalent disclosures are now required by law under the *Directors' Remuneration Report Regulations 2002 (SI 2002/1986)* – see CHAPTER 9 DIRECTORS' REMUNERATION AND BENEFITS);
- if grants under executive share option or other long-term incentive schemes are awarded in one large block, the report should explain and justify this;
- the report should include disclosure of the pension entitlement earned by each individual director, calculated on one of the alternative bases recommended by the Faculty of Actuaries and the Institute of Actuaries – however, companies should make clear that transfer values cannot meaningfully be added to annual remuneration;
- if any annual bonuses or benefits in kind are pensionable, the report should explain and justify this;
- the disclosure of the amounts received by, and commitments made to, each director under his/her remuneration package (including share options and pension entitlements) should be subject to audit; and
- the report should disclose details of any directors' service contracts that provide for, or imply:
  - a notice period in excess of one year (and the reasons for the longer period should be explained); or
  - predetermined compensation on termination which exceeds one year's salary and benefits.

No changes to these provisions are proposed in the Higgs Report. The FSA Listing Rules also require disclosure of the unexpired term of any service contract for a director proposed for election or re-election at the forthcoming meeting, or a statement that he/she does not have a service contract. For accounting periods ending on or after 31 December 2002, *CA 1985* has been amended to require all quoted companies to prepare a statutory directors' remuneration report. The contents of the remuneration report are considered in more detail in **CHAPTER 9 DIRECTORS' REMUNERATION AND BENEFITS.**

## Relations with shareholders                                        6.42

## At a glance                                                        6.43

---

- Section C of the Combined Code sets out governance principles in respect of relations with shareholders.
- The best practice provisions cover the following issues:
  - dialogue with shareholders;
  - constructive use of the AGM.
- The Government is proposing a number of measures to improve the quality of shareholder input to the AGM.

---

## Combined Code Principles                                           6.44

Section C of Part 1 of the Combined Code identifies two principles on relations with shareholders:

- companies should be ready, where practicable, to enter into a dialogue with institutional shareholders based on the mutual understanding of objectives; and
- companies should use the AGM to communicate with private investors and encourage their participation.

The Higgs Report proposes some wording changes to these principles, but no substantial amendments.

## Dialogue with major shareholders                                   6.45

The Combined Code does not currently include any detailed provisions on the recommended dialogue with major shareholders. The Higgs Report proposes the introduction of the following best practice provisions:

- the board should disclose in the annual report the steps taken to ensure that the members of the board, and the non-executive directors in particular, develop an understanding of the views of major shareholders;
- the senior independent director should attend sufficient regular meetings of management with a range of major shareholders to develop a

balanced understanding of the themes, issues and concerns of share-holders, and should communicate these views to the non-executive directors and, where appropriate, to the board as a whole;

- non-executive directors should be able to attend regular meetings with major investors and should expect to attend if requested by major share-holders;
- on appointment, non-executive directors should meet major investors as part of the induction process.

The introduction of recommendations on meetings between the non-execu-tive directors and major shareholders is an interesting development. It has been generally accepted until now that the chief executive and finance direc-tor should be the main channel of communication between investors and the company. The chairman should be the main channel of communication with institutional investors on matters of concern and that a direct approach to the senior independent director has been seen as a last resort and an indication that something is seriously amiss. Views have been divided on whether the institutional investors should have more regular contact with the independent non-executives and companies have generally been reluctant to allow *ad hoc* meetings to take place.

This is an area that was bound to be controversial with some feeling that this encourages 'two tier thinking' and divisiveness. Early press comment focussed on this but Higgs clearly stated that he believed in the unitary board and the chairman's role as leader.

A sensible balanced approach will need to taken in practice. Otherwise the time commitment for non-executives and the senior independent non-execu-tive in particular will become too great and a deterrent.

## Constructive use of the AGM                                    6.46

Part 2 of the Combined Code currently includes four best practice provisions on constructive use of the AGM:

- companies should count all proxy votes and, except where a poll is called, should indicate the level of proxies lodged on each resolution, and the balance for and against, after the resolution has been dealt with on a show of hands;
- separate resolutions should be proposed on each substantially separate issue, and in particular a resolution should be proposed on the annual report and accounts;
- the chairman of the board should arrange for the chairmen of the audit, remuneration and nomination committees to be available to answer questions at the AGM; and
- companies should arrange for the notice of the AGM and related papers to be sent to shareholders at least 20 working days before the meeting.

The Higgs Report proposes the retention of these provisions, with an additional recommendation that all non-executive directors should attend the AGM. Perhaps more controversially, so should representatives from institutional investors.

## Accountability to shareholders 6.47

The Cadbury Report summarised the relationship between the board and the company's shareholders as follows:

- the shareholders, as owners of the company, elect the directors to run the business on their behalf, and hold them accountable for its progress and development;
- the directors report to the shareholders on their stewardship of the company and its assets; and
- the shareholders appoint external auditors to provide an independent check on the company's financial statements.

The Cadbury Committee considered suggestions on how the accountability of directors to shareholders might be strengthened but concluded that shareholders should continue to make their views known to the board through direct communication and through attendance at annual general meetings. The Committee also noted that shareholder organisations set up to represent shareholder interests generally might provide an opportunity for individual shareholders to act collectively if they wish. Whilst shareholders cannot be involved in the detailed direction and management of their company, they are entitled to insist on a high standard of corporate governance, evidenced by compliance with the Combined Code.

## Government proposals for change 6.48

The Government White Paper *Modernising Company Law* issued in July 2002 includes a number of measures designed to improve the quality of shareholder input at the AGM and in particular to give shareholders adequate opportunity to raise matters of concern. The proposals include changes to the timing of the AGM, a requirement for annual accounts and reports to be distributed more quickly after the year end, a requirement for quoted companies to publish both their preliminary announcement and their annual accounts and reports on a website, new provisions on the circulation of members' resolutions and statements, greater powers for proxies at meetings and new requirements on the conduct and results of polls.

## Accountability and audit 6.49

## At a glance 6.50

- Section D of the Combined Code sets out governance principles in respect of accountability and audit.
- The best practice provisions cover the following issues:

- financial reporting, including going concern;
- internal control; and
- audit committees and auditors.
- The Higgs Report and the Smith Report propose significant revision of the current provisions on audit committees and auditors.

## Combined Code Principles                                        6.51

Section D of Part 1 of the Combined Code identifies three principles on accountability and audit:

- **Financial reporting:** The board should present a balanced and under-standable assessment of the company's position and prospects;
- **Internal control**: The board should maintain a sound system of inter-nal control to safeguard the shareholders' investment and the company's assets; and
- **Audit committee and auditors**: The board should establish formal and transparent arrangements for considering how they should apply the financial reporting and internal control principles mentioned above, and for maintaining an appropriate relationship with the company's auditors.

The Higgs Report proposes that these principles are retained without signifi-cant amendment. The Cadbury Report discussed the presentation of a balanced and understandable assessment of the company's position in the context of recognised accounting practice. The accounts are required by law to show a true and fair view and they should give the highest level of disclo-sure consonant with presenting reports that are understandable, and without causing damage to the company's competitive position. The Cadbury Report also emphasised that balance involves dealing with setbacks as well as successes and that words are as important as figures. These issues are explored in more detail in CHAPTER 10 FINANCIAL REPORTING.

## Financial reporting                                             6.52

The best practice guidance in Part 2 of the Combined Code currently includes three provisions on financial reporting:

- the directors should explain their responsibility for preparing the accounts, next to a statement by the auditors about their reporting responsibilities;
- the board should consider interim reports, and other price-sensitive public reports and reports to regulators, as well as information that has to be presented under statutory requirements; and
- the directors should report that the business is a going concern, with supporting assumptions or qualifications as necessary.

The Higgs Report proposes retaining these provisions, with certain wording changes which remove any confusion over the location of the directors' and auditors' statements within the annual report and accounts and clarify that the board's responsibility to present a balanced and understandable assessment extends to all financial reporting documents.

## Internal control 6.53

The best practice guidance in Part 2 of the Combined Code includes two provisions on internal control:

- the directors should, at least annually, review the effectiveness of the company's (or group's) system of internal control and should report to shareholders that they have done so – the review should cover all controls, including financial, operational and compliance controls and risk management; and
- companies which do not have an internal audit function should periodically review the need for one.

The Higgs Report proposes retaining these provisions, with a small amendment to the second one to require an annual (rather than periodic) review of the need for an internal audit function.

## Audit committee and auditors 6.54

The best practice guidance in Part 2 of the Combined Code includes two provisions on the audit committee and the relationship with the company's external auditors:

- the board should establish an audit committee of at least three non-executive directors with written terms of reference dealing clearly with its authority and duties; a majority of the members should be independent non-executive directors and the members of the audit committee should be named in the company's annual report and accounts; and
- the duties of the audit committee should include keeping under review the scope and results of the audit, its cost effectiveness, and the independence and objectivity of the auditors; where the auditors also provide a substantial level of non-audit services, the committee should keep the nature and extent of these services under review, seeking to balance the maintenance of objectivity and value for money.

## Proposed changes in respect of audit committees 6.55

The proposals in the Higgs Report are based on the recommendations set out in 'Audit Committees: Combined Code Guidance' (the Smith Report - see CHAPTER 2 AUDIT MATTERS). They retain the essence of the existing provisions, but cover them in much greater detail as follows:

- the board should establish an audit committee of at least three members, all of whom should be independent non-executive directors, and at least one of whom should have significant, recent and relevant financial experience;

- the main role and responsibilities of the audit committee should be set out in written terms of reference and should include:
  - monitoring the integrity of the financial statements of the company and reviewing significant financial reporting judgements contained in them;
  - reviewing the company's internal financial control system and, unless addressed by a separate risk committee or by the board itself, risk management systems;
  - monitoring and reviewing the effectiveness of the company's internal audit function;
  - making recommendations to the board in relation to the appointment of the external auditor and approving the remuneration and terms of engagement of the external auditor;
  - monitoring and reviewing the external auditor's independence, objectivity and effectiveness, taking into account relevant UK professional and regulatory requirements; and
  - developing and implementing policy on the engagement of the external auditor to supply non-audit services, taking into account relevant ethical guidance;
- the audit committee should be provided with sufficient resources to undertake its duties;
- the annual report should include a separate section describing the role and responsibilities of the audit committee and the actions taken by the committee to discharge those responsibilities; and
- the chairman of the audit committee should be present at the AGM to answer questions, through the chairman of the board.

These provisions are amplified further by the detailed guidance set out in the Smith Report.

## Institutional investors                                             6.56

## At a glance                                                         6.57

---

- There is a significant degree of common interest between individual shareholders and institutional shareholders.
- Institutional shareholders will usually have more access to boards than individual shareholders.
- Section E of the Combined Code sets out governance principles in respect of institutional investors.
- The best practice provisions currently include provisions on shareholder voting but not on the other principles relating to institutional investors.
- Detailed guidance for institutional investors is issued by the Institutional Shareholders' Committee (ISC) and other similar organisations.
- The Higgs Report proposes a new best practice provision on dialogue with companies.

---

## Role of institutional shareholders 6.58

The Cadbury Report noted that institutional shareholders hold the majority of shares in listed companies, but emphasised that in many cases they hold them on behalf of individuals (eg as members of pension schemes or beneficiaries of insurance policies) and that there is a significant degree of common interest between individual shareholders and institutional shareholders. In particular, both have the same interest in standards of financial reporting and corporate governance. Since the publication of the Cadbury Report there has in fact been a rapid growth of active private investors. This is attributed to a variety of factors, including the interest generated by the growth of the dotcom industry (despite its subsequent problems), technological development (the internet has made it much easier to buy and sell shares) and the substantial growth of journalism on personal financial issues. However, there is no doubt that institutional investors continue to represent a very significant proportion of shareholders and are in a unique position to develop closer links with the companies in which they invest. The Cadbury Report drew attention to three key issues critical to the development of a constructive relationship between companies and their shareholders:

- the need for institutional investors to encourage regular contact at senior executive level to exchange views and information on strategy, performance, board membership and quality of management;
- the need for institutional investors to make positive use of their voting rights and to exercise their votes on a regular basis; and
- the need for institutional investors to take a positive interest in the composition of boards and the appointment of non-executive directors with appropriate experience and independence.

These issues were developed further by the Hampel Committee in the Combined Code, although the Committee did not put forward any disclosure requirements on compliance with the principles or provisions relating to institutional shareholders. However, they indicated their hope that these shareholders would disclose to the relevant companies, and possibly also to the public as a whole, the extent to which they are following the principles and provisions set out in the Combined Code.

## Communication with shareholders 6.59

The Cadbury Report raised the following issues in respect of communication with shareholders:

- institutional shareholders will usually have more access to boards than individual shareholders, but there is still a need for companies to maintain parity between shareholders wherever possible – a board should therefore ensure that any significant statements concerning the company are made publicly so that they are equally available to all shareholders;
- in communicating with institutional shareholders, there is always a risk

of the company disclosing inside information – price-sensitive information should only be disclosed with the prior consent of the shareholder (who will then be unable to deal in the company's shares until the information has been made public); and

● in order to develop long-term relationships, it is important for a company to communicate its strategy to the major shareholders – similarly shareholders should inform the company if they have concerns over particular aspects of the business.

## Combined Code Principles                                    6.60

Section E of Part 1 of the Combined Code identifies three principles in relation to institutional investors:

● **Shareholder voting**: Institutional shareholders have a responsibility to make considered use of their votes;
● **Dialogue with companies**: Institutional shareholders should be ready, where practicable, to enter into a dialogue with companies based on the mutual understanding of objectives; and
● **Evaluation of governance disclosures**: When evaluating governance arrangements, and in particular those relating to board structure and composition, institutional shareholders should give due weight to all relevant factors drawn to their attention.

The Higgs Report proposes retaining these principles with minor wording amendments. The best practice guidance in Part 2 of the Combined Code does not include any provisions on the evaluation of corporate governance disclosures and none are proposed in the Higgs Report.

## Shareholder voting                                          6.61

The best practice guidance in Part 2 of the Combined Code currently sets out three provisions on shareholder voting:

● institutional shareholders should endeavour to eliminate unnecessary variations in the criteria which each applies to the corporate governance arrangements and performance of companies in which they invest;
● on request, institutional shareholders should make available to their clients information on the proportion of resolutions on which votes were cast and non-discretionary proxies lodged; and
● institutional shareholders should take steps to ensure that their voting intentions are being translated into practice.

The Higgs Report proposes retaining these three provisions with minor wording amendments and adding the following additional provision:

● institutional shareholders should be expected to attend AGMs where practicable.

## Institutional Shareholders' Committee (ISC)    6.62

The Institutional Shareholders' Committee (ISC) represents the interests and concerns of institutional investors, with representatives from the Association of British Insurers (ABI), the National Association of Pension Funds (NAPF), the Association of Investment Trust Companies (AITC) and the Investment Management Association (IMA). The ISC has issued guidance to institutional investors covering issues such as communication with boards, the use of voting rights, board composition, directors' remuneration and takeover bids. On the subject of shareholder voting, the guidelines note that institutional investors should support boards by positive use of their voting rights unless they have good reason for doing otherwise. Where an institutional investor considers it appropriate to vote against a particular proposal, the issue should be raised with the board in good time to allow for the problem to be considered and, if possible, a satisfactory solution found. If a solution proves impossible, it may be appropriate for a spokesperson to attend the meeting to explain why the proposal is being opposed. A poll should also be demanded in such cases, to ensure that the vote is properly recorded.

## Voting guidelines    6.63

Voting guidelines are regularly issued to institutional investors by organisations such as NAPF, ABI and Pensions Investment Research Consultants (PIRC), based on their assessment of the key current issues. Issues that have received most focus in recent times include directors' remuneration (including incentive schemes, service contracts and notice periods), the independence of non-executive directors and issues relating to the external audit (eg the level of non-audit services provided by the auditors, connections between the directors and auditors, reappointment or changes in the appointment of auditors, and the role and constitution of the audit committee). Directors are well advised to keep track of the current issues being raised by these organisations so that they can be forewarned of any difficulties that are likely to arise at the AGM. Relevant information can usually be found on their websites and in some cases will be circulated to larger listed companies in advance of the publication date for their annual reports and accounts.

## Dialogue with companies    6.64

The best practice guidance in Part 2 of the Combined Code does not include any provisions on dialogue between institutional investors and companies. The Higgs Report proposes the following provision:

● institutional shareholders should apply the principles set out in the Institutional Shareholder's Committee's Code of Activism which should be included in fund manager contracts.

The ISC guidance makes the following points in respect of communication between companies and institutional investors:

- Institutional investors have a strong obligation to exercise their influence in a responsible manner. Many already have effective channels of communication, either directly or through advisers, with the boards of companies in which they invest. The ISC recommends that such channels should be developed more widely to make the communication process more effective.

- Formal methods of communication with shareholders (for instance, through the annual reports and accounts, shareholder circulars, and the right to attend meetings) may not be sufficient to establish the type of relationship which enables directors and shareholders to obtain a deeper understanding of each other's aims and requirements.

- Institutional shareholders should take positive steps to encourage regular and systematic contact at senior executive level on both sides, so that views and information can be exchanged on strategy, performance, board membership and quality of management. This will enable shareholders to get a better understanding of management's objectives, the problems it is facing and the quality of those involved, and also focus the attention of management on the expectations and requirements of shareholders.

- Institutional investors do not wish to become insiders and price sensitive information should generally not be transmitted during such regular contact. In exceptional circumstances, if a board needs to consult its institutional investors on issues which are price sensitive, the investors will need to accept that their ability to deal in the company's shares will be suspended. Companies must not make such disclosures inadvertently or without the consent of the institutional investor.

## Reporting requirements                                        6.65

## At a glance                                                   6.66

---

- Listed companies are required to make an annual statement on the extent of their compliance with the Combined Code.
- The annual report of a listed company must include a statement from the directors on going concern.
- The directors of listed companies must report to shareholders that they have reviewed the effectiveness of the company's system of internal control.
- A separate directors' remuneration report must be prepared by all quoted companies.
- The Combined Code includes recommendations on certain other disclosures which should be given in the annual report.

---

## Statement on compliance with the Combined Code      6.67

For accounting periods ending on or after 31 December 1998, the Financial Services Authority (FSA) Listing Rules require each listed company to include in its accounts:

- a narrative statement of how it has applied the principles set out in Part 1 of the Combined Code, with explanations to enable the shareholders to evaluate how the principles have been applied; and
- a statement on whether or not it has complied throughout the accounting period with the best practice provisions set out under headings A to D of Part 2 of the Combined Code, with details of, and the reasons for, any areas or periods of non-compliance.

The preamble to the Combined Code emphasises that neither the form nor the content of the compliance statement has been prescribed. Directors are therefore given a free hand to explain their corporate governance policies in the light of the principles set out in the Code and any special circumstances that may have led the directors to take a particular approach. Certain aspects of the company's statement on compliance with the Code must be reviewed by the auditors (see CHAPTER 2 AUDIT MATTERS).

## Going concern                                                       6.68

The Combined Code recommends that the directors should report in the annual report and accounts that the business is a going concern, with supporting assumptions or qualifications as necessary. This disclosure was originally recommended by the *Cadbury Code of Best Practice* but did not become fully effective until additional guidance was issued to directors in the document *Going concern and financial reporting – guidance for directors of listed companies* published in November 1994. In the case of listed companies, the inclusion of a statement on going concern is now a direct requirement of the FSA Listing Rules and the statement must also be reviewed by the auditors. This reporting requirement is considered in more detail in CHAPTER 12 GOING CONCERN.

## Internal control                                                    6.69

The Combined Code recommends that the directors conduct an annual review (as a minimum) of the effectiveness of the company's (or group's) system of internal control and report to shareholders that they have done so. The review should cover all aspects of internal control, rather than just internal financial control, but there is no longer a requirement for the directors to express an opinion on the effectiveness of the system. Guidance on reviewing internal control and reporting under the Combined Code was developed by a working party of the Institute of Chartered Accountants in England and Wales chaired by Nigel Turnbull. Their final report *Internal Control – Guidance for directors on the Combined Code* (often referred to as the Turnbull Report) was published in September 1999 and clarifies what is expected of the board of a listed company in terms of:

- applying Principle D.2 in Part 1 of the Combined Code (maintaining a sound system of internal control to safeguard the shareholders' investment and the company's assets);
- determining the extent of their compliance with the best practice

guidance set out in provision D.2.1 of Part 2 of the Combined Code (review of the effectiveness of the system of internal controls); and

- determining the extent of their compliance with the best practice guidance set out in provision D.2.2 of Part 2 of the Combined Code (consideration of whether an internal audit function should be established).

Transitional provisions applied for accounting periods ending before 23 December 2000 to give directors adequate time to develop and implement procedures to enable them to report on internal control in line with this guidance. The FSA Listing Rules require full compliance for accounting periods ending on or after 23 December 2000. This reporting requirement is considered in more detail in **CHAPTER 14 INTERNAL CONTROL**. The directors' statement on internal control must also be reviewed by the auditors.

## Remuneration of directors                                      6.70

The Combined Code recommends, and for accounting periods ending on or after 31 December 2002 *CA 1985* requires (in the case of a quoted company), details of the company's remuneration policy and extensive information on the remuneration received by each individual director to be disclosed in a separate directors' remuneration report. These requirements are considered in more detail in **CHAPTER 9 DIRECTORS' REMUNERATION AND BENEFITS**. The auditors are required to audit certain aspects of these disclosures.

## Other disclosures                                               6.71

The Combined Code also recommends the disclosure of certain other information in the company's annual report. In particular, it recommends disclosure of the following:

- the membership of the main board committees (audit, remuneration, nomination);
- the name of the senior independent director; and
- an explanation of the directors' responsibility for preparing the accounts;

Under the Higgs proposals, additional disclosures will also need to be given each year on:

- the roles, responsibilities, processes and activities of the main board committees;
- the number of meetings of the board and its main committees, together with individual attendance;
- a statement on whether the non-executive directors have met without the chairman or executives present;
- identification of the chairman and chief executive, and the chairmen of the main board committees;
- identification of the non-executive directors that are considered by the board to be independent;

- the reasons for considering a director to be independent if there are relationships or circumstances that might be deemed to affect this;
- where relevant, an explanation of why external advice or open advertising has not been used in the appointment of directors;
- whether performance evaluation is taking place and how it is conducted;
- the steps taken to ensure that members of the board, and the non-executive directors in particular, develop an understanding of the views of major shareholders;
- an explanation of how the company's policy on the provision of non-audit services by the external auditor provides adequate protection of auditor independence;
- where relevant, the reasons why an internal audit function is not considered necessary; and
- where relevant, a statement from the audit committee explaining its recommendation on the appointment, reappointment or removal of the external auditor and the reasons why the board has taken a different position.

Under the latest proposals, the board will also be required to publish:

- a high level statement of which decisions are taken by the board and which are taken by management;
- the terms of reference of the nomination and remuneration committees; and
- the terms and conditions of appointment of the non-executive directors.

## Smaller companies                                                    6.72

As has been said above Higgs came to the conclusion that

> 'There should be no differentiation in the Code's provisions between larger and smaller companies.'

He did, however:

> 'recognise that it may take some time for smaller listed companies to comply with the new provisions and in the interim they, will need to explain why they cannot do so and what steps they are taking'

and that they should therefore be given more time to comply.

Whilst this sounds sensible in the context of the Higgs review and hard to argue with, there is already a big issue for smaller companies in terms of the value they get from being listed and the costs and time involved in being so. The extra costs of the recommendations in the Higgs report may just tip the balance for some.

# 7. Corporate Strategy

## Introduction                                                    7.1

## At a glance                                                     7.2

---

- Market strategy should be decided on the basis of quality market intelligence, rather than merely statistical information
- A company's mission statement should be clear in terms of target and aspirations.
- A board should unite behind a strategy once it has been chosen, even if the choice was not a unanimous one.

---

In the definition of the board's role on **PARAGRAPH 1.2** 'Right Strategy' was at the top of the list and involvement in strategy is frequently described as the most enjoyable aspect of the non-executive's role. The company's strategy will have a fundamental effect on whether value is created or destroyed. What was meant by 'Right Strategy' was:

> 'To ensure that the business has the right strategy, that it is being implemented and monitored and that there is a good process for formulating and adapting it.'

But what do we mean by strategy and what role should the board and a non-executive actually be performing in relation to strategy? From the board's point of view 'Strategy' should not simply include the strategy for the business but also the strategy for the company. The two are clearly linked and the linkage and impact of one on the other should be well understood. For example the board of a private company which has decided that the company should be listed or sold may elect a different strategy for the company's business than one choosing to remain in a private situation with the same owners. There are of course many definitions of strategy; the one we would like to use is:

'The way we are going to achieve our vision'.

Naturally this assumes that there is an agreed vision. If there isn't then any attempt at coming up with a strategy is flawed.

The executive, led by the chief executive, has responsibility for executing the agreed strategy for the business. The chairman has responsibility for executing the strategy for the ownership of the business. The board's role is to ensure that there is good process for developing strategy, choosing the strategy to be adopted and ensuring that the CEO has the best chance of leading its successful execution.

The three key elements from the board's point of view are:

- analysis – assessing the current position.
- developing options – determining a vision and strategic options.
- choice – making a judgement, and
- execution – implementing, monitoring and adapting the chosen strategy

The purpose of this chapter is not to explore the many different frameworks, tools and techniques for formulating strategy but rather to focus briefly on the non-executive's role in the process. Strategy ought to be an an area where a non-executive is able to add significant value through their experience and knowledge of other markets and companies. They may also add considerable value through helping to develop the company's approach to the process of developing strategy. However it is the quality of their strategic judgement that is likely to be their most significant contribution.

## Analysis – assessing the current position                    7.3

The chief executive must take responsibility for formulating strategy and developing a series of strategic options within the context of the board's vision for the company. Good chief executives with experienced boards are likely to draw on the experience of their board in doing this before they seek approval for their particular chosen strategy. A chief executive who presents the strategy as a *fait accompli* without proper involvement of his or her colleagues beforehand is undermining the board.

Good chairmen and chief executives will also have a finely developed understanding of different shareholder views and appetites for risk so that they avoid developing a vision or strategy which fails to get the support of the board as a whole.

The board should also be prepared to adapt the vision for the company in the light of strategic analysis. Many companies at the start of this decade had to redefine their ambitions in the light of a difficult economic environment, geopolitical tension and weak capital markets. A higher degree of external uncertainty inevitably led to more conservative and flexible strategies being adopted.

A natural starting point is an analysis of the company's position and the environment that it is operating in. Most businesses will conduct this regularly so it shouldn't be new. Richard Koch's book *The Financial Times Guide to Strategy* provides an excellent summary of the many different tools and techniques for doing this.

A non-executive will want to feel that high quality market intelligence underpins any analysis that is undertaken and that the analysis contains a lot more than regurgitated market statistics. High quality market intelligence is the basis for providing an in depth understanding of the strategic variables and drivers of value growth. Qualitiative information is usually just as valuable as quantitative, especially with regard to customers and competitors. The non-executive will also need to understand the key assumptions being made, as well as receiving a realistic competitor analysis. There may be certain strategic parameters which have been set for some time and left unchallenged.

For example, perhaps the business is conglomerate in nature. It is important for the board to recognise these parameters and have a process for determining at suitable frequency whether they are still appropriate or need to changed.

A lot of board time can be taken up discussing the minutiae of strategy when there may in fact only be a limited number of critical things to decide upon. We call these the key strategic variables.

## What are these key strategic variables?                    7.4

For most companies comprising a collection of activities or business units choices on the following will result in the overall strategy. A few key questions are included for each on the basis that each of these topics is worth a book in their own right.

## *Market*                                                    7.5

- What business activities and markets does the company choose to compete in?
- What is the basis upon which the company chooses to compete?
- Which distribution channels should the company supply its products and services through?
- What approach should the company take towards marketing alliances and partnerships?

## *Financial* 7.6

- What level of financial risk is acceptable?
- What is the required overall return of the group?
- What is the company's strategy with regard to its investors?
- How will financial control will be exercised?

## *Operations* 7.7

- What will the company make/do itself and what will be contracted out?
- What degree of flexibility in capacity is appropriate?
- What approach should the company take towards production alliances and partnerships?
- How should operations processes be managed to maximise both financial and non-financial objectives?

## *Human resources* 7.8

- What kind of employer does the company want to be?
- If the company consists of several subsidiaries or divisions, does it want consistent policies and for there to be mobility across them?
- What approach is taken towards career development and succession planning?
- What remuneration policy is appropriate?

## *Acquisition* 7.9

- What is the company's strategy with regard to organic growth and growth through acquisition?
- If there is an acquisitive strategy are there clear criteria for selection of opportunities and processes for induction and review?

## *Alliance/partnering* 7.10

- Should the company have alliances, joint ventures or partnerships with other companies?
- If so what form should they take?
- What criteria are there for entering into such arrangements?

However the key strategic variable is often none of the above but the 'board's ambition and appetite for risk'.

For example, a decision to be a world class business in its chosen sectors will impact on all of the above, adding cost in the short term in anticipation of gaining a sustainable advantage in the long term. A lower ambition may produce higher financial returns and lower risk in the short term.

At several points over the last century the conglomerate corporate model has been in fashion. At the start of the 2000s it is not the dominant corporate model in most of the developed economies. The true conglomerate is in a different position to other businesses with regard to strategy, though many of the same principles hold good. For the conglomerate the strategic variables will probably relate to just three things:

- what level of return is acceptable from companies owned by the conglomerate?;
- how does the conglomerate exercise financial control over those companies?; and
- what companies should the conglomerate own or sell?

## Developing options – determining a vision and strategic options      7.11

For some a vision for the company should be market based and realistic in the sense that it takes full account of the company's own capabilities and those of other players in its markets. Many visions centre around leadership of a particular market and a description of the core value proposition. They are then expressed as mission statement in motivational terms from a customer, staff and other key audience point of view.

If the company is expressing its vision in terms of leadership then there should be clarity over what it means by leadership and how it will be measured. Leadership could mean many things. To some it is biggest in the market, to others it means having the best performing products. To others it means most innovative or available, highest brand awareness and so on.

In his book *Hidden Champions* Helmut Simon gave an interesting analysis of a group of German *mittlestand* (mid-sized private) companies who had defined their markets very tightly in terms of product and had been able to build world leading positions in terms of quality of products, market share and profitability as a result of this focus. Their pragmatic approach to developing a vision and their absolute conviction to organising themselves to achieve it was in his view a key to their success.

Interestingly a highly successful company which has an entirely different approach to this is Microsoft, whose stated mission is far more social in nature and doesn't mention the word leadership. Their current mission is:

> 'To enable people and businesses throughout the world to realize their full potential'

Another highly successful business in a different sector, Southwest Airlines has the following mission statement

> 'dedication to the highest quality of customer service delivered with a sense of warmth, friendliness, individual pride, and company spirit.'

Neither of these two businesses are lacking in commercial zeal and these statements should not be taken as if both organisations are charities.

A new vision statement can be used to re-energise a company and galvanise its staff if it has been through a period of difficulty or has previously had a confused direction. One of the most successful demonstrations of this was the 'World's favourite airline' vision used to reenergise British Airways in the 1980s.

With regard to developing strategic options as has been said, the chief executive and his executive colleagues are responsible for developing a recommended strategy and a small number of credible alternatives for the board to consider as a whole.

Most businesses choose the mechanism of an annual strategic plan as a way of providing a focal point for producing a comprehensive and up-to-date analysis and confirming or revising their vision. This process is often also intended as a way of involving and obtaining buy-in from people within the business. It is important for the non-executive to understand and feel comfortable with the key assumptions upon which the recommendations of the executive are based.

It is normal if the company hits difficulty or a new chief executive is brought in from outside that a strategic review outside the regular cycle will take place. This may be done with the assistance of a firm of strategy consultants. If this is the case the non-executive needs to be comfortable that a rigorous selection process has taken place, that there is clarity over the role of the consultants and that their work is appropriately priced and monitored. The reasons for choosing to solicit external help should also be clear. Knowledge, expertise, process skills and resource are the usual reasons for a firm being brought in to assist.

## Choice: making a judgement                                    7.12

How do boards select which strategy to adopt? If they have been through the stages described above then there will have been a recommendation put forward by the chief executive which they will have had prior input.

In Gordon Donaldson's Strategic Audit article in the Harvard Business Review he put forward the idea, somewhat cynically, that boards in the US normally only really get involved in strategy when

> 'there is a retirement of CEO, a precipitous fall in profitability or an unsolicited takeover attempt.'

Believing that the strategy of the business is fundamental to the building or destruction of shareholder value he advocates the creation of a strategic audit committee for larger corporations. Strategic audit committees are rare even in the US and most boards determine strategy through the conventional approach of preparing a plan and then having an awayday to allow sufficient time to discuss it ahead of formal approval at a subsequent board meeting.

A traditional board meeting where there are other items on the agenda is a difficult environment for a rigorous strategic debate. It is essential if an awayday approach is to be taken that its purpose is clear and that there is significant preparatory work undertaken to ensure that the board's time is used to maximum effect on the day.Tips for holding awaydays are contained in **PARAGRAPH 3.19**.

It is important that the board is united behind the strategy chosen even if there have been differences of view in developing it. Fundamental differences of view over the future strategic direction may mean that a non-executive feels they ought to resign.

In reaching the point of being able to agree to a certain strategy the board will have considered the feasibility of execution and the implications in terms of resources, financial and human in particular. Therefore at this stage in the process the non-executive just has to be satisfied that there is a good process under development for turning the strategy into action.

## Execution                                                7.13

From the non-executive's point of view this is very straightforward as the task for executing the board's chosen strategy falls to the chief executive and the executive directors. It might be, especially in smaller businesses, that he or she is asked to support certain elements. This is normally though with regard to shareholder issues or key appointments rather than operational detail.

The board's role is to ensure that there is good process for developing strategy, choosing the strategy to be adopted and ensuring that the CEO has the best chance of leading its successful execution.

A critical element of execution is the communication of the strategy internally and externally. Alignment of these is essential. The strategy should be able to be articulated in a few key bullet points and easily memorable. Leading companies will tend to test whether the strategy is well understood and agreed with when they are undertaking staff and investor surveys.

With regard to monitoring strategy there are a number of key questions for the non-executive to address and these are:

- How will the board monitor progress against the agreed strategy?
- What measures is the board using to know what effect the strategy is having on shareholder value?
- How will the board be sufficiently informed as to know when the strategy should be adapted?

Critical to this will be monitoring the key assumptions central to the strategy. In order to do this the non-executive needs to be on top of the relevant performance data. If the company has its own market intelligence capability this is an easier task. If not then published information or specific analyses will be required.

If the strategy is wrong then the sooner it is recognised and corrective action is taken the better. This does however often mean a credibility issue for the leadership of the company and this is why sometimes there is a longer gap between recognition and action than there should be. It is a very important aspect of the non-executive's role to be alive to this issue especially when they themselves have endorsed the strategy in the first place.

# 8. Directors' Duties and Liabilities

## General duties                                                          8.1

## At a glance                                                             8.2

- The general rules on the role and duties of a company director are set out in common law and complex case law.
- As part of the current modernisation of company law, the Government is proposing to introduce a statutory statement of the general principles by which all directors are bound.
- A company director has fiduciary duties to the company (as a separate legal entity) and to its members as a whole, in addition to various legal responsibilities that apply to anyone running a business.
- A director must act in accordance with the company's constitution and in the way most likely to promote the success of the company for the benefit of the members as a whole.
- A director may not delegate his/her powers and must maintain independence of judgement.
- A director must exercise appropriate care, skill and diligence.
- A director should not enter into a transaction involving a personal interest unless he/she has disclosed that interest as required by company law.
- A director or former director must not use company property or information for his/her own benefit unless such use has been properly authorised.

- A director or former director must not accept any benefit conferred by a third party unless acceptance has been properly authorised, or the benefit is necessarily incidental to the proper performance of his/her role as director.
- A company is permitted to provide indemnity insurance for its directors.

## *Statutory position* 8.3

The general rules on the role and duties of a company director are laid out not in companies' legislation itself but in complex and often inaccessible case law developed over many years. This can make it difficult for directors, especially those in smaller companies, to gain a good understanding of their overall responsibilities. The steering group responsible for the current review of company law has therefore proposed the introduction of a statutory statement of principles on directors' general duties. The Government White Paper *Modernising Company Law* issued in July 2002 confirms the intention to adopt this approach and includes a draft Schedule setting out the principles which directors will be expected to follow (see **8.6** below). The steering group suggested that the statement of directors' duties should also be given on Form 288a so that each director acknowledged his/her understanding of the role when signing to confirm acceptance of the appointment. However, the Government concluded that this might give a false impression that it was a comprehensive statement of directors' responsibilities, and also noted that the duties will apply, regardless of whether the director signs an acknowledgement of them. The White Paper therefore proposes that Companies House should instead send a general information leaflet to all new directors. It is envisaged that there will be at least two versions of the leaflet (for private and public companies respectively), and that these will summarise all the duties and responsibilities imposed on directors by companies legislation and insolvency law.

## *General legal responsibilities* 8.4

A variety of legal responsibilities apply to the directors of a company in the same way as to anyone else involved in running a business (eg as a partner or sole trader) – for instance, the duty to comply with law and regulations in respect of employment, health and safety, public liability, consumer protection, VAT, excise duties and other taxes.

## *Fiduciary duty* 8.5

The position of a company director is, however, very different to that of someone running a business in partnership or as a sole trader, in that he/she is in a position of trust and consequently has a fiduciary duty both to the company (as a separate legal entity) and to the members who have invested in the company. This is a wide-ranging responsibility, but the main elements may be summarised as follows:

- the directors must comply with the company constitution and use their powers under it for proper purposes;
- the directors must run the company for the benefit of the members as a whole;
- the directors must always act in the interest of the company as a whole, and not for the benefit of an individual shareholder or creditor;
- the directors should act fairly as between members;
- a director should not profit personally from his/her position within the company and should avoid any conflict of interest - where a potential conflict of interest arises, the director has a duty to declare his/her personal interest to the company;
- a director has an obligation to perform his/her duties with reasonable skill and care and must maintain independence of judgement.

## *Proposed statement of principles* 8.6

The recent company law review recommended that a statement of directors' duties should be incorporated into company law, the intention being to clarify the present position by making the details more accessible and understandable, rather than to make significant changes to current law and practice. The Government White Paper *Modernising Company Law* issued in July 2002 includes for comment a draft clause and a draft Schedule setting out the general principles by which company directors are bound. The principles are set out under the following headings:

- Obeying the constitution and other lawful decisions;
- Promotion of company's objectives;
- Delegation and independence of judgement;
- Care, skill and diligence;
- Transactions involving conflict of interest;
- Personal use of the company's property, information or opportunity; and
- Benefits from third parties.

If the legislation is finalised as it stands, directors will have a duty to comply with all of the principles set out in the Schedule, and former directors will have a continuing duty to comply with the principles in the final two sections.

The company law review had also recommended the inclusion of special duties that would come into effect when a director knew, or should know, that the company was likely to be unable to meet its debts as they fall due, or that there was no reasonable prospect of the company avoiding going into insolvent liquidation. The Government has concluded that this would be a very finely balanced judgement and that the fear of personal liability might lead to excessive caution. It does not, therefore, propose to incorporate any aspects of insolvency law into the statutory statement of directors' duties, although attention will be drawn to the requirements of insolvency law in the guidance document for new directors (see **8.3** above).

*Directors' Duties and Liabilities*

## Constitution and law 8.7

Directors have an obligation to act in accordance with the company's constitution and with decisions taken under that constitution, and must exercise their powers for the proper purpose.

## Promotion of the company's objectives 8.8

A director must act honestly and in good faith, and in the way that will be most likely to promote the success of the company for the benefit of its members as a whole. In reaching decisions, he/she must also take account of all the material factors that it is practicable to identify. The guidance in the draft legislation notes that this includes:

- the likely consequences in both the short and the long term, so far as a person of care and skill would consider them relevant; and
- all other factors that a person of care and skill would consider relevant, including the need for the company to:
  - foster business relationships with its employees, suppliers and customers;
  - consider the impact of its operations on the community and the environment;
  - maintain a reputation for high standards of business conduct; and
  - achieve outcomes that are fair between members.

## Delegation and independence of judgement 8.9

A director must not delegate any of his/her powers unless authorised to do so by the company's constitution or by a decision taken under that constitution. Directors must also maintain their independence of judgement and should not commit themselves to act in accordance with the wishes of another party. However, the guidance notes that a director who has entered into an agreement which restricts his/her power to exercise independent judgement is not prevented from acting in accordance with the agreement where to do so is:

- appropriate, in his/her independent judgement; and
- in accordance with the other general principles set out in the draft Schedule.

## Care, skill and diligence 8.10

A director must exercise the care, skill and diligence which would be exercised by a reasonably diligent person with both:

- the knowledge, skill and experience which may reasonably be expected of a director in his position; and
- any additional knowledge, skill and experience which he/she has.

## *Conflict of interest*     **8.11**

A director should not authorise, permit or arrange for the company to enter into a transaction in which he/she has a personal interest unless that interest has been disclosed in accordance with company law. For instance, the company's constitution may permit directors to have a personal interest in company transactions provided that the interest is disclosed to the other directors. Similarly, a director should not enter directly into a transaction with the company unless that interest has been appropriately disclosed.

## *Personal use of company assets*     **8.12**

A director should not receive any personal benefit as a result of his/her position as a director of the company. A director or former director must therefore not use for his/her own benefit, or for the benefit of another party, any property or information of the company, or any opportunities of the company of which he/she became aware whilst performing the role of director, unless:

- that use has been proposed to the company and agreed by ordinary resolution; or
- in the case of a private company, that use has been proposed to and authorised by the board and nothing in the company's constitution invalidates that authorisation; or
- in the case of a public company, the constitution includes a provision enabling the board to authorise such use, and the use has been proposed to and authorised by the board in accordance with the constitution.

The draft guidance emphasises that, in this context, the board means the board of directors acting without the participation of the director concerned. It is also proposed that the requirements should not apply to a use to which the director has a right under a contract or other transaction which he/she has entered into with the company, or which he/she (as director) has authorised, permitted or arranged for the company to enter into.

## *Benefits from third parties*     **8.13**

The draft Schedule also prohibits a director or former director from accepting any benefit conferred as a result of his/her powers as director, or by way of reward for any exercise of those powers, unless the benefit is conferred by the company or:

- acceptance of the benefit has been proposed to the company and company has consented to it by ordinary resolution; or
- the benefit is necessarily incidental to the proper performance of any of his/her functions as director.

**Directors' Duties and Liabilities**

## *Indemnity and insurance for directors*      **8.14**

*Section 310* of *CA 1985* prevents a company from exempting a director or officer of the company from, or indemnifying him/her against, any liability in respect of negligence, default, breach of duty or breach of trust. However, the company is permitted to provide insurance against such a liability and it can also indemnify a director or other officer against the cost of defending any proceedings in which judgement is given in his/her favour or in which he/she is acquitted. A company's articles of association will usually include a provision on indemnity for the directors and officers of the company in these circumstances, to prevent them having to meet any costs personally.

## More specific duties      **8.15**

## At a glance      **8.16**

---

- A director has a duty to give the company written notification of any interests that he/she holds in shares or debentures of the company or group, and of any changes in those interests.
- Directors and other employees must ensure that they do not infringe provisions on insider dealing when entering into transactions involving the company's shares and debentures.
- A director has an obligation to disclose to the other directors any personal interest in a contract, transaction or arrangement involving the company – this requirement extends to interests held by persons connected with the director.
- Directors have a duty to provide appropriate information and explanations to the auditors.
- Where a private company intends to act by means of a written resolution, the directors have a duty to arrange for a copy of the resolution to be sent to the auditors.
- Directors have a duty to keep proper accounting records and to prepare annual accounts for the company or group.
- Under insolvency law, a liquidator can apply to the court for a director or former director to contribute personally to the company's assets if he/she knew, or should have known, that there was no prospect of the company avoiding going into insolvent liquidation.
- Any person who is knowingly a party to a company carrying on business for any fraudulent purpose, including an intent to defraud creditors, is guilty of an offence.

---

## *Disclosure of interests in shares and debentures*      **8.17**

Under *section 324* of *CA 1985*, each director and shadow director has a duty to give written notification to the company of any interest that he/she holds in the shares or debentures of the company or group, and the company is obliged to record these in a register of directors' interests which must be available for public inspection. The definition of 'interests' for this purpose is very wide and is specifically extended by *section 328* of *CA 1985* to include interests held by the director's immediate family (ie spouse and children/step-children under the age of 18). All interests, and any subsequent changes, must be notified to the company within 5 days of the interest arising or changing. Failure to comply with the requirements can result in imprisonment, or a fine, or both. Directors must take particular care when dealing in the company's shares and debentures that they do not infringe the rules on insider dealing set out in the *Criminal Justice Act 1993*. Directors and employees of listed companies should also comply with the Model Code that forms part of the the FSA Listing Rules, or with any more stringent requirements adopted by the company in relation to dealing in the company's listed securities (see **8.51** below).

## *Disclosure of interests in contracts*     **8.18**

Under *section 317* of *CA 1985*, a director has an obligation to disclose at a meeting of the directors any interest (whether direct or indirect) that he/she has in a contract, transaction or arrangement entered into by the company, or which the company proposes to enter into. The disclosure requirement extends to the interests of a person connected with the director, including:

- the director's spouse and children (including stepchildren);
- a body corporate with which the director is associated;
- a trustee (acting in that capacity) of any trust which includes amongst the beneficiaries:
    - the director;
    - the director's spouse, children or stepchildren;
    - any body corporate with which he is associated;
    - a partner (acting in that capacity) of the director or of any person connected with him;
    - a Scottish firm in which the director, or a person connected with him, is a partner.

The requirement to disclose specifically includes any loans, quasi-loans and credit transactions between the company and the director (see **8.26** below). The director must make the disclosure at the first meeting at which the proposed contract, transaction or arrangement is discussed, or at the first meeting after the director, or a person connected with him/her, has acquired a disclosable interest in a contract, transaction or arrangement with the company. A shadow director is required to give written notice to the directors of a disclosable interest before the meeting at which disclosure would otherwise have been required. Directors are also permitted to give general notice that they are connected with a particular company or firm and are therefore to be regarded as interested in any contract, transaction or arrangement with that entity. Whether the director can participate in any discussion or vote on the contract, transaction or arrangement will depend on the detailed provisions in the company's articles of association. If a director fails to disclose a notifiable interest, he/she is liable to a fine and may be prevented from retaining any private profits earned as a result of that interest. The contract, transaction or arrangement may also become voidable by the company.

## Duty to assist auditors 8.19

*Section 389A* of *CA 1985* grants the auditors a right of access at all times to the company's books, accounts and vouchers and entitles them to require from the directors and other officers of the company the information and explanations that they consider necessary in order to perform their duties as auditors. It is an offence for a director or other officer knowingly or recklessly to make a statement to the auditors, either orally or in writing, which conveys (or purports to convey) information or explanations which the auditors are entitled to require and which is misleading, false or deceptive. A director or officer who commits such an offence is liable to imprisonment or a fine or both. The DTI document *Modern Company Law for a Competitive Economy: Final Report* issued in July 2001 recommends that this duty (and its criminal sanction) should be extended to all company employees, and that directors should have an additional duty to volunteer information to the auditors where, under the normal standards of skill and care, they recognise (or should recognise) that it is likely to be material to the audit. The Government White Paper, *Modernising Company Law*, confirms the intention to proceed with this.

## Use of written resolutions 8.20

Private companies are permitted by *section 381A* of *CA 1985* to act by means of a written resolution rather than by a resolution of the company in general meeting or by a resolution of a meeting of any class of members of the company. Under *section 381B* of *CA 1985*, a director or secretary of the company who knows that it is proposed to seek agreement by means of a written resolution, and who knows the terms of the resolution, has a duty to arrange for a copy of the resolution to be sent to the auditors at or before the time that it is sent to the members for signature. The auditors also have the right to receive all communications relating to a written resolution that must be supplied to a member of the company under *Schedule 15A* to *CA 1985*. There are penalties for failure to comply although it is a defence for a director or secretary to demonstrate that it was not practicable to comply or that there were reasonable grounds to believe that the auditors had been informed of the proposed resolution. The recent company law review has recommended certain simplifications of the procedures for written resolutions, including removal of this duty to send a copy to the auditors.

## Financial responsibilities 8.21

The duties of the directors in respect of the maintenance of accounting records and the preparation of an annual report and accounts (including the need to make a formal statement of their responsibilities in respect of the accounts) are considered in detail in **10 FINANCIAL REPORTING**.

## *Wrongful trading* 8.22

*Section 214* of the *Insolvency Act 1986* deals with the issue of wrongful trading. Where a company goes into insolvent liquidation, this section enables the liquidator to apply to the court for a person who is, or has been, a director of the company to contribute personally to the company's assets if he/she knew, or ought to have concluded, before the winding up of the company commenced that the company had no reasonable prospect of avoiding going into insolvent liquidation. The legislation makes no specific reference to trading whilst insolvent, and it may therefore be acceptable for a company that is technically insolvent to continue trading if the directors consider that there is a genuine prospect of the company avoiding insolvent liquidation by doing so. In considering this issue, the facts that a director is expected to know, the conclusions that he/she is expected to reach and the steps that he/she is expected to take are those that would be known, reached or taken by a reasonably diligent person with both the general knowledge, skill and experience that may reasonably be expected of a person fulfilling that function, and the general knowledge, skill and experience that the director in question actually has. A director will not be personally liable in this way if he/she can demonstrate that, on first realising that insolvent liquidation was unavoidable, they took every step to minimise the potential loss to the company's creditors. A director is therefore advised to ensure that the minutes of board meetings include an accurate record of any concerns that he/she expresses in respect of the company's solvency.

## *Fraudulent trading* 8.23

Under *section 458* of *CA 1985*, every person who is knowingly a party to a company carrying on business with the intent to defraud creditors or for any fraudulent purpose, regardless of whether the company is solvent or not, is liable to imprisonment, or a fine, or both. Fraudulent trading is also covered in *section 213* of the *Insolvency Act 1986*. In this case, a liquidator is able to apply to the court for a person who is, or has been, a director of the company to contribute personally to the company's assets if, in the opinion of the liquidator, the director was knowingly a party to carrying on the company's business with the intent to defraud creditors or for any fraudulent purpose. Intent to defraud can include the company incurring additional debts when the directors were aware that there was no realistic prospect of the existing creditors being paid.

## *Additional obligations in the case of listed companies* 8.24

The continuing obligations of a listed company are set out primarily in Chapter 9 of the UK Listing Rules, but reference may also need to be made to Chapters 10 to 16. Detailed guidance is also given in *The Continuing Obligations Guide* which forms Appendix 3 to the UKLA Guidance Manual. Both the UK Listing Rules and the UKLA Guidance Manual are available from the FSA website at www.fsa.gov.uk/ukla/. There is an overriding requirement that all shareholders should be treated equally and that all price sensitive information must be notified to the Regulatory Information Service without delay. The directors of a listed company also have an ongoing obligation to take all reasonable care that any published statement, forecast or other information is not misleading, false or deceptive, and that it does not omit any information that is likely to affect its import.

## Loans to directors                                                    8.25

## At a glance                                                           8.26

- *CA 1985* generally prohibits a company from making a loan to a director of the company or its holding company, and also from guaranteeing or providing security for such a loan.
- In the case of a relevant company (broadly a public company or any member of a group including a public company), the prohibition extends to certain other transactions and arrangements.
- For these purposes, 'director' includes a shadow director and any person occupying the position of director, regardless of his/her title.
- The provisions also extend to persons connected with a director.
- There are a number of specific exceptions to the general rules, principally covering small or short-term transactions and those carried out in the ordinary course of business.
- With minor exceptions, all loans, quasi-loans and credit transactions involving directors must be disclosed in the annual accounts, regardless of whether or not they are permitted under the legislation.
- If the required disclosures are not given, the auditors must give the information in their audit report, so far as they are reasonably able to do so.
- There is no specific requirement under *CA 1985* to disclose the legality of a transaction.
- It can be helpful to set up standard procedures to identify any illegal and disclosable transactions each year, and to keep them to a minimum.
- Loans and similar transactions involving other officers of the company must also be disclosed in the annual accounts.

### *General prohibition on loans to directors*                         8.27

*Section 330(2)* of *CA 1985* generally prohibits any company from:

- making a loan to a director of the company;
- making a loan to a director of the company's holding company;
- guaranteeing a loan to a director of the company or to a director of the company's holding company; or
- providing any security in connection with a loan to a director of the company or to a director of the company's holding company.

This is intended to provide a safeguard against the directors abusing their position within the company and using company assets for their personal benefit. Loans, quasi-loans and credit transactions are specifically included in the duty to disclose that is imposed on every director by *section 317* of *CA 1985* (see **8.18** above).

## *Additional prohibitions for relevant companies*     **8.28**

A relevant company is a public company, a subsidiary of a public company, a fellow subsidiary of a public company or the holding company of a public company. In the case of relevant companies the general prohibition on loans to directors extends to certain other transactions and arrangements. A relevant company is therefore also prohibited from:

- making a quasi-loan to a director of the company or to a director of the company's holding company, or to a person connected with any such director;
- guaranteeing a loan or quasi-loan, or providing any security in connection with a loan or quasi-loan to:
  - a director of the company, or a person connected with such a director; or
  - a director of the company's holding company, or a person connected with such a director;
- entering into a credit transaction as creditor for, or guaranteeing or providing security for a credit transaction made by any other person for:
  - a director of the company, or a person connected with such a director; or
  - a director of the company's holding company, or a person connected with such a director

## *Quasi-loans*     **8.29**

A quasi-loan is a transaction between two parties (the creditor and the borrower), where the creditor pays or agrees to pay a sum on behalf of the borrower, or reimburses or agrees to reimburse expenditure incurred by the borrower, on the terms that the borrower or a person on his behalf will reimburse the creditor, or in circumstances which create a liability for the borrower or person on his behalf to reimburse the creditor. The following are examples of quasi-loans:

- the purchase of any goods or services through the company, where the company becomes liable to pay the supplier and is subsequently reimbursed by the director;
- personal use of a company credit card by the director, where the company settles the liability and the director subsequently reimburses the company;
- a season ticket loan, if the company buys the ticket on behalf of the director and the director makes subsequent repayments, either in cash or by deduction from his salary;
- any personal costs paid by the company and subsequently reimbursed

by the director (eg travel costs for a spouse who accompanies the director on a business trip).

## Credit transactions                                    8.30

A credit transaction is a transaction under which one party (the creditor);

- supplies goods under a hire purchase agreement or a conditional sale agreement;
- sells land under a hire purchase agreement or a conditional sale agreement;
- leases or hires goods in return for periodical payments;
- leases or hires land in return for periodical payments;
- otherwise supplies goods or services on the understanding that payment is to be deferred; or
- otherwise disposes of land on the understanding that payment is to be deferred.

## Directors and connected persons                        8.31

For these purposes, a director includes a shadow director and any person occupying the position of director, regardless of his/her actual title. The following are to be treated as persons connected with a director:

- the director's spouse
- a child or step-child under the age of 18 (including an illegitimate child);
- a body corporate with which the director is associated, and where the director and his/her connected persons are:
  - interested in at least 20% of the nominal value of the equity share capital, or
  - entitled to exercise, or control the exercise of, more than 20% of the voting power at a general meeting;
- the trustee of any trust, where the beneficiaries include:
  - the director;
  - his/her spouse;
  - his/her child (as defined above); or
  - a body corporate with which he/she is associated (as defined above);
- the trustee of any trust whose terms confer on the trustees a power that may be exercised for the benefit of those noted (a person acting as trustee under an employee share scheme or a pension scheme is specifically excluded);
- a partner of the director or of any person connected with the director; or
- a Scottish firm in which the director, or any person connected with him/her, is a partner or which has as a partner another Scottish firm in which the director, or a person connected with him/her, is a partner.

A person who is a director of the same company in his/her own right is not treated as a connected person of another director, even if the above criteria are met.

## Exceptions to the general prohibition                     8.32

There are a number of specific exceptions to the general prohibition on making, guaranteeing or securing loans and quasi-loans to, and credit transactions with, directors or persons connected with directors, the main ones being:

- short-term quasi-loans (*section 332* of *CA 1985*)
- inter-company loans or quasi-loans within the same group (*section 333* of *CA 1985*)
- loans of small amounts (*section 334* of *CA 1985*)
- minor transactions and transactions in the ordinary course of business (*section 335* of *CA 1985*)
- transactions at the behest of the holding company (*section 336* of *CA 1985*)
- funding of expenditure incurred in the performance of duties as a director of the company (*section 337* of *CA 1985*)

Special rules also apply in the case of banks and money-lending companies.

## Disclosure of loans to directors                          8.33

With a small number of specific exceptions, all loans and quasi-loans to, and credit transactions with, directors are disclosable in the annual accounts under *section 232* of, and *Schedule 6* to, *CA 1985* regardless of whether or not they are permitted under the legislation. The disclosure requirements specifically include any related guarantees and securities and must cover all transactions involving anyone who was:

- a director of the company at any time during the financial year;
- a director of the company's holding company at any time during the financial year; or
- a person connected with any such a director.

Under *paragraph 19* of *Schedule 6* to *CA 1985*, the fact that a transaction may have originated before an individual became a director of the company (or before a company became a subsidiary) will not exempt it from disclosure if there was an amount outstanding under that transaction during the year. For example, if an employee receives a loan from the company at the beginning of the year and repays it when he is appointed as a director of the company later in the the year, details of the loan will still be disclosable in the accounts for that year. Similar considerations apply when individuals become connected persons during the year. Under *section 237(4)* of *CA 1985*, if the disclosure requirements have not been complied with, the auditors must include the relevant details in their audit report, so far as they are reasonably able to do so.

## Exceptions to disclosure requirement     8.34

There is no requirement to disclose a transaction or arrangement which was not entered into during the year and did not exist at any time during the year (ie transactions entered into and settled in earlier years do not continue to be disclosable). Also, credit transactions and related guarantees, securities and arrangements are not disclosable if the aggregate of the values of each transaction or arrangement for that director and his/her connected persons, after allowing for any reduction of the liabilities, does not exceed £5,000. Therefore, if an individual director, together with any connected persons, does not have more than £5,000 outstanding in respect of credit transactions, the details do not have to be disclosed. There is no *de minimis* disclosure exemption in respect of loans and quasi-loans to directors and connected persons.

## No requirement to disclose legality     8.35

There is no requirement under *CA 1985* for the accounts to disclose whether a particular transaction or arrangement between a director and the company is legal or not. There is similarly no requirement for the auditors to express an opinion on the legality of any items disclosed in their audit report as a result of *section 237(4)* – they are simply required to make good any deficiencies in the disclosures required by *CA 1985*.

## Company procedures     8.36

Companies may find it helpful to develop a standard form for completion each year which requires every director to give formal confirmation that he/she has not been involved in any illegal or disclosable transactions or arrangements with the company, or to provide the relevant information. Such a form could include a summary of the requirements of the *CA 1985* to remind the director of the importance of these matters. Company procedures might also include detailed guidance in the form of a directors' code of conduct to ensure that disclosable transactions are kept to a minimum. For instance, clear rules on the way in which company credit cards are to be used and how any purchases through the company should be dealt with, may help to ensure that disclosable transactions do not arise (eg if purchases through the company are paid for by the director when the order is raised, the transaction should not come within the definition of a quasi-loan).

## Loans to other officers of the company     8.37

A company must also disclose in its annual accounts details of loans and similar transactions involving other officers of the company. Once again, there are separate rules in respect of banks and money-lending companies. There are, however, no prohibitions on making loans to officers of the company, provided that the individuals are not also directors. The detailed disclosure requirements are set out in *Part III* of *Schedule 6* to the *CA 1985*. All definitions are the same as those for loans to and similar transactions with directors. There is also a similar requirement for the auditors to give any missing disclosures in their audit report, so far as they are reasonably able to do so.

## Other transactions with directors                8.38

## At a glance                                      8.39

---

- *CA 1985* requires the annual accounts to include details of any transaction or arrangement in which a director had a material interest, either directly or indirectly.
- The board must act in good faith in deciding whether or not an interest is material for disclosure purposes.
- FRS 8 *Related Party Disclosures* also includes guidance on when a transaction should be regarded as material.
- The required details must be given individually for each director and for each relevant transaction or arrangement in the current year.
- If the required disclosures are not given, the auditors must give the information in their audit report, so far as they are reasonably able to do so.
- *CA 1985* sets out a number of exceptions to the general disclosure requirements, principally in respect of transactions between group companies and those involving only small amounts.
- Additional information may need to be given in respect of some transactions with directors, under the disclosure requirements of FRS 8 *Related Party Disclosures*.
- In the case of a listed company, a transaction that involves a related party will usually require both an announcement to the market and a circular to shareholders seeking their approval.

---

*Directors' Duties and Liabilities*

### *Disclosure of transactions*                    8.40

In addition to the detailed disclosures required for loans to directors, *CA 1985* also requires disclosure in the annual accounts of any transaction or arrangement in which a director had a material interest, either directly or indirectly. For these purposes, a director is treated as being interested in any transaction between:

- the company and the director, or a person connected with him/her, or
- the company's holding company and the director, or a person connected with him/her.

Only those transactions in which a director has a material interest are disclosable in the accounts and the interpretation of what constitutes a material interest is one of the most difficult aspects of this legislation. **8.14** above considers in more detail the duty of each director to disclose to the other directors any interest that he has in a contract, arrangement or agreement involving the company. A substantial property transaction between the company and a director may also require prior shareholder approval under *section 320* of *CA 1985*.

## *Materiality* 8.41

*Paragraph 17(2)* of *Schedule 6* to *CA 1985* provides that an interest is not material for disclosure purposes if the board of directors of the company are of the opinion that it is not material. It is generally accepted that the board must act in good faith in reaching this decision, although the legislation makes no specific statement on this. In this context, the board is defined as 'the directors of the company preparing the accounts, or a majority of those directors, but excluding in either case the director whose interest it is.' Therefore, the director involved in the transaction must not take part in the board's decision on whether or not it is material for disclosure purposes. *CA 1985* makes no mention of recording the board's decision, but it is usually advisable for the board's discussion and decision to be formally minuted. Two approaches to the interpretation of 'material' have developed:

- the relevant view – a transaction is material if knowledge of it might influence the decisions taken by the shareholders or users of the accounts, or be of specific interest to them; and
- the substantive view – a transaction is material if the director's interest in it is substantial, even though the transaction itself may be small.

One of the major problems with the substantive view is that a small interest in a major contract could be considered insubstantial and therefore not material (eg a commission of 1% payable to a director on a company contract worth £1 million), whereas many people would consider that this is precisely the sort of arrangement that the shareholders would probably want to know about. The balance has tended, therefore, to favour the relevant view, but if there is any doubt over whether a transaction involving a director, or a person connected with him/her, is one in which the director has a material interest, legal advice should be taken.

## *FRS 8 approach to materiality* 8.42

The ASB also adopted the relevant view in FRS 8 *Related party disclosures* but preserved some element of the substantial view in respect of transactions involving directors:

> 'Transactions are material when their disclosure might reasonably be expected to influence decisions made by users of general purpose financial statements. The materiality of related party transactions is to be judged, not only in terms of their significance to the reporting entity, but also in relation to the other related party when that party is:
>
> (*a*)   a director, key manager or other individual in a position to

influence, or accountable for stewardship of, the reporting entity; or

(b)     a member of the close family of any individual mentioned above; or

(c)     an entity controlled by any individual mentioned in (a) or (b) above.'

## Detailed disclosures under CA 1985          8.43

Where a director has a material interest in a transaction, the following information must be given in the notes to the accounts:

- a statement that the transaction or arrangement was made or existed during the year;
- the name of the director who has a material interest in the transaction and the nature of that interest;
- where relevant the name of the connected person involved in the transaction and the name of the director with whom he/she is connected;
- the value of the transaction or arrangement; and
- the principal terms of the transaction or arrangement (for instance, the rate of commission earned by the director in respect of a contract involving the company).

These details must be given individually for each relevant transaction during the year but comparatives for the previous year are not required. If the disclosure requirements have not been complied with, the auditors are required to include the relevant details in their audit report, so far as they are reasonably able to do so.

## Value of a transaction or arrangement          8.44

The value of a transaction or arrangement is the price that could reasonably be expected to be obtained for the respective goods, services or land if they had been supplied in the ordinary course of business and on the same terms (apart from price) as they are supplied in the transaction under consideration – in other words, the price that would normally be obtained in an arm's length transaction. If the value of any transaction or arrangement cannot be expressed as a specific sum of money, for whatever reason, its value is deemed to exceed £100,000.

## Exceptions to the general disclosure requirement          8.45

CA 1985 sets out the following exceptions to the general disclosure requirements:

- a transaction between two companies does not need to be disclosed if the director's interest in the contract arises only from the fact that he is a director of both of the companies involved in the transaction;
- a contract of service between the company and director of the company,

a director of the company's holding company, or a director of any of the company's subsidiaries does not require disclosure under these provisions of *CA 1985*;

- there is no requirement to disclose a transaction or arrangement which was not entered into during the year and did not exist at any time during the year (ie transactions entered into and settled in earlier years do not continue to be disclosable);
- an arm's length transaction between companies in the same group does not require disclosure under these provisions;
- disclosure of a transaction between group companies should only be necessary where the company has minority interests (although the wording of this part of the legislation is ambiguous); and
- disclosure is not required where the value of disclosable transactions or arrangements involving the director, including any outstanding amounts from previous years, did not at any time during the financial year exceed in aggregate £1,000 or, if more, did not exceed the lower of £5,000 or 1% of the company's net assets at the end of the financial year – for this purpose, a company's net assets are the aggregate of its assets, less the aggregate of its liabilities, including any provisions for liabilities and charges.

## *FRS 8 disclosure requirements*                                      **8.46**

FRS 8 *Related party disclosures* requires detailed disclosures to be given in respect of material related party transactions (which include transactions with directors). In the case of transactions with directors, some of these duplicate the disclosure requirements of *CA 1985*, but others may require additional information to be given in certain cases. The ASB issued FRED 25 *Related Party Disclosures* in May 2002 as part of its project to achieve convergence between UK accounting standards and international accounting standards. The Exposure Draft proposes replacing FRS 8 with requirements based on the revised IAS 24, although retaining the present UK requirement for an entity's controlling party to be named.

## *Additional requirements for listed companies*           **8.47**

In the case of a listed company, a transaction that involves a related party (eg a transaction between the company or its subsidiary and a director or substantial shareholder or their associate) will usually require both an announcement to the market and a circular to shareholders seeking their approval. Very small transactions are generally exempt from these requirements, although details must be provided in writing to the UKLA before the transaction takes place, together with:

- confirmation from an acceptable independent advisor that the terms of the transaction are fair and reasonable; and
- an undertaking to give details of the transaction in next annual report and accounts.

The definition of a related party for these purposes is complex and companies should therefore consult their professional advisers and the UKLA to clarify the precise requirements in each case.

## Share dealings by directors of listed companies 8.48

## At a glance 8.49

---

- A listed company must notify the Regulatory Information Service without delay of any dealings in the company's shares, or any grant of share options, involving a director or persons connected with them.
- The directors of a listed company are expected to comply with a company Code on share dealing that is no less exacting than the Model Code appended to the UK Listing Rules.
- Directors and relevant employees must not deal in the company's shares without receiving clearance to do so from the chairman or another designated director.
- The company must keep a written record of all requests for clearance to deal, and of the responses given to those requests.
- Exceptions to the general rule are permitted in limited circumstances.
- Any failure to comply with the Model Code (or the company's equivalent) must be notified to the UKLA.

---

### *Notification to the Regulatory Information Service* 8.50

The continuing obligations of a listed company are set out primarily in Chapter 9 of the UK Listing Rules. Detailed guidance is also given in *The Continuing Obligations Guide* which forms Appendix 3 to the UKLA Guidance Manual. Both the UK Listing Rules and the UKLA Guidance Manual are available from the FSA website at www.fsa.gov.uk/ukla/ . As part of its continuing obligations, a listed company must notify the Regulatory Information Service without delay of:

- any dealings in the company's shares by directors (and persons connected with them) notified to the company under *sections 324* to *328* of *CA 1985* (see **8.17** above); and
- any grant of options to a director or a person connected with him.

### *Compliance with the Model Code* 8.51

The Model Code is appended to Chapter 16 of the UK Listing Rules and is designed to ensure that directors and certain other relevant employees, and persons connected with them, do not deal in the company's securities when they may be in possession of unpublished price sensitive information. Listed companies must require their directors and other relevant employees to comply with a Code on share dealings that is no less exacting than the Model Code and are free to impose more stringent requirements if they wish. The company's list of relevant employees for this purposes may change, depending on what is happening in company – for instance, there may be a small group of people who are permanently on the list and a larger group who are added or deleted depending on the nature of any unpublished price sensitive information at a particular point in time. Directors and relevant employees must not deal in the company's shares without receiving clearance to do so from the chairman or another designated director. Clearance cannot be given if there is any unpublished price sensitive information, even if the individual director or employee is not aware of that information. The company must keep a written record of all requests for clearance to deal, and of the responses given to those requests. If permission to deal is granted, it is recommended that only a short period is allowed for the dealing to take place (eg 24 hours) and that there is a requirement to reconfirm the clearance if there is any delay beyond this.

### *Exceptions in limited circumstances* 8.52

Paragraph 20 of the Model Code lists the dealings which are not subject to the Code and which can therefore take place at any time without prior clearance. In certain circumstances, grants of share options may be permitted during a prohibited period and the exercise of options during such a period may also be allowed in limited circumstances, but sale of the resulting securities will generally not be permitted. Permission to sell, but not to buy, may also be given in exceptional circumstances – the Model Code gives as an example a pressing personal financial commitment that cannot otherwise be satisfied. Directors may also be given permission to acquire qualification shares in certain circumstances.

### *Breaches of the the Code* 8.53

Any failure to comply with the Model Code (or the company's equivalent) must be notified to the UKLA as soon as possible. The UKLA will also contact the company if it becomes aware of an unnotified breach, to request an explanation. The UKLA may take disciplinary action and may require notification of the circumstances of the breach to the Regulatory Information Service.

# 9. Directors' Remuneration and Benefits

## At a glance                                                                9.1

- Directors' remuneration – issues for the non-executive director
- Share options
- Disclosure of directors' remuneration
- The directors' remuneration report
- Directors' service contracts
- Appendix 1: Contents of the directors' remuneration report
- Appendix 2: Example of director's service contract

## Directors' remuneration                                                    9.2

Before getting into the detail of what has become a very complex and sensitive subject, it is important from the non-executive director's point of view to consider the following, whether they are on the remuneration committee or not.

- What are the objectives?
  - there should be an overarching objective to build shareholder value;
  - there should be an alignment of the remuneration schemes and the performance objectives of the company; and
  - remuneration schemes for directors should be to attract and retain relevant talent.

- What principles should the board apply in designing and implementing the directors' remuneration?
  - Be market driven.
  - Be commercial and fair.
  - Comply with legal and accounting standards.
  - Avoid unnecessary complexity.
  - Be tax efficient for company and director.
- What is the process by which the board makes the key decisions with relation to directors' remuneration?
  - The board process
  - A process for ensuring legal compliance
  - Accounting compliance
  - Investor approval and
  - Ensuring the engagement of the key participants
- How will directors' remuneration issues be communicated?
  - Internally; and
  - Externally

Increasing complexity in the instruments used to reward directors combined with higher levels of disclosure on directors' remuneration, a perception of a widening gap between director and non-director remuneration and a greater degree of investor and media scrutiny have made this subject a considerable challenge for non-executive directors.

It is therefore very important that the non-executive keeps up-to-date with the latest trends, best practice and debate on the subject. A good example of the importance of this, and one covered in detail below, would be the level of knowledge required to contribute to a debate on the implications of the latest proposals on accounting for payments made in the form of shares.

The key driver of process in this area should be the remuneration committee, supported if appropriate by professional consultants. **CHAPTER 18 REMUNERATION COMMITTEES** covers this in considerably more detail.

Disclosure appears to have become a bigger and bigger issue each year and is covered in detail below. The number of pages given over to the disclosure on directors' remuneration in many companies now exceeds that used to describe the activities of the business.

One particular aspect of directors' remuneration which has been the subject of considerable debate in the last few years has been share options.

## Share options                                                                  9.3

The strong performance of capital markets and high merger and acquisition activity of the late 1990s led to an environment where for many directors share options became their largest assets. This was at its most extreme in the US, and in particular Silicon Valley, but flowed over into companies in a wide range of sectors across the world.

The following extract from *Directors Dilemmas* which was published at the very beginning of 2000 prior to the crash captures the issues well and recognises the trouble ahead.

---

## The stock option dilemma 9.4

'Stock options have been described as the best way of aligning shareholder and employee interests. They have also been used enthusiastically in many early stage businesses as a component of salary because they don't consume cash. Their growth has been extraordinary and they have generated significant capital wealth and a sense of ownership among groups who were unlikely to experience it any other way. Just look at the impact on the housing market in Northern California. Their 'Heads you win, tails you don't lose' quality has made them extremely popular with those receiving them. No downside, only opportunity cost has proven easy to sell.

However there has been some questioning in the Wall Street Journal and elsewhere about their effectiveness in their spiritual home, the United States. The concern is that contrary to their objective, they are in fact causing job-hopping and short-termism. The high technology companies in Silicon Valley are given as an example. Young avaricious technologists have been job hopping from company to company on the basis of where is likely to show the highest stock appreciation, cashing in their chips when there has been significant growth and moving on quickly. I really don't think such practice is common and I haven't observed it myself but it is an interesting thought.

One other share option myth is that they are free to the company. Sure they don't consume the business's cash. They do however result in dilution for shareholders. A good scheme is one that has been carefully considered with regard to the basis of their grant, their pricing and the manner in which they can be exercised. It is also likely to have performance hurdles that must be met before any exercise can take place.

Realistically, the growth in value may come more from timing, the growth in the stock market and the contribution of others than the individual's own contribution. A scheme may confuse brilliance with a buoyant stock market. In this way they are aligned with shareholders!'

---

*Directors Dilemmas* also contains five case studies on directors remuneration issues including the repricing of options, determining the level and pricing of equity incentives.bonuses relating to takeover bids and so on.

## The debate on accounting for share options 9.5

The recent debate really has its origins in the US. In 1991 the Financial Accounting Standards Board (FASB) floated a draft of a proposed new accounting standard. FASB felt that there wasn't 'a level playing field in the reporting of management incentive compensation'. It contrasted the treatment of cash bonuses with options. Companies that rewarded management with cash bonuses were required to report a compensation expense for the amount of the bonus paid, thereby reducing net income. Companies that rewarded management with stock options did not have a comparable reduction in net income. FASB's proposal was that, at the time a company awarded a stock option to an employee, it record an expense for the 'fair value of the option'. It did not give guidance as to how the fair value should be calculated but the implication was that the most commonly used method at the time, the Black-Scholes Option Pricing Model, would be what people would use.

A simple explanation of this is to consider that if the company sold the option in the public market, it would receive a cash payment from the buyer. By giving the option to the employee, the company was foregoing the cash it would receive if it sold the option. FASB proposed that the 'fair value' of the option, as determined by the Black-Scholes Model, or some other valuation model, should therefore be recorded as an expense.

There was a strong adverse reaction to the FASB suggestion. Essentially companies argued that employee stock options were important incentives and lobbied hard to get FASB to back down. This they effectively did by reducing the suggestion to simply one of disclosure of the effect.

The dramatic falls in capital markets and the high profile failures of several companies whose directors were alleged to have inflated profits to increase the value of their options led to a reopening of the debate in the US and in the UK.

There are several issues.

- Does expensing a share option at the time of award really provide a level playing field in accounting for remuneration?
- What will be the impact on the use of share option schemes?
- Will expensing improve corporate governance?

The arguments for and against go as follows.

**For:**

- Financial accounts should present a 'true and fair' view of a company's financial performance and financial position. Where payment for services (or more exceptionally, for goods) is made in the form of shares or share options, standard setters argue that there is an undeniable expense that should be recognised in the accounts.
- Expensing options provides a level playing field so that companies using cash bonuses and companies using stock options will be treated in the same way.
- It will improve corporate governance by reducing or eliminating incentives to inflate income, earnings per share or other measures.

**Against:**

- Regarding improved corporate governance, some would argue that unscrupulous directors will not be deterred simply by the expensing of options.
- Expensing options is just an accounting matter and has no cash impact. It is very likely that analysts will remove the option expense from the income statement to obtain a clear view of the company's performance. This may then lead to companies including a pro forma income statement which excluded the option expense.
- Wider employee share option schemes are likely to be the main victim of this move, reducing both motivation and focus on shareholder value.
- There are alternatives such as caps on the amount of options granted to board members.

The standard setters in most countries appear to be in agreement that executive and employee share packages should be charged as an expense. This is despite considerable lobbying from companies against the move. The UK Accounting Standards Board (ASB) published FRED 31 'Share-based Payment' in November 2002. This sets out proposals for a UK accounting standard based on the International Accounting Standards Board's (IASB's) exposure draft ED 2 which was published simultaneously. The draft standard is based on the principle that when a company receives services or goods in exchange for a share-based payment, it should recognise an expense (based on fair value) over the period in which the services are rendered or as the goods are received. The standard is intended to apply to all UK entities (both listed and unlisted) and to all share-based payment transactions, including employee share option schemes. The current proposal is that the new standard should come into effect for accounting periods beginning on or after 1 January 2004.

The collapse of investor confidence and the transparency of financial data are the capital markets' main priorities. If the choice is between mollifying concerned investors – by agreeing to recognise the cost of share options – and fighting against standard accounting practice, boards are likely to choose the former. Indeed in the US several influential people and companies have already adopted, or announce their intention to adopt, the approach.

Legendary investor Warren Buffett has been particularly vocal on the subject and Coca Cola, General Electric and several other leading US businesses have announced plans to expense options. In August 2002 the UK bank HSBC announced that it would become one of the first UK companies to do so. It also disclosed that expensing share options woul have cost over £80m in the first six months of 2002.

There is little published research into the wider impact this change will have. However it was reported in Financial Director magazine that the corporate governance consultancy Institutional Shareholder Services (ISS) revealed that at least ten of Britain's largest companies offer share option schemes so

*Directors' Remuneration and Benefits*

generous that they potentially account for more than 10% of their market value.

## Disclosure of directors' remuneration 9.6

## At a glance 9.7

---

- *CA 1985* requires detailed disclosures on directors' remuneration to be given in the notes to the accounts.
- Separate disclosure requirements apply for quoted and unquoted companies.
- Additional requirements also apply to listed companies under the FSA Listing Rules and the Combined Code.
- Aggregate disclosures must be given in respect of emoluments, contributions to defined contribution retirement schemes, share options, amounts payable under long-term incentive schemes and the number of directors accruing benefits under defined benefit retirement schemes.
- Slightly reduced disclosure requirements apply in the case of small companies.
- Additional aggregate information must be given by quoted and AIM companies.
- The auditors are required to include any missing information in their audit report.
- The money value of any benefits in kind must be included in emoluments.
- Bonus payments that require shareholder approval should normally be included in emoluments in the year in which they are approved.
- Details of directors' share options must also be given in the directors' report.
- Awards under long-term incentive schemes are disclosable when the director becomes entitled to receive payment.
- All pension schemes must be classified as either defined contribution or defined benefit for disclosure purposes.
- Amounts paid to, or receivable by, a person connected with a director must be included in the disclosures.
- Particular difficulties can arise in groups of companies, especially if all directors' remuneration is paid by the holding company.

---

## Disclosure under Companies Act 1985 9.8

A company's annual accounts must include detailed information on remuneration paid to, or receivable by, anyone who was a director during the year. The disclosure requirements cover all amounts receivable by the directors in respect of their services as directors of the company (and, where relevant, of its subsidiaries), regardless of who actually makes the payment. The legislation requires basic disclosures to be given by all companies, and then makes a clear distinction between quoted and unquoted companies in requiring more detailed information to be given. The requirements are broadly similar for accounting periods ending before 31 December 2002, although greater detail is required in the case of quoted companies, but the *Directors' Remuneration Report Regulations 2002 (SI 2002/1986)* introduce some significant changes to the disclosure requirements for quoted companies for accounting periods ending on or after 31 December 2002. For these purposes, a quoted company is defined as a company whose equity share capital is:

- included in the Official List of the London Stock Exchange;
- officially listed in an EEA State; or
- admitted to dealing on the New York Stock Exchange or the Nasdaq exchange.

## Basic accounts disclosures for all companies 9.9

The basic requirement is that every company should disclose in the notes to the accounts:

- the aggregate of the emoluments paid to, or receivable by, the directors in respect of their qualifying services (which include services as director of a subsidiary or in the management of the company or group);
- the aggregate value of any contributions paid by the company in respect of directors into a pension scheme where the benefits depend on the level of contributions paid (ie defined contribution schemes – see Chapter 18 Pension Arrangements for Employees);
- the number of directors who are accruing retirement benefits under money purchase schemes; and
- the number of directors who are accruing retirement benefits under defined benefit schemes.

The contributions made during the year to defined benefit retirement schemes do not have to be disclosed. Slightly reduced disclosure requirements apply in the case of small companies. Emoluments are defined in *CA 1985* as including salary, bonus, fees, benefits in kind, expense allowances (if these are chargeable to UK income tax) and amounts paid on acceptance of office as director. This list is not intended to be exhaustive and any other similar amounts paid to, or receivable by, directors will therefore be disclosable. Share options, pension contributions and amounts payable under long-term incentive schemes are specifically excluded from the definition of emoluments as they are subject to separate disclosure requirements.

## Quoted and AIM companies 9.10

In addition to the above aggregate information, quoted companies and those whose equity share capital is listed on the Alternative Investment Market (AIM) must disclose:

- the aggregate gains made by directors on the exercise of share options; and
- the aggregate of the amounts paid to, or receivable by, directors under long term incentive schemes in respect of qualifying services and the net value of any assets (other than cash or share options) receivable by directors under such schemes.

## Avoiding duplication                                      9.11

If any of the required details are readily ascertainable from other information included with the accounts, such as a remuneration report (see **9.18** below), they generally do not have to be disclosed again. The one exception is aggregate gains on the exercise of share options which must always be shown separately in the notes to the accounts. In practice, if the detailed information is included in a separate directors' remuneration report, it is helpful for the notes to the accounts to include a cross-reference to where it can be found.

## Audit requirements                                        9.12

If the accounts do not include all of the required disclosures in respect of directors' emoluments and other benefits, or transactions between the company and its directors or other officers, the auditors must include a statement of the missing details in their audit report, so far as they are reasonably able to do so. In the case of listed companies, the FSA has extended this requirement to cover disclosures required under the Listing Rules and it also applies to certain elements of the information that must be included in the directors' remuneration report (see **9.18** below).

## Benefits in kind                                          9.13

Emoluments specifically include the estimated money value of benefits in kind received by a director otherwise than in cash. The most common benefits in kind are:

- company car;
- free or subsidised accommodation;
- insurance for the benefit of the director (eg private health cover, indemnity insurance, personal accident cover);
- loans at preferential interest rates;
- relocation costs (unless the relocation is clearly for business purposes).

Some of these may also be disclosable in the annual accounts as loans or transactions with directors (see **8 DIRECTORS' DUTIES**). Share options are subject to separate disclosure requirements and are therefore specifically excluded from emoluments for disclosure purposes. The main difficulty with benefits in kind is establishing an appropriate and realistic money value for the benefit. In most cases, market value will provide the best estimate of money value.

## Bonus payments 9.14

Provision should usually be made in the accounts for bonuses in the year in which they are earned. Where a bonus payment to directors requires approval by the shareholders before the directors are entitled to receive it, it is usual to treat the bonus as being receivable by the directors (and therefore disclosable within directors' emoluments) in the year in which shareholder approval is given, even though the bonus may have been charged to the profit and loss account in an earlier period.

## Share options 9.15

In addition to the disclosures on share options referred to in 9.5 above, the directors' report (or the notes to the accounts) must give detailed information on directors' interests (including options) in the shares in or debentures of the company or any other body corporate in the same group. Interests include those held by the directors' close family. Certain exemptions apply in the case of wholly-owned subsidiaries. These disclosures are considered in more detail in **CHAPTER 10**. In the case of listed companies, extensive disclosures must also be given in the directors' remuneration report (see **9.18** below).

## Long-term incentive schemes 9.16

Under *CA 1985*, amounts payable under long-term incentive schemes are disclosable when they are paid to or receivable by the director. The director must therefore have the right to receive a sum before it becomes disclosable. Amounts should therefore normally be disclosed in the year in which the director becomes entitled to receive payment. In the case of a long-term incentive scheme, the director will not usually be entitled to receive payment until all the specified conditions have been met. Even though it will usually be necessary to accrue for the payments in each accounting year, these sums will not become disclosable until all the relevant conditions have been met and the director becomes entitled to receive payment. As with annual bonuses, this will not always match the actual timing of the payment. Complex schemes which extend over a number of years will sometimes include the provision of a guaranteed minimum payment to the directors once a specified target has been achieved. In this case, the guaranteed minimum payment will become disclosable in the year in which the target is achieved, as this is when the directors become entitled to the minimum payment. Further disclosures on long-term incentive schemes must be given in the directors' remuneration report (see **9.18** below).

## Pension arrangements 9.17

For the purposes of the *CA 1985* disclosures referred to in **PARAGRAPH 9.4** above, all pension schemes must be classified as either defined contribution or defined benefit schemes (see **CHAPTER 18 PENSION ARRANGEMENTS FOR EMPLOYEES**). Any death in service benefits are to be disregarded when classifying a pension scheme for disclosure purposes. A pension scheme under

Directors' Remuneration and Benefits

which a director will be entitled to receive both money purchase benefits and defined benefits is classified as a defined benefit scheme for disclosure purposes. Where a scheme provides for the director to receive money purchase benefits or defined benefits, whichever is the greater, the company is allowed to assume for disclosure purposes that the benefits will be whichever appears more likely at the end of the financial year in question. Listed companies must also given additional details on directors' pension arrangements in the directors' remuneration report.

## Payments to and from other parties      9.18

Amounts paid to or receivable by a person connected with a director or a body corporate controlled by him are specifically included within the disclosure requirements. Disclosure therefore cannot be avoided by arranging for the payment to be made to a connected party. In the case of payments to a company owned by the director, the emoluments note to the accounts usually includes an explanation that some or all of the payments have been made through the company. Emoluments also include all relevant amounts in respect of a director's services paid by, or receivable from the company, the company's subsidiary undertakings and any other person, unless the director must in turn account to the company or any of its subsidiary undertakings for the amounts received.

## Payments to third parties      9.19

The accounts must also disclose the aggregate amount paid to, or receivable by, third parties for making available the services of any person as a director of the company or otherwise in connection with the management of the affairs of the company or group. The most common example of this is an arrangement whereby a substantial investor in a company (eg a bank or venture capital company) has the right to appoint a director to the board of the investee company and payment for the services of this director is made to the investor rather than to the director himself.

## Particular problems in groups of companies      9.20

In some groups all directors' remuneration is paid by the holding company. Recharges may be made to subsidiary undertakings to reflect the cost of the services of their directors, but this will not always be done. This can cause difficulties over the disclosure of directors' remuneration in the accounts of the holding company and the subsidiaries. Directors' remuneration in the accounts of the holding company will comprise:

- remuneration paid to directors of the holding company in respect of their services to the company and management of the company and group; and
- if any holding company directors are also directors of one or more of the subsidiaries, remuneration paid to them for their services in relation to these companies.

Remuneration paid to those who are directors of subsidiaries but who are not directors of the holding company is not disclosable in the accounts of the holding company. The same disclosure requirements apply in the holding company's accounts, regardless of whether some or all of the remuneration costs are recharged to the subsidiaries.

## Disclosure in the accounts of subsidiaries          9.21

Where the holding company recharges the subsidiaries with the cost of remunerating their directors, each subsidiary should disclose as directors' remuneration the amount paid to the holding company in respect of directors' services to the company. If the holding company makes a global recharge to the subsidiaries to cover general management costs, including directors' remuneration, but the element for directors' remuneration cannot be separately identified, an appropriate apportionment should be made for disclosure purposes. Where the holding company does not recharge the subsidiaries with the costs of remunerating their directors, the costs borne by the holding company are still disclosable as directors' remuneration in the accounts of the subsidiary – it is not acceptable to simply disclose the fact that the directors have been remunerated by the holding company and not quantify the amount that they have received. However, it may be helpful to explain that this cost has been borne by the holding company and is not charged in the subsidiarys accounts.

Where directors of a subsidiary are also directors or employees of the holding company, it is sometimes argued that the holding company remunerates them only for their services to the holding company and that they receive no remuneration in respect of their services as directors of the subsidiary. The validity of this argument will usually depend on the amount of time that the director or employee devotes to the subsidiary company. If the time is relatively small it may be acceptable that he/she does not receive remuneration for services as a director of the subsidiary. In this case, a brief explanation should be included in the subsidiary's accounts.

## Compensation for loss of office          9.22

The aggregate compensation for loss of office paid to, or receivable by, directors and former directors must also be disclosed. Compensation for loss of office constitutes a separate category of payment to directors and should not be included in the figure for directors' emoluments for the period. Where compensation payments include non-cash benefits, these should be included in the disclosures at their estimated money value and the nature of the benefit must be disclosed. Many compensation payments to directors will also require shareholder approval under *CA 1985*, although this is not usually required for genuine payments in respect of damages for breach of contract or for pensions in respect of past services. If significant non-cash items are included, the compensation payments may also require approval under the provisions on substantial property transactions in *section 320* of *CA 1985*. Where a retired director continues to have an involvement with the company in a part-time or consultancy capacity, any payments in excess of normal market rates for the work performed may well include an element of compensation for loss of office, in which case the details should be disclosed.

## Directors' remuneration report                                    9.23

## At a glance                                                        9.24

---

- For accounting periods ending on or after 31 December 2002, the directors of a quoted company are required to prepare a separate directors' remuneration report.
- Certain elements of the directors' remuneration report are subject to audit.
- The general meeting at which the annual reports and accounts are laid must include a resolution inviting the shareholders to approve the directors' remuneration report.
- The content of the directors' remuneration report is specified in the legislation and includes:
  - detailed information on the remuneration paid to each individual director;
  - a statement on the company's future remuneration policy;
  - an explanation of any performance-related elements of remuneration;
  - details of pension entitlements earned under a defined benefit retirement scheme;
  - details of service contracts and any related compensation commitments; and
  - comparative information on shareholder return for the last five years.
- The legislation also specifies which elements of the directors' remuneration report should be included in summary financial statements.

---

## Requirements of CA 1985                                           9.25

For accounting periods ending on or after 31 December 2002, the directors of a quoted company are required to prepare a directors' remuneration report containing the detailed information specified in a new *Schedule 7A* to *CA 1985*. Current directors and those who have served as director in the preceding five years are given a specific duty to disclose relevant information to the company to enable the report to be prepared. The report must be formally approved by the directors and must be signed on behalf of the board by a director or by the company secretary. A signed copy must be delivered to the registrar as part of the company's annual reports and accounts. The auditors are required to report on the auditable part of the report (which is defined as the part covering the detailed disclosures on remuneration received by the directors) and to include any missing information in their audit report, so far as they are reasonably able to do so.

## Combined Code recommendations 9.26

The preparation of a separate directors' remuneration report has been a recommendation under the Combined Code for a number of years and, for listed companies, a requirement of the FSA Listing Rules. The contents of the report required under the new legislation are similar to those previously required by the Code and the FSA rules, but include some additional disclosures. In particular, the report must now include a line graph showing the total shareholder return for the last five years on:

- a holding of the class of equity shares whose public trading has resulted in the company meeting the definition of a quoted company; and
- a hypothetical holding of shares, based on a broad equity market index, together with the name of index and why it was chosen.

## Shareholder approval 9.27

Under the legislation, the general meeting at which the annual reports and accounts are laid must include a resolution enabling the shareholders to approve the directors' remuneration report, and details of the resolution must be set out in the notice of the meeting. However, the legislation notes that this requirement does not mean that the entitlement of any individual to the remuneration shown in the report is conditional on the resolution being passed. For accounting periods ending before 31 December 2002, there was no requirement for the report prepared under the Combined Code recommendations or FSA Listing Rules to be formally approved by the shareholders.

## Contents of the remuneration report 9.28

The detailed contents required by *CA 1985* are set out in APPENDIX 9A to this chapter in the form of a disclosure checklist. The contents are divided into two sections in the legislation (those subject to audit and those not subject to audit) and this is reflected in the layout in APPENDIX 9A. The legislation generally requires the detailed information to be given in tabular form and in a way that links the information to each director by name. A limited degree of aggregation is permitted in the disclosure of information on share options where the required details would otherwise result in a disclosure of excessive length. One of the potential problems here is the considerable amount of detail that may need to be given in the report. In presenting the disclosures, companies need to make a particular effort to ensure that the information that is likely to be of most interest to shareholders does not become obscured by the sheer volume of detail.

## Pension entitlements 9.29

Defined benefit retirement schemes usually link pension entitlement to final salary or average salary over a fixed period (say the last three years). The Greenbury Report suggested that, in these circumstances, the best measure of the pension entitlement earned by an individual director during the year was the present value of the additional entitlement earned as a result of the additional length of service, any increase in salary and any changes in the scheme, less any pension contributions made by the director during the period. The Report also recommended that any major changes compared with the previous year should be explained. These recommendations did not totally solve the problem, however, as there are two possible methods of calculating pension entitlement: the accrued benefit method and the transfer value method. A consultation exercise did not produce any clear consensus on which approach should be used for disclosure purposes – directors and companies were generally in favour of the accrued benefit method, whilst investors and their representatives generally preferred the transfer value method. The Faculty of Actuaries and the Institute of Actuaries therefore put forward recommendations proposing two separate disclosures for each director:

- the increase in his/her accrued pension entitlement, excluding any annual inflation adjustment made to all deferred pensions; and
- the transfer value of the increased benefit, disclosed either as a figure calculated on the basis of actuarial advice, or by giving sufficient information for shareholders to make a reasonable assessment of the value.

These recommendations were accepted by the FSA and were incorporated in the Listing Rules, together with a requirement to disclose the total accrued pension entitlement of each director at the end of the financial year.

## *Disclosure of transfer value* 9.30

Where a transfer value is disclosed, it should be calculated in accordance with Actuarial Guidance Note 11 (GN11) but should not include any deduction for underfunding. The Combined Code notes that companies may wish to make clear in the report that transfer values represent a liability of the company, not sums paid (or due) to the individual directors.

## *Disclosure of additional information* 9.31

Where the company adopts the approach of providing additional information, this should normally include:

- the current age of the director;
- the normal retirement age of the director;
- any contributions paid or payable by the director during the year under the terms of the scheme;
- details of spouse and dependants' benefits;
- details of early retirement rights and options, and expectations of pension increases after retirement (whether guaranteed or not); and
- discretionary benefits for which allowance is made in transfer values on leaving, and any other relevant information which will significantly affect the value of benefits.

Voluntary contributions and benefits should not be included in any of these disclosures.

## Share performance graph                                      9.32

In the case of the share performance graph, there is no requirement to disclose information for periods before the new regulations came into effect – in the early years, therefore, information will be given for one to four years as appropriate. The legislation includes detailed guidance on calculating total shareholder return for this purpose.

## Summary financial statements                                 9.33

The provisions of *CA 1985* on summary financial statements are amended to require, in the case of a quoted company, the inclusion of either the whole of the directors' remuneration report or, as a minimum:

- aggregate information on directors' remuneration (see **9.4** above);
- the statement of the company's policy on directors' remuneration for future years; and
- the performance graph summarising shareholder return.

## Directors' service contracts                                 9.34

## At a glance                                                  9.35

---

- The Combined Code includes specific provisions on the notice periods and compensation arrangements for directors.
- A comprehensive service contract for each executive director can help to prevent misunderstandings.
- Each non-executive director will usually have a contract for services.
- *CA 1985* includes provisions on the retention and location of directors' service contracts.
- Members of the company are entitled to inspect directors' service contracts.
- Shareholder approval is required for any contract giving a director a right of employment for more than 5 years, unless the company can give unconditional notice at any time.

---

## Service contracts and compensation                           9.36

The best practice guidance on directors' service contacts and compensation in the Combined Code (see **CHAPTER 6 CORPORATE GOVERNANCE**), as revised by the Higgs Report, includes the following provisions:

- notice or contract periods should be set at one year or less;

- if it is necessary to offer longer notice or contract periods to directors recruited externally, these should reduce after the initial period;
- the remuneration committee should consider what compensation commitments (including pension contributions) directors' service contracts would entail in the event of early termination– in particular, the committee should consider the advantages of providing explicitly in the initial contract for such compensation commitments other than in the case of removal for misconduct; and
- where the initial contract does not provide explicitly for compensation commitments the remuneration committee should, within legal constraints, tailor their approach in the case of early termination to the wide variety of circumstances – the broad aim should be to avoid rewarding poor performance while dealing fairly with departure in other circumstances, and to take a robust line on reducing compensation to reflect the departing director's obligations to mitigate loss.

## Service contracts for executive directors 9.37

An executive director is in effect an employee of the company and it is appropriate that the terms and conditions of his/her appointment should be set out in a written contract of service between the director and the company. A comprehensive service contract can help to prevent misunderstandings and provides a useful point of reference if problems arise. Non-executive directors have a very different role to executive directors and the terms and conditions of their appointment will usually be set out in a contract for services. A service contract for an executive director should normally include:

- specific duties of the director, including the amount of time to be spent on company activities (this may be particularly important where the individual also holds posts such as non-executive directorships in other businesses);
- remuneration, including details of any arrangements involving:
  - ○ benefits in kind (eg private health cover, accommodation, company car);
  - ○ bonus schemes;
  - ○ long-term incentive plans;
  - ○ share options;
- holiday entitlement;
- arrangements in the case of prolonged absence through illness;
- pension arrangements;
- required notice period, and procedures in the case of dismissal;
- compensation arrangements in the event of early termination of the contract; and
- confidentiality arrangements.

Other issues may need to be covered, depending on the circumstances. The Institute of Directors publishes a specimen contract of service for executive directors and this is reproduced in **APPENDIX 9B** to this chapter.

## Contracts for services of non-executive directors 9.38

The main role of non-executive directors is to make a positive contribution to the development of company strategy, and on matters such as company performance, standards of conduct and corporate governance issues. It is helpful to all parties for the terms of their appointment to be set out in a written contract for services. This will usually specify:

- the expected commitment, in terms of attendance at meetings of the board and its sub-committees; and
- fee arrangements.

## Companies Act 1985 requirements 9.39

Where a director has a written contract of service with the company, *section 318* of *CA 1985* requires the company to retain a copy of the contract at one of the following locations:

- the company's registered office;
- the place where the register of members is kept (if this is not the registered office); or
- the company's principal place of business (provided that this is in the part of Great Britain where the company is registered).

If a director does not have a written contract of service, the company must keep a written memorandum of the terms of his/her appointment. The same rules apply to a variation of a director's contract. A parent company is also required to keep copies of service contracts between its subsidiaries and their directors, or a written memorandum of the terms if these contracts are not in writing. Copies of all contracts and memoranda must be kept in the same place. If they are not kept at the registered office, the company must notify the Registrar of Companies of where they are held and of any changes in location. *Section 318(6)* of *CA 1985* emphasises that these arrangements apply equally in the case of shadow directors. However, there is no formal requirement for a company to retain a copy of a contract, variation or memorandum when the unexpired term is less than 12 months, or where the contract can be terminated by the company within the next 12 months without the payment of compensation.

### *Director working outside the UK* 9.40

Where a director of the company, or of one of its subsidiaries, is required under his/her contract to work wholly or mainly outside the UK, the company is not required to keep a copy of the contract, but it must keep a memorandum giving the director's name and the provisions of the contract relating to its duration. In the case of a contract for a director of a subsidiary, the name and place of incorporation of the subsidiary must also be recorded in the memorandum. These memoranda must be kept in the same place as the contracts and memoranda relating to the other directors.

Directors' Remuneration and Benefits

## Inspection of contracts                              9.41

Under *section 318(7)* of *CA 1985*, any member of the company is entitled to inspect the copies of the directors' contracts of service (or the memoranda where there is no written service contract) without charge. If the company refuses to allow a member to inspect a contract or memorandum, the court can require immediate inspection.

## Shareholder approval for contracts for more than five years                                                   9.42

Under *section 319* of *CA 1985*, a director cannot be given the right of employment with the company (or, where relevant, with the group) for a period of more than five years under an agreement which does not not allow the company to give unconditional notice at any time, unless this term of the contract has been first approved by the company in general meeting (or, in the case of a private company, by written resolution). Employment is defined as including employment under a contract for services. Where the director is also a director of the company's holding company, prior approval to the arrangement must normally be given by the shareholders of both the subsidiary and the holding company (unless the subsidiary is wholly-owned, in which case prior approval of the arrangement by the shareholders of the subsidiary is not required).

A written memorandum setting out the proposed agreement must be available for inspection by the members at the company's registered office for a period of at least 15 days before the meeting and at the meeting itself. In the case of a private company where agreement is to be by written resolution, a copy of the memorandum must be sent to each member before, or at the same time as, the resolution is provided for signature.

A term included in a director's contract in contravention of *section 319* of CA *1985* is void, and the agreement is deemed to include a term entitling the company to terminate the agreement at any time by the giving of reasonable notice.

## *Series of agreements*                               9.43

*CA 1985* includes special provisions to prevent a company entering into a series of shorter agreements with the same director in an attempt to avoid the requirement for shareholder approval of a contract that in effect extends for more than five years.

## Checklist for the recommended contents of the remuneration report                                      9.44

This checklist is based on the requirements of *CA 1985* (which apply for accounting periods ending on or after 31 December 2002, the recommendations in the Combined Code and current FSA Listing Requirements. The second column indicate the origin of the disclosure requirement. Additional details may need to be given, depending on the specific circumstances of the company.

*A    Contents subject to audit*

The following information must be disclosed and is subject to audit:

| | |
|---|---|
| ● for each director who served during the financial year, the total amount of: | FSA Listing Rules |
| ○    salary and/or fees; | |
| ○    bonuses; | |
| ○    expense allowances that are chargeable to UK income tax; | |
| ○    any compensation for loss of office and similar payments; | |
| ○    the estimated money value of any benefits in kind; and | |
| ○    the sum total of all these amounts, and the equivalent total for the previous financial year. | Sch 7A, CA 1985 |
| ● the nature of any element of a remuneration package which is not cash; | Sch 7A, CA 1985, Combined Code, FSA Listing Rules |
| ● for each director who served during the financial year, the number of shares subject to a share option (distinguishing between those with different terms and conditions) at: | Sch 7A, CA 1985, Combined Code |
| ○    the beginning of the year, or the date of appointment if later; | |
| ○    the end of the year, or the date of ceasing to be a director if earlier. | Sch 7A, CA 1985, Combined Code, FSA Listing Rules |
| ● information on share options awarded, exercised and lapsed during the year, and any variations to terms and conditions; | Sch 7A, CA 1985, Combined Code, FSA Listing Rules |
| for each share option that was unexpired at any time during the year: | |
| ○    the price (if any) paid for its award; | |
| ○    the exercise prices; | |
| ○    the date from which the option can be exercised; and | Sch 7A, CA 1985 |

**Directors' Remuneration and Benefits**

| | |
|---|---|
| ○ the date on which the option expires; | |
| ● a summary of any performance criteria upon which the award or exercise of a share option is conditional, and any changes made in the year; | Sch 7A, CA 1985, Combined Code, FSA Listing Rules |
| ● for any share option exercised during the year, the market price at the time of exercise; | Sch 7A, CA 1985, Combined Code, FSA Listing Rules |
| ● for each share option that was unexpired at the end of the financial year; | |
| ○ the market price at the year-end date; and | |
| ○ the highest and lowest market price during the year; | Sch 7A, CA 1985, Combined Code, FSA Listing Rules |
| ● for each director who served during the financial year, details of interests in long-term incentive schemes, showing: | |
| ○ interests at the beginning of the year, or the date of appointment if later; | |
| ○ awards during the year, showing whether they crystallise in the year or in subsequent years; | |
| ○ the money value and number of shares, cash payments or other benefits received during the year; and | |
| ○ interests at the end of the year, or on ceasing to be a director if earlier; | Sch 7A, CA 1985 |
| ● for each disclosed interest in long-term incentive schemes, the date by which the qualifying conditions have to be fulfilled and details of any variations in the terms and conditions made during the year; | Sch 7A, CA 1985 |
| ● for each scheme interest that has vested during the year, details of any shares, the amount of any money and the value of any other assets that have become receivable as a result; | Sch 7A, CA 1985, Combined Code, FSA Listing Rules |
| ● for each director who served during the financial year and and has rights under a defined benefit retirement scheme: | ⟶ |

| | |
|---|---|
| O details of any changes during the year in their accrued benefits under the scheme; | |
| O the accrued benefits at the end of the year; | |
| O the transfer value of the accrued benefits, calculated as recommended by the Institute of Actuaries and Faculty of Actuaries (see **9.24**); and | |
| O the equivalent transfer value at the end of the previous year and the difference between this and the current transfer value, after deducting any contributions made by the director in the current year; | |
| ● for each director who served during the financial year and has rights under a money purchase retirement scheme, details of the contributions paid or payable by the company during the year; | Sch 7A, CA 1985, FSA Listing Rules |
| ● details of certain excess retirement benefits paid to directors or former directors; | Sch 7A, CA 1985 |
| ● details of any significant awards to former directors (eg compensation for loss of office, pensions); | Sch 7A, CA 1985, FSA Listing Rules |
| ● for each director who served during the financial year, the aggregate amount of any consideration (including any benefits in kind) paid to, or receivable by, a third party for making available the services of the individual as a director. | Sch 7A, CA 1985 |

**B Contents not subject to audit**
The following information is required to be disclosed, but is not subject to audit:

| | |
|---|---|
| ● the names of the members of any committee that considered directors' remuneration during the year and the names of any other individuals (whether directors or not) who provided advice or services to that committee, together with details of the nature of the advice or services; | Sch 7A, CA 1985 |

| | |
|---|---|
| • a statement of the company's policy on directors' remuneration for the forthcoming year and for subsequent financial years, drawing attention to any factors specific to the company – this must include for each individual who has served as a director between the end of the financial year under review and the date on which the annual reports and accounts are laid before the members: | Sch 7A, CA 1985, Combined Code, FSA Listing Rules |
| ○ a detailed summary of any performance conditions in respect of awards under share option or long-term incentive schemes; | |
| ○ an explanation of why these performance conditions were chosen; | |
| ○ a summary of the methods used in assessing whether the performance conditions are met, and why those methods were chosen; | |
| ○ if any performance condition involves comparison with external factors, a summary of the factors to be used and the identify of any companies or index used for comparison purposes; | Sch 7A, CA 1985 |
| • a description of, and explanation for, any significant changes to the terms and conditions of entitlement under share option or long-term incentive schemes; | Sch 7A, CA 1985 |
| • an explanation of why any entitlements under share option or long-term incentive schemes are not subject to performance conditions; | Combined Code, FSA Listing Rules |
| • an explanation of, and justification for, any grants under share option or other long term incentive schemes that are awarded in one large block; | Listing Rules |
| • a statement of the company's policy on the granting of options or awards under employee share schemes and other long term incentive schemes and an explanation and justification of any departure from that policy during the year; | Sch 7A, CA 1985 |

| | |
|---|---|
| ● the relative importance of elements of remuneration that are related to performance and those that are not; | Sch 7A, CA 1985 |
| ● a summary of the company's policy on the duration of directors' service contracts and on notice periods and termination payments under those contracts; | |
| ● the following information on the contract of service, or contract for services, of each person who served as a director during the financial year: | |
| ○ date of the contract, the unexpired term and any notice period; | |
| ○ any provision for compensation on early termination; and | |
| ○ sufficient information on any other provisions to enable a member to estimate the company's liability in the event of early termination of the contract; FSA Listing Rules | |
| ● the unexpired term of any directors' service contract of a director proposed for election or re-election at the forthcoming AGM, and if any such director does not have a service contract, a statement of that fact; | Combined Code, FSA Listing Rules |
| ● an explanation of any service contracts which provide for, or imply, notice periods in excess of one year, or which include provisions for pre-determined compensation which exceeds one year's salary and benefits; | Sch 7A, CA 1985, FSA Listing Rules |
| ● an explanation for any significant awards during the year to former directors (eg compensation for loss of office, pensions); | Combined Code |
| ● an explanation of, and justification for, any annual bonuses or benefits in kind that are pensionable; and | Sch 7A, CA 1985 |
| ● a line graph showing the total shareholder return for the last five years on: | ⮕ |

245

| | | |
|---|---|---|
| ❍ | a holding of the class of equity shares whose public trading has resulted in the company meeting the definition of a quoted company; and | |
| ❍ | a hypothetical holding of shares, based on a broad equity market index, together with the name of index and why it was chosen. | Sch 7A, CA 1985 |

# 10. Financial Reporting

## Accounting standards                                            10.1

## At a glance                                                     10.2

- Accounting standards are developed in the UK by the Accounting Standards Board (ASB) under the auspices of the Financial Reporting Council (FRC), and a detailed consultation programme is undertaken for each new standard.
- Accounting standards apply to all accounts that are required to show a true and fair view, although they need not be applied to immaterial items.
- Each accounting standard is effective from the date specified in the standard, although early adoption is usually encouraged.
- Accounting standards should generally be regarded as applying to all transactions, unless an individual standard requires a different approach.
- Care is required over the early adoption of accounting treatments proposed in ASB Discussion Papers or FREDs, especially where they represent the updating of an existing accounting standard.
- Directors are generally required to state whether the accounts have been prepared in accordance with applicable accounting standards.
- Additional disclosures must be given if the company departs from applicable accounting standards when preparing its annual accounts.
- The Urgent Issues Task Force (UITF) considers interpretational issues arising from existing accounting and company law requirements.

Financial Reporting

- The Financial Reporting Review Panel (FRRP) enquires into accounts that appear to depart from the requirements of company law, accounting standards and UITF Abstracts.
- From 2005, the group accounts of listed companies will have to comply with international accounting standards.
- The Government is proposing certain changes to the way in which detailed rules on accounting and financial reporting are developed and enforced.
- Certain smaller entities are permitted to adopt the Financial Reporting Standard for Smaller Entities (FRSSE) in place of other accounting standards.
- Statements of Recommended Practice (SORPs) set out recommended accounting practice for specialised sectors or industries.

## The present regime                                                   10.3

Accounting standards are currently developed in the UK by the Accounting Standards Board (ASB) under the auspices of the Financial Reporting Council (FRC). Both bodies were established in 1990, together with the Financial Reporting Review Panel (FRRP) and the Urgent Issues Task Force (UITF). The structure of these bodies can be summarised as follows:

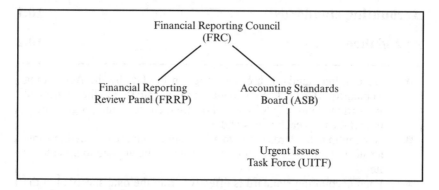

Prior to 1990, standards were developed by the Accounting Standards Committee (ASC). At its first meeting, the ASB formally adopted all existing accounting standards (22 at the time) developed by the ASC, but many of these have now been revised or superseded by new standards issued by the ASB. Standards issued by the ASC were described as Statements of Standard Accounting Practice (SSAPs) and those issued by the ASB are described as Financial Reporting Standards (FRSs). Some of the present accounting standards are therefore in the form of SSAPs whilst others are FRSs, but all have the same status for practical purposes.

## Development of accounting standards                                    10.4

Potential topics for accounting standards are identified by the ASB from its own research and also from external sources, and ASB staff then undertake a programme of consultation and research, considering conceptual issues, existing practice in the UK, any existing pronouncements (both in the UK and abroad), and the practical implications of introducing new requirements in the UK. A Discussion Paper is usually prepared setting out the main issues and inviting comments on the ASB's initial proposals. Following this initial consultation, a Financial Reporting Exposure Draft (FRED) is published to give those who are interested a chance to comment on the proposals and to enable the ASB to assess the likely level of acceptance. The draft document may be amended in the light of the comments received, but the final decision on the content of an FRS rests with the ASB.

## Scope and application of accounting standards 10.5

Accounting standards apply to all accounts that are required to show a true and fair view of the profit or loss for the financial period and of the state of affairs of an entity at its balance sheet date. Consequently they apply not only to companies and groups, but also to unincorporated entities if these are required to prepare accounts that show a true and fair view. However, the requirements of accounting standards need not be applied to items that are considered immaterial in the context of the accounts as a whole. They also do not override any exemption from disclosure that is available by law. In its guidance, the ASB emphasises that, when applying accounting standards, preparers of accounts should follow the spirit and reasoning behind the requirements as explained in the standards themselves and in the ASB's *Statement of Principles for Financial Reporting*. The report published in 2003 by the DTI Co-ordinating Group on Audit and Accounting Issues (CGAAI) as part of the post-Enron review endorses the need for accounting standards to be based on conceptually sound principles rather than detailed prescriptive rules, but also notes that such an approach requires companies and their auditors to be prepares to apply the standards responsibly and with integrity and not in a way that skews the underlying economic reality of the company's performance.

## Effective date of accounting standards 10.6

Each accounting standard is effective from a specific date set out in the standard. The date chosen by the ASB will take into account the fact that companies may need time to put detailed procedures into place in order to comply with the new accounting requirements. However, the effective date set by the ASB is the latest date by which compliance must be achieved, and early adoption of new accounting standards is usually encouraged. The question sometimes arises as to whether new requirements apply to all transactions or only to those arising after the effective date of the standard. The ASB's general view is that the requirements of accounting standards should be regarded as applying to all transactions, regardless of when they took place, unless a particular accounting standard specifies a different approach. Care is also required over the early adoption of accounting treatments proposed in Discussion Papers and FREDs. If the subject matter of a

**Financial Reporting**

Discussion Paper or FRED is not covered by an existing accounting standard, the exposure document may be regarded as indicative of best practice and it may therefore be acceptable to adopt the accounting treatment proposed, bearing in mind that the the final FRS may impose slightly different requirements. If the subject matter of the Discussion Paper or FRED is already covered in an accounting standard, the existing standard remains in force until it is replaced and accounts must therefore be prepared in accordance with the existing standard, even if it is expected that the standard will be superseded by new requirements. In these circumstances, it may be appropriate to explain the effect of the new proposals in a note to the accounts.

## Disclosure of compliance with accounting standards   10.7

*Paragraph 36A* of *Schedule 4* to *CA 1985* requires the directors to state whether the company's accounts have been prepared in accordance with applicable accounting standards. There is an exemption from the disclosure requirement (but not from the requirement to follow applicable standards) for companies that qualify as small or medium-sized under the legislation. If there has been a departure from applicable accounting standards, particulars must be given, together with the reasons for the departure. The *Foreword to Accounting Standards* and FRS 18 *Accounting Policies* also require disclosure of the financial effect of a material departure from accounting standards.

## Applicable accounting standards   10.8

*Section 256* of *CA 1985* defines accounting standards as 'statements of standard accounting practice issued by such body or bodies as may be prescribed by regulations'. Applicable accounting standards are those that are relevant to the company's circumstances and to the accounts. For the purposes of UK company law, FRSs and SSAPs constitute 'accounting standards'.

## Role of the UITF   10.9

The role of the Urgent Issues Task Force (UITF) is to help the ASB to fulfil its aim of responding promptly on urgent matters as they arise. The UITF considers issues that are covered by an existing accounting standard or a provision in company law but where conflicting or unacceptable interpretations have developed, or seem likely to develop. Having considered the issue and reached a conclusion, the UITF issues its consensus in the form of an Abstract, which usually becomes effective shortly after publication. Once it is in force, a UITF Abstract has the same authority, scope and application as an accounting standard and therefore forms part of standard accounting practice.

## Role of the FRRP   10.10

The Financial Reporting Review Panel (FRRP) enquires into accounts that appear to depart from the requirements of company law, accounting standards and UITF Abstracts, including the requirement to show a true and fair view.

To date, reviews have concentrated on the accounts of public companies and larger private companies, but technically all companies come within the remit of the FRRP unless they qualify as small or medium-sized under *CA 1985*. At present, the FRRP does not review accounts on a routine basis but acts on matters drawn to its attention, either directly or indirectly. Qualified audit reports, press comment and referrals by individuals or companies can all result in an enquiry. Where revision of the accounts is considered necessary, the FRRP usually tries to reach voluntary arrangement with the directors, but it can seek a court order for revision of the accounts under *section 245B* of *CA 1985* if it is unable to reach a satisfactory agreement with the directors.

The CGAAI report issued in January 2003 (see **10.5** above) includes the following recommendations in respect of the work of the FRRP:

- a financial reporting regime is only credible if accounting standards are applied in a consistent and rigorous way – effective arrangements for the enforcement of accounting standards are therefore essential;
- the FRRP should develop a pro-active element to its work – the proposal is that this should involve a risk-based selection of accounts for review and should encompass all published information issued by listed companies, including interim reports and preliminary announcements;
- The Financial Services Authority (FSA) should have a greater role in the enforcement process and in particular in identifying the risks to be investigated and the selection of accounts for review by the FRRP – the FRRP and FSA are asked to develop and agree a memorandum of understanding to clarify their respective roles and responsibilities in this process; and
- the Government should explore the scope for opening a legal gateway to enable information to be passed between the Inland Revenue and the FSA, FRRP and DTI to help in the identification of high-risk accounts.

Some changes to the current powers of the FRRP may be needed in order to implement these proposals.

## European regulation of quoted groups                    10.11

In June 2002, European ministers ratified a Regulation that will require quoted companies to prepare group accounts in accordance with international accounting standards. This will come into effect in January 2005 and will mean that responsibility for the financial reporting of quoted groups will be passed to a European level. Individual governments will have no power to reduce or increase the quoted group financial reporting requirements laid down in Brussels – their jurisdiction will be limited to unquoted companies and groups, and single-entity quoted companies. In preparation for these changes, the new International Accounting Standards Board (IASB) is in the process of revising a number of its existing standards and proposals for 12 revised standards were issued in May 2002. At the same time, the ASB issued a series of exposure drafts of proposed new UK accounting standards, based

251

on the IASB's improved standards. These represent the first major step towards aligning the text of UK accounting standards with international accounting standards in preparation for 2005. The ASB plans to introduce the new standards in the UK at the same time as the IASB issues the final versions of its own revised standards. This is expected to be in the first quarter of 2003.

## Government proposals for change                                  10.12

Following the recent company law review, the Government White Paper *Modernising Company Law* published in July 2002 proposes some changes to the way in which requirements on the form and content of accounts will be developed in future. As noted above, quoted companies preparing group accounts will have to comply with the requirements of international accounting standards from 2005. For other companies, the company law review proposed that most of the detailed requirements on accounts should be removed from company law and that the power to prescribe detailed rules on accounting and financial reporting in its widest sense should be devolved to a new Standards Board, developed from the ASB but with a suitably adapted membership and constitution. The review also recommended the creation of a successor body to the FRRP to enforce compliance with accounting and other disclosure requirements, with an extended remit covering all the documents associated with annual financial reporting. However, the DTI has subsequently published a consultation document on the possible extension of the EU Regulation on the adoption of international accounting standards. Member states have the option of extending the application of the Regulation by:

- permitting or requiring quoted companies to prepare individual accounts in accordance with IASs; and
- permitting or requiring some or all unquoted companies to prepare their group and/or individual accounts in accordance with IASs.

The consultation document notes that the Government does not currently have a preferred option on these issues, but expects to come to a decision early in 2003, based on the results of the consultation. The proposals for a new institutional framework for the development of UK accounting standards could consequently prove to be superfluous.

## Financial Reporting Standard for Smaller Entities (FRSSE)                                                     10.13

A Financial Reporting Standard for Smaller Entities (FRSSE) was first published in November 1997 and came into immediate effect. A number of revised versions have been published, the latest one becoming effective in June 2002. The FRSSE may be adopted in financial statements that are intended to give a true and fair view of the financial performance and financial position of companies that qualify as small under *CA 1985* and of other entities that would qualify if they were incorporated under *CA 1985*. If the FRSSE is adopted, this fact must be stated in the accounts. The contents of the FRSSE are based on other accounting standards, but definitions and accounting requirements are set out in a more straightforward manner, and more complex issues that are not expected to arise in smaller entities are excluded. The document is reviewed on an annual basis so that its requirements are kept up to date with developments in accounting practice. An appendix to the FRSSE links its requirements with those in accounting standards, and where issues arise that are not specifically covered in the FRSSE, those preparing the accounts are required to have regard to other standards and UITF Abstracts as a means of establishing current practice. The FRSSE includes a specific additional requirement for the accounts to disclose any personal guarantees given by the directors in respect of company borrowings.

## SORPs 10.14

Statements of Recommended Practice (SORPs) set out recommended accounting practice for specialised sectors or industries. They are developed by bodies representing the appropriate sector or industry and are supplementary to accounting standards, legislation and other regulations affecting the business. Bodies wishing to develop a SORP are expected to meet criteria laid down by the ASB and to develop the SORP in accordance with the ASB's Code of Practice. The ASB will review the proposed SORP and, where appropriate, issue a 'negative assurance' statement for publication in the document, confirming that:

- the SORP does not appear to contain any fundamental points of principle that are unacceptable in the context of current accounting practice; and
- the SORP does not conflict with an accounting standard or with the ASB's plans for future accounting standards.

The contents of a SORP do not override the requirements of accounting standards, UITF Abstracts or relevant legislation. The ASB Code of Practice specifically notes that the fact that a SORP has not been updated does not exempt relevant entities from complying with more recent accounting standards and UITF Abstracts. If new standards and Abstracts conflict with the provisions of a SORP, those provisions cease to have effect. FRS 18 *Accounting Policies* requires specific disclosures to be given in the accounts when an entity comes with the scope of a SORP.

## The true and fair view 10.15

## At a glance 10.16

- *CA 1985* requires all company and group accounts to show a true and fair view.
- The interpretation of what constitutes a true and fair view will vary over time, based largely on the requirements of the accounting standards in force at the time.

**Financial Reporting**

- The ASB 'Foreword to Accounting Standards' considers the status of accounting standards in the context of UK company law
- In certain exceptional circumstances, directors are required to depart from the specific accounting requirements of *CA 1985* – this is commonly referred to as the use of the true and fair override.
- Specific disclosures must be given in the accounts whenever the true and fair override is used.

## Requirement for accounts to show a true and fair view                                                10.17

*CA 1985* requires a company's balance sheet to give a true and fair view of the state of affairs of the company at the end of the financial period and the profit and loss account to give a true and fair view of the profit or loss for the financial period then ended. A similar requirement applies to group accounts. Where compliance with the provisions of the legislation is not sufficient for the accounts to give a true and fair view, the additional information necessary to achieve a true and fair view must be given in the accounts or the notes to the accounts. The true and fair view requirement applies to the accounts of all companies, regardless of their size.

## What constitutes a true and fair view?                                                10.18

Although the concept of the true and fair view lies at the heart of financial reporting in the UK, there is no clear definition, in the legislation or elsewhere, of what constitutes a true and fair view. This is essentially a question of judgement and, as a legal concept, it can only be interpreted by the Court. It is a dynamic concept and the interpretation of what constitutes a true and fair view will vary over time, based largely on the accounting standards in force at any given date. New accounting standards are developed, and existing standards revised, to take account of changes in business practice and in the general economic climate, and an accounting treatment that was accepted as giving a true and fair view ten years ago will not necessarily achieve such a view today.

## Impact of accounting standards                                                10.19

The interpretation of 'true and fair' will usually be governed by generally accepted accounting practice and, in particular, the requirements of accounting standards. Each accounting standard states that it applies to all financial statements that are required to show a true and fair view. The *Foreword to Accounting Standards*, issued in 1993 by the Accounting Standards Board, considers the status of accounting standards in the context of UK company law, and an appendix to the document sets out an opinion by Miss Mary Arden QC (now the Honourable Mrs Justice Arden) on the true and fair requirement. This includes detailed consideration of the relationship between accounting standards and the legal requirement for company accounts to show a true and fair view. The main points set out in the Opinion are:

- although the true and fair requirement is a question of law and must therefore be interpreted by the Court, this cannot be done without evidence of the practice and views of accountants – the more authoritative the practices and views, the more ready the Court will be to follow them;
- *CA 1985* now gives statutory recognition to accounting standards;
- *CA 1985* requires disclosure of non-compliance with accounting standards rather than compliance with them – the Court is therefore likely to infer that accounts will usually follow accounting standards in meeting the true and fair requirement and that any departure from accounting standards needs to be explained and disclosed in the accounts;
- once an accounting standard has been issued, the Court is likely to hold that compliance with the standard will be necessary for accounts to show a true and fair view – this view is likely to be strengthened by the extent to which the standard is subsequently accepted in practice;
- the converse will not necessarily apply, and a lack of support for an accounting standard will not automatically lead the Court to conclude that a true and fair view can be achieved without compliance with the standard;
- the fact that a departure from an accounting standard is disclosed in accordance with the requirements of *CA 1985* does not necessarily mean that the departure is permitted under the legislation.

It is advisable to read the full Opinion in any case where departure from an accounting standard is being contemplated.

## True and fair override          10.20

If, in special circumstances, compliance with the provisions in the legislation would be inconsistent with the requirement for the accounts to show a true and fair view, *CA 1985* requires the directors to depart from those requirements and make specific disclosure of this in the accounts. This is commonly referred to as the use of the true and fair override. A departure from the requirements of *CA 1985* might arise in one of two ways. Firstly, some accounting standards specifically require departure from the requirements of the legislation in order to achieve a true and fair view – examples include the non-depreciation of investment properties under SSAP 19 *Accounting for Investment Properties*, the treatment of certain exchange gains and losses under SSAP 20 *Foreign Currency Translation*, and the non-amortisation of certain categories of goodwill under FRS 10 *Goodwill and Intangible Assets*. Secondly, in very rare and exceptional circumstances, it may be necessary to depart from the requirements of accounting standards in order to achieve a true and fair view – the legislation requires accounts to be prepared in accordance with applicable accounting standards and a departure from these will therefore constitute a departure from the requirements of *CA 1985*.

## Disclosing use of the true and fair override          **10.21**

Where the directors depart from the requirements of *CA 1985*, the accounts must give:

- particulars of the departure;
- the reasons for the departure; and
- the effect of the departure.

FRS 18 *Accounting Policies* deals with these disclosure requirements in more detail and requires the following information to be given:

- a clear and unambiguous statement that there has been a departure from the requirements of company law, accounting standards or UITF Abstracts, as appropriate, and that the departure is necessary in order to achieve a true and fair view;
- a statement of the treatment that company law, accounting standards or UITF Abstracts would normally require and a description of the treatment actually adopted; and
- a description of how the position shown in the financial statements is different as a result of the departure – this should include quantification of the effect except where this is already evident in the financial statements themselves, or where the effect cannot be quantified (in which case the circumstances must be explained).

FRS 18 requires this information to be given in the note to the accounts on compliance with applicable accounting standards, or to be cross-referenced to this note. If the departure continues in future years, the disclosures must be given each year, with comparatives. If the departure applies only to the figures for previous year, the disclosures must still be given in respect of those figures.

## Materiality                                                **10.22**

## At a glance                                                **10.23**

- An item is generally regarded as material to the financial statements if its misstatement or omission might reasonably be expected to influence the decisions or assessments made by a user of the financial statements.
- The requirements of accounting standards should generally be applied to all material transactions, regardless of when they took place.
- Key factors in assessing the materiality of an item include its size, its nature and the surrounding circumstances.
- In making the assessment, information should be viewed from a user's perspective.
- Both the quantative and the qualitative aspects of an item or transaction should be taken into account when assessing its materiality.

## Nature of materiality                                     10.24

Paragraph 3.29 of the ASB's *Statement of Principles for Financial Reporting* describes materiality as a threshold quality in that it provides a cut-off point for establishing whether an item needs to be considered in detail in relation to the accounts. The document goes on to explain that:

> 'An item of information is material to the financial statements if its misstatement or omission might reasonably be expected to influence the economic decisions of users of those financial statements, including their assessments of management's stewardship. Whether information is material or not will depend on the size and nature of the item in question judged in the particular circumstances of the case.'

The Statement also emphasises that the inclusion of immaterial information can impair the understandability of the other information provided. Immaterial information should therefore be excluded. Materiality is different to the qualitative characteristics of financial information that are discussed in the *Statement of Principles* (ie relevance, reliability, comparability and understandability), because these represent the characteristics that information must have if it is to be useful to a user of the accounts. The materiality of an item should be considered before its other qualities are assessed, because:

- if the information is not material, it cannot be useful to a user of the accounts and therefore does not need to be considered further;
- if the information is material, it will be useful to a user of the accounts, and its qualitative characteristics will therefore need to be assessed.

## Influence on the decisions of users                       10.25

The main issue to be considered in establishing whether an item is material or not is whether a user of the accounts may make a different decision if the relevant detail or information is made available to him. A wide range of users of accounts is identified in the *Statement of Principles*, including:

- existing investors, taking decisions on whether to increase, hold or sell their investments;
- potential investors, deciding whether or not to invest in the entity;
- employees and prospective employees, assessing the ability of the entity to provide secure employment opportunities, remuneration and retirement benefits;
- lenders, taking decisions on whether to maintain, increase or decrease the level of financing provided to the entity;
- suppliers and customers, taking decisions on whether to trade with the entity; and
- the general public, assessing the contribution of the entity to the local economy.

**Financial Reporting**

## Requirements of accounting standards 10.26

Paragraph 13 of the *Foreword to Accounting Standards* states that accounting standards need not be applied to immaterial items and this is repeated in the introductory note to each accounting standard. The Foreword also emphasises that the requirements of accounting standards should generally be applied to all material transactions, irrespective of the date of the transaction. Many accounting standards refer to material items in one context or another. For example, accounting standards may require:

- disclosure of material items – for instance, exceptional items under the requirements of FRS 3 *Reporting financial performance*;
- disclosure of material differences where items are calculated under different methods – for instance, the disclosure of historical cost profits or losses under FRS 3 *Reporting financial performance*;
- disclosure of material events or conditions – for instance, the sale or termination of an operation under FRS 3 *Reporting financial performance*;
- the application of a specific accounting treatment to material items – for instance, adjusting the accounts for certain material post balance sheet events under SSAP 17 *Accounting for Post Balance Sheet Events*; and
- the application of a specific accounting treatment where material events or transactions occur – for instance, accounting for transactions on the basis of their economic substance under FRS 5 *Reporting the substance of transactions*;

## Assessing materiality 10.27

The materiality of an item (or an error) will therefore usually need to be assessed in relation to:

- the accounts as a whole;
- the total (or totals) in which it is (or should be) included;
- the individual profit and loss account heading or balance sheet heading in which it is (or should be) included;
- other related items in the profit and loss account and balance sheet; and
- the corresponding figure (or figures) for the previous year.

## *Key factors to consider* 10.28

The materiality of an individual item cannot be assessed in isolation. There are three key factors, all of which are important to the assessment:

- the size of the item;
- the nature of the item; and
- the surrounding circumstances.

For instance, it is not possible to say whether an item (or an error) of £35,000 is material without also knowing its nature and the reasons why it arose.

Knowing the size alone is not sufficient. It is also not possible to deal with the question of materiality on a purely mathematical basis – the final assessment will often be subjective and will invariably require the exercise of judgement. Whilst percentage guidelines may be helpful as part of the assessment process (eg whether an item represents (say) 5% or more of the profit for the year, or (say) 10% or more of a particular balance sheet or profit and loss account heading), they should not be used as the sole means of assessing whether or not an item is material for accounting purposes.

## *Nature of an item* 10.29

The following points should usually be taken into account when considering the nature of an individual item or error:

- the event or transaction that gave rise to it;
- the legality of the event or transaction and its likely consequences;
- the identity of any other parties, and their relationship to the reporting entity;
- the relevant profit and loss account or balance sheet heading; and
- any other related disclosure requirements, either in *CA 1985* or in accounting standards.

## *User's perspective* 10.30

It is also important to consider both the context of the item in the accounts and the way in which the information provided may be used. A user will rarely make decisions on the basis of accounting information for one year only – he/she is more likely to:

- compare the latest information with the details for previous years, identify any trends and use this information to make projections and forecasts for future years; and
- compare the latest information with equivalent information in respect of similar entities.

The impact that the information may have on decisions made by the user is of primary importance when assessing materiality. It is therefore important to view the information (or potential lack of it) from the user's perspective.

## Qualitative aspects of transactions 10.31

The Financial Reporting Review Panel criticised the 1995 group accounts of RMC Group plc for failing to disclose an expense that the Panel considered to be material. The issue related to restrictive trade practices fines and related legal costs totalling just under £5m which were paid by a subsidiary during 1995. The matter originally arose in 1988 and details of the legal action had been given in the group accounts each year. The 1994 accounts disclosed the matter as a contingent liability. The 1995 accounts of the subsidiary disclosed the payment of the fines, but no mention of them was made in the group accounts. The group profits for the year were £173m, and the costs of £5m were presumably not considered to be material in the context of the group results. The Panel took the view that the nature and circumstances of the fines were such that they should have been drawn to the attention of users of the group accounts. Their decision was based on guidance in the ICAEW statement *The Interpretation of Materiality in Financial Reporting* and the ASB *Statement of Principles* (in its draft form at that stage). The Panel has therefore emphasised that qualitative aspects of significant transactions need to be considered as well as quantitative ones.

## Other issues to consider                                      10.32

Other issues that may affect the assessment of whether an item or error is material include:

- whether there is already an element of estimation or approximation in the calculation of the item - for instance, the valuation of long term contracts will usually involve an assessment of the expected outcome, whereas the amount due to a creditor can often be calculated with a reasonable degree of precision;
- whether the inclusion or exclusion of an item, or correction or non-correction of an error, has the effect of:
  - reversing a trend;
  - turning a profit into a loss, or vice versa;
  - changing the margin of solvency shown in the balance sheet; or
  - altering the degree of compliance with debt covenants;
  these are considered to be 'critical points' and may indicate that it is appropriate to use a lower materiality level than might otherwise be the case;
- an item that is small in the context of the accounts may nevertheless be material, depending on the circumstances – for instance, where a particular item of income or expenditure would normally be large, the fact that it is small in the current year may be relevant to a user of the accounts;
- as well as considering the materiality of individual items, it will usually be necessary to consider similar items in aggregate as well, as the total may be material, even if the individual components are not.

## Exclusion of immaterial items                                10.33

The consideration of materiality is equally important in establishing whether certain details need not be shown separately in the accounts. For instance, reporting in detail on items that are not material, and which are therefore not useful to a user of the accounts, may result in information that is relevant and useful becoming obscured. However, certain information must always be disclosed to meet the requirements of *CA 1985*, even though it may not appear to be material in the context of the accounts.

## Statement of directors' responsibilities     **10.34**

## At a glance     **10.35**

- Audited accounts that are required to show a true and fair view should include a formal statement of the directors' responsibilities in respect of the accounts.
- If the directors do not make such a statement, the auditors must include a description of the directors' responsibilities in their audit report.
- The statement should cover the requirements for the directors to:
    - prepare accounts that show a true and fair view;
    - select suitable accounting policies and apply them consistently;
    - make judgements and estimates that are prudent and reasonable;
    - state whether applicable accounting standards have been followed;
    - prepare accounts on a going concern basis unless this is inappropriate;
    - keep proper accounting records;
    - safeguard the assets of the company; and
    - take reasonable steps to prevent fraud and other irregularities.
- In the case of small and medium-sized companies, no reference needs to be made to the adoption of applicable accounting standards.
- A different statement of directors' responsibilities is required where the company is exempt from having its annual accounts audited.
- The wording of the statement may need to be adapted in the case of specialised businesses and unincorporated entities.

## Requirement to include a statement of responsibilities in the annual accounts     **10.36**

The inclusion of a formal statement of directors' responsibilities in respect of the accounts is addressed in Statement of Auditing Standards 600 (SAS 600) *Auditors' reports on financial statements*. This standard applies in all cases where audited accounts are required to show a true and fair view. Auditors are required to refer in their report to a description of the responsibilities of the directors in respect of the accounts and to distinguish the responsibilities of the auditors from those of the directors. If a statement of the directors' responsibilities is not given in the accounts, or if the statement given is not considered adequate, the auditors must include an appropriate description of the directors' responsibilities within their audit report. In the case of listed companies, the FSA requires the directors to include in the annual report a narrative statement on how it has applied the principles set out Part 1 of the Combined Code, together with details of, and reasons for, any areas of non-compliance. Part D.1.1 of the Combined Code recommends that the directors

*Financial Reporting*

explain their responsibility for preparing the accounts next to a statement by the auditors clarifying their reporting responsibilities. The purpose of both statements is to help shareholders understand the respective roles and responsibilities of the directors and the auditors.

## Presentation of the statement 10.37

It is always preferable for the directors to make a separate statement of their responsibilities for the accounts rather than leaving this to be dealt with by the auditors. The Combined Code recommendation that the directors' statement is given 'next to' the statement of the auditors' responsibilities has been widely interpreted in practice, and the directors' statement is often given above or below the auditors' report, or on the immediately preceding page. It is also acceptable for the statement to be given within the directors' report or in a separate corporate governance report, although this will usually have the disadvantage of separating the information from the summary of the auditors' responsibilities. The Higgs Report proposes changing the wording of Provision D.1.1 in the Combined Code to remove any potential confusion over the location of the respective statements.

## Content of the statement 10.38

The following matters should be covered in the directors' statement:

- the requirement under company law for directors to prepare annual accounts giving a true and fair view of the profit or loss for the year and of the state of affairs of the company (and, where relevant, the group) at the end of the year;
- in preparing those the accounts, the requirement for the directors to:
    - select suitable accounting policies;
    - apply those accounting policies on a consistent basis;
    - make judgments and estimates that are prudent and reasonable;
    - state whether applicable accounting standards have been followed, subject to any material departures disclosed and explained in the accounts; and
    - prepare the accounts on a going concern basis unless it is not appropriate to presume that the company will continue in business;
- the requirement for the directors to:
    - keep proper accounting records;
    - safeguard the assets of the company; and
    - take reasonable steps to prevent and detect fraud and other irregularities.

The statement on compliance with applicable accounting standards need not be given where the company qualifies as small or medium-sized under *CA 1985*.

## Example wording 10.39

SAS 600 suggests the following wording for the statement:

### *Example: Statement of directors' responsibilities for the accounts* 10.40

---

Company law requires the directors to prepare financial statements for each financial year which give a true and fair view of the state of affairs of the company and of the profit and loss of the company for that period. In preparing those financial statements, the directors are required to:

- select suitable accounting policies and then apply them consistently;
- make judgments and estimates that are reasonable and prudent;
- state whether applicable accounting standards have been followed, subject to any material departures disclosed and explained in the the financial statements; *
- prepare the financial statements on the going concern basis unless it is inappropriate to presume that the company will continue in business.

The directors are responsible for keeping proper accounting records which disclose with reasonable accuracy at any time the financial position of the company and to enable them to ensure that the financial statements comply with the *Companies Act 1985*. They are also responsible for safeguarding the assets of the company and hence for taking reasonable steps for the prevention and detection of fraud and other irregularities.

* Not required for companies that qualify as small or medium-sized under *CA 1985*.

---

The directors of most companies choose to make the statement in terms of their general responsibilities, as set out above. It is equally acceptable for the statement to be made in more positive terms, for instance by stating that the directors are of the opinion that appropriate accounting policies have been adopted and applied consistently.

## Impact of audit exemption 10.41

Where a small company is exempt from an audit under *section 249A* of *CA 1985*, a different statement of directors' responsibilities is required. The legislation specifies the content of the statement and requires it to be given on the balance sheet, above the signature of director(s).

## Specialised businesses and unincorporated entities 10.42

SAS 600 applies to all audit reports on accounts that are required to show a true and fair view. The wording of the statement of directors' responsibilities may need to be amended to reflect the specific requirements applying to specialised businesses (for instance banks and insurance companies). In the case of unincorporated entities (such as charities and pension funds) the responsibilities of the directors, managers or trustees may not be so clearly defined and may vary quite considerably between apparently similar entities. Care must be taken to ensure that the statement given in the annual accounts properly reflects the responsibilities actually in place under the relevant constitution or trust deed.

## Form and content of company accounts 10.43

## At a glance 10.44

---

- *CA 1985* offers a choice of four formats for the profit and loss account and two formats for the balance sheet – once a format has been chosen, it must be used consistently from year to year unless there are good reasons for making a change.
- Certain additional items must be shown in the profit and loss account and additional information or analyses must be given in the notes to the accounts.
- Accounting standards generally require more detailed disclosures to be given in the notes to the accounts – some add new items to the standard formats or require additional statements to be included in the accounts.
- The ASB has issued proposals for replacing the profit and loss account and statement of total recognised gains and losses with a single performance statement.
- Comparative figures must be given for each item in the profit and loss account and balance sheet, and most disclosures in the notes to the accounts.
- CA 1985 and accounting standards prescribe the principles to be adopted when preparing accounts.
- Accounting standards require accounts to reflect the commercial substance of the transactions undertaken by the company.

---

## Prescribed formats 10.45

*CA 1985* requires a company to use one of the prescribed formats set out in the legislation for the profit and loss account and for the balance sheet. The legislation provides a choice of four formats for the profit and loss account and two formats for the balance sheet – these are all set out in *Paragraph 8* of *Schedule 4* to *CA 1985*. The directors can choose which format to adopt in each case, but once a format has been selected, it must be used consistently year by year unless there are good reasons for changing to another format. If a format is changed (for instance, where a change in activity makes an alternative profit and loss account format more appropriate to the company's business), details of the change must be disclosed in the accounts and the reason for the change must be explained. The formats do not generally indicate where sub-totals should be drawn and the directors are therefore free to decide on this themselves, subject to the additional disclosure requirements of accounting standards (see **10.47** below). The profit and loss account and balance sheet formats require additional information or analyses to be given for certain items. These disclosures are usually given in the notes to the accounts, together with other detailed disclosures required by the legislation.

## Additional profit and loss account disclosures        10.46

In addition to the details set out in the standard formats, the legislation requires every profit and loss account to show:

- the profit or loss on ordinary activities before taxation;
- the aggregate amount of any dividends paid and proposed (and the aggregate amount of any proposed dividends, unless this is shown in the notes to the accounts); and
- any amounts to be transferred to or from reserves.

## Requirements of accounting standards        10.47

Accounting standards also require additional disclosures to support figures shown in the profit and loss account and balance sheet. The additional details are usually required to be given in the notes to the accounts, except in the case of FRS 3 *Reporting Financial Performance* which requires:

- the separate disclosure of 'operating profit' on the face of the profit and loss account;
- all figures from turnover through to operating profit to be analysed into amounts relating to continuing, discontinued and newly-acquired operations – as a minimum, the figures for turnover and operating profit must be analysed in this way on the face of the profit and loss account;
- separate disclosure on the face of the profit and loss account of:
    - profits and losses on the sale or termination of operations;
    - costs of a fundamental reorganisation or restructuring that has a material effect on the nature and focus of operations; and
    - profits or losses on the disposal of fixed assets (other than marginal adjustments to depreciation charged in previous years).

FRS 3 also requires annual accounts to include a statement of total recognised gains and losses, to draw together all gains and losses recognised during the financial period, and a reconciliation of movements in shareholders' funds The same standard also deals with the definition and disclosure of exceptional items and extraordinary items (although the latter are now very rare, as a result of the stringent definitions in FRS 3). FRS 1 *Cash Flow Statements* requires the presentation of a cash flow statement in the format specified in the standard. FRS 14 *Earnings per share* sets out detailed requirements on the calculation and disclosure of earnings per share – the standard applies to all companies whose shares are publicly traded (or about to become publicly traded) and to any company which chooses to disclose earnings per share on a voluntary basis.

## Expected future developments

10.48

In December 2000, the ASB issued FRED 22 *Revision of FRS 3: Reporting Financial Performance* which proposes some significant changes to present disclosure requirements. The proposals represent an agreed international approach to reporting financial performance and replace the present profit and loss account and statement of total recognised gains and losses with a single performance statement showing all the gains and losses recognised during a financial period. The proposed performance statement is divided into three sections:

- operating;
- financial and treasury; and
- other gains and losses.

It is proposed that dividends should not be reported in the performance statement as they represent transactions with shareholders rather than elements of financial performance. *CA 1985* currently requires dividends to be shown in the profit and loss account, and the ASB is therefore discussing with the DTI the possibility of changing the law. The Government notes in the White Paper *Modernising Company Law* issued in July 2002 that it supports the view that the profit and loss account should become a wider performance statement reporting all gains and losses, and indicates that current moves to modernise EC Directives include similar proposals. The recommendations are now being taken forward as a joint ASB/IASB project and a further exposure draft is expected in the middle of 2003.

## Comparative figures

10.49

Comparative figures must be given for each item in the profit and loss account and balance sheet and for most of the additional information that has to be disclosed in the notes to the accounts. Where any figure reported in the accounts is not directly comparable with the equivalent amount for the previous year, the comparative figure must be adjusted and details, together with the reason for the adjustment, must be given in the notes to the accounts. Accounting standards also include detailed requirements on the disclosure of comparative figures, and in particular on the use of prior period adjustments to account for changes in accounting policies and the correction of fundamental errors.

## Accounting principles

10.50

*CA 1985* requires company accounts be based on the principles of going concern, consistency, accruals and prudence. These principles apply to all companies, regardless of size, and are considered to have such general acceptance that there is no requirement to refer to the fact that they have been followed when preparing the accounts – a company is presumed to have observed them unless its accounts state otherwise. The directors are only permitted to depart from the accounting principles where there are special reasons for doing so and the accounts must disclose particulars of the departure, the reasons for it and the financial effect. Detailed guidance on the principles that should be followed when preparing annual accounts, including practical interpretation of the *CA 1985* requirements, can be found in the ASB's *Statement of Principles for Financial Reporting* and in FRS 18 *Accounting Policies*. Brief details are set out below.

## *Going concern* 10.51

*CA 1985* does not provide any detailed guidance on going concern. FRS 18 describes the going concern basis as the hypothesis that the entity is to continue in operational existence for the foreseeable future. When preparing accounts, the standard requires the directors to assess whether there are any significant doubts about the entity's ability to continue as a going concern and requires financial statements to be prepared on a going concern basis unless:

- the entity is being liquidated or has ceased trading; or
- the directors have no realistic alternative but to liquidate the entity or to cease trading.

In these circumstances the entity may, if appropriate, prepare the financial statements on a different basis. Additional disclosures may need to be given in the notes to the accounts where uncertainties affect the assessment of going concern, and the directors of listed companies are specifically required to make a formal statement on going concern each year (see CHAPTER 12 GOING CONCERN).

## *Consistency* 10.52

Accounting policies provide a framework within which assets, liabilities, income and expenditure are recognised, measured and presented in financial statements, and they help to improve the comparability of financial information. Both *CA 1985* and FRS 18 require accounting policies to be applied consistently within an accounting period and from one financial year to the next. However, situations will inevitably arise from time to time which make it necessary for an entity to change one or more of its accounting policies. For instance, a new accounting standard may have been introduced which requires a different accounting treatment to the one previously adopted, or the nature or scale of activities may have changed so that an existing accounting policy is no longer acceptable. FRS 18 requires accounting policies to be regularly reviewed, and sets out specific accounting and disclosure requirements that apply whenever an accounting policy is changed.

## Accruals

**10.53**

*CA 1985* requires all income and charges relating to the financial year to be taken into account, regardless of the date of receipt or payment. FRS 18 also requires adoption of the accruals method of accounting, which it describes as requiring 'the non-cash effects of transactions and other events to be reflected, as far as is possible, in the financial statements for the accounting period in which they occur and not, for example, in the period in which any cash involved is received or paid'. Provision must therefore be made for all expenses and losses relating to the year in question, and for income and profits relating to that year, subject to the requirement for prudence (see **10.54** below).

## Prudence

**10.54**

*CA 1985* requires the amount of any item in the accounts to be determined on a prudent basis. In particular, only profits realised at the balance sheet date should be included in the profit and loss account, and all losses or liabilities which have arisen (or are likely to arise) in respect of the current financial year or any previous financial year must be taken into account. This includes any liabilities or losses that only become apparent between the balance sheet date and the date on which the accounts are formally approved and signed by the directors. FRS 18 does not deal with prudence as such, but emphasises the need for financial information to be reliable and also the legal requirement that only realised profits are to be included in the accounts. The standard notes that profits should be treated as realised for accounting purposes only when they have been realised in the form of cash or of other assets, the ultimate cash realisation of which can be assessed with reasonable certainty. In the section on reliability, FRS 18 makes the following points:

- under conditions of uncertainty, financial information is reliable if it has been prudently prepared (ie a degree of caution has been applied in exercising judgement and making necessary estimates);
- it is not necessary to exercise prudence where there is no uncertainty; and
- it is not appropriate to use prudence as a reason for creating hidden reserves or excessive provisions, deliberately understating assets or gains, or deliberately overstating liabilities or losses.

## Substance over form

**10.55**

Under FRS 5 *Reporting the Substance of Transactions*, accounts are required to reflect the commercial substance of the transactions entered into by the reporting entity rather than their legal form (where this is different). The commercial substance of a transaction is not always easily identifiable, especially where:

- the principal benefits of an asset are in some way separated from legal ownership;

- the transaction involves options or conditions that are not commercially realistic (for instance, where the terms of an option mean that it is virtually certain not to be exercised); and
- the overall commercial effect of a series of transactions is different from the apparent effect of the individual transactions.

When assessing the substance of a transaction, the standard requires greater emphasis to be given to the aspects of the transaction that are likely to have a practical commercial effect. Where an overall commercial effect is achieved by a series of transactions, the standard requires the series to be considered as a whole rather than as individual transactions. FRS 5 is deliberately conceptual rather than factual in nature to prevent transactions being structured so as to circumvent prescribed rules.

## Form and content of group accounts     10.56

## At a glance     10.57

---

- Group accounts must be prepared in the form of consolidated accounts and must generally include the accounts of the parent company and all its subsidiaries.
- *CA 1985* and FRS 2 *Accounting for Subsidiary Undertakings* set out detailed rules on what constitutes a subsidiary undertaking.
- In certain circumstances, a subsidiary undertaking is permitted or required to be excluded from the consolidated accounts.
- The assets, liabilities, profits, losses and cashflows of certain other entities ('quasi-subsidiaries') may also need to be included in the group accounts, even if these entities do not meet the legal definition of a subsidiary undertaking.
- The results of associates and joint ventures should be normally be included in group accounts using the equity method of accounting.
- *CA 1985* and accounting standards include detailed rules on the preparation of consolidated accounts and on accounting for acquisitions and mergers.
- Directors must ensure that the financial year of each subsidiary undertaking coincides with that of the parent unless there are good reasons against this.

---

## Consolidated accounts     10.58

Group accounts must be prepared in the form of consolidated accounts and must include the accounts of the parent company and all its subsidiary undertakings. The only exception to this rule is where a subsidiary undertaking is required or permitted by the legislation, or by accounting standards, to be excluded from the consolidation. The requirements of accounting standards, particularly FRS 2 *Accounting for Subsidiary Undertakings*, must also be taken into account. The prescribed formats (with appropriate adaptations) and the true and *fair* requirement apply to group accounts in the same way as to individual company accounts.

## Definition of subsidiary undertaking                                10.59

The detailed rules on what constitutes a subsidiary undertaking are set out in *section 258* of *CA 1985* and in FRS 2. The focus of these definitions is the ability of the parent to control the subsidiary. Although *CA 1985* uses terms such as 'exercises a dominant influence' and 'managed on a unified basis', it does not expand on these. FRS 2 gives detailed guidance on how these terms should be interpreted for practical purposes. *Schedule 10A* to *CA 1985* provides guidance on the interpretation of voting rights for the purpose of establishing whether an entity is a subsidiary undertaking.

## Exclusion of a subsidiary from the group accounts            10.60

*Section 229* of *CA 1985* permits a subsidiary undertaking to be excluded from the consolidation if:

- severe long-term restrictions hinder the parent's ability to exercise its rights over the assets and management of the entity; or
- the interest is held exclusively for resale.

FRS 2 includes detailed guidance on the conditions that should be met for exclusion to be justified on these grounds, but where the conditions are met the standard requires exclusion rather than permitting it. FRS 2 also prescribes the accounting treatment to be adopted in each case: a subsidiary excluded on the grounds of long-term restrictions should be accounted for as a fixed asset investment and an interest held exclusively for resale should be accounted for as a current asset investment. Both *CA 1985* and FRS 2 require a subsidiary undertaking to be excluded from the consolidation where its activities are so different from the rest of the group that its inclusion in the consolidation would be incompatible with the true and fair view requirement, but both emphasise that this situation is expected to be extremely rare in practice – in particular, a straightforward diversification of activities will not justify exclusion on these grounds. *CA 1985* also permits a subsidiary to be excluded from the consolidation in two other situations:

- where inclusion would not be material for the purpose of achieving a true and fair view (if two or more subsidiaries are involved, materiality must be assessed on an aggregate basis) – FRS 2 makes no reference to this as accounting standards are only intended to apply to material items;
- where the necessary information cannot be obtained without undue expense or delay – FRS 2 does not permit exclusion on these grounds.

In any case where a subsidiary is excluded from the consolidation, both *CA 1985* and FRS 2 require detailed disclosures to be given in the accounts.

## Quasi-subsidiaries 10.61

An undertaking may in effect be controlled by another entity, and generate benefits for that entity, without meeting the definition of a subsidiary undertaking set out in *CA 1985* or FRS 2. Such an undertaking is described as a 'quasi-subsidiary' in FRS 5 *Reporting the Substance of Transactions* and the standard generally requires the assets, liabilities, profits, losses and cash flows of the quasi-subsidiary to be included in the group accounts of the 'parent' in order to reflect the true substance of the arrangements. Consideration of whether an entity meets the definition of a 'quasi-subsidiary' must take into account:

- who gains the benefit from the entity's net assets;
- who bears the inherent risks relating to the net assets; and
- who directs the operating and financial policies of the entity.

Risk is defined in the standard as including the potential to gain as well as the possible exposure to loss, and the ability to prevent others from gaining access to benefits or from directing the entity's policies are equally relevant to the assessment.

## Associates 10.62

It has become common practice for companies and groups to carry out part of their business activities through entities that are not subsidiary undertakings but over which the investor nevertheless has a considerable degree of influence. An associate is defined as an entity, other than a subsidiary, in which the investor has a participating interest and over whose operating and financial policies the investor exercises significant influence. *Section 260(1) of CA 1985* defines a participating interest as an interest held on a long-term basis for the purpose of securing a contribution to activities through the exercise of control or influence. FRS 9 *Associates and Joint Ventures* gives detailed guidance on the practical application of this definition and of the term 'significant influence'. A shareholding of 20% or more will usually constitute a participating interest, although it is possible to rebut this presumption in certain cases. Although it would be inappropriate to consolidate fully the results, assets and liabilities of an associate into the group accounts, it is also accepted that it would be misleading to ignore the nature of the relationship and account for the associate in the same way as other investments (for instance, by simply reflecting any dividends received as income in the profit and loss account). Both *CA 1985* and FRS 9 therefore require the results of associates to be included in the accounts using the equity method of accounting. Under this method, the investing group's share of the profit or loss of the associate is included in the profit and loss account, and its share of the underlying net assets of the associate is included in the group balance sheet.

## Joint ventures 10.63

FRS 9 also includes detailed guidance on the definition of a joint venture and requires such an entity to be accounted for using the gross equity method of accounting. This is broadly the same as the equity method of accounting but with two additional disclosure requirements:

- the investor's share of the turnover of the joint venture must be shown in the consolidated profit and loss account; and
- the investor's share of the gross assets and liabilities of the joint venture should be shown in the consolidated balance sheet.

Care is needed in the presentation of these figures to ensure they are not confused with those of the group, or do not appear to be included as part of the totals for the group. Further disclosures must be given where a major part of the business is conducted through joint ventures.

## Consolidation rules                                                    10.64

Both *CA 1985* and FRS 2 set out detailed rules on the preparation of consolidated accounts, the main points being that:

- uniform accounting policies should be used throughout the group to determine the amounts to be included in the group accounts – where (in exceptional circumstances) this is not possible, full details of the differences must be disclosed in the accounts;
- where assets held by any group undertakings include profits or losses arising from intra-group transactions (for instance, where items in stock have been purchased from another group company at more than cost price), the full amount of the profit or loss must be eliminated when preparing the consolidated accounts;
- amounts due to and from undertakings included in the consolidation, and income and expenditure relating to transactions between them, must be eliminated from the consolidated accounts; and
- the amount of capital and reserves attributable to shares held by any minority interests, and the profit or loss on ordinary activities (and any extraordinary items) attributable to them, must be shown separately in the consolidated accounts – *Schedule 4A* to *CA 1985* amends the balance sheet and profit and loss account formats to provide additional headings for these disclosures.

There are also detailed rules in the legislation, and in particular in accounting standards, on accounting for acquisitions and mergers and for any goodwill that arises on consolidation.

## Acquisitions and mergers                                               10.65

There are currently two permitted methods of accounting for the combination of existing businesses – acquisition accounting and merger accounting. Merger accounting can only be used when the stringent criteria set out in *CA 1985* and FRS 6 *Acquisitions and Mergers* are met. Most business combinations are therefore accounted for as acquisitions. Under this method of accounting, the assets and liabilities of the acquired entity are brought into the group accounts at fair value as at the date of acquisition, and the results of the entity are included in the group accounts only from the date of acquisition. FRS 7 *Fair Values in Acquisition Accounting* sets out rules on how the fair value of each type of asset and liability should be established. Any difference between the purchase consideration and the aggregate fair value of the assets and liabilities acquired constitutes purchased goodwill.

## Goodwill                                                                10.66

Goodwill is a means of recognising that the value of a business as a whole is often more than the aggregate value of the underlying assets and liabilities. Neither *CA 1985* nor FRS 10 *Goodwill and Intangible Assets* permits internally-generated goodwill to be recognised on the balance sheet. Goodwill is therefore only recognised for accounting purposes when it is purchased as part of a business acquisition. When a company buys an unincorporated business, any goodwill acquired will be recognised on the company's own balance sheet along with the other business assets and liabilities acquired. When a company acquires a business by buying shares in another company, any goodwill acquired is recorded only when the accounts of the company and its new subsidiary are consolidated to form group accounts. Goodwill arising in a company's own accounts and goodwill arising on consolidation must be accounted for in accordance with FRS 10. The standard requires purchased goodwill to be capitalised as an asset and amortised over its useful economic life. There is a rebuttable presumption that the useful economic life of goodwill is no more than 20 years. If it can be demonstrated that the expected life of the goodwill is indefinite, the asset should not be amortised but a detailed impairment review must be carried out each year. This treatment will require use of the true and fair override, as *CA 1985* requires all goodwill to be amortised. Annual impairment reviews must also be carried if the goodwill is amortised over a period of more than 20 years. FRS 10 sets out separate requirements on accounting for negative goodwill, which arises when the purchase consideration is less than the aggregate fair value of the assets and liabilities acquired.

## Accounting date of subsidiary undertakings                            10.67

Under *CA 1985*, the directors of a parent company must ensure that the financial year of each subsidiary undertaking coincides with that of the parent unless, in their opinion, there are good reasons against this. In this case, *CA 1985* requires the group accounts to include:

- the latest accounts of the subsidiary undertaking, provided that these are for a period ending not more than three months before the financial year end of the parent company; or
- interim accounts for the subsidiary made up to the financial year end of the parent company.

FRS 2 *Accounting for Subsidiary Undertakings* sets out more stringent rules, requiring the accounts of all subsidiary undertakings included in the consolidated accounts to be for the same accounting period and made up to the same accounting date as the accounts of the parent, as far as is practicable. Where a subsidiary has a different financial year end, interim accounts should therefore be prepared for consolidation purposes. Only if this is not practicable should the latest accounts of the subsidiary be used, and even then adjustments must be made to reflect any changes in the intervening period if these have a material effect on the group accounts. The standard also requires additional disclosure in the notes to the accounts when a subsidiary prepares its accounts to a different accounting date, or for a different accounting period, from that of the parent company.

## Directors' Report                                              10.68

## At a glance                                                     10.69

---

- Directors are required to prepare a formal report for each financial year – where the company is required to prepare group accounts, the directors' report must also provide information for the group as a whole.
- The detailed contents of the directors' report are prescribed in *CA 1985*.
- The auditors are specifically required to consider whether the information presented in the directors' report is consistent with the annual accounts.
- The report must include a fair review of the development of the business during the year and the position at the end of the year.
- The ASB has issued a non-mandatory Statement 'Operating and Financial Review' to provide a framework for the discussion of a company's performance and financial position.
- Detailed disclosures must be given on directors' interests in shares and share options.
- Extensive disclosures on political donations and expenditure are required as a result of the *Political Parties, Elections and Referendums Act 2000.*
- The Government has issued proposals for replacing the directors' report with a supplementary statement and, in the case of large companies, an Operating and Financial Review.

---

## Requirement to prepare                                         10.70

*CA 1985* requires the directors to prepare a report for each financial year. The detailed contents of the report are specified in the legislation. The report must be approved by the board and signed on their behalf by a director or by the company secretary. Where the company is required to prepare group accounts under *CA 1985*, the directors' report must also provide the required information for the group as whole – however, disclosure requirements in respect of the directors relate only to the directors of the parent company.

## Consistency with the accounts    10.71

The information given in the directors' report must be consistent with any related information given or included in the annual accounts. The auditors are specifically required to consider whether the directors' report is consistent with the accounts and to report any inconsistencies in their report, although in practice they will usually seek to resolve these through discussion and adjustment where appropriate.

## Fair review of the business    10.72

Although *CA 1985* requires the report to include a fair review of the business, it does not specify a format or indicate what should be covered in the review. The main objective is to provide narrative commentary to support the details shown in the profit and loss account and balance sheet, to help the user to understand the company's performance and financial position. The report should be balanced and cover both good and bad aspects of the year. *CA 1985* also requires the directors to give an indication of likely future developments. It is usually advisable to keep this part of the report relatively general in nature, particularly in the case of listed companies, so that comments made by the directors cannot be deemed to constitute a profit forecast.

## ASB 'Operating and Financial Review'    10.73

The ASB issued a non-mandatory Statement *Operating and Financial Review* in July 1993 to provide a framework for the discussion, within the annual report, of the main factors underlying a company's financial perform- ance and financial position. A revised version of the Statement was published in January 2003 and provides a broader framework for the discussion of busi- ness performance than its 1993 predecessor. The current version sets out the principles that directors should follow when preparing an Operating and Financial Review (OFR) together with detailed guidance on their practical application. In particular, the statement now includes:

● guidance on describing the business, its objectives and its strategy in order to put the directors' discussion of performance and financial posi- tion into context;

● a recognition that business objectives and performance may encompass both financial and non-financial measures (eg corporate social respon- sibility);

● a recommendation that the directors explain the strengths and resources of the business, especially any which are not reflected in the balance sheet, together with action taken to enhance future performance;

● a proposal that the OFR should highlight the accounting policies which are key to understanding the entity's performance and financial posi- tion, focussing in particular on any policies to which the results are particularly sensitive; and

● in the light of an increasing use of 'pro-forma' figures, a recommenda- tion that where information from the financial statements has been adjusted for inclusion in the OFR, this fact should be highlighted and a reconciliation provided.

Although the Statement has been prepared with listed companies in mind, the ASB notes that it is also applicable to larger entities. To some extent, the recommendations in the Statement overlap with a number of the current *Companies Act 1985* requirements in respect of the directors' report and the contents of the ASB document can therefore provide useful guidance on the discussion of relevant issues in the directors' report.

## *Principles to be applied*           **10.74**

The ASB Statement sets out the following principles that should be adopted by the directors when preparing an OFR or similar report.

- **Purpose:** The OFR should set out the directors' analysis of the business, to help the user assess likely future performance. The OFR should therefore discuss:
  - the nature and dynamics of the business, its objectives and the strategies adopted to achieve those objectives;
  - significant features of performance in the period, including the main influences on performance, the likely effect of any known trends and the potential effect of any risks; and
  - the financial position, including capital structure and treasury policy, and factors likely to affect that position.
- **Audience:** An OFR will often be of interest to a wide range of users, but should focus on matters which are relevant to investors and should be written in a clear and readily understandable style. It should not assume detailed prior knowledge of the business or its principal operating environment.
- **Time-frame:** The OFR should identify trends and factors relevant to a user's assessment of future performance and the achievement of long-term business objectives, concentrating on those that have affected performance in the current year and are expected to affect the financial performance and financial position of the business in future years. The impact of significant post-balance sheet events should be discussed, and reference should be made to any comments in previous OFRs that have not been borne out by events.
- **Reliability:** Information in the OFR should be neutral, free from bias and complete, dealing even-handedly with both good and bad aspects. The guidance is not intended to result in the duplication of information provided elsewhere in the annual report, but cross-references should be given where appropriate to ensure that balance is maintained and users are not misled by the apparent ommission of information.
- **Comparability:** The disclosures should be sufficient to enable a user to compare the information with that for previous periods and with information about other entities in the same industry or sector, although this should not prevent the approach to disclosure evolving over time or differing from that adopted by similar entities. Accounting policies that

are key to understanding the entity's performance and financial position should be highlighted in the OFR, with a focus on any policies to which the results are particularly sensitive and any policies that have changed during the year.

- **Measures:** An OFR will usually include a range of financial and non-financial measures and comparability will be enhanced if these are widely used within the industry or sector, or more generally. The measures used should be defined, the calculation methods and any related assumptions should be explained, and the source of the underlying data should be disclosed. Any changes in the measures or calculation methods, or in the underlying accounting policies, should be highlighted and explained, The OFR should also identify and comment on the key performance indicators used by the directors in managing the business. In the light of an increasing use of 'pro-forma' figures, the document also recommends that where information from the financial statements has been adjusted for inclusion in the OFR, this fact should be highlighted and the figures reconciled with those shown in the financial statements.

## Directors' share interests 10.75

The disclosure requirements on directors' share interests are extremely complex, particularly as the wording or meaning is not always clear. Interpretations and opinions consequently vary on precisely what needs to be included in the disclosures. For the purposes of the disclosures, the term 'director' includes shadow directors, and an interest in shares or debentures is given the very broad definition set out in *Paragraph 1* of *Schedule 13* to *CA 1985*, so that any interest of any kind whatsoever in relevant shares or debentures constitutes a disclosable interest. A director's interests are also deemed to include any interests held by his/her immediate family, which in this context means the director's spouse, infant children and infant step-children - it does not include parents, brothers, sisters or children over the age of 18. However, if any members of the director's immediate family are also directors of the company, their interests are separately disclosable and are therefore not deemed to be interests of the director. Where a director of a wholly-owned subsidiary is also a director of its holding company and his/her interests will therefore be disclosed in the directors' report for the holding company, the information does not need to be given by the subsidiary, although in this case it is usual to explain where the details can be found. In the case of a listed company, directors' shareholdings must be analysed between beneficial and non-beneficial holdings, and the information must also be updated to within one month of the date of the notice of the AGM.

## Directors' share options 10.76

In addition to the disclosures on directors' interests required by *CA 1985*, UITF Abstract 10 *Disclosure of Directors' Share Options* recommends that the directors' report or accounts include extensive information on the granting and exercise of directors' share options. The Abstract applies to all companies but, unlike other UITF pronouncements, is non-mandatory.

However, in the case of listed companies, the FSA Listing Rules in effect require compliance with UITF Abstract 10. The Abstract has been withdrawn for accounting periods ending on or after 31 December 2002, on the basis that quoted companies are now required to give equivalent disclosures under the *Directors' Remuneration Report Regulations 2002 (SI 2002/1986).*

## Political donations                                      10.77

The *Political Parties, Elections and Referendums Act 2000* came into effect on 16 February 2001. In the context of political donations by companies it broadly requires:

- prior shareholder approval for political expenditure within the EU and for aggregate donations to EU political organisations of more than £5,000 by a company and its subsidiaries in any twelve month period beginning with the company's 'relevant date' (see below);
- disclosure of the detailed names and amounts where the aggregate amount of political expenditure and political donations in the EU by a company or group exceeds £200; and
- disclosure of the aggregate amount paid or donated to non-EU political parties (in this case there is no *de minimis* amount).

Where a payment or donation is to be made by a subsidiary, prior approval must also be obtained from the shareholders of the holding company. Wholly-owned subsidiaries of UK holding companies are exempt from the disclosure requirements, on the basis that the details will be given in the holding company's accounts. If these requirements are not followed, the directors will be personally liable to make good the amount paid or donated and to pay damages for any loss suffered by the company. In the case of non-compliance by a subsidiary, the directors of the holding company will also be personally liable.

A company's relevant date is the date of its AGM, if one is held within 12 months of 16 February 2001, or 16 February 2002 – whichever of these is the earlier. Shareholder approval must be in place for any payments or donations made after this date. The new disclosures must be given in the directors' report for financial years starting on or after the first anniversary of the relevant date. For instance, if a company with a 31 December year-end holds an AGM on 1 August 2001, this will become its relevant date (because it is earlier than 16 February 2002) and prior shareholder approval must be obtained for all political payments and donations made after that date. The new disclosure requirements will apply for the directors' report for the year ending 31 December 2003 (ie the first financial period starting after 1 August 2002, which is the anniversary of the relevant date).

## Government proposals for change                           10.78

Following the recent company law review, the Government White Paper *Modernising Company Law* published in July 2002 proposes removing the present requirement for a narrative directors' report and replacing it with a requirement for the directors to provide a short supplementary statement, to meet the EU requirement for a 'fair review' and provide a location for other necessary disclosures not covered in the accounts. The precise contents of the supplementary statement will be established by Parliament. The detailed reporting by the directors of small companies will be limited to this supplementary statement. Larger companies will be required to prepare an Operating and Financial Review in addition to the supplementary statement. The Government proposes to adopt the company law review recommendations in establishing the initial regime for this. The requirement for an OFR will therefore apply to companies who meet two out of the three following criteria:

|  | *Public companies* | *Private companies* |
|---|---|---|
| Turnover more than | 50 million | 500 million |
| Balance sheet total more than | 25 million | 250 million |
| Number of employees more than | 500 | 5,000 |

Auditors will be required to report on the adequacy of the preparation process and compliance with applicable rules. The intention is that the new legislation will prescribe the contents of the OFR in general terms, but that detailed requirements will be developed by the new Standards Board (see **10.12** above). The White Paper notes that the Government welcomes the update of the ASB's Statement 'Operating and Financial Review' (see **10.74** above) and it therefore seems likely that the revised Statement will form the basis for any new reporting requirements.

## Summary financial statements                                   10.79

## At a glance                                                     10.80

- Subject to certain conditions, listed companies are permitted to issue a summary financial statement to their shareholders in place of the full annual accounts and reports.
- The Government proposes to extend this facility to all companies.
- Each shareholder retains the right to receive a copy of the full annual accounts and reports.
- The minimum content of a summary financial statement is prescribed in *CA 1985*.
- A summary financial statement must also include certain statements to clarify its status, together with a special report from the auditors.
- Research has shown that companies see both advantages and disadvantages in preparing a summary financial statement, but shareholders are more likely to read a summary document than the full accounts and reports.

Financial Reporting

- There are two practical approaches to preparing a summary financial statement.
- Many companies include more than the minimum contents in a summary financial statement.

## Background                                                          10.81

Legislation permitting listed companies to issue a summary financial statement to their shareholders in place of the full annual report and accounts was first introduced in *CA 1989*. The timing of the legislation coincided with the significant increase in the number of individual shareholders as a result of the Government's privatisation programme. In 1995, a number of changes were made to the administrative process to try and encourage a greater take-up of the option, but the number of companies who issue summary financial statements remains comparatively low. Following the recent company law review, the Government White Paper *Modernising Company Law* issued in July 2002 confirms that the option to prepare a summary financial statement will be retained in the new legislation and proposes extending the option to all companies. The contents of the statement are to be widened, so that it becomes a summary of all reporting documents – in practice, this is the approach that most companies already adopt. The Government proposes that detailed rules on the form and content of the summary financial statement should in future be developed by the new Standards Board and that summary financial statements should come within the remit of the successor to the FRRP (see **10.12** above).

## Right to receive full accounts                                      10.82

Even if a company decides to take advantage of the option to prepare a summary financial statement, each shareholder and other person entitled to receive the accounts retains the right to receive a copy of the full annual accounts and report in respect of any financial year. The company cannot issue summary financial statements in place of the full accounts and report without first ascertaining that the entitled individual is happy to receive them – this must be done by following one of the consultation processes set out in the legislation.

## Form and content of summary financial statements      10.83

The summary financial statement must be derived from the company's annual accounts and directors' report and the following minimum content of the statement is specified in the legislation:

- a summary of the directors' report, including:
    - fair review of development of the business;
    - important post balance sheet events;
    - likely future developments in the business;
    - names of those who were directors during the year; and

- amount recommended to be paid as dividend (if not shown in the summary profit and loss account);
- a summary profit and loss account, including;
  ○ turnover;
  ○ income from shares in group undertakings and participating interests;
  ○ other interest receivable and similar income, and interest payable and similar charges;
  ○ profit or loss on ordinary activities before taxation;
  ○ tax on profit or loss on ordinary activities;
  ○ profit or loss on ordinary activities after tax;
  ○ extraordinary income and charges, after tax;
  ○ profit or loss for the financial year;
  ○ aggregate of dividends paid and (if not shown in the summary directors' report) dividends proposed;
- for accounting periods ending before 31 December 2002, the aggregate information on directors' emoluments required by *Paragraph 1(1)* of *Schedule 6* to *CA 1985*;
- for accounting periods ending on or after 31 December 2002, either the whole of the directors' remuneration report or, as a minimum:
  - the aggregate information on directors' remuneration required by *CA 1985, Sch 6, para 1(1)*;
  - the statement of the company's policy on directors' remuneration for future years; and
  - the performance graph summarising shareholder return;
- a summary balance sheet, showing a single amount for each item that is assigned a letter in the *CA 1985* standard formats.

Comparative figures must be given for each item and, where the company is required to prepare group accounts, consolidated figures must be presented. In practice, most companies who issue summary financial statements include more than the minimum information – in particular, summarised cash flow information and corporate governance reporting is usually included (see **10.89** below). Separate requirements apply for banking and insurance companies and groups.

## Other statements to be included                     10.84

The summary financial statement must be signed by a director on behalf of the board and the name of the signing director must be stated. The document must also include:

- a clear statement that it is only a summary of the information given in the company's annual accounts and directors' report;
- a formal statement, in a prominent position, that the summary does not contain sufficient information to allow as full an understanding of the results and state of affairs of the company or group as the full documents would, and that members and other entitled persons have the right to obtain a copy of the full accounts and reports, free of charge;

- a clear statement of how members and other entitled persons can obtain the full accounts and reports for the current year, and how they can elect to receive these in future years in place of the summary financial statement.
- a report from the auditors on whether:
  - the summary financial statement is consistent with the full accounts and reports for the relevant financial year;
  - the summary financial complies with the requirements of *section 251* of *CA 1985* and the related Regulations; and
  - their report on the full accounts was qualified or contained a statement under *section 237(2)* of *CA 1985* (inadequate accounting records or returns, or accounts not in agreement with the records or returns) or *section 237(3)* of *CA 1985* (failure to obtain all the information and explanations that the auditors consider necessary).

## The purpose of summary financial statements　　10.85

The provisions allowing listed companies to prepare and issue summary financial statements were introduced to recognise the fact that the needs of shareholders and other users of the accounts can vary quite significantly. The disclosures required by accounting standards and companies legislation are becoming increasingly complex, and whilst the information now required may be highly relevant to technically sophisticated users of accounts, it is evident that many private shareholders are confused by the volume of detail given in a full set of accounts. In some cases the level of detailed disclosures can actually obscure the key information that private shareholders require from the accounts. The main aims of the summary financial statement are to remove most of the more complex disclosures and concentrate on the key issues that are of relevance to individual shareholders, and to enable companies to present this key information in a user-friendly manner, for instance by making appropriate use of charts and graphs.

## Perceived advantages and disadvantages　　10.86

A working party established by the Institute of Chartered Accountants in England & Wales (ICAEW) reported in 1996 on the results of research amongst companies on why they decided to produce or not to prepare a summary financial statement, and amongst shareholders on the relative merits to them of full accounts and a summary financial statement ('Summary Financial Statements: The Way Forward' – ICAEW July 1996). The main reasons given for not making use of summary financial statements were:

- potentially higher production costs, especially in the first year, and no significant cost savings anticipated in subsequent years;
- the additional administrative burden;
- that the use of a summary financial statement would run counter to the present philosophy of providing fuller information to shareholders.

The main advantages reported by companies who had issued summary financial statements were better communication with shareholders and actual cost savings. The point on actual cost savings is particularly interesting. Whilst the majority of companies who decided to prepare summary financial statements did so primarily to improve communication with their shareholders, nearly all of them found that the exercise also achieved some cost savings. It may be that companies not currently using summary financial statements are being unnecessarily pessimistic in their assessment of the costs and the additional administrative effort required. It should be emphasised that most of the research referred to in the report was undertaken before the changes introduced by the *Companies (Summary Financial Statement) Regulations 1995 (SI 1995/2092)* which simplified the consultation process with shareholders and may already have helped to alleviate some of the concerns over costs and administration.

## Views of shareholders                                                10.87

The ICAEW report also summarised the results of a survey to assess the reactions of shareholders to summary financial statements. This indicated a high degree of enthusiasm for summary financial statements amongst shareholders. The key conclusions from the research were:

● shareholders were more likely to read some or all of the summary financial statement than to open and read the full accounts, and that a summarised document is therefore helpful in improving communication with shareholders;
● where a summary financial statement was made available, a very high proportion of shareholders (in the order of 90%) opted to receive the summary rather than the full annual report and accounts.
● the summarised results, chairman's statement and overall business review were the most widely read parts of the document;
● other financial information, the report by the auditors and any additional details (for instance on corporate governance issues) were generally not widely read by shareholders; and
● there was a clear preference for a short document rather than a longer one.

A further point highlighted by the research was that very few companies had carried out any direct consultation with shareholders to try and identify their specific needs and ensure that these were being satisfied, despite the fact that the research amongst companies had indicated that shareholder pressure would encourage them to consider preparing a summary financial statement.

## A practical approach to producing summary financial statements                                            10.88

There are essentially two approaches to the preparation of a summary financial statement:

- the production of two completely separate and free-standing documents – the summary financial statement and the full annual report and accounts; and
- the production of a summary financial statement and a supplementary document containing additional information – in this case, the summary financial statement and the supplementary document together constitute the full annual report and accounts.

The second approach is by far the more common in practice. Failure to consider this method of preparation may be one of the factors that explains why companies not preparing summary financial statements quote potentially higher costs (or no anticipated cost savings) as one of the reasons against using them, whilst those preparing summary financial statements have achieved actual cost savings. A potential disadvantage of the second approach is that analysts and other technically-minded users of the accounts may find it irritating to have to refer to two documents. However, this can usually be overcome by careful planning of the contents of each part of the document and clear cross-referencing.

## Usual contents of summary financial statements      10.89

There is a broad consensus amongst companies who do prepare summary financial statements on the basic contents of the document. These invariably go beyond the minimum contents laid down in Regulations and usually comprise:

- financial highlights;
- chairman's statement;
- an operational review of the business, which often makes extensive use of colour photographs and other illustrations;
- the summarised profit and loss account and balance sheet;
- summarised cash flow information;
- information on directors' remuneration; and
- financial calendar.

Corporate governance issues are also usually referred to in the summary financial statement, but the level of detail given varies. Despite the preference for short documents highlighted in the shareholder research, summary financial statements these days are often substantial documents, with many being between 20 and 40 pages in length.

## Interim reports      10.90

## At a glance      10.91

- The FSA Listing Rules require listed companies to issue an interim statement each year, giving details of their results for the first half of the financial year.

- The FSA Listing Rules require the interim statement to be notifed within 90 days of the period end – the ASB Statement 'Interim Reports' recommends that it is issued within 60 days of the period end.
- There is no formal requirement for the auditors to review or report on the interim statement but directors often arrange for this to be done as a separate engagement.
- FSA requirements on the minimum contents of an interim statement are now broadly consistent with the recommendations set out in the ASB Statement 'Interim Reports'.
- A management commentary on the results for the first half of the year should be included in the interim statement.
- The interim statement should be prepared on the basis of the company's normal accounting policies and should take account of any change in accounting policy that is to be implemented in the accounts for the full financial year.
- Earnings per share should be calculated and disclosed in the same way as in the annual accounts.
- The ASB Statement includes detailed guidance on the measurement and recognition of income and expenditure in the interim statement.
- Comparative figures should cover both the corresponding interim report and the last full financial year.
- An interim statement must include the formal statements that have to be given in non-statutory accounts.

## Requirement to prepare an interim report　　　　10.92

The FSA Listing Rules require listed companies to issue an interim statement each year, giving details of their results for the first half of the financial year. The FSA requirements on the minimum content of an interim statement have now been brought broadly into line with the recommendations set out in the ASB Statement *Interim Reports* (see **10.95** below). Companies may issue information on a more regular basis, and quarterly reporting is required for innovative, high-growth companies which apply for listing under Chapter 25 of the UK Listing Rules. The FSA is currently considering whether quarterly reporting should be introduced for all listed companies. Where a listed company changes its accounting reference date and the change results in an accounting period of 14 months or more, the FSA Listing Rules require publication of a second interim report covering either the period to the previous accounting reference date or a period ending not more than six months before the new accounting reference date.

## Timing and distribution　　　　10.93

For listed companies, interim reports form an important part of the process of communicating with shareholders and with the financial market as a whole, enabling readers to monitor the progress and development of the business and assess the impact of recent events. The reaction of the financial markets to information given in interim reports can be significant and many companies provide more than the minimum details required. The interim report should be distributed to all shareholders and the ASB Statement *Interim Reports* recommends this is done within 60 days of the period-end. However, the UK Listing Rules currently allow a slightly longer timescale for the preparation of the interim report, requiring it to be notified within 90 days of the period-end.

## Review by the auditors                                                  10.94

There is currently no formal requirement for auditors to review or report on interim reports before they are published. The ASB Statement *Interim reports* recommends disclosure of the extent to which the information given in the interim report has been audited or reviewed. APB Bulletin 1999/4 *Review of Interim Financial Information* sets out guidance on the procedures that should be undertaken where auditors are asked to review an interim report, although it notes that the directors (or, where relevant, the Audit Committee) may ask the auditors to carry out specific agreed procedures as an alternative to this. Where an interim report is reviewed in accordance with the APB guidance, the FSA Listing Rules require the auditors' review report to be published as part of the interim report. The latest guidance on the wording of the review report can be found in APB Bulletin 2001/2 *Revisions to the Wording of Auditors' Reports on Financial Statements and the Interim Review Report*. Because the recommended review work is limited in scope, and does not constitute an audit, the auditors will normally report in terms of 'negative assurance' - in other words, they report that nothing has come to their attention to indicate that material modification is required to the information presented in the report. APB Bulletin 1994/5 recommends that, where the scope of the work agreed between the directors and auditors is less than that set out in the Bulletin, the directors should describe the interim report as 'neither audited nor reviewed'.

## Contents of an interim report                                           10.95

The ASB published its Statement *Interim Reports* in September 1997 in response to issues raised in the Cadbury Report, the objective being to improve the timeliness, quality, relevance and consistency of the information published in interim reports. The ASB Statement is non-mandatory but it sets out best practice for companies that are required to publish an interim report, and all listed companies are encouraged to follow its recommendations. It is particularly helpful to have formal guidance on the principles to be followed in dealing with some of the potentially difficult issues that can arise. The principles set out in the guidance are equally relevant to reports produced on a more regular basis. The recommended contents for an interim report are:

- a balanced narrative commentary on the main factors influencing performance during the period and the financial position at the period end;
- a summarised profit and loss account, showing:
    - turnover;

- operating profit or loss;
- net interest payable/receivable;
- profit or loss on ordinary activities before tax;
- tax on profit or loss on ordinary activities;
- profit or loss on ordinary activities after tax;
- minority interests;
- profit or loss for the period;
- dividends paid and proposed;
- a statement of total recognised gains and losses;
- a summarised balance sheet, showing:
  - fixed assets;
  - current assets:
    - stocks;
    - debtors;
    - cash at bank and in hand;
    - other;
  - creditors: amounts falling due within one year;
  - net current assets/liabilities;
  - total assets less current liabilities;
  - creditors: amounts falling due after more than one year;
  - provisions for liabilities and charges;
  - capital and reserves;
  - minority interests;
- a summarised cash flow statement, showing:
  - net cash inflow/outflow from operating activities;
  - returns on investments and servicing of finance;
  - taxation;
  - capital expenditure and financial investment;
  - acquisitions and disposals;
  - equity dividends paid;
  - management of liquid resources;
  - financing;
  - increase/decrease in cash.

## Other disclosures                    10.96

The ASB Statement recommends the following additional disclosures:

- where relevant, amounts relating to associates and joint ventures should be shown separately in the summarised profit and loss account;
- turnover and operating profit in respect of any acquisitions or discontinued operations should be shown separately on the face of the summarised profit and loss account – for this purpose, operations are to be regarded as discontinued if the sale or termination was completed in the interim period, or by the earlier of the date of approval of the interim report or three months after the end of the interim period;
- segmental analyses of turnover and profit or loss before interest should

287

be given, using the same business and geographical classifications as in the annual accounts;

- any exceptional items occurring in the interim period should be disclosed, including items required to be shown separately in the profit and loss account under FRS 3 *Reporting financial performance* (ie profits and losses on the sale or termination of an operation, costs of a fundamental reorganisation or restructuring, and profits and losses on the disposal of fixed assets); and
- reconciliations of operating profit to operating cash flow and the movement of cash to the movement in net debt should be given.

The following should be clearly stated:

- the period covered by the interim report;
- the date on which the interim report was formally approved by the board of directors; and
- the extent to which the information in the interim report has been audited or reviewed.

The results of operations that are in the process of discontinuing, or which are expected to be classified as discontinued in the accounts for the full financial year, may be shown separately in the notes to the interim report.

## Management commentary                                    10.97

Because the interim report is intended to update shareholders and other interested parties on the company's performance since the latest annual accounts, the management commentary should focus on recent events, activities and circumstances. The commentary should therefore discuss the financial information shown in the interim profit and loss account, statement of total recognised gains and losses, balance sheet and cash flow statement in the context of events since the previous financial year end. It is important that the review does not concentrate solely on performance in the period, as shown in the profit and loss account, but also considers related issues such as working capital, liquidity and net debt. Significant trends and events mentioned in the commentary should be supported by the figures shown in the primary statements or by additional disclosures in the notes. Additional information should be given where this is necessary for an understanding of the significant items in the primary statement (for instance, additional information about company borrowings may need to be given if this is a significant issue).

The Statement recommends that the management commentary on the interim figures explains the reasons for significant movements in key indicators and gives a balanced view of the perceived trends within the business, so that readers of the report can understand the main factors influencing the company's performance during the period under review and its position at the end of that period. The report should therefore discuss both positive and negative aspects of the interim period. Where the business is seasonal, it will be particularly important to provide sufficient information for readers to understand the interim results in the context of the full financial year. The commentary should also draw attention to any events and changes occurring during the interim period that are likely to have a significant impact in the second part of the year, even though they may not have affected the company's performance in the period under review. Where relevant it should also cover significant changes in fixed assets and investments, capital structure, financing, commitments and contingencies.

The management commentary included in an interim report is not intended to be as detailed as an operating and financial review presented as part of the annual accounts and reports. However, the guidance in the ASB Statement *Operating and financial review* (see **10.73**) may be useful in helping to identify key issues that should be discussed in the interim report.

## Accounting policies                                           10.98

Interim reports should be prepared using the company's normal accounting policies and should include a statement that the policies are the same as those disclosed in the last published accounts, or explain any differences. Where it is known that a change in accounting policy is to be made in the accounts for the full financial year, the interim report should normally be prepared on the basis of the new policy, all relevant comparative figures should be restated and the cumulative effect on opening reserves should be disclosed. If the interim figures are not presented on the basis of the new accounting policy, the estimated financial effect of the change in policy should be disclosed. Any other prior period adjustments (for instance, to correct fundamental errors) should be reflected in the interim report in the same way as changes in accounting policy.

## Earnings per share                                             10.99

Basic earnings per share should be calculated from the interim results and disclosed in the interim report in the same way as in the full annual accounts. If the company adopts a policy of disclosing additional calculations of earnings per share in its annual accounts, the same details should be given in the interim report.

## Basis of presentation of financial information      10.100

One particular issue that arises in the case of an interim report is whether the interim period is treated as part of an annual reporting cycle or as a discrete accounting period, distinct from the annual cycle. The ASB Statement recommends that the latter method is used so that the measurement and recognition of income and expenditure is consistent with the annual accounts. Specific guidance is given in the Statement on accounting for items such as bonuses, profit-sharing arrangements and volume discounts that will normally only be calculated at the end of the financial year. The treatment depends on whether there is an obligation at the end of

**Financial Reporting**

the interim period to transfer economic benefits as a result of past events. For instance, if a profit-related bonus is to be paid at the end of the year, it will be appropriate to recognise a proportion of this in the interim period, based on the profit earned to date, if past practice shows that the company has a constructive obligation to make the payment. A genuinely discretionary bonus paid at the end of the year would not be recognised in the interim figures. However, the Statement also notes that it will sometimes be necessary to look at the expected income or expense for the full year in order to calculate the amount to be recognised in the interim period. The most obvious example here is taxation and considerable guidance is given on this. The likely effective tax rate for the full year should be calculated, expressed as a percentage of the expected results for the full year, and this percentage should be applied to the interim profit or loss to calculate the interim tax charge. More detailed calculations may be needed where different tax jurisdictions are involved or where different tax rates apply to material categories of income. Other points to note in relation to the presentation of financial information in interim reports are:

- the results of foreign group entities should be translated in line with the company's usual accounting policy;
- asset revaluations will not usually be required for interim report purposes, although certain disclosures are recommended; and
- materiality should be assessed in relation to the interim period rather than the expected results and financial position at the end of the financial year.

## Comparative figures                                      10.101

Comparative figures for the summarised profit and loss account, statement of total recognised gains and losses and summarised cash flow statement should cover the corresponding interim period in the previous year and also the last full financial year. This is to help provide a meaningful view of the company's performance to date, especially where the business is seasonal. In the case of the balance sheet, the critical comparative figures are those for the last full financial year, although those for the corresponding interim period may also be given.

## Statutory disclosure                                     10.102

Where an interim report contains information for a full financial year of the company or information as at the company's normal financial year (for instance, comparative profit and loss account information for the previous financial year, and comparative balance sheet information as at the end of the last financial year), the interim report will constitute 'non-statutory accounts' under *section 240* of *CA 1985* and must include the statements required by that section.

# Preliminary announcements         10.103

# At a glance         10.104

- The FSA Listing Rules require listed companies to make a preliminary announcement of their annual results and dividends within 120 days of the year-end.
- The ASB Statement *Preliminary announcements* encourages companies to make their preliminary announcement within 60 days of the year-end and to issue their accounts and reports as soon as practicable thereafter.
- The audit of the underlying accounts should be substantially complete before the preliminary announcement is issued.
- The FSA requires directors to obtain agreement from the auditors before the preliminary announcement is issued and to give details in the announcement of any qualification of the auditors' report.
- Companies are encouraged to make their preliminary announcement widely available in order to maintain parity between shareholders.
- FSA requirements on the minimum contents of a preliminary announcement are now broadly consistent with the recommendations set out in the ASB Statement.
- The management commentary should discuss the results for the second half of the year as well as the company's overall performance and financial position.
- The preliminary announcement should be prepared on the basis of the company's normal accounting policies – any changes in accounting policy should be explained and the financial effect should be disclosed.
- Earnings per share should be calculated and disclosed in the same way as in the annual accounts.
- Comparative figures should cover the last full financial year – companies are also encouraged to disclose the figures for the second half of the year, with comparatives.
- A preliminary announcement must include the formal statements that have to be given in non-statutory accounts.

# Requirement to prepare a preliminary announcement         10.105

The FSA Listing Rules require listed companies to notify a preliminary statement of annual results and dividends immediately after it has been approved by the board. Under the current Listing Rules, the preliminary announcement must be notified within 120 days of the end of the accounting period, although an extension of this deadline may be granted in exceptional circumstances. The minimum contents required by the Listing Rules are broadly in line with those set out in the ASB Statement *Preliminary Announcements*. Technically, this document is non-mandatory but it sets out best practice on

**Financial Reporting**

the form and content of preliminary announcements and listed companies are therefore encouraged to follow its recommendations. In many ways, interim reports and preliminary announcements are very similar in nature. Both communicate new information on the company's performance and financial position and, in each case, the reaction of the financial markets to the information given can be significant.

## Timing of preliminary announcement      10.106

The ASB Statement encourages companies to issue their preliminary announcement within 60 days of the financial year-end, and to issue the full report and accounts (and, where relevant, the summary financial statement) as soon as practicable thereafter, although it acknowledges that individual circumstances may make it impractical for some companies to achieve this target. The FSA has therefore set a longer deadline of 120 days from the end of the accounting period. The ASB Statement also considers the need for the figures in the preliminary announcement to be reliable and the impact that this might have on the timing of publication. It recommends that:

- the audit of the draft financial statements should be substantially complete at the date of the announcement;
- all the figures in the preliminary announcement should agree with the draft financial statements on which the audit is substantially complete; and
- any non-financial information or commentary included in the preliminary announcement should be consistent with the draft financial statements and with the figures set out in the preliminary announcement.

Companies are encouraged to make their preliminary announcement as soon as the main figures have been agreed by the auditors, rather than waiting for the audit to be fully completed. This recognises that, in practice, it will usually take time to finalise the detailed notes to the financial statements and the other reports published with them, but this will not affect the reliability of the principal figures. APB Bulletin 1998/7 *The Auditors' Association with Preliminary Announcements* provides guidance on when the audit should be regarded as being substantially complete. To prevent any misunderstanding, the ASB Statement recommends that the preliminary announcement should state that the audit report on the full financial statements has not yet been signed, if that is the case.

## *Need to obtain auditors' agreement*      10.107

It is important that the information released in the preliminary announcement is reliable and the FSA therefore requires the directors to obtain agreement from the auditors before the preliminary announcement is approved for issue. APB Bulletin 1998/7 recommends that the role of the auditors in respect of the preliminary announcement is set out in writing (this is usually dealt with by including an appropriate paragraph in the audit engagement letter) and that the auditors issue a formal letter to the directors confirming their agreement to publication of the preliminary announcement. If the audit report on the financial statements is likely to be qualified, the FSA requires the preliminary announcement to include details of the nature of the qualification.

## *Distribution of preliminary announcement*     **10.108**

Interim reports are issued to all shareholders, but preliminary announcements tend to be issued only to financial analysts and institutional shareholders. The ASB Statement emphasises that all shareholders should be treated equally and encourages companies to make better use of technology (for instance, by making preliminary announcements available on the internet) and to give all shareholders the option of receiving a copy of the preliminary announcement as soon as it is issued (for instance, by establishing a pre-registration scheme or publishing an address or telephone number from which copies can be obtained). The Government White Paper *Modernising Company Law* published in July 2002 endorses the recommendation made in the recent company law review that all quoted companies should be required to make their preliminary announcement available on a website.

## *Contents of a preliminary announcement*     **10.109**

The ASB Statement recommends the following contents for a preliminary announcement:

- a balanced narrative commentary on the main factors influencing performance during the period and the financial position at the period end;
- a summarised profit and loss account, showing:
  - turnover;
  - operating profit or loss;
  - net interest payable/receivable;
  - profit or loss on ordinary activities before tax;
  - tax on profit or loss on ordinary activities;
  - profit or loss on ordinary activities after tax;
  - minority interests;
  - profit or loss for the period;
  - dividends paid and proposed;
- a statement of total recognised gains and losses;
- a summarised balance sheet, showing:
  - fixed assets;
  - current assets:
    - stocks;
    - debtors;
    - cash at bank and in hand;
    - other;
  - creditors: amounts falling due within one year;
  - net current assets/liabilities;
  - total assets less current liabilities;

- creditors: amounts falling due after more than one year;
- provisions for liabilities and charges;
- capital and reserves;
- minority interests;
- a summarised cash flow statement, showing:
  - net cash inflow/outflow from operating activities;
  - returns on investments and servicing of finance;
  - taxation;
  - capital expenditure and financial investment;
  - acquisitions and disposals;
  - equity dividends paid;
  - management of liquid resources;
  - financing;
  - increase/decrease in cash.

A reconciliation of movements in shareholders' funds only needs to be included in the when there are additional movements to be explained (ie movements other than those shown in the statement of total recognised gains and losses).

## *Other disclosures*                                    **10.110**

The ASB Statement also recommends the following additional disclosures:

- where significant, amounts relating to associates and joint ventures should be shown separately in the summarised profit and loss account;
- turnover and operating profit in respect of any acquisitions or discontinued operations should be shown separately on the face of the summarised profit and loss account in accordance with the requirements of FRS 3 *Reporting financial performance*;
- where significant, the segmental analyses of turnover and profit or loss before interest to be given in the full report and accounts should also be disclosed in the preliminary announcement;
- sufficient information should be given for readers to understand any significant changes in the effective tax rate from the previous year – in some cases, the tax charge may need to be analysed into its main components;
- any exceptional items should be disclosed, either or the face of the profit and loss account or in the notes, in accordance with FRS 3 *Reporting financial performance*;
- reconciliations of operating profit to operating cash flow and the movement of cash to the movement in net debt should be given; and
- the preliminary announcement should state the period covered and the date on which it was formally approved by the board of directors.

## *Management commentary*                               **10.111**

The aim of the management commentary in a preliminary announcement is to enable shareholders and other interested parties to understand the main factors that have influenced the company's performance during the financial year and its financial position at the year end. As well as commenting on the year as a whole, the ASB Statement recommends that management discuss and explain in particular the salient features of the second half of the year (ie the period not covered by the interim report). These represent new information for shareholders, but are often subsumed into the details of the full year without specific comment. It is also important that the review does not concentrate solely on performance in the period, as shown in the profit and loss account, but also considers related issues such as working capital, liquidity and net debt. Significant trends and events mentioned in the commentary should be supported by the figures shown in the primary statements or by additional disclosures in the notes. Additional information should be given where this is necessary for an understanding of the significant items in the primary statement. The information given in the preliminary announcement should be succinct, consistent with the details to be given in the full report and accounts, and comparable with reports previously published.

The report should discuss both positive and negative aspects of the financial year and should include adequate information on any seasonal activity, so that the impact of this can be fully appreciated. The commentary should also draw attention to any events and changes occurring during the current financial year that are likely to have a significant impact in the following year, even though they may not have affected the company's performance in the period under review. Where relevant it should also cover significant changes in fixed assets and investments, capital structure, financing, commitments and contingencies.

The management commentary included in a preliminary announcement is not intended to be as detailed as an operating and financial review presented as part of the annual accounts and reports. However, the guidance in the ASB Statement *Operating and financial review* (see **10.73**)may be useful in helping to identify key issues that should be discussed in the preliminary announcement.

## *Accounting policies* 10.112

The accounting policies used in preparing the preliminary announcement should be consistent with those in the full accounts, and the preliminary announcement should include a statement that the policies are the same as those disclosed in the last published accounts, or explain any differences. If there has been a change in accounting policy, the preliminary announcement should be prepared on the new accounting policy, all relevant comparative figures should be restated on the basis of the new policy and the cumulative effect on opening reserves should be disclosed. If any other prior period adjustments are necessary (for instance, to correct fundamental errors) these should be reflected in the preliminary announcement in the same way as changes in accounting policy.

## *Earnings per share*                                      **10.113**

Basic earnings per share should be calculated and disclosed in the preliminary announcement in the same way as in the full annual accounts. If the
company adopts a policy of disclosing additional calculations of earnings per
share in its annual accounts, the same details should be given in the preliminary announcement.

## *Comparative figures*                                     **10.114**

Comparative figures for the summarised profit and loss account, statement of
total recognised gains and losses, summarised balance sheet and summarised
cash flow statement should cover the last full financial year. The ASB
Statement also recommends that the preliminary announcement should set out
information on the second half of the year, together with comparatives for the
equivalent period in the previous year, to support the management commentary and facilitate an understanding of the company's current performance.

## *Statutory disclosure*                                    **10.115**

A preliminary announcement contains information for the current and previous financial years of the company and also information as at the company's
current and previous financial year-end. It therefore constitutes 'non-statutory accounts' under *section 240* of the *Companies Act 1985* and must include
the statements required by that section.

# Reporting on the internet                                  **10.116**

## At a glance                                               **10.117**

- Many companies now use a website to disseminate financial information, but concern has been expressed over the lack of any formal
requirements or guidance on this form of financial reporting.
- The Government has proposed that listed companies should be
required to publish their annual accounts and reports on a website.
- A Discussion Paper published by the International Accounting
Standards Committee (IASC) in 1999 set out suggested contents for
a Code of Conduct on internet reporting.
- The International Federation of Accountants (IFAC) has recently
issued guidance on issues to consider in respect of internet reporting.
- *CA 1985* now permits companies to distribute their annual accounts
and reports electronically.
- The Auditing Practices Board (APB) has issued guidance on the
steps that auditors should take when accounts are to be made available on a website or distributed electronically.
- The Institute of Chartered Secretaries and Administrators (ICSA)
has issued guidance on communicating electronically with shareholders.

## *Impact of the internet* 10.118

Research has shown that at least 80% of listed companies with websites make use of them to disseminate financial information. Following the recent company law review, the Government White Paper *Modernising Company Law* published in July 2002 proposes that all quoted companies should be required to publish their annual accounts and reports on a website as soon as practicable after they have been approved and the audit report signed, and within four months of the financial year end at the latest. However, this form of reporting goes beyond the traditional reporting boundaries and there is concern that regulators and accounting standard setters are not keeping pace with the technological changes. There is a consequent lack of any formal guidance on this form of reporting and users have no guarantee on the quality of the information presented or on its comparability with the information published by other businesses. There is particular concern that companies often fail to distinguish information that has been audited from that which is unaudited.

There is also a wide variety in the level of information provided. Some websites include only brief summary reports, some allow downloading of electronic versions of the printed financial statements and others present the full financial statements for on-screen viewing. Where the website includes only extracts of the full financial report, there is concern that users may be given a misleading impression. Many sites simply present financial information as if it were in printed form, which can make it cumbersome and inflexible. More advanced sites allow users to manipulate the underlying data to suit their own purposes, and this is expected to become more widespread as technology continues to develop.

## *Suggested Code of Conduct* 10.119

A discussion paper published in November 1999 by the International Accounting Standards Committee (IASC), which has now been superseded by the International Accounting Standards Board (IASB), concluded that a Code of Conduct for internet reporting should be developed to deal with issues of immediate concern, and that in the longer term standards should be established to deal with reporting by means of developing technologies. The paper set out the recommended content of a Code of Conduct and, although this is not a formal document, companies which are already making use of the internet for financial reporting may find it helpful to bear in mind the points raised. The recommendations include the following:

● *Consistency.* Financial information published on the internet should be consistent with similar information published in another medium (eg in printed form). If documents provided online do not include the full information from the original format, this fact should be stated and a point of contact provided for obtaining the missing information. If any information provided on the internet is additional to that provided in another form, this fact should also be stated.

- *Multiple online files.* Where financial reports are divided into separate documents for online presentation, the complete set should be listed together on the website and there should be appropriate cross-referencing between documents.
- *Boundaries of financial statements.* The boundaries of the complete set of financial statements should be clearly recognisable so that a user knows when he/she has moved out of this area.
- *Other financial information.* Where an entity includes on its website financial information or similar data that is not derived from its financial statements (eg forecasts, environmental information, social responsibility information), this information should not be presented in a manner which suggests that it conforms to an international or similar reporting standard.
- *Excerpts.* If a website includes only excerpts from a complete set of financial statements (eg just an income statement or a balance sheet, without the related notes), it should be clearly identified as an excerpt and details should be provided of how the full copy can be obtained.
- *Historical summaries.* If a historical financial summary is published on the website, the underlying accounting principles should be clearly identified. In particular, it should be clear whether the figures are those originally reported or whether they have been restated to be consistent with the requirements of new reporting standards.
- *Supplementary information.* Supplementary information that would not otherwise be widely available (eg data for analysts' briefings, press releases, other investor relations material) should be provided online for the benefit of all shareholders.
- *Auditors' report.* It should be clear which information is subject to an audit opinion, and any qualification in the auditors' report should be clearly noted. If information is provided in more than one language, but only the primary language financial statements were audited, this fact should be stated in the translated versions.
- *Stability.* All pages should be identifiable and re-creatable to enable users to bookmark them and return to the data in future.
- *Archiving.* Once financial information has been made available online, it should be archived and should not be removed from the site. Archived information should be clearly identified as such to avoid confusion with more recent material.
- *Dating.* All pages should show clearly the date of origin and the date of the last amendment.
- *Downloads.* Key data should be provided in a format that can be downloaded for off-line analysis. As a minimum, the statutory filings made by the entity in its primary jurisdictions should be downloadable.
- *Notification of updates.* Users should be informed of significant changes to the website, either through an e-mail notification service or by providing a date order listing of changes.
- *Currency conversions.* If the website offers a facility for changing the reporting currency on the basis of period-end or average exchange rates, this 'convenience translation' should be clearly identified for

what it is and should state that it does not conform to the translation requirements of accounting standards.

- *Responsibility*. Users have a right to presume that the entity is taking legal responsibility for the accuracy and completeness of the financial information provided on its website. If this is not the case, this fact should be clearly stated. Any data on the site that was created outside the company should be clearly identified and its source noted.
- *Security*. All reasonable precautions should be taken to prevent unauthorised alteration of the data. The discussion paper proposes that, once a Code of Conduct is developed, websites providing financial information should be required to state their compliance with the Code, or specify any departures.
- *Other recommendations*. Other recommendations in the discussion paper include the following:
  - listed companies should prepare their websites in such a way that business reporting information for investors is clearly distinguished from promotional and other material;
  - auditors of listed companies should be responsible for ensuring that audited and unaudited information on the website is clearly distinguished; and
  - auditors of listed companies should ensure that the company conforms fully to the Code of Conduct where it claims to do so, or that any deviations are noted in the audit report.

## *Subsequent guidance from IFAC*     10.120

In August 2002, the International Federation of Accountants (IFAC) published *Financial Reporting on the Internet*. This has been developed by IFAC staff in the course of work on other projects and builds on the IASC discussion paper. The paper has not been formally approved by IFAC and consequently does not have the status of a formal IFAC document. It is intended to stimulate discussion and provide guidance to companies currently using the internet to report financial information. It considers issues under the following headings:

- *Internet Reporting Policy – Matters of principle*: This summarises management's responsibility for considering:
  - the type of information to be provided;
  - the involvement of the auditor;
  - the format in which the information will be provided; and
  - when the information will be provided.
- *Internet Reporting Policy – Practical issues: This covers:*
  - the need to distinguish clearly between audited and unaudited information;
  - the need to distinguish between information intended to supplement the financial information (eg press and analysts briefings) and promotional or marketing information;
  - the use and maintenance of hyperlinks to third party internet sites (eg financial analysts);

Financial Reporting

- the inclusion of third party analyses and information on a company website;
- the frequency of changes to financial information provided on a website.
- *Internet Reporting Policy – Control issues: This covers:*
  - controls over the approval of information provided on a website;
  - the security of financial information provided on a website;
  - the need to state clearly how users can obtain further information in either electronic or written form.
- *Management's responsibilities for content: This includes guidance on:*
  - ensuring the consistency of financial information to be provided on a website;
  - the need to establish retention policies for website material;
  - dealing with changes in accounting policy.
- *Timeliness:* This discusses the need for website information to be clearly dated and the need to ensure that any requirements on the release of price sensitive information are complied with.
- *Content – Financial information:* This deals with publication of the auditors' report, interim financial reporting, and the disclosure of aggregated, disaggregated or additional financial information on a website.
- *Security:* This emphasises management's responsibility for preventing the corruption or distortion of financial information on a website by employees (either accidentally or intentionally) or by third parties. As well as ensuring that changes are properly authorised, the controls and procedures should enable all changes to be detected and monitored.
- *Other issues:* Other issues covered in the paper include the translation of financial information into other languages, the provision of information in a format that can be downloaded and procedures to inform interested parties of changes to the website.

The paper can be downloaded free of charge from the Bookstore (under the 'Other' category) on the IFAC website at http://www.ifac.org/Store/

## *Satisfying legal requirements by electronic means* 10.121

The *Companies Act 1985 (Electronic Communications) Order 2000 (SI 2000/3373)* came into force on 22 December 2000 and clarifies that references to sending accounts and reports to those entitled to receive them include:

- sending copies by electronic communication to the address notified to the company for that purpose by the person entitled to receive the documents; or
- where the company and the person entitled to receive the accounts so agree, publishing the documents on a website, notifying the person in the manner agreed that they have been published in this way and providing him/her with both the address of the website and details of where and how the documents may be accessed on the website.

## *Auditing Practices Board guidance*      **10.122**

APB Bulletin 2001/1 *The Electronic Publication of Auditors' Reports* was published in January 2001. This is effective for accounting periods commencing after 22 December 2000 and provides guidance on:

- the work that auditors should do when an entity decides to publish its annual financial statements on a website or distribute financial statements to shareholders by electronic means; and
- adjustments that should be made to the auditors' report when this is to be published electronically – for instance to identify which information is covered by the report and which accounting and auditing standards have been applied (given that information on a website will be available worldwide).

The Bulletin also emphasises that the directors are responsible for ensuring that financial information made available on a website is not amended or tampered with.

## *ICSA guidance on electronic communications*      **10.123**

The Institute of Chartered Secretaries and Administrators (ICSA) has also issued *Electronic Communications with Shareholders: A Guide to Best Practice.* This sets out 25 points of recommended best practice together with detailed guidance for directors and employees on issues such as:

- points to consider before offering the facility to shareholders;
- what to do if electronic communication fails;
- keeping records to establish proof of sending;
- separate identification of statutory and audited material on the website; and
- security issues, including systems to check that statutory and audited information made available on a website has not been tampered with.

Further details can be found on the ICSA website (http://www.icsa.org.uk/) and copies of the full text can be obtained from ICSA, 16 Park Crescent, London W1B 1AH.

# 11. Fraud and Illegal Acts

| | |
|---|---|
| **Understanding fraud** | **11.1** |
| **At a glance** | **11.2** |

- Fraud encompasses the use of deception to obtain unjust or illegal financial gain, and intentional misrepresentations affecting the financial statements.
- The nature of fraud usually depends on the type of business, the reason for the fraud and who is perpetrating it.
- The view that fraud is a victimless crime is rapidly losing ground.
- Recent terrorist attacks and accounting scandals have heightened the general awareness of fraud and the damage that it can cause to the economy.
- A principal theme is the need for a major change in business culture and attitudes.
- Fraud may involve an individual or a group of people, and may involve management, employees or third parties (or a combination of these).
- The two key factors that encourage fraud are motive and opportunity.
- Accounting manipulation is usually driven by business pressures, whereas other forms of fraud are usually driven by personal pressures.
- Unidentified or temporary weaknesses in systems and controls can increase the inherent risk of fraud.
- The internet creates increasing opportunities for high speed and high frequency fraud.

- Increased regulation is likely to be imposed as a result of the accounting recent scandals.
- The primary role of the Fraud Advisory Panel is to raise awareness of the social and economic damage caused by fraud.
- Useful information can be found on websites dedicated to the issue of fraud.

## *What is fraud?* 11.3

There is no single definition of fraud. Auditing Standards describe fraud as comprising:

- the use of deception to obtain unjust or illegal financial advantage; and
- intentional misrepresentations affecting the financial statements.

Fraud may involve physical theft or misappropriation of cash or goods, recording transactions with no substance (such as payments to fictitious employees or suppliers) and falsifying or altering accounting and other records to cover up theft or misappropriation. It also includes the manipulation or distortion of data, either for tangible gain (for instance to increase the payments under bonus or commission schemes) or simply to present the details in a more favourable light (for instance, to meet targets, show improved results or enhance share performance). The nature of fraud often depends on the type of business, the reason for the fraud and who is perpetrating it. Certain businesses, particularly those involving access to high levels of cash or movable goods, are particularly vulnerable to fraud involving personal gain for the fraudster. In this context, the more common types of fraud include the theft of cash or stock, the submission of false expense claims and purchasing frauds involving false invoices or fictitious suppliers. Financial information will usually be misstated in these cases, but primarily to cover up the fraudulent activity rather than as an end in itself. Fraud involving the intentional misrepresentation of financial information is more likely to be driven by the need to meet or exceed performance targets, either for a business segment or for the business as a whole, and is much more likely to involve those in more senior positions within the business.

## *A low profile issue?* 11.4

Fraud has tended to be given a relatively low profile within the business community. Concerns over the impact of adverse publicity have resulted in many companies being reluctant to report and follow up any frauds that are identified and it is therefore difficult to estimate the true cost of fraud, although the report *The Economic Cost of Fraud* produced for the Home Office by National Economic Research Associates (NERA) towards the end of 2000 suggested that it could be in the order of £14 billion per annum. However, the view that fraud is a victimless crime is rapidly losing ground as everyone becomes more aware of the impact that serious fraud can have on the general public in terms of business failures (and thus reduced employment opportunities), loss of (or reductions in) pensions and savings, higher insurance premiums, higher banking costs and, potentially, higher taxes.

## Impact of recent events     11.5

The terrorist attacks in New York and Washington in September 2001 and various accounting scandals that have come to light in recent months, especially those at Enron and Worldcom, have all served to heightened the general awareness of fraud and the damage that it can cause to the business economy. There has been an increased focus on the use of fraud and money laundering to secure funds to support terrorist activity, and on the need for tighter legislation and controls to prevent this. Similarly, the various accounting scandals have highlighted how quickly share prices and the investment markets can collapse when business confidence is destroyed. Whilst these are large, high profile businesses, the issue of fraud, the damage it can cause and the need to prevent it, are equally relevant in a smaller, owner-managed company.

## Need for culture change     11.6

One of the principal themes emerging from recent events is the need for a major change in business culture and attitudes. Various initiatives have been developed in recent years, including the Combined Code (and its predecessor Codes), to try and create a business culture of transparency, integrity and accountability. This is something that must come from the top of an organisation – it will only happen if the board is prepared to recognise the issue and take appropriate action, setting a strong example at board level. In particular, it is important to encourage a climate of openness and trust, where all employees accept the responsibility for upholding high standards and feel confident in reporting any concerns to management. The Government has also expressed concern that awards of large share options packages to senior executives might be creating 'perverse incentives' rather than encouraging the achievement of performance targets. Both the Combined Code and the new regulations for quoted companies on the Directors' Remuneration Report require the disclosure of detailed information on the use of share options and other long-term incentive schemes (see CHAPTER 6 CORPORATE GOVERNANCE and CHAPTER 9 DIRECTORS' REMUNERATION AND BENEFITS), and the Government has instigated further examination of the use of such schemes.

## Who perpetrates fraud?     11.7

Fraud on a company may involve a single individual or a group of individuals, and may be committed by management, employees or third parties. In many cases, a degree of collusion will be needed in order to perpetrate the fraud. Employee or management fraud intended to achieve personal gain will often be committed with third party help, and those committing fraud from outside the organisation will often need internal assistance. For instance, many purchasing frauds require collusion between a supplier and an employee involved with purchases transactions. The two key factors that encourage fraud are motive and opportunity. The motive for fraud can be very wide-ranging. Accounting manipulation is usually driven by business pressures, such as:

- the need to achieve or exceed budgets and targets;
- the need to maintain or improve the share price;
- the need to secure additional funding; and
- the need to support weak or failing ventures.

The demands on senior management are not only internal and there is particular concern that the attitude of financial analysts and commentators is fuelling the development of an aggressive attitude to earnings management within the business community. Unrealistic reporting deadlines can also put undue pressure on senior management. Other types of fraud are more likely to be driven by personal pressures, such as those arising from excessive greed, an attempt to resolve personal financial difficulties, general career dissatisfaction or a desire for revenge.

## *Nature of fraud*      **11.8**

Accounting manipulations that amount to fraud include:

- the creation of false sales;
- the deliberate overstatement of assets;
- the deliberate suppression of liabilities;
- failure to take account of the substance of all elements of a transaction (ie recognising only those elements that help to achieve the required overstatement or understatement of income, expenses, assets or liabilities);
- delaying or advancing income or expenditure;
- manipulation of pricing agreements; and
- inappropriate use of reserves.

In the case of other types of fraud, the opportunity is usually greatest where there are limited deterrents or little chance of the fraud being discovered. Many of those who commit this type of fraud are opportunists, and unidentified, or even temporary, weaknesses in systems and controls can make the company especially vulnerable. New business activities, changes to management information systems, changes in management, the prolonged absence of key individuals and weakened controls as a result of reduced staffing levels can all increase the inherent risk of fraud. There can also be particular problems in areas where management are heavily reliant on specialist expertise. For instance, if the management team has only limited computer expertise, they may in effect place heavy reliance on relatively junior employees in areas where there is enormous scope for manipulation. It is usually inevitable that what begins as a small fraud will grow, particularly where accounts manipulation is involved, either as an end in itself or to cover up a fraud of a different type. If income for the current year has been inflated in order to show the required level of performance, further inflation is going to be needed in the next accounting period in order to maintain the 'growth'.

## *Internet fraud* 11.9

Fraud is now more organised than ever before and the internet has opened up increasing opportunities for high speed and high frequency frauds. Relatively common internet frauds include identity fraud, credit card fraud and the theft of confidential data. Particular care is needed when developing websites, as poor programming and website design can result in relatively easy but unauthorised access being given to data, which can then be corrupted or used for fraudulent purposes. Also, encryption techniques will sometimes not be as sound as they appear and may therefore not give the required degree of physical security over data.

## *Reaction to recent accounting scandals* 11.10

The reaction to recent accounting scandals is likely to result in an increased regulatory cost for business generally, although there is a strong awareness of the need to avoid creating regulatory overload and to weigh the perceived advantages of certain measures against the potential adverse consequences. In particular, the Higgs Report, the Smith Report and the DTI post-Enron reports propose the following:

- a considerably more demanding role for audit committees in ensuring proper protection of shareholder interests in relation to financial reporting and internal control and a requirement for audit committees to report in detail on their activities each year;
- a specific requirement for audit committees to carry out an annual assessment of the qualifications, expertise, resources, effectiveness and independence of the external auditors;
- a requirement for auditors of listed companies and other public interest entities to publish detailed information, covering whole firm financial information, organisational structure and reward systems, how quality is achieved and monitored, and the policies and procedures used to manage threats to independence;
- the development of more detailed guidance on auditor independence, and in particular on the provision of non-audit services to audit clients, and an enhanced role for the audit committee in developing company policy on this;
- new measures for regulating the accountancy profession and for monitoring the performance of audit firms with listed and other public interest clients; and
- an enhanced role for the Financial Reporting Review Panel (FRRP) in monitoring and enforcing compliance with accounting standards.

The reviews decided against the mandatory rotation of auditors on the grounds that there are sensible and effective alternatives to this. The above issues are considered in more detail in CHAPTERS 2 and 10.

## *The Fraud Advisory Panel*     **11.11**

The Fraud Advisory Panel was established in 1996, on the initiative of the Institute of Chartered Accountants in England and Wales (ICAEW), and it acts as a focal point for the generation and exchange of ideas and information aimed at fighting fraud in its various forms. The members of the Panel are drawn from the legal and accountancy professions, industry and commerce, the academic world, the police and a range of government and quasi-governmental bodies. The work of the Panel is directed by a Steering Group and is carried out by a series of working parties. The Panel's primary role is to raise awareness of the social and economic damage caused by fraud, and in particular to:

- develop proposals to reform the law and public policy on fraud;
- develop proposals to enhance the investigation and prosecution of fraud;
- advise business on fraud prevention, detection and reporting;
- assist in improving fraud related education and training in business and the professions; and
- establish a more accurate picture of the extent, causes and nature of fraud.

Its most recent publication is a guide and checklist entitled *Fighting Fraud: A guide for SMEs* (available from the Fraud Advisory Panel section of the ICAEW website at icaew.co.uk, together with other Fraud Advisory Panel publications). Membership of the Panel is open to individuals and corporate bodies that share its values. Further information can be obtained from the Fraud Advisory Panel, Chartered Accountants' Hall, PO Box 433, Moorgate Place, London, EC2P 2BJ (telephone 020 7920 8721; fax 020 7920 8536; e-mail FAP@icaew.co.uk).

## *Other information*     **11.12**

Other useful sources of information on fraud issues include the Fraud website at www.fraud.org.uk and the Fraud Prevention website maintained by the National Working Group on Fraud on behalf of the Association of Chief Police Officers (ACPO) – this can be found at www.uk-fraud.info/ and includes a particularly useful 'Alert' section giving details of the most recent fraudulent schemes. It also has an extensive links page to other relevant sites.

## Responsibility for fraud prevention and detection 11.13

## At a glance 11.14

- Company directors have a collective responsibility for taking reasonable steps to prevent and detect fraud and other irregularities.
- An internal audit function can help management to identify and assess fraud risk and develop appropriate systems and controls.
- External auditors are required to plan their work so that they have a reasonable expectation of detecting material errors and misstatements arising from fraud, but do not have a responsibility to detect all fraud or error that may exist within a business.
- The role of the audit committee is to provide assurance that the board's collective responsibility for financial matters and internal control is being properly discharged.

### *Collective responsibility of directors* 11.15

The directors have joint and several responsibility for safeguarding the assets of the company, and must therefore take reasonable steps to prevent and detect fraud and other irregularities. This is specifically referred to in the statement of the directors' responsibilities that must be published as part of the annual accounts (see CHAPTER 10 FINANCIAL REPORTING). Although it may be helpful for management purposes to allocate the management of security issues to a specific director or other senior individual within the organisation, the directors always retain collective responsibility for the prevention and detection of fraud.

### *Role of internal audit* 11.16

Internal auditors are not responsible for designing and implementing systems, nor for the prevention and detection of fraud. However, the work of an internal audit function can help management to identify and assess potential risks within the business, and to develop appropriate systems and controls to reduce these risks to an acceptable level. This includes the inherent risk of fraud. The internal audit function provides a useful source of information for management on what is actually happening within the organisation. Its remit is generally much wider then the prevention and detection of fraud, and includes providing assurance on issues such as the completeness and accuracy of the company's accounting and other records, and the overall efficiency of the operations. However, by focusing its efforts on the effectiveness of the company's system of internal control, reporting any weaknesses and concerns and recommending appropriate changes to policies, procedures and controls, an internal audit function can help the directors to demonstrate that they are paying due attention to their responsibility for safeguarding the company's assets. Internal auditors can also be commissioned to undertake special assignments to assist management in the development of the business. These might include occasional more detailed forensic checks on accounting and other operational controls designed to limit the opportunity for fraud. Further information on establishing and operating an internal audit function is given in CHAPTER 2 AUDIT MATTERS.

## *Role of external auditors* 11.17

For many years there has been a commonly held, and misconceived, view that the detection of fraud is an important aspect of the role of the external auditors. The auditing profession has made considerable efforts in recent years to explain the role and responsibilities of external auditors, and the nature of an audit, in an attempt to eliminate this 'expectation gap'. External auditors are appointed to express an independent opinion on the annual financial statements. Their work is therefore directed towards identifying any potentially material misstatements in the accounts, including any that arise as a result of fraud and other irregularities. Auditors are required to plan their work so that they have a reasonable expectation of detecting material errors and misstatements arising from fraud. In carrying out their work, the external auditors will review the company's systems and controls, carry out certain test checks, and report to management any weaknesses and concerns that they identify, but the external audit should not be relied upon to detect all fraud and irregularities that may exist within the organisation. The auditors will usually emphasise this in their report to management on significant issues that have come to their attention during the audit (see CHAPTER 2 AUDIT MATTERS). If the company does not have an internal audit function, the directors might consider arranging for the external auditors to carry out more detailed forensic checks on the systems and controls as a separate exercise from time to time. If the external auditors do detect, or have reason to suspect, fraud during the course of their work, they will normally report this to the directors. However, separate arrangements may apply where the auditors suspect that directors are involved in the fraud, or in the case of regulated businesses. If the company has an audit committee, the auditors may report through that committee if they have reason to believe that executive directors may be involved in the fraud.

## *Role of the Audit Committee* 11.18

The precise role of the audit committee must be tailored to the needs of the individual company, but broadly the role of an audit committee is to provide assurance that the board's collective responsibility for financial matters and internal control is being properly discharged. The audit committee's responsibilities will usually include reviewing the results of the work of the external auditors and, where relevant, the internal auditors, and ensuring that points brought to the attention of management are being properly followed up and actioned. The terms of reference for the audit committee will usually include a general provision for the committee to consider other issues defined by the board from time to time, and this might include an annual review of procedures to prevent fraud and irregularities, and the operation and effectiveness of the company's ethical code and its 'whistle-blowing' procedures. The existence of an audit committee can help to demonstrate a climate of discipline and control within the business and can provide a useful forum, independent of the executive management team, for the finance director, external auditors and head of internal audit to raise issues of concern where necessary. Further information is given in CHAPTER 2 AUDIT MATTERS.

## Minimising the risk of fraud                          11.19

## At a glance                                           11.20

> • Fraud risk should be managed in a way that reduces it to an acceptable level.
> • Rigorous personnel procedures, for both permanent and temporary staff, can help to reduce the risk of fraud.
> • The likelihood of fraud arising should be assessed for each area of the company's activities (including those that are peripheral to the main business), and the controls to prevent each fraud risk should be identified.
> • Steps should be taken to correct any missing or weak controls.
> • The importance of management attitude and the general ethos of the organisation cannot be overemphasised.
> • Biometrics can now be used to improve the security of access controls.
> • All businesses should be aware of the risks of becoming inadvertently involved in money laundering.

### *Managing the risk*                                   11.21

Fraud is one of the many inevitable risks that any business faces. The risk of fraud arising can never be wholly eliminated, but it can be managed and reduced to an acceptable level by taking practical, common sense precautions and making use of cost-effective accounting and operational controls. Careful planning should enable appropriate controls to be introduced without disrupting the efficient operation of the business. However, the potential benefit of reducing risk to an acceptable level must always be balanced against the cost of doing so. If the directors decide not to take steps to reduce a potential risk, on the basis that the ongoing cost of doing so is too great, it is important that they do so with a clear understanding of the possible consequences.

### *Personnel procedures*                                11.22

Rigorous personnel procedures can help to reduce the risk of fraud. It is particularly important to take up references for all potential new employees and to follow these up thoroughly. Organisations frequently fail to confirm the qualifications and experience of prospective employees, follow up any apparent gaps in the previous employment record or investigate further any issues that may be referred to, however obliquely, in references from former employers. Consideration should also be given to introducing the same procedures for temporary staff, particularly where they are to work in areas of the business that could be particularly susceptible to fraud. If temporary staff will have the same access to company records and assets as permanent employees, there is little justification for less rigorous personnel checks. Where the business makes regular use of temporary staff through employment agencies, it will usually be appropriate to check that the agency has adequate procedures in place on this. If certain services are contracted out to other organisations (for instance, cleaning or maintenance services) it will usually be sensible to confirm that the main contractor carries out thorough checks on his employees and that proper records are maintained of who is working at each location at any given time. This is especially important when the individuals have regular access to the company's premises at times when management and staff are not usually present. Contracts of service for employees should normally provide for immediate suspension on the suspicion of fraud, to help prevent further loss and to preserve security over company records and assets. Similar arrangements may be appropriate for temporary staff and for contracted services.

## *Review and assessment of activities*                    **11.23**

The initial step in minimising the risk of fraud is to identify all the company's activities and assess the likelihood of fraud arising in each area. This review should encompass all those activities that are peripheral to the main business but which may nevertheless provide scope for material fraud. In many ways these activities often represent a higher risk as they can easily be overlooked and are frequently not subjected to the same degree of scrutiny as the key aspects of the business. For instance, peripheral activities might include the disposal of fixed assets, or the management of the company's car fleet. It is important to recognise that giving one person access both to company assets and to the related accounting or operational records significantly increases the opportunity for fraud. Hence the frequent emphasis by auditors on the need for segregation of duties wherever practicable. If at all possible, the following five aspects of a transaction should be fully segregated:

- initiation;
- authorisation;
- execution;
- custody of any related assets; and
- recording in the accounting records.

If segregation is not possible (for example, due to the small size of the organisation and the limited number of staff available) compensating checks and controls should be introduced. Business operations in remote locations will also usually present a higher risk of fraud – a higher degree of autonomy may be necessary for a remote operation to function efficiently, but this will usually bring with it an increased risk of abuse.

## *Assessment of controls*        **11.24**

Having identified the fraud risks, the next step is to identify the controls that are already in place to prevent fraud wherever a potential risk arises. This should highlight any areas where:

- there is an absence of appropriate controls;
- controls are weak; or
- there is a lack of appropriate management information.

Steps can then be taken to introduce new or enhanced controls and to improve the flow of information. In some cases, the analysis may reveal an excess of controls in a particular area, which might enable some rationalisation and provide scope for additional controls in weaker areas. It is important to remember that a control that is effective in preventing errors will not necessarily be effective in preventing fraud (eg a determined fraudster can easily forge an authorisation signature). It is also essential to confirm that the controls identified do actually operate in practice.

## *Management attitude*        **11.25**

The importance of management attitude and the general ethos of the organisation cannot be overemphasised. Fraud is much less likely to be perpetrated in a culture that is honest and open. It is essential that the directors make their views on the unacceptability of fraud and dishonesty explicit and that they lead by example, by setting out clear rules (and not bending them) and ensuring that all business practices are honest and above board. Employees should be left in no doubt as to the consequences of involvement in fraud. Management can impress this on their staff by:

- having a clear company policy on fraud, publicising this within the organisation and drawing it to the attention of third parties, such as customers and suppliers;
- including fraud awareness in staff induction programmes;
- incorporating on-going fraud awareness training into staff development programmes and emphasising that all employees have a responsibility for the prevention and detection of fraud;
- having a confidential 'whistle-blowing' procedure (see **11.23** below);
- developing a fraud response plan, to make it clear that action will be taken promptly and effectively if fraud is identified (see **11.28** below);
- following up all allegations of fraud sensitively but thoroughly, and being prepared to take action against any perpetrators of fraud who are identified.

Implementing an effective system of internal control, and monitoring it regularly, helps to ensure that transactions are recorded accurately and that company assets are safeguarded. It also demonstrates to the employees that the directors take their responsibilities in this area seriously. A relaxed management attitude towards procedures and controls sends the opposite message. Rewarding staff for appropriate attention to control and compliance issues, as well as for financial performance, can also help to highlight the importance of these issues to the business as a whole.

## *Biometrics* 11.26

A relatively recent development is the increasing use of biometrics to help protect a business against fraud – for instance, the use of techniques such as facial recognition, finger print recognition and iris recognition gives a much higher level of access security than a system of passwords.

## *Money laundering* 11.27

Certain businesses, in particular those in the financial services sector, will be subject to stringent legal requirements in respect of the identification and reporting of money laundering and it is essential that such businesses have procedures and controls in place to ensure that they fulfil their duties in this area. However, any business could potentially be an unwitting party to money laundering and it is therefore advisable to ensure that management and staff are aware of the need to question unusual and potentially dubious transactions and know who to inform in such circumstances. Cash oriented businesses are particularly attractive to money launderers.

## Detection of fraud 11.28

## At a glance 11.29

---

- All managers and staff should be aware of the potential warning signs of fraud.
- A clear, straightforward procedure for 'whistle-blowing' by employees can be of significant help in the detection of fraud.
- Any business areas performing differently from expectations should be investigated.
- The use of management override of internal controls should be carefully monitored.
- Any seemingly unusual behaviour by employees should be investigated.
- Any apparently unusual transactions should always be investigated.
- The company should maintain its own fraud record and analyse the information for any particular patterns.

---

## *Awareness of warning signs* 11.30

Many frauds come to light by accident or as a the result of a tip-off, but putting procedures in place to detect fraud can help to ensure that any irregularities come to light at an early stage and that any loss is minimised. They can also act as a useful deterrent. It may be helpful to allocate the management of security issues, including the prevention and detection of fraud, to a specific individual within the organisation. However, all members of the management team, and preferably all employees, need to be aware of the potential warning signs of fraud and to be constantly alert for them. Experience has shown that when fraud is detected, the warning signs have often been apparent for some time but have either not been noticed by management or have been noted but not acted upon. A strong system of internal controls should help to ensure that any irregularities are highlighted. However, regular monitoring is important, both to check that the controls are actually operating as intended (for instance, staff may be tempted to take short cuts to save time) and to ensure that controls are kept up to date as the business develops (for instance, new activities may not be adequately covered by existing controls, or organisational changes may have inadvertently resulted in a control lapsing). It is also important to consider whether management can override the controls and, if so, how often this is done in practice. An internal audit function can provide valuable assistance on these points. Taking prompt and appropriate action on weaknesses in systems and controls highlighted by the auditors (both external and internal) helps to demonstrate management's commitment to operating an effective system of internal control.

## *Whistle-blowing procedures* 11.31

The company should develop and publicise a clear, straightforward system for 'whistle-blowing' by employees. This will only operate satisfactorily if there is a climate of openness, honesty and trust and if employees feel confident that they will not suffer personally as a result of raising their concerns. Options to consider include reporting:

- through the line manager – although such a system will need to provide for cases where the employee suspects the line manager of being implicated in the fraud;
- directly to an identified member of senior management;
- directly to an identified member of the audit committee; or
- through a confidential fraud telephone hotline (which may be either internal or external).

It is generally inadvisable to use e-mail for this purpose. Whatever method best suits the company's circumstances, it is important that employees see that their concerns are taken seriously and are properly followed up, and that confidentiality is maintained. Where suspected fraud is reported in good faith, the employee will usually be protected under the *Public Interest Disclosure Act 1998*. The effective operation of the 'whistle-blowing' procedures should be regularly reviewed.

## *Business areas performing unexpectedly* 11.32

Directors should ensure that regular checks are carried out, using performance indicators relevant to the business, to identify any areas that are performing differently from expectations. For example, where a business area regularly performs better than expected, it is possible that the results are being manipulated, whilst a business that is consistently falling below expectations could potentially be the subject of cash or purchasing frauds. Wherever possible, financial information should be reviewed in conjunction with non-financial data as this may help to highlight any inconsistencies (for instance, it should be possible to review payroll totals in conjunction with independently prepared details of employee numbers). The most useful performance indicators will depend on the nature of the business, but those in common use include:

- gross margin – significant fluctuations could indicate manipulation of sales figures, purchasing fraud or theft of stock;
- stock turnover – significant fluctuations could indicate theft of stock, or purchasing fraud;
- debtors: sales ratio (average debtor days) – significant fluctuations could indicate manipulation of sales figures, or teeming and lading of cash received;
- age analysis of debtors – increase in old balances could indicate cash fraud;
- creditors: purchases ratio (average creditor days) – significant fluctuations could indicate purchasing fraud;
- average pay per employee – significant increase could indicate payments to fictitious employees.

Unusual trends or fluctuations should be thoroughly investigated, and apparently plausible explanations should always be corroborated. It is also worth remembering that too much consistency might in itself be suspicious. It has been known for a business unit to perform exactly in line with budget each year – on further investigation, it transpired that the unit had in fact performed consistently above budget and that management and staff had colluded to divide the excess profits between them.

## *Opportunity for management override*      **11.33**

Directors should be constantly aware of situations where line managers and senior employees may have the opportunity to override internal controls, or to arrange for figures to be presented in a more positive light. This can be a particular problem where an autocratic individual occupies a senior post, or in the case of remote operations, where local management may need a higher level of autonomy for the operation to function efficiently. These situations should be subject to careful monitoring and, in the case of other locations, regular visits should be made to check on what is actually happening in practice. An internal audit function can be very useful in this situation. The setting of performance targets and the operation of incentive schemes are well accepted methods of managing businesses. However, both require careful monitoring and review on a regular basis. The setting of over-ambitious targets can encourage manipulation of the figures to show the desired result, and this can be a particular problem where employee earnings are directly affected by the financial performance of the business (for instance, through bonus schemes, profit sharing schemes, sales commission or earn out arrangements).

## *Staff issues* 11.34

Low staff morale can generate a higher risk of fraud, and a high level of staff turnover could be indicative of general management problems and potential fraud. Disaffected staff may be tempted to cut corners or not operate controls properly, or may be tempted to take advantage of systems weaknesses as revenge for lack of job satisfaction or to redress the feeling that they are not being adequately rewarded for their efforts. Independent debriefing of leavers can sometimes highlight the existence of fraudulent activity or concerns over dishonest business practices that would not otherwise have come to light. Any seemingly unusual behaviour by employees should be investigated. For example:

- A reluctance to take regular holidays may be due to the need to conceal an ongoing fraud. Fraud can often come to light during a sudden and unexpected absence of the person perpetrating it. Some organisations have a rule that staff must take at least two consecutive weeks' holiday each year – both for the physical well-being of the employee and to reduce the opportunity for long-term fraud to go undetected.

- Regular late-working by individual employees, whether paid or unpaid, should always be investigated and monitored – it may result from a need to cover up fraudulent activities in the absence of other members of staff. There are numerous examples of apparently diligent, long-standing employees working long hours, seemingly for the benefit of the company, but in fact to conceal their fraudulent activity. A trusted employee can be in a powerful position, especially if management have become relaxed about monitoring his/her activities.

- A refusal to change jobs or accept a promotion, or the consistent failure by a manager to delegate certain activities, may all be due to the need to conceal an ongoing fraud.

- An apparent discrepancy between an employee's earnings and his/her lifestyle is a common indicator of fraud.

## *Unusual transactions* 11.35

Management should always investigate apparently unusual transactions – for instance, an individual transaction that cannot immediately be explained or which seems to lack commercial substance or sense, or an unexpected quantity of a particular type of transaction, such as an abnormally high level of sales credit notes or an unusually large number of outstanding items on the bank reconciliation (especially if they seem to have been outstanding for some time). Frequent or regular systems breakdowns may also be a warning signal – they can provide a useful opportunity to conceal transactions or manipulate financial information.

## *Collating information on fraud* 11.36

An issue that is often overlooked is the potential benefit of a company maintaining its own record of suspected and actual fraud, and analysing this to see if any particular patterns emerge. This may be helpful in the ongoing development and monitoring the company's response to fraud.

## Developing a fraud response plan 11.37

## At a glance 11.38

* A fraud response plan sets out company policy on fraud and the action to be taken when fraud is suspected.
* The plan should explain who will lead the investigation and the detailed procedures that will be followed.
* The fraud response plan should be regularly reviewed to ensure that it is kept up to date.

## *Benefits of a fraud response plan* 11.39

A fraud response plan should include the general company policy on fraud and should also set out the action to be taken when fraud is suspected. Having a detailed fraud response plan in place helps to ensure that everyone is clear about the action that needs to be taken if and when fraud is identified or suspected. Thinking about the issues in advance helps management to ensure that all the relevant aspects are covered. It is much more difficult to react promptly and effectively without a plan to follow. In particular, a detailed document setting out the policies and procedures to be followed in the case of fraud has the following benefits:

* it demonstrates that management is in control of the situation;
* it can help to minimise the risk of further loss once the fraud has been detected;
* it should improve the chance of recovering the loss already incurred, or of maximising the amount recovered;
* it can help the company to minimise the potential adverse commercial effect (for instance, where supplier or customer accounts are affected).

It also provides a clear statement to employees that the directors are not prepared to condone fraud and will take appropriate action against anyone found to be involved in fraudulent activity.

## *Contents of the plan* 11.40

The plan should include:

* a clear statement of company policy on fraud, and in particular who should be contacted when there is any suspicion of fraud;

- who will take responsibility for leading any investigation of suspected fraud;
- relevant legal and personnel procedures. As noted above, it will usually be helpful to ensure that employment contracts provide for any employee suspected of fraud to be suspended immediately and either isolated or removed from the premises. The company should adopt a consistent policy for staff throughout the organisation – employees can be given the wrong message if (say) management are treated more leniently than other members of staff;
- specific procedures for securing the company's assets and records when fraud is suspected, both to prevent further loss and to ensure that potential evidence is not destroyed – for instance, the procedures might include changing locks, security passes and computer passwords. Particular care is needed in these days of advanced computer technology – it has been known for a suspended employee to delete vital information by accessing the company's records from a remote computer terminal;
- procedures for carrying out a detailed investigation into the suspected fraud – this may be done internally or may require specialist assistance. In particular, the gathering of supporting evidence will usually require expert knowledge to ensure that it is sufficiently reliable for use in a prosecution;
- procedures for making contact with the police, the company's insurers or the business regulators (where relevant);
- procedures for making internal reports on the issue (eg to the audit committee or main board);
- the company's policy on seeking the recovery of funds; and
- procedures for dealing with any publicity issues that might arise from the fraud.

It also important that the directors should be seen to act immediately to enhance controls over the business area that was the subject of the fraudulent activity.

## *Regular review* 11.41

The fraud response plan should be subject to regular review to ensure that it takes account of any recent changes – for instance, new developments within the business, changes resulting from the development of new technologies and any new external reporting requirements.

## *Checklist: prevention and detection of fraud* 11.42

> This checklist summarises some of the key issues that need to be considered when dealing with the prevention and detection of fraud. It should not be regarded as comprehensive – other issues may need to be taken into account, depending on the particular circumstances of the business.

- Are all directors made fully aware of their collective responsibility for the prevention and detection of fraud?
- Do the directors encourage a business culture that is open and honest, and lead by example?
- Has the company developed a clear policy on fraud and is this:
  - widely publicised amongst employees?
  - drawn to the attention of third parties (eg customers and suppliers)?
- Do the company's personnel procedures ensure that:
  - The stated qualifications and experience of new employees are verified?
  - Any apparent gaps in the employment record of new employees are investigated?
  - References are taken up for all new employees?
  - Any points raised in employee references are followed up?
  - The same procedures are applied for temporary as well as permanent staff?
  - Where agency staff are used, the company understands the level of checking that has been carried out by the agency?
  - Where a service is contracted out to a third party, the company understands the level of checking carried out by the contractor, especially where individuals will be given access to the company's premises outside normal working hours?
  - All employment contracts and other service contracts provide for immediate suspension on the suspicion of fraud?
  - All employees are required to take at least two consecutive weeks' holiday each year?
  - Regular late-working by employees is monitored and investigated?
  - An independent debriefing interview is held with all leavers?
- Is fraud awareness included in staff induction programmes?
- Is on-going fraud awareness training incorporated into staff development programmes?
- Does the company have a confidential 'whistle-blowing' procedure?
- Is the effectiveness of the 'whistle-blowing' procedure subject to regular review?
- Are staff rewarded for appropriate attention to compliance and control issues as well as for financial performance?
- Has the company assessed the likelihood of fraud arising:
  - In each principal area of the business?
  - In each peripheral area of the business (eg disposal of fixed assets, management of company car scheme)?
- Has the company identified and assessed the controls that operate to prevent fraud in each case where a potential risk arises and taken steps to:
  - introduce new controls where gaps are evident?
  - strengthen potentially weak controls?
  - ensure the proper flow of relevant management information?

■ rationalise any areas where excessive bureaucracy has been identified?

● Has the company confirmed that the identified controls are actually operating in practice?

● Do the company's procedures ensure that, as far as practicable, the following aspects of each business transaction are segregated:

■ initiation;

■ authorisation;

■ execution;

■ custody of related assets; and

■ recording in the accounting records?

● Are procedures and controls regularly reviewed and updated to take account of developments in the business?

● If the company is subject to legal requirements in respect of money laundering, have appropriate procedures and controls been put in place?

● Are all directors and staff aware of the issues relating to money laundering, and the risk of the company becoming inadvertently involved?

● Are all directors and staff made aware of the potential warning signs of fraud?

● Is the use of management override of controls monitored and reviewed?

● Have appropriate performance indicators been identified for each aspect of the business?

● Are all variations from expected performance, and any unusual trends, thoroughly investigated and explanations corroborated?

● Is the use of incentive schemes and performance targets monitored and reviewed, to confirm that it is not encouraging manipulation of the underlying figures?

● Are regular control visits made to remote business locations?

● Do the company's procedures ensure that all unusual transactions are investigated?

● Do the directors collate information on actual and suspected fraud within the business and review this for any particular patterns?

● Does the company have an up-to-date fraud response plan setting out:

■ the company policy on fraud?

■ who will lead any investigation into suspected fraud?

■ the detailed procedures that will be followed, covering in particular:

○ suspension and isolation/removal of relevant individuals;

○ protection of the company's records and assets;

○ gathering of reliable evidence;

○ contact with relevant third parties (eg police, insurers, regulators); and

○ internal reporting?

■ the company's policy on seeking recovery of funds?

■ procedures for dealing with any related publicity issues?

# 12. Going Concern

| Background and current guidance | **12.1** |
|---|---|
| At a glance | **12.2** |

- Company law and accounting standards generally require annual accounts to be prepared on a going concern basis.
- Under the Combined Code, directors should report in the annual report and accounts that the business is a going concern, with supporting assumptions or qualifications where necessary.
- The document 'Going Concern and Financial Reporting – Guidance for Directors of Listed Companies' sets out the principles that directors should follow in relation to going concern.
- Additional guidance on the subject of going concern can be found in Statement of Auditing Standards 130 (SAS 130) *The going concern basis in financial statements*.

## *Accounting requirements* 12.3

The *Companies Act 1985* (*CA 1985*) specifies that, for accounts purposes, a company is presumed to be carrying on business as a going concern, but gives no further guidance on this issue. Detailed guidance on the use of the going concern basis when preparing accounts is provided in Financial Reporting Standard 18 (FRS 18) *Accounting policies*. UK Auditing Standards also require the annual report of each company to include a statement of the directors' responsibilities for the preparation of the the accounts and this should also refer to the use of the going concern basis (see CHAPTER **10** FINANCIAL REPORTING).

## *Significance of the going concern assumption* 12.4

The use of the going concern basis for the preparation of accounts is of particular significance when assessing the appropriateness of the accounting policies adopted. Some items in the accounts would be unchanged if the entity was not considered to be a going concern, but others might be significantly affected by this. For instance, fixed assets are usually included in the accounts at cost or valuation, depreciated to reflect the proportion of the life of the asset that has been used up in the business to date. The balance sheet value of the assets essentially represents their value to the business as a going concern, but will not necessarily represent the amount that would be realised if the individual assets had to be sold. If an entity is being liquidated or has ceased trading, a different accounting treatment may therefore need to be adopted for these assets. Other costs and liabilities may also need to be included in the accounts – for instance, penalties for the breach or early termination of contracts such as leases and other rental agreements.

## *Combined Code recommendations* 12.5

The Combined Code recommends that the directors should report in the annual report and accounts that the business is a going concern, with supporting assumptions or qualifications as necessary. This disclosure was originally recommended by the *Cadbury Code of Best Practice* but did not become fully effective until additional guidance was issued to directors in the document *Going concern and financial reporting – guidance for directors of listed companies* published in November 1994. In the case of listed companies, the inclusion of a statement on going concern is now a direct requirement of the FSA Listing Rules and the statement must also be reviewed by the auditors.

## *Joint Working Group Guidance* 12.6

The guidance set out in *Going concern and financial reporting – guidance for directors of listed companies* was developed by a Joint Working Group (JWG) and sets out the governance principles that directors should adopt in relation to going concern. The guidance is addressed primarily to listed companies, but it was hoped that the clarification of the concept of going concern would be of general benefit to all entities and would assist directors in meeting their obligations under *CA 1985*. The document has three main objectives:

- to explain the significance of going concern in relation to financial statements;
- to describe the procedures that an explicit statement on going concern may entail; and

- to recommend appropriate disclosures.

## *Other guidance* 12.7

Additional guidance on the subject of going concern can be found in Statement of Auditing Standards 130 (SAS 130) *The going concern basis in financial statements*. Although this was developed to assist auditors when considering going concern, some of the issues raised may also be of help to directors when making their annual assessment of whether the company is a going concern. In particular SAS 130 sets out illustrative summaries of financial, operational and other indicators of potential going concern difficulties, including:

*Financial indicators of potential going concern difficulties*

- An excess of liabilities over assets.
- Net current liabilities.
- Necessary borrowing facilities not yet agreed.
- Default on terms, or potential breaches of covenants, in respect of loan agreements.
- Significant liquidity or cash flow problems.
- Major losses or cash flow problems since the balance sheet date.
- Substantial sales of fixed assets which are not to be replaced.
- Major restructuring of debt.
- Major debt repayment falling due without adequate facilities to cover this.
- Inability to pay debts as they fall due.
- Denial of, or reductions in, terms of trade credit by suppliers.

*Operational indicators of potential going concern difficulties*

- Fundamental changes in the market, or in technology, to which the entity is unable to adapt.
- Forced reductions in operations (eg as a result of new legislation).
- Loss of key management or staff.
- Labour difficulties.
- High level of dependence on limited product lines in a depressed market.
- Loss of key customers.
- Loss of key suppliers.
- Technical developments which render a key product obsolete.

*Other indicators of potential going concern difficulties*

- Major litigation, where an adverse judgement may threaten the entity's existence.

## Directors' assessment of going concern 12.8

## At a glance 12.9

> - Going concern is defined as the hypothesis that the entity is to continue in operational existence for the foreseeable future.
> - The term 'foreseeable future' is not defined, but additional disclosures should be given when the period considered by the directors is less than twelve months from the date on which the accounts are approved.
> - When preparing the company's annual accounts, the directors should give formal consideration to the issue of going concern each year and should assess in particular whether there are any factors which cast doubt on the entity's ability to continue in operational existence.
> - Factors to take into account include forecasts and budgets, cash flow and borrowing requirements, contingent liabilities, market developments and financial adaptability.
> - The directors' consideration of going concern should normally be updated when the interim report is formally reviewed by the board.

### *Basis of preparation of accounts* 12.10

FRS 18 generally requires financial statements to be prepared on a going concern basis unless:

(i)   the entity is being liquidated or has ceased trading; or
(ii)  the directors have no realistic alternative but to liquidate the entity or to cease trading.

In these circumstances the entity may, if appropriate, prepare its financial statements on a different basis (although this is rare in practice). The JWG guidance emphasises that it will not usually be appropriate to adopt the going concern basis for the accounts if there is any intention or need to enter into a scheme of arrangement with the company's creditors, make an application for an administration order or put the company into administrative receivership or liquidation. However, the restructuring of a business, even on a major scale, is a relatively common practice these days and will not usually result in the going concern basis being an inappropriate basis for the preparation of the accounts.

### *Definition of going concern* 12.11

FRS 18 *Accounting Policies* describes the going concern basis as the hypothesis that the entity is to continue in operational existence for the foreseeable future and notes that this basis will usually provide the most relevant information to users of the accounts. The standard therefore requires directors to assess, when preparing accounts, whether there are any significant doubts about the entity's ability to continue as a going concern. In making this assessment, the directors must take into account all available information about the foreseeable future. The guidance in the standard emphasises that the degree of consideration needed in order to make this assessment will vary depending on the circumstances of the entity. If there is a history of profitable operations with ready access to financial resources when required, and this situation is expected to continue, the consideration of going concern may be less detailed than when there are concerns over issues such as expected profitability, the ability to meet debt repayment schedules and the availability of alternative sources of finance.

## *What is the foreseeable future?* 12.12

Neither accounting standards nor *CA 1985* explain the term 'foreseeable future' and the JWG guidance emphasises that it is not appropriate to set a minimum period to which the directors should pay particular attention when considering the issue of going concern. However, the guidance does make the following points:

- any consideration involving the foreseeable future involves making judgements about future events which are inherently uncertain;
- in general terms, the degree of uncertainty increases significantly the further into the future the consideration is taken;
- the judgement is valid only at the point in time at which it is made.
- in assessing going concern, the directors should take into account all the information of which they are aware at the time the judgement is made, and their statement on going concern should be made on the basis of the information that is known to them at the date on which they approve the financial statements.

Although no minimum review period is specified, the guidance does note that where the period considered by the directors has been limited, for example, to a period of less than one year from the date of approval of the financial statements, the directors should consider whether additional disclosure should be made to explain the assumptions underlying the adoption of the going concern basis. FRS 18 now requires additional disclosures to be given in the accounts in these circumstances.

## *Procedures to be carried out* 12.13

In order to be able to make the required statement on going concern each year, the directors will need to:

- give formal consideration to the issue of going concern;
- consider whether there are any factors which cast doubt on the entity's ability to continue in operational existence for the foreseeable future, and whether the going concern basis is appropriate for the financial statements;

- consider whether additional disclosure is necessary in the annual report and accounts;

It is not acceptable for directors to simply assume that the business can be treated as a going concern without carrying out any procedures to confirm this. However, many of the recommended procedures will already be carried out by directors and senior management for other purposes, such as the development of strategic plans, the preparation of budgets and forecasts, and risk management. All that may be necessary in these circumstances is to summarise the procedures already carried out, and the issues arising from them, and for the directors to consider whether any additional procedures need to be undertaken to cover any aspects that have not already been adequately dealt with. In practice, much of the work will be done prior to the approval of the accounts, but because the directors are required to make their assessment on the basis of the information known to them on the date on which the accounts are approved, they will need to update their review to take account of any changes in circumstances that have arisen since the detailed procedures were carried out.

## *Factors to consider*          12.14

Many different factors will be relevant to a consideration of whether a company is a going concern, and these will vary with the nature of the business under review. Some factors will be within the control of the directors, others may be external and therefore outside their direct control. Similar factors will need to be taken into account in preparing budgets and forecasts and the directors should therefore have a good understanding of the most significant issues for their company. The JWG guidance sets out examples of major areas that directors will usually need to consider in order to identify whether they are, or could become, significant in relation to going concern – the list is not intended to be exhaustive but rather to indicate the sort of factors that should be taken into account when considering going concern. The areas identified in the guidance are:

- forecasts and budgets;
- borrowing requirements;
- liability management;
- contingent liabilities;
- products and markets;
- financial risk management; and
- financial adaptability.

An appendix to the document sets out detailed procedures that may be followed, although the guidance emphasises that these should not be regarded as checklists, partly because not all of the procedures will be relevant in every case, and also because procedures which are not listed may be appropriate in certain circumstances. Each of the main areas is considered briefly below.

## *Forecasts and budgets* 12.15

Budgets and cash flow forecasts should be prepared for at least the period to the next balance sheet date. Alternatively, they may be prepared on a rolling basis covering a twelve month period. Subsequent periods will usually be covered by medium or long-term plans, giving a general indication of how the business is expected to perform. Directors should bear in mind the need to consider a period of at least twelve months from the date on which they formally approve the accounts (see **12.12** above). Budgets and forecasts will usually be supported by a detailed summary of the underlying assumptions and the directors will need to confirm that these are reasonable. Directors may also wish to carry out sensitivity analyses on the figures, particularly where the timing of cash receipts may be uncertain or the level of activity may vary significantly. Other factors that may need to be considered include:

- whether the budgets and forecasts need to be updated for changes in the assumptions or actual results to date;
- the interaction between assumptions;
- whether the budgets and forecasts provide adequately for rising costs;
- whether the budgets and forecasts take appropriate account of seasonal fluctuations;
- the accuracy of budgets and forecasts in previous years – it may be appropriate to document and analyse significant variances and consider whether these are likely to arise again in the current year.

## *Borrowing requirements* 12.16

The facilities available to the company should be reviewed and compared in detail to cash flow forecasts for at least the period to the next balance sheet date. It will often be appropriate to carry out sensitivity analyses on the critical assumptions when making this comparison, to identify whether facilities would be adequate even in a worst case scenario or whether covenants would be likely to be breached in these circumstances. The directors should seek to ensure that there are no anticipated shortfalls in facilities against requirements, no arrears of interest and no other breaches of covenants. There may be mitigating factors which would enable the directors to cope with any potential problems, for instance where they have scope to alter the amount or timing of significant cash flows. Any potential deficits, arrears or breaches that cannot be covered should be discussed with the company's bankers at an early stage to determine any action that needs to be taken and to prevent problems crystallising if possible. The onus is on the directors to be satisfied that appropriate and committed financing arrangements are in place.

## *Liability management* 12.17

The directors should ensure that the company's financial plans indicate appropriate matching of cash outflows with cash inflows. It is particularly important to ensure that cash outflows include all known liabilities, such as loan repayments, payments of tax and VAT, and any commitments which may be off-balance sheet (for instance, certain leasing commitments, or forward exchange contracts). It may also be appropriate to consider whether the company is particularly dependent on individual suppliers, and the impact that a failure in supply might have on the company's ability to meet its cash outflows.

## Contingent liabilities                                       12.18

The directors should review the company's exposure to contingent liabilities, including:

- liabilities experienced in the past and which might recur, such as legal proceedings, and those arising from guarantees, warranties and product liability claims not covered by insurance; and
- new contingencies that may arise in the future, such as environmental clean-up costs or future decommissioning costs.

## Products and markets                                         12.19

The directors should consider the size and strength of the market, the company's market share, and whether the market may change as a result of economic, political or other factors. In more complex businesses, this will usually need to be done by major product line. Depending on the nature of the business, this review may also need to take into account technical research and development, to confirm that this is adequate and can be maintained at an appropriate level for the foreseeable future. Other factors that may need to be considered include:

- product quality and expected life;
- the adequacy of the company's marketing strategy;
- the adequacy of the company's costing system, and in particular whether costs are updated on a regular basis;
- the customer mix, and in particular whether the business is dependent on a small number of significant customers – if so, the risk of losing one or more of them and the likelihood of finding alternative sales markets may also need to be assessed;
- the level of dependence on inter-group trading and the financial implications of this.

## Financial risk management                                    12.20

Directors should identify which financial risks are most significant for their company and their current approach to managing these. For instance, financial risks might include exposure to fixed price contracts or to significant fluctuations in foreign currency exchange rates. Sensitivity analyses may need to be performed if assumptions on factors such as interest rates and foreign currency are particularly critical to the cash flow forecasts.

## *Other factors* 12.21

The JWG identifies a number of other factors that may need to be taken into account in particular circumstances, including:

- recurring operating losses or fluctuating profits and losses;
- the impact of dividend arrears;
- non-compliance with statutory capital requirements;
- the impact of labour difficulties;
- the potential impact of the loss of key management and staff, and the likelihood of finding suitable replacements quickly;
- the potential impact of the loss of a key patent or franchise;
- the impact of long-overdue debtors, or high stock levels;
- the impact of potential losses on long-term contracts;
- the potential impact of the company's fixed asset replacement policy (eg if funds are not available to replace assets regularly, there is the potential for increased maintenance costs, higher levels of down-time or quality control problems).

## *Financial adaptability* 12.22

Financial adaptability is the ability of the company to take effective action to alter the amounts and timings of cash flows to respond to unexpected needs or opportunities. Financial adaptability can help to mitigate any of the factors discussed above in relation to going concern. Consideration of financial adaptability might include reviewing:

- the ability to dispose of assets or postpone the replacement of assets, or to finance assets from other sources (eg leasing rather than outright purchase);
- the potential for obtaining new sources of finance;
- the possibility of extending or renewing loans, or restructuring debt;
- the possibility of raising additional share capital.

## *Overall assessment and conclusion* 12.23

Once they have carried out all the individual procedures that they consider appropriate, the directors should determine the likely outcome by considering the range of potential outcomes and the probability of their occurrence and taking into account the implications of any interaction between the various factors. In practice, this will usually be evidenced by the board:

- considering a paper summarising the going concern position of the company;
- discussing the implications of the issues; and
- reaching a formal conclusion on going concern.

If the directors become aware of any factors that cast doubt on the ability of the entity to continue in operational existence for the foreseeable future, they will need to carry out additional detailed investigations to determine the extent of the problem and to decide how the company can best respond to it. They will also usually need to make additional disclosure in the annual report and accounts.

### Interim reporting                                                    12.24

Going concern will not usually be considered in the same level of detail in the context of an interim report as in the case of the annual report and accounts. However, the JWG guidance notes that at the time that the interim report is approved, the directors should review their previous work on going concern and see whether any of the significant factors identified at that time have changed in the intervening period to such an extent as to affect the appropriateness of the going concern presumption. More information on the preparation of interim reports is given in Chapter 10 'Financial Reporting'.

### Application of the guidance to groups                                12.25

In the case of a group, the JWG guidance notes that the directors of the parent company should make a going concern statement in relation to both the parent company and the group as a whole. However, the statement in respect of the group should not be taken as implying that each of the individual companies within the group is considered to be a going concern.

## Disclosures in respect of going concern                               12.26

## At a glance                                                           12.27

- The JWG guidance includes illustrative wording for the directors' statement, depending on the company's circumstances.
- Some companies give additional details on the steps that the directors have taken in reaching their conclusions.
- Where the directors conclude that the company is unlikely to continue in operational existence for the foreseeable future, they will usually need to take legal advice on the wording of their statement.
- In some situations it is good practice to confirm in the notes to the accounts that the going concern basis has been adopted and why this is considered appropriate.
- Where the period considered by the directors has been limited to a period of less than twelve months from the date on which the accounts are formally approved by the directors, this fact must be disclosed in the notes to the accounts.
- The statement can be presented in a separate section of the annual report and accounts dealing with corporate governance issues or within the Operating and Financial Review.

## *Making a formal statement on going concern*     **12.28**

Having carried out appropriate procedures, the directors should be able to reach one of three possible conclusions:

(i)    there is a reasonable expectation that the company will continue in operational existence for the foreseeable future, and the going concern basis is therefore appropriate for the financial statements;

(ii)    there are factors that cast doubt on the ability of the company to continue in operational existence for the foreseeable future, but the directors consider that it is still appropriate to use the going concern basis in preparing the financial statements; or

(iii)    it is unlikely that the company will continue in operational existence for the foreseeable future and it may therefore not be appropriate to use the going concern basis in preparing the financial statements.

In the case of listed companies, the JWG guidance sets out recommendations on the disclosures that should be given in each of these circumstances in order to comply with the Combined Code. It is important to remember that FRS 18 also requires certain disclosures to be given in the annual accounts in the situations (ii) and (iii) above, and that these apply to all companies, not just those whose shares are listed.

## *Going concern presumption appropriate*     **12.29**

Where the directors conclude that there are no indications to suggest that the company will be unable to continue in operational existence for the foreseeable future, and that the going concern presumption is therefore an appropriate basis for the preparation of the accounts, the JWG guidance suggests the following basic disclosure:

> 'After making enquiries, the directors have a reasonable expectation that the company has adequate resources to continue in operational existence for the foreseeable future. For this reason, they continue to adopt the going concern basis in preparing the accounts.'

The implication of this recommendation is that details of the 'supporting assumptions or qualifications as necessary' specifically required by the Combined Code only need to be given where there are some doubts or uncertainties over the continuation of the business. A number of companies have gone beyond the basic disclosure suggested in the guidance, and have given details of the steps that the directors have taken in reaching their conclusions, along the following lines:

> 'The directors have reviewed the company's budget for 200X and outline plans for the following two years. After taking into account the cash flow implications of the plans, including proposed capital expenditure and reorganisation costs, and after

comparing these to the company's committed borrowing facilities, the directors are satisfied that it is appropriate to prepare the accounts on a going concern basis.'

## *Going concern basis used despite certain doubts*      **12.30**

If there are some doubts or uncertainties over the appropriateness of the going concern basis for the accounts, the directors should explain the circumstances by giving details of:

- the factors that give rise to the problems (including any external factors that are beyond their control); and
- the action being taken to deal with the problem.

For instance, such a situation might arise where loan convenants have been breached so that the loan has technically become repayable on demand, and the facility is in the course of being renegotiated. The JWG guidance sets out the following example of how the disclosure requirements might be met in these circumstances:

> 'The company is in breach of certain loan covenants at its balance sheet date and so the company's bankers could recall their loans at any time. The directors continue to be involved in negotiations with the company's bankers and as yet no demands for repayments have been received. The negotiations are at an early stage and, although the directors are optimistic about the outcome, it is as yet too early to make predictions with any certainty. In the light of the actions described ...... the directors consider it appropriate to adopt the going concern basis in preparing the accounts.'

## *Going concern basis not appropriate*      **12.31**

Where the directors conclude that the company is unlikely to continue in operational existence for the foreseeable future, they may need to prepare accounts on an alternative basis, such as a break-up basis. This situation is expected to arise only rarely in practice, but in these circumstances the directors will have to state that, in their opinion, the company is no longer a going concern. They will usually need to take legal advice on the wording of such a statement. The fact that the company is not considered to be a going concern does not necessarily mean that it is insolvent, but the directors will need to give appropriate consideration to this and in particular to the wrongful trading provisions of the *Insolvency Act 1986*.

## *Other situations where disclosure may be appropriate*      **12.32**

Unless a formal statement on going concern is needed in order to comply with the Combined Code, it is not usually considered necessary to disclose the use of the going concern basis in the accounts – users are entitled to assume that is has been adopted in the absence of any information to the contrary.

However, where it is not apparent from the accounts themselves that the entity is a going concern (eg where the entity has made a loss during the year and the balance sheet shows net liabilities), it is good practice to confirm that the accounts have been prepared on the going concern basis and to explain why the directors consider this to be appropriate. For instance, it may be that a parent undertaking has formally agreed to make ongoing financial support available to the reporting entity and that the directors have taken this into account in their going concern assessment. The following disclosures illustrate how this situation might be explained:

## *Example 1 – Going concern disclosure: Subordination of balance due to parent undertaking*

The company's parent undertaking has confirmed that it will not seek repayment of the amount owed to it until the company?s other liabilities have been met in full. Having considered this and all other information available to them up to the date on which the financial statements were approved, the directors consider that it is appropriate to prepare the financial statements on a going concern basis.

## *Example 2 – Going concern disclosure: Ongoing financial support from parent undertaking*

The company's parent company has confirmed that it will continue to make available such financial support as is required to enable the company to continue to trade for the foreseeable future. Having considered this and all other information available to them up to the date on which the financial statements were approved, the directors consider that it is appropriate to prepare the financial statements on a going concern basis.

## *Period considered less than one year* 12.33

Where the period considered by the directors has been limited to a period of less than twelve months from the date on which the accounts are formally approved by the directors, FRS 18 requires this fact to be disclosed in the notes to the accounts and it may also be advisable to refer to this in the Combined Code statement on going concern (see **12.12** above).

## *Location of the directors' statement* 12.34

The JWG guidance suggests that the directors' statement on going concern should be given in the Operating and Financial Review, as the detailed discussion and analysis given in this review will usually help to put the going concern statement into context. However, given that the review is a historical statement, the directors may need to incorporate additional information for going concern purposes (eg new factors that have arisen, or that are expected to arise). In practice, many companies present the going concern statement as part of a separate section of the annual report and accounts dealing with corporate governance issues rather than as part of the Operating and Financial Review. However, where FRS 18 requires disclosures to be given in respect of going concern issues, these details must be given in the accounts themselves and it will usually be advisable to cross-reference the directors' statement to the disclosures.

---

## Checklist: assessment of going concern

This checklist summarises some of the issues that directors may need to consider when assessing whether the company is a going concern. Not every item will be relevant to every company. Similarly, the checklist should not be regarded as comprehensive – other factors may need to be taken into account, depending on the specific circumstances of the company.

**A    Financial indicators of potential going concern difficulties**
- Is the company incurring recurrent operating losses?
- Is the company experiencing fluctuating profits and losses?
- Is the company having difficulty in paying its debts (including tax, VAT and any off-balance sheet commitments) as they fall due?
- Are there any indications that the company's suppliers are withdrawing or reducing the terms of trade credit offered?
- Is the company experiencing significant liquidity or cash flow problems?
- Does the company have an excess of liabilities over assets?
- Does the company have net current liabilities?
- Has the company defaulted on the terms of existing loan covenants or breached the terms of existing loan agreements?
- Does the cashflow forecast indicate that the company will require additional borrowing facilities that have not yet been agreed?
- Is the company experiencing difficulty in meeting the interest cost on borrowings?
- Is a major restructuring of debt required?
- Does the company have major debt repayment falling due without adequate facilities to cover this?
- Have major cash flow problems developed since the balance sheet date?
- Have significant losses arisen since the balance sheet date?
- Has the company been forced to sell substantial fixed assets without replacement?
- Does the company have significant exposure to fluctuations in exchange rates?
- Does the company have significant exposure to losses arising on fixed price contracts?

**B    Operational indicators of potential going concern difficulties**
- Is the company having difficulty in adapting to fundamental changes in the market?

---

- Is the company having difficult in adapting to fundamental techno-logical change?
- Is the company heavily dependent on a limited range of products or services in a depressed market?
- Have recent technical developments rendered a key product or service obsolete?
- Has the company lost key customers?
- Has the company lost key suppliers?
- Has the company been forced reduce the level of its operations (eg as a result of new legislation, environmental issues etc)?
- Has the company lost key members of management or staff?
- Is the company experiencing difficulties in recruiting the appropri-ate calibre and number of staff?
- Is the company encountering problems with labour-related organisa-tions (eg trade unions)?
- Is the company experiencing quality control problems?
- Is the company experiencing significant uninsured warranty or product liability claims?
- Has the company lost significant patents, licences or franchises?
- Is the company incurring increased maintenance costs and down-time as a result of an inability to fund the replacement of fixed assets?

**C     Other indicators of potential going concern difficulties**
- Is the company involved in major litigation, where an adverse judge-ment may threaten the continuation of the business?
- Has the company given significant guarantees that are likely to be called upon?
- Are significant commitments likely to arise from environmental issues or new legislation?

*Checklist: going concern review*

This checklist summarises the main steps that directors should take when carrying out an annual review of going concern. The checklist should not be regarded as comprehensive - other steps may need to be taken, depend-ing on the specific circumstances of the company.

- Review the company's budgeting process and consider whether the resulting budget is appropriate for going concern review purposes – for instance, does the budget represent the best estimate of the results for the review period or has it been prepared with additional objectives in mind (eg to set performance targets) which might result in it being over-optimistic?
- Review the assumptions made during the budgeting process – for instance, those on:

- general issues such as inflation, interest rates and the economy;
- individual items of income and expenditure;
- customer demand;
- the availability of supplies and labour;
- the availability of finance;
- the incidence of product and warranty claims;
- the outcome and impact of contingent liabilities and guarantees.

Are the assumptions:

- realistic?
- consistent with each other?
- still valid at the time of the going concern review?

● Review the impact on the budget of changes in critical assumptions.

● Review the company's cashflow forecast and consider:
  - whether adequate financing is already available or whether additional facilities need to be negotiated;
  - if the term of any of the facilities is due to end within the period reviewed, whether confirmation should be sought of the likely continuation of that facility;
  - the impact of any changes in critical assumptions.

● Consider whether any other factors cast doubt on the company's ability to continue operations for the foreseeable future (see Going Concern Checklist below).

● Consider whether the going concern assumption is appropriate and whether any additional disclosures need to be given in the accounts.

● Prepare a memorandum on going concern for formal consideration by the main board.

● Prepare a statement on going concern for inclusion in the annual report (listed companies only).

# 13. Insurance

| Introduction | 13.1 |
|---|---|
| At a glance | 13.2 |

> ● All directors are advised to carry Directors' and Officers' liability insurance.

This chapter concerns insurance for the directors themselves as opposed to insurance for the company. This is known commonly as 'Directors and Officers liability insurance' or 'D&O cover'. It is of course one of the duties of a non-executive to ensure that the company is appropriately insured for the relevant risks it faces. The insurance of directors has become a highly technical area and it is important to take relevant professional technical and legal advice before entering into any such arrangements. For the avoidance of doubt the authors assume the reader will seek such advice and we therefore accept no responsibility.

In the 2003 3i/IRS survey 98% of the directors in the sample had directors' indemnity insurance.

Following the collapse of Enron, the seventh biggest business by market capitalisation in the United States, in 2001 most insurers across the world reviewed the cover that they were prepared to provide. They also reviewed the rates for which they were prepared to provide that cover as well as the conditions and exclusions contained in their policies.

It is possible to design a policy to suit the specific requirements of any company, but as most companies now have these polices for their directors the major insurers have designed template policies. One decision a director has to take is whether they want to take out an individual policy or whether they are comfortable with the policies provided by the companies on whose boards they serve.

Members of The Institute of Directors can take advantage of the personal indemnity policy it has arranged with Chubb Insurance Company of Europe.

## What are you insuring against? 13.3

In our research we reviewed policies from a range of insurers. What was striking was that many of these policies were much clearer about what cover they were not providing than that which they were.

The purpose of a D&O policy is to provide cover for loss, including defence expenses, arising from claims made by third parties against the directors personally for wrongful acts.

A wrongful act is typically described as:

'any actual or alleged act, error, omission, misstatement, mislead- ing statement or breach of duty by the director in their capacity as a director or officer of the company.'

Policies from the leading insurers will normally include provisions for advance payment of legal expenses.

What they will not cover is described in detail under 'Exclusions' below but here are a few of the highlights.

- Any litigation or actions which commenced before the inception of the policy.
- Situations where the director has been acting fraudulently or dishonestly.
- Actions brought outside the specified jurisdictions stated in the policy.
- Physical damage to humans or tangible property.
- Not always but usually, directorships in companies with negative net worth.

## How are most policies structured? 13.4

Each insurer will have their own preferred presentational style but most poli- cies contain the following elements:

- a Schedule for the insurance certificate;
- the insuring agreement;
- definitions;
- exclusions;

338

- conditions;
- discovery period; and
- extensions.

A brief description of each of these elements and points to consider is provided below.

## *A Schedule for the insurance certificate*      **13.5**

This will normally list the following details:

- company or companies to which the policy refers;
- principal address of the company;
- policy period;
- limit of liability in the aggregate and specifically for individual directors if relevant;
- retention;
- retroactive period;
- acquisition limit; and
- premium.

If the company has or intends to have subsidiaries then it is important for the directors of the holding company to understand the extent of their liability for actions arising from the activities of these subsidiaries. Policies should contain an automatic cover for subsidiaries clause for subsidiaries below a specified percentage of the assets of the Group. The same will be the case for future acquistions.

Policy periods tend to be very precise, for example, stating the hour that the cover commences and ceases.

The limit of liability in aggregate means the limit for all of the directors, executive and non-Executive. Some policies also include specific amounts for individual directors, for example the chairman or chief executive. The limit will generally include:

- retention relates usually to an amount held back by the insurer. This is common in the USA and Canada; and
- retroactive period.

## *The Insuring Agreement*      **13.6**

This will simply state that the insurer will pay on behalf of the insured all loss which the insurer is legally liable to pay to the extent that they are not indemnified by the company. Most will specify that this includes defence expenses. If the one you are considering doesn't then it is of questionable value!

## *Exclusions* 13.7

In the UK these will typically be the following:

- for death, bodily injury, sickness or disease;
- acts which are found by a court to be fraudulent or dishonest;
- any personal profit or gain for which the insured was not legally entitled;
- any circumstances where there is collusion between the person bringing the action and the insured;
- actions brought in certain jurisdictions. (these may be insurer specific); and
- no payment for the directors' own time spent in defending claims.

## *Conditions* 13.8

These relate to the:

- manner in which claims are made;
- process for making claims and paying advances; and
- arrangements for retention;

as well as any conditions the insurer may determine because of the nature of business or the history of individual directors.

## *Some other practical issues to consider* 13.9

In UK if the policy premium is paid for by the company it is deemed to be a taxable benefit.

You are only covered if the premium has been paid.

How do you know that the premium has been paid if it is a company rather than individual policy? The simplest way is to have your interest in the policy noted with the insurer and diarise when the premium falls due to be paid.

# 14. Internal Control

## Requirements on internal control 14.1

## At a glance 14.2

- Under the Combined Code, directors should review the effectiveness of the company's system of internal control at least annually and report to shareholders that they have done so.
- Guidance on reviewing and reporting on internal control is set out in 'Internal Control – Guidance for Directors on the Combined Code' (often referred to as the 'Turnbull Report').
- The form or content of the directors' statement on internal control is not prescribed in detail by the Combined Code or the related guidance.

## The Combined Code 14.3

Paragraph D.2.1 in Part 2 of the Combined Code requires the directors to conduct an annual review (as a minimum) of the effectiveness of the company's (or group's) system of internal control and to report to shareholders that they have done so. Their review should cover all aspects of internal control, rather than just internal financial control. However, there is no longer a requirement for them to express an opinion on the effectiveness of the system.

## *Turnbull guidance* 14.4

Guidance on reviewing internal control and reporting under the Combined Code was developed by a working party of the Institute of Chartered Accountants in England and Wales chaired by Nigel Turnbull. Their final report *Internal Control – Guidance for Directors on the Combined Code* (often referred to as the Turnbull Report) was published in September 1999 and clarifies what is expected of the board of a listed company in terms of:

- applying Principle D.2 in Part 1 of the Combined Code (maintaining a sound system of internal control to safeguard the shareholders' investment and the company's assets);
- determining the extent of their compliance with the best practice guidance set out in provision D.2.1 of Part 2 of the Combined Code (review of the effectiveness of the system of internal controls); and
- determining the extent of their compliance with the best practice guidance set out in provision D.2.2 of Part 2 of the Combined Code (periodic consideration of whether an internal audit function should be established).

Transitional provisions applied for accounting periods ending before 23 December 2000 to give directors adequate time to develop and implement procedures to enable them to report on internal control in line with this guidance. The FSA Listing Rules require full compliance for accounting periods ending on or after 23 December 2000.

## *Aims of the working party* 14.5

The objective of the Internal Control Working Party was to develop guidance that:

- can be tailored to the circumstances of an individual company;
- identifies sound business practice, by linking internal control with risk management and placing emphasis on the key controls that a company should maintain;
- provides meaningful high level information and avoids extensive disclosure that does not add to a user's understanding; and
- will remain relevant and be capable of evolving with the business environment.

This approach is in line with the Preamble to the Combined Code, in which the Hampel Committee emphasised that it was not their intention to prescribe the form or content of the various reporting statements required by the Code, but rather that companies should be free to explain their governance policies in the light of the principles set out in the Code and in the context of any special circumstances specific to the company.

# Risk management and internal control 14.6

# At a glance 14.7

> - The Turnbull guidance is based on the principle that companies will adopt a risk-based approach to establishing a system of internal control, and that the review of its effectiveness will be part of the normal process of managing the business.
> - The directors of a parent company are responsible for reviewing and reporting on internal control for the group as a whole.
> - An effective system of internal control should provide reasonable assurance against business failure, material error, fraud or breaches of regulations.
> - A sound system of internal control includes policies and processes to safeguard company assets, identify and manage liabilities, maintain proper records and generate information that is timely, relevant and reliable.

## *Importance of risk management and internal* 14.8

Internal control is one of the main elements in the management of risk, along with the transfer of risk to third parties (eg through insurance arrangements), the sharing of risk (eg through participation in joint ventures) and contingency planning. The risks that any entity faces will inevitably change as the business develops and the environment in which it operates evolves. Companies must therefore regularly review and evaluate the risks to which they are exposed. The aim will usually be to manage and control business risk rather than to attempt to eliminate it completely. The Turnbull guidance is based on the principle that companies will adopt a risk-based approach to establishing of a system of internal control and to the regular review of its effectiveness. The review of the effectiveness of the internal control system should therefore be part of the normal process of managing the business rather than a specific exercise carried out only in order to comply with the recommendations of the Combined Code.

## *Group perspective* 14.9

The guidance notes specifically that references to a company should be taken, where relevant, to refer to a group. The directors of a parent company are therefore responsible for reviewing the effectiveness of internal control from the perspective of the group as a whole and for reporting to the shareholders on this. Where the board's report does not cover any joint ventures or associates of the group, this fact should be disclosed.

## *Responsibility for the system of internal control*     **14.10**

The detailed work involved in establishing, operating and monitoring a system of internal control should be carried out by individuals with the necessary skills, technical knowledge, objectivity and understanding of the business, its objectives, the industries and markets in which it operates and the risks that it faces. The detailed work will usually be delegated by the board to management and all employees are likely to have some responsibility for internal control as part of their accountability for achieving objectives. However, the board as a whole retains ultimate responsibility for the company's system of internal control. It must therefore set appropriate policies on internal control and satisfy itself on a regular basis that the system is functioning well in practice and that it is effective in managing the risks that the business faces.

## *Factors to consider*     **14.11**

A system of internal control can never provide absolute protection against business failure, material error, fraud or breaches of regulations, but it should be able to provide reasonable assurance against these problems. In determining policies on internal control and assessing what constitutes a good system of internal control in the particular circumstances of the company, the board should consider:

- the nature and extent of the risks that the company faces;
- the extent and categories of risk that it regards as acceptable for the company to bear;
- the likelihood of the risks crystallising;
- the company's ability to reduce the incidence, and impact on the business, of risks that do crystallise; and
- the costs and benefits of operating relevant controls.

The limitations on any system of internal control include human fallibility, management override of controls and the risk of unforeseen events and circumstances arising.

## *Definition of internal control*     **14.12**

A system of internal control is defined in the guidance as encompassing the policies, processes, tasks, behaviours and other aspects of the company that, taken together:

- facilitate its effective and efficient operation by enabling it to respond appropriately to significant risks (including business, operational, financial and compliance risks);
- help to ensure the quality of internal and external reporting; and
- help to ensure compliance with applicable laws and regulations.

They include policies and processes to safeguard company assets from loss, fraud or inappropriate use, identify and manage liabilities, maintain proper records and generate information that is timely, relevant and reliable.

## *Elements of a sound system of internal control*          14.13

A sound system of internal control should reflect the company's control environment (see **15.14** below) and organisational structure, and should include:

- control activities;
- information and communication processes; and
- processes for monitoring the continuing effectiveness of the system.

The internal control system should be embedded in the company's operations and should form part of its culture. It must be capable of responding promptly to new risks as the business develops and should include procedures for reporting immediately to management when significant control weaknesses or failures are identified. The information provided to management might include regular reports on progress against the company's business objectives (eg by using agreed performance indicators) together with information on issues such as customer satisfaction and employee attitudes.

## *Control environment*          14.14

A company's control environment is usually considered to include:

- a commitment by directors, management and employees to competence, integrity and a climate of trust (eg leadership by example, development of an appropriate culture within the business);
- the communication to all managers and employees of agreed standards of behaviour and control consciousness, which support the business objectives and risk management and internal control systems (eg written codes of conduct, formal disciplinary procedures, formal procedures for the appraisal of performance);
- clear organisational structures, which help to ensure that authority, responsibility and accountability are clearly defined and that decisions and actions are taken by the appropriate individuals;
- clear communication to employees of what is expected of them, and of their freedom to act (eg in respect of customer relations, service levels, health and safety issues, environmental matters, financial and other reporting issues);
- allocation of sufficient time and resources to risk management and internal control; and
- provision of relevant training on risk and control issues, so that management and employees develop the necessary knowledge, skills and tools to support achievement of the company's objectives and the effective management of risk.

Internal Control

# Reviewing the effectiveness of internal control 14.15

## At a glance 14.16

- The board as a whole must form its own view on the adequacy of the review of internal control.
- The precise role of the audit committee will vary between companies.
- There should be a defined process for the board's review of the effectiveness of the internal control system each year, to provide adequate support for the directors' statement in the annual report.
- The Turnbull Report recommends that companies without an internal audit function should review annually whether there is a need to establish one.

## *Role of the audit committee* 14.17

The board may delegate to the audit committee or other board committees certain aspects of the review of the effectiveness of the system of internal control (for instance, those aspects that are particularly relevant to their activities), but the board as a whole should form its own view on the adequacy of the review after due and careful enquiry. In other words, it will not be sufficient for the audit committee alone to review the effectiveness of the system of internal control. The audit committee should report formally to the board, who should then take a collective decision on the adequacy of the review. The precise role of the audit committee will vary between companies and will depend on factors such as the size, style and composition of the board and the nature of the principal risks that the business faces. The audit committee will usually consider financial controls, but may also be asked by the board to act as the focal point for reviews of the wider aspects of internal control. These issues should be considered by the board when the terms of reference for the audit committee are established and reviewed (see CHAPTER 2 AUDIT MATTERS).

## *The process of the review* 14.18

There should be a defined process for the board's review of the effectiveness of the company's system of internal control, to provide adequate support for the statement made by the directors in the annual report. The board should take account of all the information available to it up to the date on which the annual report is approved and signed. The board should not rely solely on the monitoring processes that form part of the business operations, but should receive and review regular reports on internal control, and should also carry out a specific annual exercise to support the statement in the annual report and to ensure that all significant aspects of internal control have been covered.

## Suggested approach                                          14.19

The Turnbull guidance suggests the following approach:

- there should be an agreed procedure for the board (or relevant committee) to receive and review regular reports on internal control from management or others qualified to prepare them (eg internal audit);
- the reports should provide a balanced assessment of the areas covered and should identify both the significant risks involved and the effectiveness of the internal control system in managing those risks;
- the board (or relevant committee) should:
  - consider the key risks and assess how they have been identified, evaluated and managed;
  - assess the effectiveness of the internal control system in managing those risks, taking into account the impact of any weaknesses or control failings that have been reported;
  - consider whether appropriate and prompt action is being taken to remedy weaknesses or failings;
  - consider whether the findings indicate a need for more extensive monitoring of the internal control system;
- the board should carry out a specific annual assessment to support the statement in the annual report – this assessment should cover:
  - changes since the last review in the nature and extent of significant risks;
  - the company's ability to respond effectively to change (both internal and external);
  - the scope and quality of the ongoing monitoring of the system of internal control, including where appropriate the internal audit function;
  - the extent and frequency of reporting to the board (or relevant committee) of the results of the monitoring process, enabling it to build up a cumulative assessment of the state of internal control and the effectiveness with which risk is managed;
  - the incidence of major control weaknesses or failings identified during the period and the extent to which they have resulted in unforeseen outcomes or contingencies that have had, could have had, or may in future have, a material impact on results;
  - the effectiveness of the year-end financial reporting process.

Where significant control weaknesses or failings are identified, the board should determine how these arose and should reassess the effectiveness of management's ongoing processes for designing, operating and monitoring the system of internal control.

## Review of the need for an internal audit function          14.20

The best practice guidance in Part 2 of the Combined Code recommends that companies without an internal audit function should review from time to time the need to establish one. The Turnbull guidance recommends that this should be done at least annually and that the review should take into account:

- whether the board has other means of obtaining sufficient and objective assurance on the effectiveness of the company's system on internal control;
- whether there are any trends or current factors in the company's internal environment, markets or other aspects of its external environment that have increased, or are expected to increase, the risks faced by the company – for example:
  - changes in organisational structure, reporting processes or information systems;
  - changes in key risks as a result of changes in products or services, entry into new markets, or changes in regulatory requirements;
  - adverse trends apparent from the monitoring of the internal control system; or
  - increased incidence of unexpected or unacceptable results.

Where there is an internal audit function, the Turnbull guidance recommends that the board should review its remit, authority, resources and scope of work, also on an annual basis. The role of an internal audit function is considered in more detail in CHAPTER 2 AUDIT MATTERS.

## The annual statement on internal control          14.21

## At a glance          14.22

- The annual statement should summarise the process that the board has applied, including where relevant the role of the audit committee, and acknowledge the board's responsibility for the system of internal control.
- In the case of listed companies, the auditors are required to review the directors' statement on internal control and to report any concerns in their report on the annual accounts.

## *Minimum disclosure*          14.23

The board's annual statement on internal control should provide users of the annual report and accounts with meaningful, high-level information. Particular care should be taken to ensure that the statement does not give a misleading impression. As a minimum, the board should disclose where applicable that:

- there is an ongoing process for identifying, evaluating and managing key risks;
- this has been in place for the year under review and up to the date of approval of the annual report and accounts; and

- this process accords with the relevant guidance on internal control and is regularly reviewed by the board.

The statement should also summarise the process that the board has applied in reviewing the effectiveness of the system of internal control, including where relevant the role of the audit committee or other committees. The board may also want to provide additional information to help users of the report and accounts understand the company's risk management processes and the internal control system.

## *Where one or more of the statements cannot be made*    14.24

If the board is unable to make any of these disclosures, this fact should be stated and the board should explain what action is being taken to rectify the situation. Where relevant, the board will also have to disclose that they have failed to conduct a review of the effectiveness of the company's system of internal control, or that they have not reviewed the need for an internal audit function if they do not already have one (see **15.20**). Where weaknesses in internal control have resulted in significant problems which have been disclosed in the annual accounts, the board should describe the processes that it has applied to deal with the internal control aspects of the problems.

## *Acknowledgement of responsibility*    14.25

The statement should also include an acknowledgement that the board is responsible for the company's system of internal control and for reviewing its effectiveness, together with an explanation that such a system can only provide reasonable and not absolute assurance against material misstatement or loss.

## *Reporting by auditors*    14.26

Where directors are required by the FSA Listing Rules to include in the annual report and accounts a statement on compliance with the Combined Code and on going concern, the Listing Rules also require these statements to be reviewed by the auditors. In the case of the compliance statement, the auditors' review is only required to cover certain aspects, but these specifically include the directors' statement on internal control. Under the latest professional guidance, the auditors are required to explain this reporting requirement in the section of their report that sets out their responsibilities as auditors. If the auditors are not satisfied with the adequacy of the corporate governance disclosures and cannot resolve the problems through discussion with the directors, they are required to report their concerns in a separate paragraph as part of their opinion on the financial statements, but this will not constitute a qualification of their report on the annual accounts.

## Checklist: internal control       **14.27**

This checklist summarises the issues that directors may need to consider in relation to internal control and is based on the ICAEW guidance document *Internal Control – Guidance for Directors on the Combined Code*. The checklist should not be regarded as comprehensive – directors may need to consider other issues, depending on the specific circumstances of the company.

- Does the company have clear business objectives and have these been communicated to all management and staff?
- Do the directors and senior management demonstrate an appropriate commitment to competence, integrity and the development of a climate of trust?
- Does the board adopt a professional approach to financial reporting?
- Has the company developed agreed standards of behaviour to support business objectives and risk management?
- Has it communicated these standards to all management and staff, for instance by means of:
  - written codes of conduct;
  - formal appraisal procedures;
  - formal disciplinary procedures; and
  - performance reward schemes?
- Does the company have a clear organisational structure, with clearly defined lines of authority, responsibility and accountability?
- Are decisions and actions throughout the company properly co-ordinated?
- Does the organisational structure ensure that decisions are taken at an appropriate level and by appropriate individuals?
- Are sufficient time and resources allocated to risk management and internal control?
- Are management and staff provided with relevant training on business risk and internal control issues?
- Has the company developed a formal analysis of key risks, covering:
  - operational risk (both internal and external);
  - financial risk;
  - compliance risk;
  - other risks?
- Is business risk assessed on an ongoing basis and is the analysis of key risks regularly updated to take account of new developments, both within the business and externally?
- Have clear policies and strategies been developed to deal with significant risks identified in the assessment?
- Does management have a clear understanding of the level of risk that is regarded as acceptable to the board?
- Have appropriate communication channels been put into place to enable individuals to report suspected fraud, breaches of law or regulations, or other irregularities?

- Does the board receive regular reports on progress against business objectives and the related risk factors – for instance:
  - performance reports;
  - relevant performance indicators;
  - customer service levels;
  - quality control;
  - customer satisfaction; and
  - employee attitudes?
- Does the board, or an appropriate committee, receive and review regular reports on internal control and:
  - consider how the key risks have been identified, evaluated and managed;
  - assess the effectiveness of the internal control system in managing those risks;
  - consider whether the company's financial and other information systems capture relevant, reliable and up to date information;
  - consider whether the company's financial and other information systems deliver appropriate information to the right individuals at the right time?
- Has the potential impact of identified internal control weaknesses or failures been properly established and considered?
- Has prompt and effective action been taken to deal with any internal control weaknesses or failures that have been identified?
- Are there appropriate procedures to confirm that agreed action is actually taken in practice?
- Has the board carried out a specific annual assessment to support the internal control statement in the annual report (see **15.19**)?
- If the company has an internal audit function, has the board (or an appropriate committee) reviewed its remit, authority, resources and scope of work?
- If the company does not have an internal audit function, has the need to establish one been formally considered?

Internal Control

# 15. Investor Relations

- Investor relations are vital for a company to build the investor base it wants.
- A prospective non-executive should carry out due diligence on the company's shareholders before agreeing to join.
- A non-executive can find a public-to private transaction challenging, especially where protecting shareholders' interests are concerned.
- The increasing sophistication of media relations, and the growth of the internet, have increased the scope of investor relations.

An 'Investor Relations' strategy is predicated on an 'Investor' strategy. Inevitably the current shareholder base will have been shaped by the history of the company. This may or may not be the ideal mix for the company. If not ideal then the board clearly needs to decide what investors it requires before it develops and executes a strategy for managing communications with them. Moving from a current mix to an ideal one is much easier if the company's performance is strong and the general investment climate is healthy.

As we write this first edition of this Non-Executive Director's Handbook the capital markets are under severe pressure and the economic environment is challenging. A natural consequence of this is that it is much tougher to achieve the shareholder base you desire whether you are public or private. Good investor relations are therefore critical.

## Objectives of a typical investor relations strategy     15.3

The objectives of a typical investor relations strategy are for the company to have:

- the investors it wants;
- a good understanding of what those investors require;
- a group of shareholders who support the company's vision and strategy; and
- cost effective communications;

and for shareholders to have:

- an accurate understanding of the company's vision, strategy and performance;
- the feeling that the objectives that they have for their shareholding are being met; and
- confidence in the board and the governance of the company.

If these objectives are met then the company will have a strong, well informed and supportive shareholder base to assist its development in a cost effective way.

The strategy must also recognise the importance of representing the company in a balanced way, being positive yet minimising the chances of disappointing investors. The board also needs to be conscious of any divergence in messages being given to any of the business's key audience groups.

Many companies, public and private, have widespread employee share ownership so it is therefore important that there is also good internal communication on shareholder issues and that these are consistent with external messages.

## Who takes part in investor relations?     15.4

There are several important groups of people who take part in and influence investor relations for companies. The key groups are the shareholders, the board and its principal advisers. The exact mix and the relative importance of each group naturally depends upon the specific company.

- Shareholders who may be from several categories (institutional, venture capital or private equity, private, family, trade, current and former employees).
- Executive directors, most notably the chief executive and finance director.

- Investor relations director (if public and relevant).
- The chairman.
- The senior independent non-executive director (or deputy chairman).
- Non-executive directors.
- Brokers who oversee the relationship with institutional investors.
- Market makers.
- Financial PR advisers.
- Bankers or other providers of finance to the company.
- Financial journalists.
- Equities analysts(the house analyst employed by the broker and others who follow the company).

## What should the non-executive director's role be in investor relations?                                     15.5

At a minimum it should be to ensure that there is an appropriate investor relations strategy, that the right resources are in place to achieve the agreed strategy and that there is good visibility of the performance of investor relations. The non-executive must also possess a good understanding of what the company's investors expect from the non-executive directors of the company. Whether public or private there will be certain key dates and documents that the non-executive will need to be available for or to approve. They therefore need to be aware of these and make themselves available as appropriate.

For public companies the finance director will typically have the primary responsibility for developing and implementing the investor relations strategy. The degree of sophistication varies. Larger public companies will have dedicated investor relations teams, regularly survey investor views, have the benefit of comprehensive investor information on their website and so on. In smaller public companies the finance director will be able to delegate less.

No matter what the size or nature of ownership of the company the balance between making investors keen to keep or increase their investment and reflecting a fair perspective on the outlook for the company is a critical one to achieve.

The principal points of contact between investors and the company will tend to be the chief executive, finance director and chairman. Indeed in the Higgs report, which focussed on larger listed companies, the section on 'Relationships with shareholders' contains the following remarks:

> '...only rarely do non-executive directors hear at first hand the views of major shareholders. The majority of non-executive directors (52 per cent) surveyed for the review never discuss company business with their investors. Within the FTSE 100, contact is rarer still: only about one in five FTSE 100 non-

354

> executive directors discuss company business with investors once a year or more often.'

and

> 'Qualitative research undertaken for the review showed that in normal circumstances non-executive directors and shareholders have only minimal direct contact. Interviews with investors revealed that rarely do they speak directly with non-executive directors, and only then where there is a serious problem. Even in these circumstances, discussion often centred on director remuneration rather than on wider strategy or governance issues.'

So it is likely to be the case that many private company non-executives have greater contact with investors than their public counterparts. In venture capital backed situations where often the investing institution has introduced the non-executive this will certainly be the case.

Whether there is a high level of contact or not, the non-executive's reputation and standing with investors is important. Non-executives with high investor credibility, whether that is with a small group of family investors or Wall Street, can add considerable value to the company.

## Understanding the shareholder                                  15.6

Understanding who the shareholders are and what their objectives might be is an important part of the due diligence a non-executive will undertake before agreeing to accept the appointment. (See **PARAGRAPH 1.23** for due diligence checklist). The context is important and if shareholders do for whatever reason have differing objectives the non-executive needs to understand what they are and how he or she is going to deal with them.

It is sometimes hard in practice to achieve the ideal level of knowledge, either because of the company's situation, the circumstances of the appointment, or the logistical challenge involved, especially if there are large numbers of shareholders of different types. It is also sometimes the case that investors aren't clear themselves about what they want from their investment.

Achieving the desired level of understanding may be easier in private companies than in listed ones. The number of shareholders is usually smaller, the executive management are frequently the major shareholders, and if there are venture capitalists involved they will have clearly stated intentions. However in family companies with diverse groups of shareholders it can be just as difficult as for a listed company.

The new or prospective non-executive needs to go about the process of understanding shareholder views sensitively, especially in circumstances where shareholders are not used to being asked or there are obvious differences. So the first thing they need to do is to agree with the chairman how they will do

Investor Relations

this. He will also need to be careful when gathering views from shareholders to recognise the risks of expressing any views which diverge from those given by the chairman, chief executive or finance director.

## What do the company's brokers do?                    15.7

The broker may be part of an integrated investment banking house which is providing a range of other services to the company. The non-executive director needs as part of his due diligence to understand who is providing key advisory services to the company as well as the links between the Company's various advisors.

In summary the broker's job is to supply institutional investors with the information that they need on the company and give the company honest feedback on how investors view the company and the stock.

The brokers will generally oversee, co-ordinate or manage the company's contacts with institutional shareholders. This is especially the case at or around the time of the announcement of key results or significant events (eg major acquisition or fund raising).

They will employ what is known as an analyst, typically known as the 'House analyst' who essentially acts as the 'expert' on the company. The London Stock Exchange's excellent guide to IR *A practical guide to investor relations* sums up their position as follows:

> 'While the house analyst's research must be objective to be credible, and is intended to form the basis of commercial investment decisions by institutions and other investors, it is widely accepted by the market that the house analyst will generally be unable to take a highly critical position on the company or its stock.'

In 2002 in the wake of the Enron, Worldcom and Global Crossing scandals in the US there was increased focus on the role of brokers and house analysts in particular.

It is important that the management, usually the finance director and, if relevant, the IR director, put sufficient time and effort into ensuring that the house analyst and the broker have an appropriate depth of understanding of the company and the markets in which it operates.

For even large businesses there will be a limited number of other analysts who cover the company in any depth. In the UK this tends to be fifteen to twenty depending upon the size and importance of the sector the company is operating in. This is a highly competitive job and the nature of the people who do it is that they are very bright and aggressive.

Brokers should also monitor activity in the shares of the company and produce accurate summaries of the shareholder register. Many larger listed companies circulate as part of their regular board reports a summary from the brokers of key movements since the last report. This monitoring is valuable input to the IR strategy and to determining communications priorities. It is important for the company to learn whether the sale of entire holding is a vote of no confidence in the business or simply a programmed reduction as part of a wider strategy to reduce holdings of a particular profile.

As with any of the key advisers to the company the non-executive will want to ensure that they are happy with the selection. It is, however, unusual for them to be too actively involved in the process. Contact is normally limited to the presentations that the brokers may make to the board, usually at the time of results or significant events.

## Market Makers                                            15.8

Every company quoted on SEAQ, the London Stock Exchange's quote driven system, must have at least two market makers quoting two-way process in its shares. The house broker will normally want to be one of these.

Non-executive directors have little if any contact with market makers.

## Special issues for smaller quoted companies (SQCs)      15.9

It is often argued that investor relations has become particularly challenging for SQCs. Several reasons are given for this including:

- consolidation of the fund management industry. The impact of which means there are few analysts following the company or even the sector;
- indexation. The consequence of which is that analysts are focussed on analysing indices rather than companies;
- low liquidity which undermines the economics of doing the analysis; and
- the difficulties of raising capital.

As a consequence the non-executive often has a greater role to play in supporting the chairman, chief executive and finance director in smaller quoted companies.

The Waterstone report for the UK's Department of Trade and Industry (DTI) in 1999 highlighted the challenges. In our view the situation has become worse rather than better. A survey undertaken by BDO published in 2003 of over 100 directors of listed companies capitalised between £10 and £200m showed that:

- 66 per cent felt that the stock market didn't fairly value their company.
- 48 per cent of them felt constrained by lack of access to equity funds.
- 51 per cent said that they would consider a public-to-private transaction within the next year or two.
- 54 per cent of them wouldn't consider a flotation if they were a private company.

Interestingly, as part of the same survey, 83 institutional fund managers were also interviewed with the following results:

- 64 per cent felt that the stock market failed to value fairly companies with a sub-£250m capitalisation;
- 41 per cent felt that the growth potential of profitable smaller companies was being constrained by lack of access to new equity funds; and
- 58 per cent felt that there wasn't enough analyst coverage of smaller quoted companies.

## Public-to-private transactions – issues for the non-executive director                                  15.10

The authors feel that the level of level of disenchantment described above is unhealthy and probably unsustainable. One solution for those companies who don't feel that they are receiving sufficient benefit from being a public company is to go private.

Venture capital and private equity funds have significant capital to fuel the growth in public-to-privates. However the process of going private is not straightforward. The lack of concentrated shareholding blocks in many smaller quoted businesses often means that it is difficult to make a transaction happen in practice. Other barriers to public-to-private transactions have been the costs, regulatory compliance issues and the perceived risk by the initial bidder that the company is put into play and they might lose.

A non-executive can be placed in an awkward situation in a public-to-private. Achieving fairness for existing shareholders whilst meeting the legitimate needs of management and their backers, as well as competing offerors for the company, is inherently difficult. Non-executive directors therefore need to be aware of the process and the issues involved. In particular they should be aware of the specific provisions in the takeover code which relate to their role.

The first thing to be clear about is whether they are acting as an independent non-executive director. A general definition of independence is provided in the Higgs report (see **PARAGRAPH 1.6** for details). However as the definition of 'independence' in the Takeover Code in relation to these transactions has yet to be amended in the light of Higgs we would encourage the reader to refer to the Takeover Code description and seek advice.

The easiest circumstance is where the Non-executive has no ongoing role on the board post-transaction. In this circumstance as a director the non-executive will want to ensure that a proper process is being followed and that the conflicts of interest which arise are managed properly. An important part of any public-to-private process is the flow of information to the various interested parties. The non-executive will want to be assured that these are conducted in the right way.

Any non-executive who becomes involved in a potential public-to-private must obtain good advice and should learn from the experience of others who have gone through the process before.

Clarity over each director's position is essential from the outset whether they are executive of non-executive. The target's board should constitute an 'Independent committee'. This is an express requirement of the Code. The committee should comprise only those directors of the target who are not in the buyout team. One of the first roles of that independent committee will be to consider whether it is appropriate for confidential information to be disclosed to the buyout backers. The release of the information should only then occur if an appropriate confidentiality agreement is executed beforehand.

The non-executive has to be aware of the duties of the management team in the process. The buyout team should declare their conflict and cannot and should not join in with the recommendation of the independent members of the board in an expression of views on the offer. However, they will still need to take responsibility for other information contained in any circular or advertisement issued by the target and in particular the responsibility statement that is part and parcel of any document issued by the bidder on behalf of the buyout team.

The executive directors and any non-executive directors who are making the bid owe fiduciary duties to the company and must observe the necessary due process that is established by the Takeover Code and company law. So they must act in the interests of the company and should not put themselves in a position where their duty to the company may conflict with their own personal interests. Accordingly they should not withhold information from the company's shareholders, that if provided to them, would enable the shareholder to negotiate a better price.

However there are practical issues to overcome if they are to achieve this. Firstly, the duty of confidentiality as well as insider dealing laws preclude the management from disclosing either unpublished price sensitive information or other confidential information in breach of their contractual and fiduciary duties to their backers. The challenge is that they will need to do this before they can make an offer and the venture capitalist will need access to financial information that is available to the management but not to the public generally.

This type of information belongs to the company and cannot be made available to the financial backers without the prior consent of the independent directors who must authorise its release. Failure to comply could result in the management team losing their jobs and facing a claim for damages if the release of the information caused financial loss to the business.

The Code expressly requires any information given by the buyout team to their backers to be given equally and promptly to any other competing bidders or potential bidders. It is one of the jobs of the independent commit-tee to monitor the information given by the target company (including members of the buyout team acting in their role as employees or directors of the target) to the buyout team's backers.

The Code further provides that the board of the target must appoint compe-tent independent financial advisors. If the existing financial advisors to the company are particularly closely connected with the buyout team, the inde-pendent committee must consider appointing new financial advisors to advise on the merits of the proposal. The Code stipulates that whenever requested, the buyout team must promptly furnish to the independent direc-tors or their advisors all information which has been furnished by the buyout team to its external financial backers (venture capitalists and bankers).

As can be seen there are several different information flows and the disclo-sure obligations differ on the important distinction of who has generated the information and in what capacity and to whom it is given. Information generated by the management of the target company in their capacity as members of the buyout team does not need to be supplied to a competing bidder. However, that same information has to be supplied to the independ-ent directors.

An express requirement of the code is that absolute secrecy be maintained right from the preliminary stages of the proposed buyout. This is to guard against rumour or speculation which may cause an untoward movement in the share price causing a need for an announcement. A crucial aspect in this regard is the obligation on the buyout team or its advisors to consult with the takeover panel if negotiations or discussions concerning the potential offer are about to be extended to include more than a very restricted number of people.

The board as a whole will also need to consider, as early as possible, the remuneration arrangements for independent directors in the course of the offer period and whether any termination payment is to be made to those directors.

This is important for a number of reasons. At the conclusion of the offer, whether successful or unsuccessful, there will need to be a clear understand-ing of what is owed to the directors by the target company. Proper consideration needs to be given to existing letters of appointment so as to ensure that no breach of *section 312* of the *Companies Act 1985* occurs. Moreover, it helps to avoid any subsequent allegations that the independence of the directors has been impaired.

In addition to all of the above, the Institutional Shareholders' Committee has issued practice guidelines for buyouts of public companies. They are entirely consistent with the Takeover Code as should be expected but the following are worthy or particular note.

- No buyout proposal is likely to be favourably received unless there has been a strong independent non-executive presence on the board of the target for some time
- It is unlikely that any buyout is going to be treated seriously without a sympathetic initial response and final recommendation by the independent non-executive directors of the target.
- it is not appropriate for the bidders to deploy as advisers those who had previously been employed by the target unless the independent non-executives clear that proposal or the independents feel that they would be better protected by appointment of new advisors.

One other area for non-executive input relates to the approval of documents. The main document is the offer document itself. This should be prepared in accordance with the provisions of the Takeover Code and the listing rules. The Code requires that any document issued to the shareholders by the buyout bidder must include a statement accepting responsibility for the information contained and this is not a task to be undertaken lightly. It requires absolutely accuracy as to the form and content of the offer document.

There will then be documentation relating to the financial backers of the buyout. This will be reflected in a shareholders' agreement. This is effectively the agreement between the venture capitalists and the management team and any other shareholders of the new company.

The venture capitalist will appreciate that warranties from the shareholders in the public offer is not feasible, but will want to obtain warranties and disclosures from any director that it can get them from. This approach is designed as much to flush out any issues as shift financial risk.

When it comes to the financing of the bid the Code requires that there be certainty of funds to prevent bids being made flippantly without financial backing. So the buyout team will have to have certainty of funding. In a private buyout funding is usually signed up at the same time as all the other documents are signed. In a public-to-private buyout the funding needs to be signed up prior to the announcement of a firm intention to make the offer even though it won't complete until some time later.

Another aspect the non-executive needs to be aware of is 'Financial Assistance'. In most cases the buyout will involve a leveraged financial structure and the providers of the debt will be looking to the assets of the target company as security. The rules prohibiting the giving of financial assistance in connection with the purchase of shares in the target company absolutely preclude those assets being secured until the company is a private company. Conversion to private status will not take place until after the compulsory acquisition of dissenting shareholders is completed so the funding structure of a buyout invariably consists of a staged process.

In conclusion these transactions are highly complex, uncertain and require a great deal of planning from the outset. It is critical for the non-executive

Investor Relations

to understand the process and be clear on what their own role in the process is.

## Media relations                                              15.11

The financial media in most developed markets are sophisticated and need to be dealt with in a highly professional manner. In the UK there are a limited number of key titles and journalists who will be relevant to a particular company, unless the company is a retail or consumer branded business. The company also needs to consider electronic media in addition to print and broadcast.

The key role for non-executives in media relations is to ensure that the company has an appropriate strategy, to be aware of how successful that strategy is and support it as relevant. This support is unlikely to include representing the company in the media and more likely to include support with the selection process of advisers and the introduction of useful contacts.

Larger businesses may have more than one adviser and may have specialists for their product and corporate public relations activities.

A non-executive who is experienced in this area may be able to add considerable value simply by imparting this experience through advice to the key spokesmen ie the chief executive, chairman and finance director. These are the people that investors and the press really want to see. An experienced non-executive may also help in other ways, for example helping the company to avoid the dangers of publicity stunts borne out of exuberance. If the media lose trust or confidence their audiences are likely to do the same shortly afterwards.

Active non-executives will want to be aware of the company's key media spokesmen and messages and be assured that there is integration and consistency with marketing communications to other audiences.

## Investor relations with private investors              15.12

For public companies with large numbers of retail investors, communications can be a challenge for the following reasons.

- The cost of communications materials.
- Handling queries and questions from shareholders.
- The nature of Annual General Meetings in the UK.
- The regulatory requirements relating to the provision of information to shareholders.

The channels of communication are straightforward:

- personal contact;
- mail;

- shareholder meetings (eg Annual General Meeting);
- internet;
- regional/Retail brokers.

For public companies, personal contact other than at the AGM or through enquiry handling is uneconomic. The main channels used are mail, internet and through using the increasingly sophisticated regional and retail brokers.

In private companies where the number of shareholders is far smaller, personal contact is the main method.

## The impact of the internet on investor relations    15.13

The development of the internet has driven several changes to the nature of investor relations, especially with retail investors. The internet boom of the late nineties expanded the numbers of people buying shares in most of the developed economies, particularly in the United States. Trading through the internet also expanded and changed the economics of share buying. However, probably the most fundamental and long lasting change from the retail shareholder's point of view has been in relation to the provision and speed of communication of information.

From the company's point of view the main benefits arise from the greater efficiency and reduced cost of providing information direct to the shareholder. Some argue that the greatest benefit of all has been the development of the FAQ ('Frequently Asked Questions') sections on company websites.

The company which has won most plaudits, and probably spent most money on web-based investor relations is BP plc (www.bp.com investor centre section)

The Department of Trade and Industry-sponsored report chaired by Tim Waterstone in 1999 'Private investors – improving share liquidity for smaller quoted companies' (see the Bibliography in **APPENDICES**) contains a useful checklist of 'desirables' for a website. These includethe following.

---

- Annual report in HTML or PDF format.
- Summary of last five years' financial data.
- Archive of press releases.
- Automatic information updates (eg major announcements).
- Event calendar (eg reportmg dates, dividend dates, meetings).
- Frequently Asked Questions section.
- Links to industry sites.
- Shareholder profile.
- Analyst coverage.
- Information/ text/video clips from key presentations.

---

One very important point to note on investor communication through

Investor Relations

websites is that the sequencing of the release of information must not in any way compromise the regulatory obligations of the company.

## Share dealing and Price Sensitive Information (PSI)    15.14

Non-executive directors are bound by the same rules as any other director when it comes to dealing in shares (see **PARAGRAPH 6.52**).

## What did the Higgs report say about the non-executive director's relationships with shareholders?    15.15

There was a whole section devoted to it in the report. This is covered in **CHAPTER 13**. There was particular sensitivity over the role of senior independent non-executives in investor relations in the published reactions to the report. Most adverse comment centred on the dangers of the senior independent director usurping the chairman's role.

The report clearly states that the primary channel of communication between the company and investors should be the CEO, FD and chairman. The senior independent director should be a safety valve when this isn't working. The suggested increase in contact between SINEs and institutions was to ensure that SINE's have earlier awareness of an issue and a mechanism for institutions to express it.

## Useful reference points    15.16

- LSE *A practical guide to investor relations* is excellent
- The Myners Report
- The Quoted Companies Alliance (www.qcanet.co.uk)
- ABI guidelines www.abi.org.uk
- NAPF guidelines www.napf.co.uk The National Association of Pension Funds (NAPF) is the principal body representing the interests of the occupational pension's movement. At the beginning of 2003 members' schemes accounted for more than £700 billion of pension fund assets invested on behalf of more than 8 million people. The NAPF therefore has considerable influence.
- Investor relations society www.ir-soc.org.uk
- FSA (www.fsa.gov.uk) The Financial Services Authority
- Proshare – www.proshare.org.uk

# 16. Nominations Committees

| | |
|---|---|
| **Introduction** | **16.1** |
| **At a glance** | **16.2** |

- The Higgs Report has made a number of recommendations on nomination committees.
- It is advisable to have a backup plan, in case of emergency.

For most listed companies the purpose of a nominations committee is straightforward and that is to 'ensure that there is a formal and transparent procedure for appointing new directors to the board and to make recommendations to the board on *all* new board appointments'.

'*All*' means executive, non-executive and of course the chairman.

We have included the sample terms of reference for a nominations committee in the APPENDICES. ICSA have also produced a very helpful guidance note (020321) which is available on their website.

In Derek Higgs' Review of the role and effectiveness of non-executives, which was focussed on listed companies, he says that:

'Almost all FTSE100 companies have a nominations committee, compared to only 30 per cent of companies outside the FTSE350. However, interviews conducted for the review suggested that where the nominations committee does exist, it is the least developed of the board's committees, usually meeting irregularly and often without a clear understanding of the extent of its role in the appointment process.'

We expect that following the publication of Higgs Report and the recommendations it makes with regard to the recruitment and appointment process for non-executives that greater focus will be placed on this committee in listed companies. This is because of the 'comply or explain' nature of his recommendations and the new proposed Combined Code for listed companies.

To quote again:

'A high level of informality surrounds the process of appointing non-executive directors. Almost half of the non-executive directors surveyed for the review were recruited to their role through personal contacts or friendships. Only four per cent had a formal interview, and one per cent had obtained their job through answering an advertisement. This situation has been widely criticised in responses to consultation.'

and

'I believe that a rigorous, fair and open appointments process is essential to promote meritocracy in the boardroom and that existing best practice for nominating and appointing directors should be universally adopted.'

He then goes on to make the following recommendations the majority of which would be incorporated into the Combined Code (see **APPENDICES**).

- All listed companies should have a nominations committee which should lead the process for board appointments and make recommendations to the board.
- The nominations committee should consist of a majority of independent non-executive directors. It may include the chairman of the board, but should be chaired by an independent non-executive.
- The chairman and members of the nominations committee should be identified in the annual report and should make publicly available their terms of reference explaining clearly their role and the authority delegated to them by the board.
- Before making an appointment, the nominations committee should evaluate the balance of skills, knowledge and experience on the board and, in the light of this evaluation, should prepare a description of the role and capabilities for a particular appointment.
- A statement should be made in the annual report detailing the activities of the nominations committee and the process used for appointments. An explanation should be given if external advice or open advertising

has not been used. The number of committee meetings and individual attendance over the course of the year should be stated.

- The nominations committee should ensure that on appointment, non-executive directors receive a formal letter of appointment setting out clearly what is expected of them in terms of time commitment, committee membership and involvement outside board meetings.
- Non-executive directors should disclose to the chairman the nature and extent of their other appointments and confirm that they will have the time available to fulfil the role.

And finally

'I therefore recommend that, when an appointment of a non-executive director is put forward for approval to shareholders, the board should explain why they believe the individual should be appointed and how they meet the requirements of the role.'

All of which appears straightforward. However there are some issues for non-executives on nominations committees.

## The existence of a committee                                      16.3

If the company is listed then there needs to be a standing committee of the board comprised of a majority of independent non-executives. In practice this will mean committees of five or more.

For non-listed companies it is more normal for the chairman and a non-executive to lead the process with active involvement of the chief executive. This may or may not be a formal committee. The board may just approve the delegation of the election process to a couple of its members and then approve, or not the recommendations that they make.

## Executive and non-executive appointments                          16.4

The Higgs Review is very clear about issues relating to the nominations committee's role in non-executive appointments as indeed it is with respect to the role of existing non-executives on the nominations committee. There is less detail with respect to executive appointments, though one would expect the same principles to apply. The authors feel that non-executives can add considerable value especially in smaller or private companies in supporting the process of senior executive appointments. This is especially true with respect to the appointment of a new finance director.

## The use of search firms                                            16.5

This is covered in detail in CHAPTER 1. We would simply reiterate that if a search firm is to be used then as with any other supplier there should be an objective selection process and they should be appropriately managed.

## Succession planning                                    16.6

Derek Higgs stated in his review that:

> 'The committee should satisfy itself that processes and plans are
> in place for orderly succession for appointments to the board and
> to senior management to maintain an appropriate balance of skills
> on the board. I recommend that the Combined Code include refer-
> ence to this important role for the nominations committee.'

Many boards have what is sometimes described as the 'falling under a bus
list'. This is a simple list of the current board and who in the event of a tragic
accident, physical or commercial, would replace them. These generally work
on the assumption that a direct replacement is made.

Succession planning for the key roles of chief executive and chairman is
covered in **PARAGRAPH 3.7**.

## Linkage with the remuneration committee               16.7

An important part of any appointment process will be the determination of the
terms and conditions of the appointment. Consequently there needs to be
strong linkage between the nominations and remuneration committees. Most
nominations committees will receive guidance from the remuneration
committee at an early stage in a recruitment process as to what terms should
be offered for the process. This tends to be more straightforward for non-
executive appointments, where it is common for all non-executives to be paid
fees on the same basis, than for executive appointments.

## Interaction with the chairman                          16.8

In the Higgs Report he says that the nominations committee may include the
chairman but should be chaired by an independent non-executive. This did
not receive much press attention at the time of publication but we believe is
a significant development. As leader of the board team the chairman should
play an active and involved role in team selection. Higgs' suggestion with
respect to larger companies is again another attempt to reduce the risk of
over-concentration of power. For smaller companies and especially private
ones the chairman will often chair the nominations committee.

Sir Adrian Cadbury in his excellent book 'Corporate governance and
Chairmanship' has a different view to Higgs:

> 'I believe that the chairman of the board should wherever possi-
> ble chair this committee, since it is chairmen who are responsible
> for the working of their boards and who should therefore play a
> leading part in selecting their team.'

The sensitive area is obviously to do with the succession of the chairman himself. If the nominations committee has done its job with regard to planning then the candidate will be an existing non-executive director. For example it may have been a selection requirement of one of the existing non-executives that they be capable of becoming chairman.

According to the Higgs Report the new chairman should be deemed to be independent (definition in the **APPENDICES**) at the time of his or her appointment.

The more challenging situation is where there is no internal candidate and the nominations committee needs to look outside. What role should the existing chairman play here? Clearly this depends upon the circumstances of his retirement. If he is being removed for underperformance then his role is obviously limited. If on the other hand he is retiring positively then he may have a lot to offer the process. This is definitely a situation where judgement is required and where, if there is a strong non-executive supporting the chairman, it is far easier to manage whether they are formally described as the senior independent non-executive or not.

Given the critical importance of the relationship between the chairman and chief executive it is essential that the chief executive is appropriately involved in the selection of any new chairman.

## Interaction with the chief executive                    16.9

Any board appointment will be a significant matter for the chief executive and the best CEOs will be actively engaged in the process. For example in recruiting top executive talent they will be the key salesman in the process as well as the key decision maker on who should be selected.

When it comes to non-executive appointments no decent potential non-executive would consider taking an appointment without meeting the chief executive and vice versa. If the chief executive is uncomfortable with a prospective non-executive then normally it is harder for the non-executive to be appointed even if there are issues with the chief executive and the non-executive is the ideal candidate.

The degree of influence a CEO has over board appointments is the cause of much debate especially in the United States and in France where power has tended to be concentrated to a greater degree in the hands of one person than in the United Kingdom. One of the roles of the nominations committee is to ensure that there is the right level of engagement of the chief executive so that they are brought into the process but do not dominate the process to the extent that the board ends up being 'a bunch of the CEO's poodles.'

## Interaction with the company's Human Resources director                                          16.10

If the company has a Human Resources director then he or she should be a key person in any recruitment or selection process. Views differ as to whether the HR director should be on the nominations committee. Technically if the nominations committee is a true sub-committee of the board then they cannot be unless they are also on the board. What typically happens therefore is that the HR director is an adviser to the committee and will attend most meetings.

The reality is that in situations where the HR director is effective they have an important and active role to play. Where they are less effective they tend to simply carry out the instructions of the nominations committee.

## What skills and experience are needed to be a member of nominations committee 16.11

The nominations committee as a whole needs to be excellent at judging people, rigorous in their selection process and good at communicating with the rest of the board. It is easier to achieve this if the members of the committee have had considerable experience of board appointments and at least one is a current or former chairman or chief executive. Good process won't in itself ensure success and often it is the most intuitive member of the nominations committee who adds the most value when it comes to key appointments. The chairman of the committee therefore needs to be a good chairman.

# 17. Pension Arrangements for Employees

## Types of pension scheme                                17.1

## At a glance                                            17.2

- The provision of good retirement benefits is often seen as an important element of the remuneration package offered to employees and the action of a responsible employer.
- Employees are increasingly being encouraged to contract out of the secondary State pension scheme and to make their own alternative provision.
- Under a defined benefit scheme, the benefits payable on retirement are fixed, either as an amount or as a proportion of salary – this is advantageous for the scheme member but the cost to the employer can fluctuate significantly over time.
- Under a defined contribution scheme, the benefits payable on retirement depend on the amount accumulated in respect of each scheme member – the employer has the benefit of a fixed cost but the employee bears the risk of the fund being insufficient to provide the level of retirement benefits hoped for.
- Employers may wish to consider alternative options to share the risks of pension provision more equitably between employers and employees.
- Any individual (and their employer) can contribute to a personal pension, provided that he/she is not already a member of an occupational pension scheme.

- From April 2001, certain individuals who are members of an occupational pension scheme can also contribute to a personal or stakeholder pension.
- All employers with five or more employees must generally give them access to a stakeholder pension scheme, unless they have made alternative pension provision.

## Introduction                                                      17.3

As we write this handbook the issue of employee pensions has become a hot political, economic and social topic. This is due to several factors including the following.

- A demographic shift in most developed nations to an older population.
- The social shift to earlier effective retirement ages.
- Significant weak performance of pension funds arising out of the collapse in stock markets in the early 2000s
- Structural issues with state pension funding and a political desire to move responsibility from the state to individuals.
- The failure of Equitable Life and the reduction in payouts from with-profits endowment policies.

The whole atmosphere around pensions has changed considerably from one where most employees thought that there was no risk to their pension to one where there is significant anxiety. It is therefore critical that non-executive directors, especially those that sit or intend sitting on remuneration committees have a good understanding of the pensions positions of the companies on whose boards they serve.

## Retirement provisions for employees                               17.4

Although most employees will qualify for State pension benefits on retirement, many people will want to make additional provision to ensure that they can maintain their lifestyle after retirement and perhaps to give themselves the option of retiring before the normal retirement age. The provision of good retirement benefits is therefore often seen as an important element of the remuneration package offered to employees and potential employees and the action of a responsible employer. Generous tax benefits are also available on contributions by employers and employees to pension schemes approved by the Inland Revenue.

## State pensions                                                     17.5

Most employees will qualify for basic State pension on retirement, although the amount that they receive will depend on whether they have a full National Insurance Contributions record, the details for which are very complex. In addition to basic pension, the State Earnings Related Pension Scheme ('SERPs') enables employees to build up a pension entitlement related to their earnings. Employees can choose to remain within SERPs, or to contract out of SERPs and participate instead in an occupational pension scheme offered by their employer or make other personal pension arrangements. SERPs is due to be replaced with a new State Second Pension ('S2P'), although there is expected to be an increasing encouragement for employees to contract out of this and make alternative pension provision in order to reduce the potential burden on government resources of present demographic trends (i.e. reducing birth rates and longer life expectancy). Consequently, many employers already offer their employees access to an occupational pension scheme, which may operate on the basis of defined benefits or defined contributions (or a combination of these), or to some form of group pension personal pension plan.

## Defined benefit schemes 17.6

A defined benefit retirement scheme is one under which the benefits payable on retirement are fixed, either as an amount or as a proportion of salary. Where benefits are defined in relation to salary they are usually based on the individual's final salary or his/her average salary for (say) the last three years before retirement. This is advantageous for the member, as he/she is assured of receiving a pension of a known amount. However, the employer has a commitment to ensure that sufficient funds are invested to enable the scheme to meet the guaranteed pension payments. The cost to the employer is consequently very dependent on a variety of factors and can fluctuate significantly over time. The cost of operating a defined benefit scheme has generally increased in recent years as a result of high salary levels, changes in life expectancy and the poor performance of the underlying investment markets. The current problems may be even more significant where past surpluses in the scheme have been used to fund improved benefits or contribution holidays. The nature of defined benefit schemes also means that they are more tightly regulated than defined contribution schemes and the accounting implications are much more complex. Defined benefit schemes are therefore generally becoming less popular with employers and many companies have opted to close their defined benefit schemes, to new members at least. Contributions to the scheme will often be paid by both the employer and the employee, but the level of the employee's contribution will usually be fixed and it is therefore the employer contribution that varies to make good any deficit in funding or, where permitted, to absorb any surplus that arises.

## *Accounting for defined benefit schemes* 17.7

FRS 17 *Retirement Benefits* was published in November 2000 and was originally intended to be fully effective for accounting periods ending on or after 22 June 2003. However, the full implementation date has now been deferred to 1 January 2005 (the date from which the adoption of international accounting standards will become mandatory for quoted groups) so that companies are not required to change their accounting treatment for retirement benefits twice within a short period of time. FRS 17 introduces significant changes to the way in which defined benefit retirement schemes are accounted for and is likely to have a significant impact on the profit and loss accounts and balance sheets of many companies. The standard specifies how scheme assets and scheme liabilities should be measured and generally requires the surplus or deficit in the scheme to be recognised as an asset or liability on the balance sheet. The continuing depressed state of the equity market increases the likelihood that deficits in funding will become apparent and that significant pension liabilities will begin to appear on company balance sheets. Many companies have been slow to prepare for the introduction of FRS 17 and to consider issues such as the potential impact of the new requirements on distributable reserves or compliance with existing loan covenants. The new standard has received a certain degree of criticism and has in some cases been quoted as the cause of companies deciding to close their defined benefit schemes and replace them with defined contribution schemes. However, the accounting standard is not the root cause of the problem – the new requirements are simply forcing directors to recognise that defined benefit retirement schemes can leave a business exposed to significant risks which need to be managed in the same way as other business risks. Further information on accounting for retirement benefits is given at **18.32-18.48** below.

## Defined contribution schemes                                          17.8

In the case of a defined contribution scheme (sometimes referred to as a 'money purchase scheme'), a fixed amount is contributed each year in respect of each member of the scheme, usually divided between the employer and employee and set as a proportion of the employee's salary. The amount contributed in respect of each individual member is accumulated in a separate account, and the pension payable to that employee will depend on the value of that fund at the date of his/her retirement. The employer therefore has the benefit of a fixed cost, but the employee bears the risk of the fund being insufficient to provide the level of pension that he/she hoped for at the time of retirement. The scheme funds may be invested in a variety of ways – in some schemes, the individual members may participate in decisions on how their particular fund is dealt with, in others this will be entirely at the discretion of the pension scheme trustees. A defined contribution scheme may be established as:

- an employer-sponsored occupational pension scheme approved by the Inland Revenue; or
- a group personal pension arrangement, under which an individual pension plan is arranged for each employee.

In the case of a group personal pension arrangement, it is not compulsory for the employer to make contributions to the scheme.

## Other options                                                          17.9

The two basic forms of pension scheme discussed above leave the risks associated with the provision of retirement benefits primarily with the employer (in the case of defined benefit schemes) or with the employee (in the case of defined contribution schemes). Some companies may feel that neither of these is entirely appropriate for them and may therefore wish to explore other options that share the risks and costs of pension provision more equitably between employer and employee. Other options that may be worth considering are considered briefly below, in a broadly reducing order of risk to the employer.

## *Shared risk final salary scheme* 17.10

A shared risk final salary scheme preserves the advantages of a defined benefit scheme in that the retirement benefits continue to be based on the employee's final salary, but there is a greater sharing of the associated risk between the employer and the employee. This sharing can be achieved by one or more of the following:

- making both the employer and employee contributions variable, depending on the results of the regular actuarial valuation;
- giving scheme members the option of paying a higher contribution in order to maintain benefits at the current level, or continuing at the current contribution level and accepting the resulting reduction in benefits; or
- providing guaranteed benefits at a relatively low level, with additional benefits granted on a discretionary basis if funding levels, or company performance, permit.

## *Career average salary scheme* 17.11

Under a career average salary scheme, retirement benefits are accrued each year in relation to the employee's salary for that year and the annual benefit is then revalued each year, up to retirement, in line with an appropriate index. Breaking the link between retirement benefits and the employee's final salary removes the impact of salary inflation during the employment period. The employee's pension on retirement is the aggregate of the revalued benefit calculated for each year of employment.

## *Hybrid schemes* 17.12

Hybrid schemes usually provide the employee with a mixture of defined benefit and money purchase benefits. For instance, a hybrid scheme might provide money purchase benefits up to a certain age (say 40) and then defined benefits for subsequent years of employment. This type of scheme can be advantageous to younger employees, who may want to transfer the money purchase benefits if their employment changes, but also gives older employees the security of defined benefits as they approach retirement age. Alternatively, a hybrid scheme may provide defined benefits on salary up to a specified level, and then money purchase benefits in respect of any salary above this. This can be particularly helpful in giving lower-paid employees the security of fixed retirement benefits whilst transferring some of the associated risk to those on higher salaries.

## Cash schemes 17.13

An employer can commit to providing a guaranteed lump sum to the employee at retirement, usually based on a proportion of final salary for each year of service, as in the case of a standard defined benefit scheme. The risk up to the date of retirement therefore continues to be borne by the employer, but the risk after retirement is transferred to the employee, who can retain part of the lump sum and use the balance to purchase an annuity.

## Insured schemes 17.14

An insured pension scheme is one under which the scheme trustees enter into an agreement with a life assurance company and pay appropriate premiums to secure the required benefits for the members and meet the costs of administering the scheme. This approach is more straightforward administratively and is therefore often favoured by smaller companies. In the case of a defined contribution scheme, a series of insurance policies may be needed to match the separate funds for the individual members.

## Personal pensions 17.15

Any individual can contribute to a personal pension, provided that he/she is not already a member of an occupational pension scheme. The individual makes contributions into an account with a personal pension provider, who invests the money on their behalf. Employers can also contribute to the personal pension plan of an employee. There are limits on the amount that an individual can contribute to a personal pension in each tax year, based on their earnings in that period and on their age. The percentage of earnings that can be contributed increases as the individual gets closer to retirement. From April 2001, members of an occupational pension scheme who earn less than £30,000 per annum, and who are not controlling directors, are allowed to contribute up to £3,600 each year to an additional personal or stakeholder pension.

## Stakeholder pensions 17.16

A stakeholder pension is a particular type of personal pension which became available from 6 April 2001 to encourage more people, especially those who are not high earners, to plan for their retirement. With effect from October 2001, the *Welfare Reform and Pensions Act 1999* and the *Stakeholder Pension Schemes Regulations 2000* (*SI 2000/1403*) require all employers with five or more employees to give their employees access to a stakeholder pension scheme, although there is no requirement for an employer to offer such access to employees earning less than the lower earnings limit under SERPs. However, an employer who operates an occupational pension scheme is exempt from the stakeholder requirement if the current scheme is open to all employees who:

- are aged over 18 and are more than five years younger than the normal retirement age under the scheme; and

- have completed one year's service with the company.

Where an existing scheme does not meet the requirements for exemption, it may be possible to make some modifications so that the employer qualifies for exemption, although the full cost of doing so will need to be carefully considered. The only commitment required from the employer is to provide the required level of access to the pension scheme – individual employees remain free to decide whether or not to join and the employer is not currently required to make any contributions to the scheme (although this may be introduced at some point in the future).

## *Group personal pension arrangement*     **17.17**

An employer is also exempt from the requirement to provide access to a stakeholder pension where a group personal pension arrangement is in place and:

- it is a term of the employment contract that all employees aged 18 or over who have completed three months' service and whose earnings are at least equivalent to the lower earnings limit have a right to join the scheme;
- the employer will pay contributions of at least 3 per cent of the employee's basic pay (or a lower amount equivalent to the contributions that the employee is willing to make);
- the employer offers a payroll deduction facility to members of the scheme; and
- the scheme does not impose any penalties on members who transfer out or stop making contributions.

## *Checklist of stakeholder pension requirements*     **17.18**

Any employer with five or more employees who is not covered by one of the above exemptions must:

- consult with employees or their representative organisations about the choice of stakeholder scheme;
- nominate a stakeholder scheme;
- provide employees or their representative organisations with contact details for the nominated scheme;
- allow representatives of the nominated scheme reasonable access to the employees; and
- enable employees to make contributions to the nominated scheme by deduction from their pay, and forward these contributions to the scheme within 19 days of the end of the month in which they were deducted.

## Pension scheme administration 17.19

## At a glance 17.20

---

- The *Pensions Act 1995* is the main legislation governing the control and management of occupational pension schemes.
- The Occupational Pensions Regulatory Authority ('OPRA') supervises the regulation of all occupational pension schemes.
- Most pension schemes are set up as trusts and established under a formal trust deed – the trustees must therefore comply with trust law as well as the more specific requirements of pensions legislation.
- Pensions legislation also gives the sponsoring employer certain duties and responsibilities.
- Most defined benefit schemes are subject to a minimum funding requirement.
- Pension scheme trustees generally have a duty to obtain audited financial statements within seven months of the end of the scheme financial year.
- The form and content of pension scheme accounts is specified in various regulations under the *Pensions Act 1995* and also in the SORP *Financial Reports of Pension Schemes.*
- Certain schemes are exempt from the requirement to appoint scheme auditors, although some of them may still require an audit under the terms of their trust deed.
- Regulations under the *Pensions Act 1995* set out the procedures that must be followed when appointing auditors and when there is a change of auditor.
- The Inland Revenue Pension Schemes Office is responsible for approving pension schemes for tax purposes, and for withdrawing approval where necessary.

---

## Pensions Act 1995 17.21

The *Pensions Act 1995* is now the main legislation governing the control and management of occupational pension schemes. The Act itself is primarily enabling legislation and the detailed requirements are set out in a long list of related regulations. The principal regulations governing financial reporting, audit and administrative requirements are:

- the *Occupational Pension Schemes (Disclosure of Information) Regulations 1996 (SI 1996/1655)*;
- the *Occupational Pension Schemes (Scheme Administration) Regulations 1996 (SI 1996/1715* as amended by *SI 1997/1405)*; and
- the *Occupational Pension Schemes (Requirement to Obtain Audited Accounts and a Statement from the Auditor) Regulations 1996 (SI 1996/1975).*

# Opra                                                                17.22

The Occupational Pensions Regulatory Authority ('OPRA') was established by the *Pensions Act 1995* to supervise the regulation of all occupational pension schemes. Its powers include:

- making directions on the provision of information to scheme members and the payment of benefits;
- suspending, prohibiting or disqualifying individuals from acting as trustees;
- appointing new or replacement trustees;
- taking action to prevent the misuse or misappropriation of scheme assets;
- winding up schemes where this is considered to be in the best interests of the members; and
- various investigative powers.

Trustees, scheme managers, sponsoring employers and professional advisers such as auditors and actuaries all have a duty to provide OPRA with information relevant to the discharge of its functions, and OPRA inspectors are given the power to enter premises and inspect relevant documents.

## Pension scheme trustees                                            17.23

Most pension schemes are set up as trusts and are established under a formal trust deed, which gives the scheme trustees responsibility for stewardship and custody of the scheme assets. Most pension schemes must therefore comply with general trust law as well as with the more specific requirements of pensions legislation, and the duties of the pension scheme trustees will usually include:

- observing the terms of the trust;
- acting at all times in the best interests of the beneficiaries of the trust;
- acting impartially between any different classes of beneficiary;
- acting prudently and making appropriate use of any particular skills and experience that they have;
- not profiting from the trust (other than as members of the scheme);
- exercising investment powers in accordance with the legislation;
- appointing professional advisers;
- maintaining specified bank accounts, books and records; and
- obtaining audited financial statements and appropriate reports from the actuary.

A trustee of the pension scheme who is also a director of the sponsoring company must take particular care not be influenced by his dual capacity. The legislation also includes specific provisions on the appointment of member-nominated trustees. Certain individuals are disqualified from acting as a trustee, including individuals with a conviction for an offence involving dishonesty or deception, undischarged bankrupts and those disqualified from appointment as a company director. OPRA (see **18.22** above) provides a number of guidance documents for pension scheme trustees to help them to understand their duties and responsibilities (for information on obtaining copies see the OPRA website at www.opra.gov.uk).

## Sponsoring employer                                          17.24

The sponsoring employer is also given a number of duties and responsibilities under the legislation, including:

- paying employer contributions in accordance with a defined schedule;
- paying employee contributions over to the scheme within 19 days of the end of the month in which they are deducted from employees' pay;
- where the employer operates the pensions payroll on behalf of the scheme, paying into a separate bank account any benefits which have not been paid to members within two days;
- a duty to disclose to the trustees or managers the occurrence of any event relating to the employer which could reasonably be considered to be of material significance to the exercise of their functions;
- a duty to disclose to the trustees or managers any information reasonably required for the proper performance of their duties or those of the professional advisers to the scheme.

Under the regulations, the power to make payments to employers may only be exercised by the trustees.

## Minimum funding requirement                                  17.25

All occupational pension schemes, other than defined contribution schemes and some statutory schemes, are currently subject to a minimum funding requirement. The trustees are required to obtain valuations of the scheme at prescribed intervals and at each valuation date after 5 April 1997 the actuary must state his opinion on whether the contributions payable under the scheme are sufficient to ensure that the minimum funding requirement will continue to be met throughout the period to the next valuation or, if it is not currently met, whether it will be met by that date. If the actuary is of the opinion that the contributions will not be adequate to achieve this, a further valuation and report by the actuary must be prepared within six months, unless the value of the scheme assets is not less than 90% of the value of its liabilities and the contribution schedule has been revised and certified by the actuary. If the value of scheme assets is less than 90% of the liabilities at the valuation date, the employer must take steps to bring the value of the assets up to 90% of the value of the liabilities within a period of one year. If the value of the scheme assets is between 90% and 100% of the liabilities at the valuation date, the employer must take steps to bring the value up to 100% within five years. The trustees have a duty to report to OPRA (see **18.22** above) any failure by the employer to take the appropriate action. The Government has indicated that the minimum funding requirement will be abolished in due course and there are outline proposals to replace it with more detailed disclosure on solvency and additional flexibility in funding, but it is likely to be a number of years before these changes are actually made.

## Financial reporting                                                17.26

Under current legislation, pension scheme trustees have a duty to obtain audited financial statements within seven months of the end of the scheme financial year. Auditors have a duty to report to OPRA (see **18.22** above) any breach of this provision by the trustees.

## Checklist for annual pension scheme report                       17.27

The annual report should comprise the following:

---

- a trustees' report, providing information on the management of the scheme and developments during the scheme year;
- an investment report, reviewing investment policy and the performance of the scheme during the year;
- a compliance statement, giving additional disclosures about the scheme required by the legislation and any other voluntary disclosures which are not sufficiently material to require inclusion in the trustees' report;
- financial statements giving a true and fair view of the financial transactions of the scheme during the year and of the disposition of its net assets at the end of the year; and
- actuarial statements – these vary depending on the nature of the scheme but will usually include an opinion from the actuary on the security of accrued rights and prospective rights, and on compliance with the minimum funding requirement.

---

The form and content of the financial statements are specified in various regulations under the *Pensions Act 1995* and the trustees are also required to state whether they have been prepared in accordance with the Statement of Recommended Practice ('SORP') 'Financial Reports of Pension Schemes', issued by the Pensions Research Accounting Group ('PRAG') under the Accounting Standards Board ('ASB') Code of Practice for the development of SORPs (see **10.15** above).

## Audit                                                              17.28

*Section 47* of the *Pensions Act 1995* requires the trustees or managers of every occupational pension scheme to appoint suitably qualified auditors. The scope of the auditors' work and the format and content of their report varies depending on the nature of the scheme. The following are exempt from the legal requirement to appoint scheme auditors:

- superannuation funds and unfunded schemes;

- money purchase Small Self-Administered Schemes (SSASs) where all members are trustees and all decisions require unanimous agreement;
- non-approved schemes;
- schemes with less than two members;
- schemes providing only death benefits and no accrued rights;
- ear-marked money purchase schemes where all benefits are secured by insurance or annuity contracts and are specifically allocated to individual members, and where all members are trustees and all decisions are by unanimous agreement; and
- certain specifically named schemes and public service schemes.

However, the trust deed for such schemes may still require an audit, even though the scheme is exempt from this requirement under the regulations. Also, certain earmarked funds that are exempt from the full audit requirement must still appoint auditors under the legislation to report on the contributions made to the scheme.

## Process for appointing auditors                     17.29

Where the appointment of auditors is required by law, the regulations lay down specific appointment procedures that must be followed. The trustees are required to send a Notice of Appointment to the auditors specifying:

- the date on which the appointment is to take effect;
- to whom the auditors are to report; and
- from whom the auditors will take instructions.

Guidance issued by the Auditing Practices Board ('APB') recommends that the Notice should also:

- state the date of the scheme year end and specify which scheme years are to be subject to audit; and
- be clear as to the name of the scheme to which the auditor is being appointed – where the appointment covers a number of schemes, there should be a separate letter for each scheme or a schedule detailing all the schemes covered.

The appointment does not become effective until the auditors have formally acknowledged receipt of the Notice of Appointment, which they are required to do within one month. They should also formally document the terms of their engagement in a letter to the trustees, to help prevent any misunderstandings over the scope of their work and the respective responsibilities of the scheme auditors, trustees and managers. If an auditor ceases to hold office for any reason, the trustees are required to make a new appointment within three months. Auditors who are invited to accept appointment after this deadline are required to report to OPRA (see **18.22** above) the breach of duty by the trustees. Auditors who resign or are removed are required to make a statement of any circumstances connected with their resignation or removal which, in their opinion, significantly affect the interests of the members, prospective members or beneficiaries of the scheme, or to state that there are no such circumstances. A copy of the statement must be included in the annual report, except where it is simply a declaration that there are no circumstances to report.

## Taxation                                                            17.30

The Inland Revenue Pension Schemes Office ('PSO') is responsible for approving pension schemes for tax purposes, and for withdrawing that approval where necessary. Almost all schemes are approved under the Inland Revenue's discretionary powers rather than under the restricted conditions set out in the *Income and Corporation Taxes Act 1988*. Approval of a scheme means that employer and employee contributions to that scheme are deductible for tax purposes. Changes to an approved scheme must be notified to the PSO and approval of the scheme will automatically lapse if the alteration is not considered to be acceptable. An exempt approved scheme is exempt from UK income tax on investment income and capital gains arising on its investments.

## Accounting for pensions and other retirement benefits                                                          17.31

## At a glance                                                         17.32

- FRS 17 *Retirement Benefits* was intended to be effective for accounting periods ending on or after 22 June 2003 but the effective date has now been deferred to 1 January 2005.
- In the case of a defined contribution scheme, the contributions payable by the employer for each accounting period are charged to the profit and loss account.
- In the case of a defined benefit scheme, the annual cost to the employer is more difficult to quantify and requires regular actuarial calculations to be carried out.
- FRS 17 requires scheme assets to be measured at fair value and scheme liabilities to be measured on an actuarial basis, using the projected unit method of valuation.
- Actuarial assumptions should be mutually compatible and should achieve the best estimate of the future cashflows that will arise.
- Scheme liabilities should be discounted at the current rate of return on a high quality bond of equivalent currency and term.
- The surplus or deficit in the scheme should generally be recognised as a separate item on the face of the balance sheet.
- FRS 17 specifies how the change in the net defined asset or liability each year should be reflected in the profit and loss account and statement of total recognised gains and losses.
- Detailed disclosures must be given in the notes to the accounts.
- Special requirements may apply where more than one employer participates in a defined benefit scheme (eg where a single scheme operates for a group of companies).

## FRS 17 'Retirement Benefits' 17.33

FRS 17 *Retirement Benefits* was originally intended to be fully effective for accounting periods ending on or after 22 June 2003. In November 2002, following a period of consultation, the Accounting Standards Board (ASB) announced that the transitional arrangements in the standard would be extended so that the new requirements become mandatory for accounting periods beginning on or after 1 January 2005. This is due to the reconsideration by the International Accounting Standards Board (IASB) of certain aspects of IAS 19 *Employee Benefits* (the corresponding international accounting standard). The IASB hopes to agree a revised standard by 2004. The transitional arrangements of FRS 17 have therefore been extended to enable quoted groups in particular to make an orderly transition to revised IASB requirements without necessitating two changes in accounting for retirement benefits within a short period of time. The ASB emphasises that the deferral of mandatory full implementation of FRS 17 reflects no weakening of its view that the UK standard is the best approach to pensions accounting, and it continues to encourage early adoption of all the requirements of FRS 17 on a voluntary basis. If the standard is not adopted early, detailed additional disclosures must be given in the notes to the accounts in the intervening years. The standard deals with how an employer should account for the costs and liabilities that arise from the provision of retirement benefits to employees, and the requirements cover all retirement benefits that an employer is committed to making, regardless of whether the commitment is statutory, contractual or implicit and wherever the commitment arises (ie in the UK or abroad). The standard is complex and only an outline of the requirements is given here. For information on obtaining copies of FRS 17 see the ASB website at www.asb.org.uk.

## Accounting for a defined contribution scheme 17.34

Accounting for a defined contribution scheme is relatively straightforward. The cost to the employer is equal to the contributions payable to the scheme for the accounting period and the charge to the profit and loss account each year will therefore represent the contributions payable by the employer in respect of that accounting period. This figure must be calculated on an accruals basis and the amount charged may therefore not be the same as the amount actually paid over to the scheme during the period. The standard specifies that the cost must be recognised in arriving at operating profit in the profit and loss account and the notes to the accounts must include the following disclosures:

- the nature of the scheme (ie the fact that it is a defined contribution scheme);
- the cost for the period; and
- any outstanding or prepaid contributions at the balance sheet date.

## Difficulties with defined benefit schemes 17.35

Under a defined benefit scheme, the employer will usually have a commitment to ensure that there are sufficient funds in the scheme to pay the appropriate benefits and may be required to make good any potential deficit in the funding of the scheme. In the case of a defined benefit scheme, therefore, the full extent of the employer's commitment is more difficult to quantify and to account for. Actuarial calculations must be carried out on a regular basis to establish the overall funding level of the scheme and to assess the level of contributions required to maintain adequate funding of the scheme. One of the particular problems is the very long-term nature of such schemes and the fact that a number of assumptions about future events will need to be made in order to carry out the calculations. Most of the detailed requirements of FRS 17 therefore deal with accounting for defined benefit retirement schemes.

## Actuarial valuations                                                17.36

Actuarial valuations provide the actuary's best estimate of the cost to the employer of providing the promised retirement benefits to employees. In carrying out a valuation, a number of assumptions about future events will need to be made and the decisions taken here can have a very significant effect on the level of contributions required. The main assumptions will cover issues such as:

- future pay increases;
- future rates of inflation;
- increases in pension payments;
- changes to the number of employees in the scheme;
- the age profile of employees; and
- expected earnings from scheme investments.

Once decisions have been reached on these factors, the actuary will assess how the scheme should be funded to ensure that adequate resources are available to meet the pension commitments as they fall due. The aim is to ensure that present and future contributions to the scheme will be sufficient to secure payment of the agreed benefits to employees as they retire.

## Valuation methods                                                   17.37

Various actuarial methods can be used to determine the liabilities of a defined benefit scheme and thus the level of contributions needed to achieve and maintain adequate funding. The two principal categories of actuarial valuation methods are:

- *accrued benefits methods* – these are based on the principle that the obligation to provide retirement benefits to an employee will be greater as that employee gets closer to retirement; and
- *prospective benefits methods* – these are based on the principle that the obligation to provide retirement benefits to an employee accumulates evenly throughout the period of that individual's employment.

FRS 17 requires scheme liabilities to be measured using the projected unit method. This is an accrued benefits valuation method under which allowance is made for projected earnings. Further guidance on this method is given in Guidance Note 26 (GN26) *Pension Fund Terminology* issued by the Faculty and Institute of Actuaries (for information on obtaining copies see the Faculty and Institute of Actuaries website at www.actuaries.org.uk).

## Measurement of scheme assets and liabilities          17.38

Under FRS 17 scheme assets should be measured at their fair value at the company's balance sheet date. Scheme assets include current assets as well as investments, and any current liabilities (such as accrued expenses) should be deducted. The standard includes specific guidance on establishing fair value for each category of pension scheme asset. Scheme liabilities comprise liabilities in respect of:

- benefits promised under the formal terms of the scheme; and
- any constructive obligations for further benefits where a public statement or past practice by the employer has created a valid expectation in the employees that these benefits will be granted.

These liabilities should be measured on an actuarial basis using the projected unit method (see **18.37** above).

## Actuarial assumptions          17.39

Actuarial assumptions underlying the valuation of scheme liabilities should be mutually compatible (ie they must reflect the underlying economic factors on a consistent basis), and they should lead to the best estimate of the future cashflows that will arise. The directors (or equivalent) have ultimate responsibility for the assumptions, but they should be set on advice given by an actuary. Any assumptions that are affected by economic conditions should reflect market expectations at the balance sheet date. The assumptions should also reflect expected future events that will affect the cost of the benefits to which the employer is committed (either legally or constructively) at the balance sheet date. Depending on the nature of the scheme these will usually include:

- expected cost of living increases;
- salary increases (where the pension is to be based on final salary); and
- expected early retirement (where the scheme gives this right to employees).

Expected future redundancies should not be reflected in the assumptions as the employer is not committed to making them. When the employer does become committed to making redundancies, the impact on the scheme should be treated as a settlement or curtailment. Also, it should not be assumed that benefits will be reduced below those currently promised (eg on the grounds that the employer will curtail the scheme at some point in the future).

## Discounting of scheme liabilities                          17.40

Scheme liabilities should be discounted at a rate reflecting the time value of money and the characteristics of the liability. This should be assumed to be the current rate of return on a high quality (AA) corporate bond of equivalent currency and term to the scheme liabilities. The FRS 17 guidance notes that, if no suitable corporate bond can be identified, the rate of return on appropriate government bonds, together with a margin for assumed credit risk spreads (from the global bond markets) may provide an acceptable alternative.

## Frequency of valuations                                    17.41

Full actuarial valuations by a professionally qualified actuary should be obtained at intervals not exceeding three years. The actuary should review the valuation at each balance sheet date and update it to reflect current conditions – for instance, the fair values of scheme assets and financial assumptions such as the discount rate may need to be adjusted each year.

## Balance sheet recognition of surplus or deficit            17.42

The surplus or deficit in a defined benefit scheme is the excess or shortfall of the value of the scheme assets over or below the present value of the scheme liabilities. The employer should recognise:

●   a liability to the extent that it reflects a legal or constructive obligation to make good the deficit; and
●   an asset to the extent that this can be recovered through reduced contributions or through refunds from the scheme.

A legal obligation to make good a deficit in the scheme may arise under the terms of the trust deed. A constructive obligation may arise if the employer has in the past acted to make good similar deficits. A scheme surplus will give rise to an asset for the employer to the extent that the employer has control over its use as a result of past events. Under most schemes, the employer's obligation will be to pay contributions at the level recommended by the actuary to keep the scheme fully funded. There will not usually be any requirement to generate a surplus in the scheme. Where a surplus does arise, it is therefore unlikely that the employer could be required to continue to make contributions to maintain the surplus. Also, the decision on whether the surplus should be used to improve scheme benefits will usually rest with the employer. In most cases, therefore, control over the use of a surplus will rest with the employer. FRS 17 gives detailed guidance on determining the amount that can be recovered from reduced contributions, reflecting refunds from the scheme in the accounts of the employer and accounting for a surplus that is used to improve benefits.

## Balance sheet presentation                                      17.43

Any unpaid pension contributions at the balance sheet date should be shown within creditors due within one year. The defined benefit asset or liability, net of any related deferred tax, should be shown separately on the face of the balance sheet as follows:

- in a balance sheet prepared under Format 1 of *Schedule 4* to the *Companies Act 1985*, after item J (Accruals and deferred income) but before item K (Capital and reserves);
- in a balance sheet prepared under Format 2 of *Schedule 4* to the *Companies Act 1985*, an asset should be shown after item D (Prepayments and accrued income) in the 'Assets' section and a liability should be shown after item D (Accruals and deferred income) in the 'Liabilities' section.

Appendix I to FRS 17 gives an example layout for this disclosure. Where an employer has more than one scheme, the total of any defined benefit assets and the total of any defined benefit liabilities should be shown separately on the face of the balance sheet.

## Performance statements                                      17.44

FRS 17 requires the change in the net defined benefit asset or liability (other than changes arising from contributions to the scheme) to be analysed into its detailed components and prescribes how each component should be reflected in the performance statements (i.e. the profit and loss account and statement of total recognised gains and losses). Broadly:

- current service cost should be taken into account in arriving at operating profit;
- the net of interest cost and the expected return on assets should be shown as other finance costs, adjacent to interest on the profit and loss account;
- actuarial gains and losses should be recognised in the statement of total recognised gains and losses.

The standard also includes detailed requirements on accounting for past service costs (which arise when an employer commits to providing a higher level of benefit than previously promised), settlements, curtailments and death-in-service and incapacity benefits. It also deals with accounting for any tax effects arising from pension costs and commitments.

## Disclosure                                      17.45

FRS 17 prescribes very detailed disclosures to be given in the notes to the accounts, the principal items being:

- the nature of the scheme (ie the fact that it is a defined benefit scheme);

- the date of the most recent full actuarial valuation on which amounts in the financial statements are based;
- contributions made in respect of the accounting period and any agreed contribution rates for future years;
- each of the main financial assumptions used at the beginning of the period and at the balance sheet date;
- a note showing the fair value of scheme assets, the present value of scheme liabilities, the resulting surplus or deficit and an analysis of the movement in the surplus or deficit during the period;
- where the defined benefit asset or liability in the balance sheet differs from the scheme surplus or deficit shown in the note, an explanation of the difference;
- a five-year summary of the difference between expected and actual returns on assets, experience gains and losses arising on scheme liabilities and total actuarial gains or losses – this disclosure is to highlight trends, which will generally be more relevant than gains or losses in one period.

The analysis of reserves in the notes to the financial statements should also distinguish the amount relating to the defined benefit asset or liability, net of related deferred tax.

## Entities with more than one defined benefit scheme     17.46

Where an employer has more than one defined benefit scheme, the required disclosures may be given in total, separately or in such groupings as are felt to be most useful (for instance, by geographical location, or where schemes are subject to significantly different risks). Where the disclosures are given in total, the assumptions should be given in the form of weighted averages or relatively narrow ranges, with separate disclosure of any items outside the range.

## Multi-employer schemes     17.47

In some cases, more than one employer may participate in the same retirement scheme. For instance, this situation is relatively common in groups of companies, where a single retirement scheme is operated for the whole group and each subsidiary participates in the scheme in respect of its own employees. If the scheme is a defined contribution scheme, the multi-employer aspect does not give rise to any particular accounting issues. Where more than one employer participates in a defined benefit scheme, the general requirement under FRS 17 is that each employer should account for the scheme as a defined benefit scheme. However, the standard recognises that this may not be appropriate or practical in every case and two specific exceptions to this general rule are therefore permitted.

- Where the employer's contributions are set in relation to the current service period only (ie they are not affected by any surplus or deficit in the scheme relating to the past service of its own employees or any other members of the scheme), the scheme should be accounted for as a defined contribution scheme – this treatment should only be adopted where there is clear evidence that the employer cannot be required to pay additional contributions relating to past service, including the existence of a third party which accepts the obligation to fund the pension payments if the scheme's assets should prove to be insufficient.

- Where the employer's contributions are affected by a surplus or deficit in the scheme but the employer is unable to identify its share of the underlying assets and liabilities in the scheme on a consistent and reasonable basis, the employer should account for the scheme as a defined contribution scheme but should disclose:
  - the fact that the scheme is a defined benefit scheme but the employer is unable to identify its share of the underlying assets and liabilities; and
  - any available information on the surplus or deficit in the scheme and the implications for the employer.

In the case of a group scheme, the second exception only enables the individual subsidiaries (and, where appropriate, the parent company in its own individual accounts) to account for the scheme as a defined contribution scheme. The scheme must still be accounted for as defined benefit scheme in the group accounts, as it does not constitute a multi-employer scheme at this level and the impracticality of identifying individual shares of the underlying assets and liabilities is no longer relevant.

# 18. Remuneration Committee

## Establishing a remuneration committee 18.1

## At a glance 18.2

- The Combined Code sets out three principles on the setting and make-up of directors' remuneration.
- A remuneration committee should be established to make recommendations to the main board on remuneration policy and to determine the remuneration package of each individual director.
- The remuneration committee should have at least three members, all of whom are independent non-executive directors of the company.
- The chairman and the chief executive should attend meetings of the remuneration committee by invitation.

## Combined Code principles 18.3

The principles set out in the Combined Code make the following points on the setting and make-up of directors' remuneration:

- levels of remuneration should be sufficient to attract and retain the directors needed to run the company successfully, but companies should avoid paying more than is necessary for this purpose;
- a proportion of executive directors' remuneration should be structured to link rewards to corporate and individual performance; and

- there should be a formal and transparent procedure for developing policy on executive remuneration and for fixing the remuneration packages of individual directors – no director should be involved in setting his/her own remuneration.

Apart from some minor wording changes, the Higgs Report does not propose any revision of these principles. The overall objective is that companies should be seen to be approaching the issue of directors' remuneration in a fair and thorough manner.

## Membership of the remuneration committee 18.4

The best practice provisions in the Combined Code currently recommend that the board should establish a remuneration committee to make recommendations to the board on the company's framework for executive remuneration and its cost, and to determine on behalf of the board specific remuneration packages (including pension rights and compensation payments) for each executive director. In order to avoid conflicts of interest, the remuneration committee should consist exclusively of non-executive directors who are independent of management and free from any business or other relationship which could materially affect the exercise of their independent judgement, and the members of the remuneration committee should be listed in the annual report to shareholders. The proposals in the Higgs Report retain these provisions without substantial amendment, except that:

- it is recommended that the remuneration committee should have at least three members;
- the new wording makes clear that the remuneration committee should have delegated responsibility for setting the remuneration of all executive directors and of the chairman, including pension rights and compensation payments, and for setting the level and structure of remuneration for senior executives;
- the remuneration committee is required to make publicly available its terms of reference, and to explain its role and the authority delegated to it by the board; and
- if executive directors or senior management are involved in advising or supporting the remuneration committee, this role should be clearly separated from their role within the business.

The Higgs Report also recommends that, other than in the case of small listed companies, no individual non-executive directors should serve on all three of the main board committees (ie audit, nomination and remuneration). Research carried out as part of the Higgs Review indicated that most listed companies already have a separate remuneration committee, and it is important that such a committee is properly constituted and has a clear remit and designated authority.

The IRS/3i 2003 survey contained a special analysis of the workings on remuneration committees. The information below is based on the responses of two hundred and eighty three members of remuneration committees. The size of the committee inevitably relates to the size of the company but this is how they responded with regard to size of the committee when asked to think about their most and least effective remuneration committees.

Directors on Remuneration Committees

So the conclusion appears to be that effective remuneration committees tend to have 3 or 4 members.

In the most effective committees 80% of the membership were non-executive directors compared with only 58% in the least effective. Given Higgs' recommendations it would have been interesting to see whether there was any difference in performance between those with only independent non-executives.

With regard to selecting a chairman for the remuneration committee there was an interesting difference in approach between the most and least effective remuneration committees.

How is the chair of the Remuneration Committee chosen?

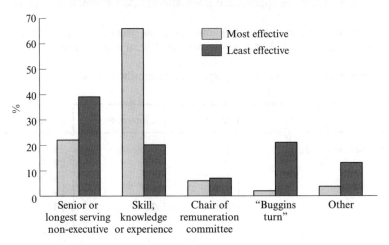

How is the chairman of the remuneration committee chosen?

So unsurprisingly chairmen chosen on the basis of their skills, knowledge or relevant experience seem to be more prevalent in the most effective and those chosen ritualistically more prevalent in the weaker committees. Chairing this committee has become an increasingly important and complex job so it is important that the chairman is chosen professionally.

There is surprisingly little training available on this subject though most of the major consultancies operating in this area provide regular update briefings.

The tenure of members was something also looked at in the IRS/3i survey. A surprisingly high number, some two thirds, had no fixed term, and there was little variation between chairman or member of the committee. This was not a topic that the sample had strong views on, believing that best practice was developing.

One observation the authors would make with regard to composition has to do with communication. It is important that at least one of the members is knowledgeable and skilled in the communication aspects of remuneration. Many highly successful companies have had issues in this area through weak communication and it is a subject the press especially in the UK are both vigilant and expert in.

## Attendance at meetings                                                18.5

Independence is considered a critical issue in this sensitive area, in which there is plenty of scope for conflicts of interest. Although membership of the committee should be restricted to independent non-executive directors, the Higgs Report emphasises that the chairman and chief executive may attend meetings when invited to do so. The present best practice provisions note that the remuneration committee should consult the chairman and/or chief executive about the proposals on the remuneration of other executive directors, and should have access to appropriate internal and external professional advice.

Membership of the remuneration committee has become an increasingly time consuming job as the chart below from the IRS/3ii survey reveals.

How many days per year do you spend on committee work?

| | Days | Chairman % | Member % |
|---|---|---|---|
| Formal meetings | 1 | 5 | 23 |
| | 2 | 41 | 27 |
| | 3 | 17 | 13 |
| | 4 | 17 | 19 |
| | 5+ | 20 | 18 |

| | Days | Chairman % | Member % |
|---|---|---|---|
| Informal | 1 | 16 | 40 |
| | 2 | 33 | 22 |
| | 3 | 18 | 14 |
| | 4+ | 33 | 24 |
| Preparation | 1 | 36 | 50 |
| | 2 | 31 | 35 |
| | 3 | 13 | 7 |
| | 4+ | 20 | 8 |

## The use of remuneration consultants                              18.6

Given the complexity of remuneration issues and the need to consider remuneration policy and quantum in relation to the market as a whole it is normal
for remuneration consultants to be employed to assist the work of the
committee.

We would suggest that the same principles be adopted as those used in choosing other professional advisers. There should be a clear role, there should be
a competitive pitch and they should be managed tightly.

## Duties of the remuneration committee                             18.7

## At a glance                                                      18.8

- The responsibilities of the remuneration committee should be set out
  in formal terms of reference, which should be made publicly available.
- These responsibilities normally include determining the following:
  - remuneration policy;
  - targets for performance-related pay;
  - pension arrangements;
  - termination payments; and
  - the individual remuneration package for each director.
- The committee is also responsible for preparing the annual report to
  shareholders on directors' remuneration.
- Where external remuneration consultants are to be used, their selection and appointment should be controlled by the remuneration
  committee.
- Performance-related elements should normally form a significant
  part of the total remuneration package for executive directors.
- The remuneration committee is responsible for setting the level and
  structure of any compensation payments to directors.

Remuneration
Committee

# Terms of reference                                          18.9

The terms of reference of the remuneration committee should set out the committee's delegated responsibilities and should be subject to annual review. The Higgs Report also recommends that the committee's terms of reference should be made publicly available. Annex E to the Higgs Report summarises the main duties of the remuneration committee as follows.

- **Remuneration policy**: The remuneration committee should determine and agree with the board the framework or broad policy for the remuneration of the chairman and of other executives, as designated by the board. The guidance notes that the remuneration committee may be asked to consider the remuneration packages of all executives at or above a specified management level, or to deal with all packages above a certain figure. In particular, the Higgs Report emphasises that:
  - O    as a minimum, the remuneration committee should have delegated responsibility for setting the remuneration for all executive directors, the chairman and the company secretary;
  - O    the remuneration of the non-executive directors should be considered by the chairman and the executive directors; and
  - O    no director or manager should be involved in setting his/her own remuneration.
- **Performance-related pay**: The remuneration committee should determine the targets for any performance-related pay schemes operated by the company.
- **Pension arrangements**: The remuneration committee should determine the policy for, and scope of, the pension arrangements for each executive director.
- **Termination payments**: The remuneration committee should ensure that contractual terms in respect of termination payments, and any payments actually made, are fair to both the individual and the company. In particular, the committee has a responsibility to ensure that failure is not rewarded and that the duty to mitigate loss is fully recognised. The guidance recommends that the committee considers agreeing a standard form of contract for the executive directors and then ensures that new appointees are offered and accept terms within the agreed level. Close co-operation will be required between the nomination and remuneration committees in order to achieve this.
- **Individual remuneration packages**: The remuneration committee should determine the remuneration of each executive director, within the terms of the agreed policy, including where appropriate the award of bonuses, incentive payments and share options. In doing so, the committee should give due regard to the recommendations in the Combined Code and related guidance and, where appropriate, any requirements of the UK Listing Authority.
- **Expenses**: The remuneration committee should agree the policy for authorising claims for expenses by the chairman and the chief executive.

- **Employee benefits**: The remuneration committee should be aware of, and advise on, any major changes in employee benefit structures within the company or group.
- **External advice**: Where remuneration consultants are to be appointed in an advisory capacity, the remuneration committee should have exclusive responsibility for establishing the selection criteria and for selecting, appointing and setting their terms of reference.
- **Disclosure**: The remuneration committee is responsible for ensuring that:
  ○ the company complies with the disclosure requirements of the *Directors' Remuneration Report Regulations 2002 (SI 2002/1986)* and of the Combined Code (see CHAPTER **9**);
  ○ the frequency of, and attendance levels at, meetings of the remuneration committee are disclosed in the company's annual report; and
  ○ the committee's terms of reference are made publicly available.

The Institute of Chartered Secretaries and Administrators (ICSA) produces a useful specimen terms of reference for a remuneration committee, and this has recently been updated to take account of the recommendations in the Higgs Report. A further example is set out in APPENDIX **18A**.

## Developing remuneration policy                    18.10

The Higgs Report notes that judgements on remuneration require sensitivity, both to the expectations of the individual directors concerned and to the concerns and perceptions of investors and other stakeholders, such as employees. The best practice provisions in the current Combined Code emphasise that the remuneration committee should:

- provide the packages necessary to attract, retain and motivate executive directors of the required quality, but should avoid paying more than is necessary;
- judge where to position the company relative to other companies, and be aware of the remuneration packages and relative performance of other companies, but use such comparisons with caution in view of the risk of increasing remuneration levels without a corresponding improvement in performance; and
- be sensitive to the wider scene, including pay and conditions elsewhere in the group, especially when determining annual salary increases

There is particular concern that external remuneration consultants are currently perceived as being too close to executive management and too willing to encourage companies to position themselves in the top quartile of their peer group. Hence the Higgs Report recommends that, where consultants are to be appointed, their selection and terms of reference should be controlled by the remuneration committee and not by the executive directors.

## Make-up of remuneration 18.11

The best practice provisions in the current Combined Code include the following points:

- performance-related elements should form a significant proportion of the total remuneration package for executive directors and should be designed to align their interests with those of the shareholder, and to give the directors a keen incentive to perform at the highest levels;
- executive share options should not be issued at a discount, except as permitted by Chapters 13.30 and 13.31 of the FSA Listing Rules; and
- in designing schemes of performance-related remuneration, the committee should follow the provisions set out in Schedule A to the Combined Code (see **18.12** below).

The Higgs Report proposes retaining these provisions, with minor amendments to the wording, and adding the following additional provision in respect of non-executive directors:

> 'levels of remuneration for non-executive directors should reflect the time and responsibilities of the role, but the remuneration of non-executive directors in share options should be avoided'.

## Performance-related pay 18.12

Schedule A to the Combined Code comprises the guidance originally set out in the Greenbury Code of Best Practice on directors' remuneration, with a number of minor wording changes. It recommends that:

- the remuneration committee should consider whether directors should be eligible for annual bonuses and, if so, performance conditions should be relevant, stretching and designed to enhance the business – upper limits should always be considered and there may be a case for part payment in shares to be held for a significant period;
- the remuneration committee should consider whether the directors should be eligible for benefits under long-term incentive schemes, and in establishing such schemes should:
  - ○ weigh traditional share option schemes against other kinds of long-term incentive schemes;
  - ○ generally ensure that shares granted and other forms of deferred remuneration do not vest, and options are not exercisable, in less than three years;
  - ○ encourage directors to hold their shares for a further period after vesting or exercise, subject to the need to finance any costs of acquisition or associated tax liabilities;
- where new long-term incentive schemes are proposed, these should be approved by the shareholders and should generally replace existing schemes, or at least form part of a well-considered overall plan

incorporating existing schemes – the total rewards potentially available should not be excessive;

- payouts or grants under all incentive schemes (including new grants under existing share option schemes) should be subject to challenging performance criteria reflecting the company's objectives, and consideration should be given to criteria which reflect the company's performance relative to a group of comparator companies in certain key variables such as total shareholder return;
- grants under executive share option and other long-term incentive schemes should normally be phased rather than awarded in one large block;
- the remuneration committee should consider the pension consequences and associated costs to the company of increases in basic salary and other changes in remuneration, especially for directors close to retirement; and
- in general, neither annual bonuses nor benefits in kind should be pensionable.

No changes to these provisions are proposed in the Higgs Report.

## Compensation payments                                    18.13

The Higgs Report also emphasises that the remuneration committee should be responsible for setting the level and structure of compensation payments for senior executives. The best practice guidance dealing with directors' service contacts and compensation currently includes four provisions:

- there is a strong case for setting notice or contract periods at, or reducing them to, one year or less - the board should set this as an objective, even though it may not be possible to achieve immediately;
- if it is necessary to offer longer notice or contract periods to directors recruited externally, these should reduce after the initial period;
- the remuneration committee should consider what compensation commitments (including pension contributions) directors' service contracts would entail in the event of early termination – in particular, the committee should consider the advantages of providing explicitly in the initial contract for such compensation commitments other than in the case of removal for misconduct; and
- where the initial contract does not provide explicitly for compensation commitments the remuneration committee should, within legal constraints, tailor their approach in the case of early termination to the wide variety of circumstances – the broad aim should be to avoid rewarding poor performance while dealing fairly with departure in other circumstances, and to take a robust line on reducing compensation to reflect the departing director's obligations to mitigate loss.

The proposals in the Higgs Report retain these provisions without significant change, although the first one is more definite that notice or contract periods should be set at one year or less, and the third one also refers to the need to ensure that the arrangements do not have the effect of rewarding poor performance.

## Issues of concern to shareholders                                     18.14

The Institutional Shareholders' Committee (ISC) represents the interests and concerns of institutional investors, with representatives from the Association of British Insurers (ABI), the National Association of Pension Funds (NAPF), the Association of Investment Trust Companies (AITC) and the Investment Management Association (IMA). The ISC issues guidance to institutional investors covering issues such as communication with boards, the use of voting rights, board composition, directors' remuneration and takeover bids. Voting guidelines are also issued regularly to institutional investors by organisations such as NAPF, ABI and Pensions Investment Research Consultants (PIRC), based on their assessment of the key current issues. Issues that have received most focus in recent times include directors' remuneration (including incentive schemes, service contracts and notice periods), the independence of non-executive directors and issues relating to the external audit (eg the level of non-audit services provided by the auditors, connections between the directors and auditors, reappointment or changes in the appointment of auditors, and the role and constitution of the audit committee). Members of the remuneration committee are therefore advised to keep track of the issues being raised by these organisations in the area of directors' remuneration. Relevant information can usually be found on their websites and in some cases will be circulated to larger listed companies in advance of the publication date for their annual reports and accounts.

## Meetings and agendas                                                  18.15

## At a glance                                                           18.16

---

- The number and frequency of meetings will vary, depending on the circumstances of the company, but the remuneration committee should meet at least once each year.
- The company secretary should act as secretary to the committee.
- Minutes of remuneration committee meetings should be circulated to all main board directors.
- The annual report should list the members of the remuneration committee and give details of the number of meetings held and the attendance levels.
- The effectiveness of the remuneration committee should be reviewed each year.

---

## Meetings of the remuneration committee                               18.17

The number and frequency of remuneration committee meetings will vary depending on the specific circumstances of the company and the precise remit of the committee, as set out in its terms of reference. The committee must meet at least once a year to prepare the company's annual remuneration report. This meeting will need to be scheduled close to the year-end to ensure the availability of the relevant information for the financial year. Further information on this report, and a checklist of the required contents, can be found in CHAPTER 9.

## Secretary                                                    18.18

It is recommended that the company secretary acts as secretary to the remuneration committee. This should ensure that the committee has access to appropriate advice on procedural or constitutional issues and should facilitate appropriate liaison and co-ordination with the other main board committees.

## Minutes                                                      18.19

The proceedings and decisions taken at meetings of the remuneration committee should be formally recorded and copies of the minutes should be circulated to all members of the main board for information. It is also good practice to keep detailed attendance records for remuneration committee meetings and for the board of directors to review these on an annual basis to confirm that each member is making an appropriate contribution to the work of the committee. Attendance information will also need to be retained in future for inclusion in the annual report on the committee's activities (see **18.20** below).

## Reporting to shareholders                                     18.20

The Higgs Report recommends that the annual report should include:

● the names of all members of the remuneration committee during the period;
● the names of any other individuals (whether directors or not) who provided advice or services to the committee, together with details of the nature of the advice or services provided; and
● the number of remuneration committee meetings and the attendance by each member.

As explained above, the remuneration committee is also responsible for the preparation of the annual report to shareholders on directors' remuneration.

## Self-assessment and appraisal                                 18.21

The Higgs Report recommends that the effectiveness of the board and each of its main committees should be reviewed annually by both the committee and the board. This might be done by considering developments generally in the role and activities of remuneration committees and discussing with the main board the extent to which the remuneration committee is considered to have fulfilled the various aspects of its terms of reference. Specific issues to consider might include:

Remuneration
Committee

- are there appropriate procedures for appointing committee members?
- does the committee have the appropriate mix of knowledge and skills?
- is the amount and nature of training and administrative support appropriate?
- are the committee's terms of reference appropriate?
- does the committee adequately fulfil its role?
- is the frequency and timing of committee meetings appropriate?
- are agendas and appropriate supporting information circulated to committee members in good time?
- does the committee's workload require a change of emphasis?
- what significant issues does the committee need to address in the coming year?

The remuneration committee should report formally to the main board each year on the results of their self-assessment. It is also best practice for the chairman of the main board, together with the executive directors, to review the contribution of individual non-executives to the work of the board, including where appropriate their activities as members of the remuneration committee.

# Appendix 18A                                                                18.22

# Specimen Terms of Reference for a Remuneration
# Committee                                                                   18.23

These specimen terms of reference are for guidance only and should be developed and adapted as necessary to suit the specific circumstances of the company or group.

**1    Constitution**
  1.1   The Board hereby resolves to establish a committee of the board, to be known as the Remuneration Committee ('the committee').

**2    Membership**
  2.1   The committee shall be appointed by the board. All members of the committee shall be non-executive directors of the company who are independent of management and free from any business or other relationship which could interfere with the exercise of their independent judgement. The committee shall consist of not less than three members. Two members shall comprise a quorum at any meeting of the committee.
  2.2   The chairman of the committee shall be appointed by the Board from amongst the independent non-executive directors.
  2.3   No member of the committee shall also be a member of both the Audit and Nomination Committee.

**3    Secretary**
  3.1   The Company Secretary or their nominee shall act as the Secretary of the committee.

**4    Meetings**
  4.1   The committee shall meet [not less than once a year][quarterly]

and at such other times as the chairman of the committee shall require.

**4.2**    Meetings shall be convened by the Secretary of the committee at the request of any committee member.

**4.3**    Unless otherwise agreed, notice of each meeting confirming the venue, time and date together with an agenda of items to be discussed, shall be forwarded to each member of the committee, any other person required to attend and all other non-executive directors, no fewer than .............. working days prior to the date of the meeting.

**4.4**    The Chief Executive, Chairman and Director of Human Resources shall attend meetings at the invitation of the committee.

**5**    **Minutes of Meetings**

**5.1**    The Secretary shall minute the proceedings and resolutions of all committee meetings, including the names of those present and in attendance.

**6**    **Authority**

**6.1**    The committee is authorised by the board to seek any information it requires from any employee of the company in order to perform its duties.

**6.2**    In connection with its duties, the committee is required by the board to select, set the terms of reference for and appoint remuneration consultants, at the company's expense.

**6.3**    Although the Committee can seek the advice and assistance of any of the company's executives, it must ensure that this role is clearly separated from their role within the business.

**7**    **Responsibilities**

**7.1**    The responsibilities of the committee shall be as follows:

    i.    To determine and agree with the board the framework or broad policy for the remuneration of the Chief Executive, the Chairman of the company and such other members of the executive management as it is designated to consider. The remuneration of non-executive directors shall be a matter for the executive members of the board. No director or manager shall be involved in any decisions as to his or her own remuneration. In order to assure his/her independence, the committee will also review and recommend to the Board the remuneration of the Company Secretary;

    ii.    In determining the company's remuneration policy, to take into account all factors which the committee deems necessary. The objective of the company's remuneration policy shall be to ensure that members of the executive management of the company are provided with appropriate incentives to encourage enhanced performance and are, in a fair and responsible manner, rewarded for their individual contributions to the success of the company.

    iii.    To liaise with the Nomination Committee to ensure that the remuneration of newly appointed executives is within the company's overall policy.

iv. To determine targets for any performance related pay schemes operated by the company and ask the board, when appropriate, to seek shareholder approval for any long term incentive arrangements.

v. Within the terms of the agreed policy, to determine the total individual remuneration package of each executive director including, where appropriate, bonuses, incentive payments and share options.

vi. To determine the policy for and scope of pension arrangements, service agreements, termination payments and compensation commitments in respect of the executive directors.

vii. In determining such packages and arrangements, to give due regard to the comments and recommendations of the Combined Code as well as the UK Listing Authority's Listing Rules and associated guidance.

viii. To review the remuneration policies of competitor companies and their relative performance, but ensure that such information is not used to create an upward ratchet of remuneration levels without a corresponding improvement in performance.

ix. To be aware of, and oversee, any major changes in employee benefit structures throughout the company or group.

x. To agree the policy for authorising the reimbursement of any claims for expenses from the Chief Executive and Chairman of the company.

xi. To prepare an annual report on the company's remuneration policy and remuneration payments, in compliance with the *Directors' Remuneration Report Regulations 2002* and the Combined Code.

## 8    Reporting procedures

**8.1** The secretary shall circulate the minutes of meetings of the committee to all members of the board.

**8.2** The committee's responsibilities and activities during the year shall be disclosed in the annual report.

**8.3** The chairman of the committee shall attend the AGM and answer questions, through the chairman of the board, on the committee's responsibilities and activities.

# 19. Risk Management

## The importance of risk management 19.1

## At a glance 19.2

- The management of business risk has become a significant main board responsibility.
- Each business must decide on the most appropriate organisational risk management structure.
- Where an executive risk management committee is appointed, its role should be set out in written terms of reference.
- If there is no risk management committee, the audit committee should be responsible for reviewing the company's risk management systems.
- Strategic and operational risks have now become the most significant issues for many companies.
- The directors should begin by identifying the company's appetite for risk.
- Companies may wish to make use of specialist resources in dealing with certain aspects of risk management.
- Risk management is not an annual compliance issue, but an ongoing exercise that should be integral to the business.

## Main board responsibility                                  19.3

There is much greater awareness today of the significance of business risk than was the case even 10 or 15 years ago. Business risk now has a very wide definition, encompassing both strategic and operational issues as well as finanical risk, and the management of business risk has become a significant main board responsibility. Good risk management needs strong leadership from the top of the organisation, and a sound system of monitoring and reporting. Many aspects of business risk are now regulated by the Government (eg health and safety, employment, product liability, environmental issues) but they nevertheless remain a compliance risk for each company, as failure to comply with the relevant requirements may itself have a significant impact on the business. There is now a general consensus that risk management is not simply a a matter of compliance but a process that can facilitate the growth and development of the company, by creating real and sustainable value as well as helping to protect investors. Good risk management also involves the management of both upside and downside risk. The focus is often on identifying and managing downside risk, but risk strategies to ensure that business opportunities are not missed are equally important.

## Organisational structure                                   19.4

Each business must decide on the most appropriate organisational risk management structure to suit its own specific circumstances. Options to consider include:

- appointing an executive risk management committee – this will usually include the CEO, finance director and the heads of the business operating units;
- appointing a head of risk management (usually at board level);
- developing an internal risk management function;
- appointing individual employees to deal with specialist issues (eg health and safety).

Businesses in the same industry or sector, facing similar risks, will often choose different risk management strategies, reflecting their differing individual circumstances. The internal audit function will also have an important role to play in the monitoring of systems and reporting of risk (see CHAPTER 2 AUDIT MATTERS). Whatever organisational structure is chosen, risk management should be seen as an intrinsic element of the company's procedures and should involve all managers and employees to some degree.

## Risk management committee                                  19.5

Where the company chooses to appoint an executive risk management committee, its role should be clearly distinguished from that of the audit committee. As with any board committee, it is advisable to develop written terms of reference, which might encompass the following remit:

- to approve the company's risk management strategy and risk management policy;
- to review reports on key risks prepared by business operating units, management and the board;
- to monitor the company's (or group's) overall exposure to risk and ensure that it remains within the limits set by the board;
- to assess the effectiveness of the company's (or group's) risk management systems;
- to provide early warning to the board on emerging risk issues and/or significant changes in the company's (or group's) exposure to risk; and
- in conjunction with audit committee, to review the company's statement on internal control with reference to risk management, prior to endorsement by the board.

If an executive risk management committee is not appointed, the Combined Code (as revised by the Higgs Report) specifically brings the review of the company's risk management systems within the remit of the audit committee (see **CHAPTER 2 AUDIT MATTERS**). Whichever approach is adopted, companies may find it helpful to develop a responsibility checklist summarising the key areas of risk and who is responsible for monitoring the relevant issues.

## Main risks                                                              19.6

Whilst the finance director will usually need to be involved in the company's risk management processes, it is important that risk management is not considered from a solely financial perspective, as this may lead to critical strategic or operating risks being underestimated or overlooked. Strategic and operational risks have now become the most significant issues for many companies. For instance, a survey by Deloitte & Touche in 1999 highlighted the following risks, in order of precedence, as being of most concern to directors:

- failure to manage major projects effectively;
- failure of corporate strategy;
- a failure to innovate;
- poor reputation and/or brand management; and
- a lack of employee motivation and poor performance.

A particular difficulty here is that traditional risk management techniques tend to focus on risks where there is relatively strong historical data, and where the potential impact and likelihood of occurrence can therefore be identified with a degree of statistical probability. Such data is rarely available to support decisions on strategic and operational issues. For instance, there is currently concern that businesses may not be taking adequate measures to deal with risks arising from emerging issues, such as e-commerce, because of a failure to understand, identify and assess the underlying risks.

## Appetite for risk                                    19.7

Regardless of which organisational structure is adopted to deal with business risk, the first step must always be for the directors to identify the company's appetite for risk – in other words, the extent to which it is willing to accept a degree of risk. Some businesses by their very nature need to accept a certain level of risk in order to be able to operate. An important factor here is for the directors to develop an awareness of the relative risks of others in the same industry or sector, highlight any differences and understand why they are willing to take an alternative approach.

## Using external resources                             19.8

Depending on the nature of the business and the potential risk areas, directors may wish to make use of specialist resources outside the company in approaching certain aspects of risk management. Areas where external consultants may be able to provide useful assistance include:

- risk assessment and risk modelling methodologies - these can be used to help identify the exposure of the business to different types of risk;
- business continuity planning, disaster recovery and crisis management, including personal safety issues (eg in hostage or similar situations);
- change/project management services; and
- specialised advice on specific areas of risk (reputation, environmental issues).

## Key points on risk management                        19.9

The key points to remember in relation to risk management are:

- risk management is not an annual compliance issue, but an ongoing exercise that should be integral to the business;
- the risk management process should be led at board level but should involve everyone in the organisation;
- the main focus should be on risks which are significant to the company as a whole;
- risk management procedures should be kept as simple and straightforward as possible;
- effective reporting mechanisms and early warning indicators should be developed as part of the risk management process.

## The risk management process                          19.10

## At a glance                                          19.11

- Management needs to understand why, how and where business risks originate.

- Each identified risk should be evaluated by assessing the likelihood of its occurrence and the potential impact on the company.
- The most appropriate approach for dealing with each identified risk should be chosen.
- Appropriate monitoring and reporting arrangements should also be put into place.
- Management must be alert to the possibility of new risks arising and take prompt action to assess and deal with these.

## Principal elements of the process      19.12

Risk management is an ongoing process that will usually involve the following steps:

- identify the risks that are inherent in the company's strategy;
- rank risks by likelihood and severity (see **19.14** below);
- agree on the appropriate approach for dealing with each risk (see **19.15** below);
- where appropriate, take action to eliminate or transfer risks;
- implement controls to manage the remaining risks;
- monitor the effectiveness of risk management actions and controls; and
- continuously improve the system, based on past experience.

## Analysing business risk      19.13

Management needs to understand why, how and where business risks originate, both inside the organisation and as a result of external factors. A variety of techniques can be used to help managers assess the likelihood of risks crystallising and quantify the potential impact on the business, both financially and in operational terms. The Turnbull guidance (see **CHAPTER 14 INTERNAL CONTROL**) uses four categories to analyse and define risk:

- business or strategic risk;
- financial risk;
- operational risk; and
- compliance risk.

An illustrative analysis of risks within these categories is given in **APPENDIX 19A**. Environmental risk may be included within compliance risk, or may need to be considered as a separate risk category, depending on its significance to the business. Other classifications of risk have been developed (eg hazard, market, enterprise) and may be found to be more helpful, depending on the nature of the company and its activities. In its briefing document 'No surprises: Working for better risk reporting' published in June 2002, the ICAEW concludes that some degree of commonality should be developed in the classification of risk in order to improve the comparability of risk reporting, but at present there is no overall consensus and each business is free to choose the analysis that best suits its own situation.

**Risk Management**

## Ranking risks by likelihood and severity                19.14

Each identified risk needs to be evaluated by assessing the likelihood of its occurrence and the potential impact on the company if the risk does crystallise. For instance, this can be done by using a risk matrix or diagram, plotting likelihood on one axis and severity of impact on the other:

This should highlight the most significant risks, so that the initial effort can be concentrated in these areas, and then move on to lower category risks. The following diagram shows the order of priority in tackling identified risks:

| High impact<br>Low likelihood<br><br>2 | High impact<br>High likelihood<br><br>1 |
|---|---|
| Low impact<br>Low likelihood<br><br>4 | Low impact<br>High likelihood<br><br>3 |

Measuring the potential impact of risk may be difficult, especially where risks are interlinked. The financial impact of each identified risk needs to be taken into account but this will not always be the only consideration and non-financial data such as staff retention and satisfaction, trend analysis, benchmarking and segmental information may also need to be considered.

## Dealing with risk                                       19.15

Once identified, each risk can be handled in one of four ways:

● **Accept:** Accepting the risk without any further action is usually only practical if it is unlikely to crystallise in practice and/or the impact on the organisation is likely to be minimal. Very few risks will come into this category.

- **Transfer:** Transferring some or all of the risk to another party might involve:
  - taking out insurance, which involves weighing the cost of the insurance against the potential impact of the risk, should it occur;
  - the use of financial market instruments (eg hedges, futures and options) to limit the company's exposure;
  - outsourcing certain activities, although this will usually involve sharing the risk rather than transferring it; or
  - including indemnities and similar risk-sharing provisions in contracts with suppliers and customers.
- **Reduce and manage:** Most risks are dealt with by reducing them as far as possible and then managing any residual risk by developing contingency plans which help to control or limit the impact if the risk crystallises.
- **Eliminate**: Where the potential impact of a risk is particularly significant, a business may have no alternative but to eliminate all possibility that the risk could crystallise (eg by ceasing a dangerous production process).

## Monitoring and reporting on risk                          19.16

Once appropriate actions have been taken, or procedures agreed, to reduce risk to an acceptable level, monitoring and reporting arrangements must be put into place to:

- confirm that the agreed actions and procedures are implemented in practice; and
- confirm that they are effective in reducing risk to the required level; or
- identify any further action that needs to be taken as a result of issues identified during the monitoring process.

The company's internal audit function will usually have a significant role to play here, and the external auditors will also provide feedback on any issues identified during their work (see CHAPTER 2 AUDIT MATTERS). The monitoring and reporting process should enable directors and managers, and subsequently the company's shareholders, to see that business risks are being properly considered and addressed on a continuous basis.

## Continuous process                                        19.17

Risk management is not a one-off exercise. The business and economic environment is changing constantly, and sometimes rapidly, and it is important for management to be alert to new risks arising from developments in business activities and from changes in legislation and the general economic climate. Methods of assessing and managing risk also change over time and directors need to keep up with developments here as well.

## Additional guidance                                     19.18

There are numerous sources of additional guidance on risk management. In particular, the ICAEW publication 'Implementing Turnbull: A Boardroom Briefing' provides a useful overview of the risk management process in the context of corporate governance. It was issued in September 1999 to help directors with the implementation of the recommendations in the Turnbull Report (see CHAPTER 14 INTERNAL CONTROL) but many of the issues raised are still relevant. The document can be downloaded from the ICAEW website at http://www.icaew.co.uk/risk, which also provides access to other detailed guidance on risk management and links to other website with articles, news items and details of training events on risk management issues.

## Reporting on risk                                        19.19

## At a glance                                              19.20

---

- Both the ASB Statement 'Operating and Financial Review' and the Combined Code recommend that directors discuss in the annual report the principal risks facing the business and how these are managed.
- Disclosures should be specific to the business and should concentrate on the most significant areas of risk.
- FRS 13 requires detailed disclosures on how financial instruments affect the company's risk profile and how risks arising from them are managed.

---

## Investor requirements                                    19.21

Investors need to have a proper understanding of the risks that a business faces, the measures used to evaluate those risks and the action taken to manage the company's exposure to risk. The ASB Statement 'Operating and Financial Review' (see **10.83**) recommends that directors discuss in the annual report the main factors underlying the company's performance and the principal risks that the business faces. The Government White Paper *Modernising Company Law* published in July 2002 proposes introducing a statutory requirement for larger public and private companies to publish such a review. The Combined Code requirements on internal control reporting cover internal control in its widest sense and specifically include risk management (see CHAPTER 14 INTERNAL CONTROL).

## Relevant disclosure                                      19.22

The present disclosure requirements are expressed in broad terms only and give directors a free hand to present the relevant issues in the specific context and circumstances of the business. An integrated risk management process should facilitate risk reporting that is relevant and concentrates on the risks that are most significant to the business. Providing a detailed listing of all the risks that the business might potentially face is more likely to mask the information that investors and other users of the report need to be able to identify. Reporting should also be balanced and should cover both 'downside risk' (ie the risk that something will go wrong) and 'volatility risk' (ie the uncertainty that gives the potential for gain as well as the risk of loss).

## Derivatives and other financial instruments          19.23

*FRS 13 Derivatives and Other Financial Instruments: Disclosures* applies to:

● all banks and similar institutions; and
● all entities that have one or more of their capital instruments listed or publicly traded on a stock exchange or market.

Insurance companies are currently excluded from the scope of this accounting standard because insurance company accounting is undergoing a general review. As its name suggests, the standard deals only with the disclosure of financial instruments and not with their recognition or measurement for accounting purposes. The disclosure requirements are very detailed and encompass both narrative and numerical information. The objective of the disclosures is to provide information on the impact that financial instruments have on the entity's risk profile, how these risks might affect financial performance and financial position and how they are being managed.

### Narrative disclosures          19.24

The narrative disclosures include:

● an explanation of how financial instruments create or change the risks that the reporting entity faces in its activities;
● the directors' approach to managing those risks; and
● a description of the objectives, policies and strategies adopted for holding and using financial instruments to manage risk.

These disclosures are mandatory under the standard, but they can be given either in the notes to the accounts or elsewhere in the annual report (for instance, as part of the OFR or corporate governance disclosures), provided that the accounts include a cross-reference to where the information can be found.

### Numerical disclosures          19.25

The numerical disclosures are intended to assist in the evaluation of the company's exposure to potentially significant risk. Separate requirements are set out for banks and similar institutions, other financial institutions, and other entities. The detailed disclosures cover:

● interest rate risk;

- currency risk;
- liquidity risk;
- fair values;
- financial instruments used for trading;
- financial instruments used for hedging; and
- certain commodity contracts.

A significant element of aggregation is encouraged to prevent key information being obscured by detail. The standard includes illustrative examples of the disclosures, covering both straightforward and complex arrangements.

## Latest proposals on financial instruments                    19.26

The ASB issued FRED 30 *Financial Instruments: Disclosure and Presentation; Recognition and Measurement* in June 2002 as part of its project to achieve convergence between UK accounting standards and international accounting standards. FRED 30 includes a proposal that all listed entities and banks should be required to comply with new disclosure requirements on financial instruments. FRS 13 *Derivatives and other financial instruments: Disclosure* will therefore be withdrawn once the new standard is finalised. The proposed effective date of 1 January 2004 assumes that the government will by then have effected various changes to companies legislation needed to implement the proposals in FRED 30 (which also include new presentation requirements and new measurement and hedge accounting requirements in certain cases), and that the IASB does not propose to make further changes to the underlying international accounting standards during 2004.

## Appendix 19A                                                   19.27

## Analysis of risks                                              19.28

The following summary provides an analysis of the more common risks faced by a business. It should not be regarded as a comprehensive listing.

| Financial risks | Operational risks |
|---|---|
| Credit risk | Reliance on key customers |
| Market risk | Reliance on key suppliers |
| Liquidity risk | Loss of key management and staff |
| Interest rate risk | Lack of business continuity |
| Currency risk | Lack of succession planning |
| Treasury risk | Skills shortage |
| Going concern difficulties | Materials shortage |
| Overtrading | Loss of significant assets |
| Unidentified liabilities | Failure of new product or service |
| Fraud | Poor customer satisfaction levels |
| Misuse of resources | Quality problems |

| | |
|---|---|
| Misstatement of financial information<br>Accounting system breakdown<br>Unreliable management information | Lack of employee motivation<br>Product liability problems<br>Loss of key contracts<br>Failure of major project<br>Failure to implement change<br>Industrial action<br>Breach of confidentiality |
| **Strategic risks**<br><br>Inappropriate business strategy<br><br>Failure to keep up with<br>   technological change<br>Failure to innovate<br>Competitive pressure on market share<br>Competitive pressure on prices<br>Poor brand management<br>Loss of reputation<br>Economic difficulties:<br>   Specific to the industry/sector<br>   General<br>Adverse Government policy<br>Inability to raise sufficient capital<br>Significant ethical problems<br>Missed business opportunities | **Compliance risks**<br><br>Breach of law, regulations or rules<br>  – eg<br><br>   Companies Act 1985<br>   FSA Listing Rules<br>   Employment law<br>   Health & safety law<br>   Environmental regulations<br>   Competition law<br><br>Significant tax errors or problems<br>Significant VAT errors or<br>   problems |

# 20. Training and Development

## Introduction 20.1

The Combined Code states that:

> 'Every director should receive appropriate training on the first
> occasion that he or she is appointed to the board of a listed
> company, and subsequently as necessary.'

The authors argue that this is a bit weak and that board training should
commence much earlier on in the careers of people in business. They should
possess the knowledge, skills and experience to perform these roles well.

One inhibitor to this has been the availability of suitable training courses. For
example few MBA programmes have contained modules on board skills
despite the fact that the ambition of most MBAs is to be on a board as soon
as they can following graduation.

There are however now a growing number of training and development
opportunities for non-executives in the UK. We have grouped these below
under four headings: the Institute of Directors, the business schools, events
run by professional intermediaries and Independent Director member organisations such as 3i's Independent Directors Programme.

## The Institute of Directors ('the IoD') 20.2

The IoD's mission statement includes the sentence:

'To raise the professional standards of directors and help them attain high levels of expertise and effectiveness by improving their knowledge and skills'.

To back this up in practice they run a regular series of courses for directors. There are some twenty eight courses in all and we have listed these in the **APPENDICES**.

The latest list can always been found on the IoD website www.iod.com.

They include courses on the roles of the:

- company director and the board for the Smaller and Medium sized enterprise (SME);
- company director and the board for the complex organisation;
- managing director, chairman, finance director, company secretary; and
- non executive director as well as a range of courses on strategy, influencing skills and financial appreciation.

The IoD also has created the Chartered Director qualification and runs a series of courses and examinations for those interested in achieving this qualification. The IoD website has an interesting interactive test you can do to see how likely you would be to qualify.

## Business Schools                                         20.3

Most of the leading business schools now have a short course available on the subject. The most developed of the UK ones is the two-day Cranfield Non-Executive Directors Seminar. Details can be found on their website link at http://www.som.cranfield.ac.uk/som/executive/execcourse.asp?page=85

These courses typically involve sessions on the legal and technical aspects of the role together with case study based role-plays on the practical aspects.

In the US the flagship course is Harvard Business School's Executive Education run by Professor Jay Lorsch, Harvard's guru on board effectiveness. The course normally attracts participants from all around the world. The material is naturally focussed on the US.

## Professional Intermediaries                              20.4

Most of the larger firms of accountants and lawyers run excellent technical briefing meetings for non-executives. KPMG and Ernst and Young also run a series of highly selective events for their larger corporate contacts. These, and those of the search firms usually take the form of expert speakers giving short addresses aimed at stimulating debate.

Training and Development

## 3i's Independent Directors Programme 20.5

3i's programme consists of 600 members in 14 countries. The members of the programme are on the boards of over 1100 3i-backed businesses as chairmen or independent directors. A range of events are organised exclusively for members in most of the countries in which 3i operates. These tend to be case study-based sessions drawing heavily on the experience of the participants. Topics include:

- coaching MDs;
- board performance and review;
- managing board disharmony;
- recruiting and retaining a high quality board.;
- how do you know a good FD when you see one?;
- internationalising businesses; and
- the independent director's role in mergers and acquisitions.

The members also have their own website, which enables them to draw on the collective experience of the group as a whole. For example:

> 'Anyone had experience of setting up joint venture manufacturing arrangements in China?'

> 'Yes I have in the X industry, these are the issues to think about and be more than happy to share our experience contacts with you.'

For any non-executive, it is important to be clear about your current knowledge skills and behaviours and to regularly review what additional training and development you need. The form of that training and development should be a healthy mix of the experiential and formal.

Finally don't underestimate the power of learning from a master of the art.

# Appendices

---

- Acknowledgements.
- Bibliography.
- Terms of reference for a Remuneration Committee.
- Terms of reference for a Nominations Committee.
- Draft letter from a chairman to a remuneration consultant.
- Draft letter from search firm to chairman with regard to appointing them to recruit a non-executive director.
- Guidance note on the subject of Independent Professional Advice.
- ICSA guidance note on Matters Reserved for the Board.
- NAPF criteria for assessing the independence of directors.
- Terms of reference for Higgs review of role and effectiveness of non-executives.
- Appointment letter for non-executive director.
- Performance Evaluation Guidance.
- Building CEO Capital article from Burson Marsteller – October 25th 2001.
- Useful websites.

---

## Acknowledgements

Baroness Hogg, Brian Larcombe, 3i Group plc
Institute of Directors
Peter M. Brown, *Independent Remuneration Solutions*
Korn/Ferry International

419

*Appendices*

Murray Steele, Cranfield School of Management
London Business School
Kogan Page
Jay Lorsch, *Harvard Business School*
INSEAD
Jay Conger, *Harvard Business School*
Sean O'Hare, *William M. Mercer*
ICSA
Sir Adrian Cadbury
Derek Higgs
David Bishop, *KPMG*
Jan Hall, Spencer Stuart

# Bibliography

- The Financial Times guide to Strategy : Richard Koch
  Financial Times/Prentice Hall ISBN 0 273 65022 X
- Harvard Business Review on Corporate Governance
  Harvard Business School Press ISBN 1 57851 237 9
- Cadbury Report: Report if the Committee on the Financial Aspects of
  Corporate Governance, Gee Publishing, 1992, ISBN: 0 85258 915 8
- Directors remuneration: A report of the study Group: Sir Richard
  Greenbury
  Gee Publishing, 1995, ISBN 1 86089 012 1
- Tolley's Finance Director's Handbook
  LexisNexis UK ISBN 0 7545 2341 1
- Tolley's Company Meetings
  LexisNexis UK ISBN 0 7545 0211 2
- Tolley's Company Secretary's Handbook
  LexisNexis UK ISBN 0 7545 1789 6
- Committee on Corporate Governance – Final Report
  Chaired by Sir Ronald Hampel, Gee Publishing, 1998,
  ISBN: 1 86089 034
- Pawns or Potentates: Professor Jay Lorsch
  Harvard Business School Press ISBN 0 87584 216 X
- Turnbull Report: Internal Control – Guidance to Directors on the
  Combined Code,
  ICAEW, ISBN: 1 84152 010 1
- Running Board Meetings: Patrick Dunne
  ISBN 0 7494 3014 1
- Directors Dilemmas: Patrick Dunne
  Kogan Page ISBN 0 7494 3043 5
- The Pocket Director B Tricker
  Economist Books
- The Independent Director survey
  Independent Remuneration Solutions and 3i
- The Independent Chairman and Non-Executive Director survey
  Top Pay research group in association with 3i 2002

- Korn/Ferry Annual Board of Directors Survey
  To obtain a copy email **global.marketing@kornferry.com**
- NAPF review
- The Company Chairman: Sir Adrian Cadbury
  Director Books Fitzwilliam Publishing Cambridge
  ISBN 0 1343 4150 3
- The Effective Director: Chris Pierce
  Kogan Page ISBN 0 7494 3551 8
- Adrian Cadbury: Corporate Governance and Chairmanship 2002
  Oxford University Press ISBN 0 1992 5200 9
- Jonathan Charkham: Keeping Good Company
  1994 Oxford University Press
- Report of the Committee on the Financial Aspects of Corporate
  Governance 1992
  Gee Publishing ISBN 0 85258 915 8
- Compliance with the Code of Best Practice
  Gee Publishing 1995 ISBN 1 86089 0067
- Directors Remuneration Gee Publishing 1995 ISBN 1 8689 036 9
- The Combined Code ISBN 1 86089 036 9
- Higgs Review of the role and effectiveness of non-executive directors
- Chairing the Board John Harper 2000 Kogan Page
- The Human Face of Corporate Governance Lynn McGregor
  Basingstoke Palgrave
- Letters to a new Chairman Hugh Parker 1990 Director Publications
- Philip Styles and Bernard Taylor Boards at Work Oxford University
  Press 2001
- Demb Ada and Neubauer F.Freidrich 1992 the Corporate Board
  Oxford Oxford University Press
- The SJ Berwin Business Guide to Directors' Responsibilities by
  Philip Goldenberg (see SJ Berwin website)
- Linda Hill HBS article
- Hugh Parker Letters to a new Chairman(1990) London Director publi-
  cations
- An international comparison of corporate governance models
  Francesco Maasen Spencer Stuart
- CEO tenure report 3i/Cranfield/Sanders and Sidney
- Corporate Boards: New Strategies for Adding Value at the Top
  Jay Conger, Edward E Lawler, David Feingold; Jossey Bass Wiley,
  2001, ISBN: 0787956201
- Family Business – Manfred Kets de Vries and Eric van der Loo
  ISBN 0415114624

# Terms of reference for a Remuneration Committee

*You will want to word this in the style of the company's other communications. What is presented below is a slightly more formal version than is necessary but easily adaptable.*

1. **Name**

   The committee shall be a standing committee of the board known as the 'Remuneration Committee'.

2. **Purpose**

   To determine on behalf of the board and the shareholders the company's broad policy for executive remuneration and the entire individual remuneration packages for the directors and as appropriate other senior executives.

3. **Members and Chairman**

   (a)  The committee shall comprise any three or more non-executive directors of the company, considered by the board to be independent for this purpose, appointed from time to time by Resolution of the board of whom one shall from time to time be appointed by the board to act as chairman.

   (b)  Notwithstanding paragraph 3(a) where a quorum would not otherwise be available for a meeting of the committee to take place the chairman and the senior non-executive director (or deputy chairman) shall have the power to co-opt any appropriate non-executive director (including themselves) as an additional member of the committee.

4. **Quorum**

   The quorum for the transaction of business by the committee shall be the chairman of the committee together with any one other member of the committee.

   In the absence of the chairman of the committee the senior independent non-executive director or, in his absence the chairman of the board or any other non-executive director they co-opt to the committee in accordance with paragraph 3 (a) can take his place.

5. **Fees**

   Additional remuneration at such a rate as the board may determine shall be payable to each member of the remuneration committee other than the chairman of the board or any other director co-opted to the committee in accordance with paragraph 3 (b).

6. **Conduct of Business**

   (a)  Meetings

   Not less than three meetings of the committee shall be held between one Annual General Meeting of the company and the next. All meetings of the committee shall be convened by the company Secretary on the instructions of the chairman of the committee or, in his absence, the member of the committee in accordance with paragraph 4 above.

   (b)  Consultation

   The Committee shall consult with the chairman of the board (if not a member of the committee) and/or the chief executive and may consult with the Human Resources director, and shall have the power to employ the services of any external remuneration consultant or other professional adviser as it thinks fit, and may invite any of such persons to attend such meetings of the committee as it considers appropriate. The budget for fees payable by the Committee to external advisers is to be agreed with the board at the beginning of each year.

(c)    Support

The company secretary shall be the Secretary to the Committee and shall provide the Committee such support and advice as it may require and shall be entitled to independent access to the chairman of the Committee at all times.

(d)    Voting

Each member of the committee shall have one vote. Note: there are three members of the Committee.

(e)    Written Resolution

A resolution in writing signed by all members of the Committee entitled to receive notice of a meeting of the Committee shall be as valid and effective as if the same had been passed at a meeting of the committee duly convened and held.

7.    **Powers of the Committee**

The Committee has the following powers, authorities and discretions.

(a)    Remuneration arrangements

Power to consider and determine, on behalf of the board, specific remuneration packages (including matters relating to pension benefits) for each of the executive directors of 'the company' and all other members of the chief executive's management Committee (called the 'executive Committee').

(b)    Termination Arrangements

Power to consider and determine, on behalf of the board, specific arrangements for the payment of compensation or other benefits to executive directors of 'The company' and any other members of the executive Committee on termination of their employment, whether by way of damages for breach of contract, pay in lieu of notice, ex gratia payment or otherwise.

(c)    Framework of Executive Remuneration

Without prejudice to the authority relating to remuneration delegated to the chief executive by Minute No XXXX, power to consider at the request of the board, and make recommendations to the board on, the company's framework for executive remuneration and its costs.

(d)    Employee Share plans

Authority to exercise or approve and authorise the exercise of all or any powers, authorities and discretions of the directors in connection with

[List of schemes]

(e)    General

Authority to exercise all or any powers, authorities and discretions at any time conferred upon the Committee by Resolution of the board.

8.  **Advisory Functions**

    The Committee shall, if requested by the chief executive to do so:

    (a)  provide its advice and guidance to the chief executive in regard to the Company's world-wide remuneration policy, both from a strategic point of view and in relation to any annual salary review, taking account of market practice and the needs of the business;

    (b)  provide its advice and guidance to the chief executive in relation to the remuneration of those individual executives who report directly to a member of the Executive Committee, and in relation to the structure and total amount of the remuneration of all other employees of the Company and its wholly owned subsidiaries; and

    (c)  provide its advice and guidance to the chief executive in regard to the amount that should be set aside for variable pay in respect of any one financial year of the Company including the amount to be provided for performance related pay, bonus participation schemes, special awards and employee share schemes world-wide.

9.  **Additional duties of chairman**

    The chairman of the committee is authorised and requested to attend (or to arrange for another member of the Committee to attend each annual general meeting of the Company to deal with shareholders' questions about directors remuneration.

## Terms of reference for a Nominations Committee

You will want to word this in the style of the company's other communications. What is presented below is a slightly more formal version than is necessary but easily adaptable. We have drawn heavily on the ICSA template.

1.  **Name**

    The committee shall be a standing committee of the board known as the 'Nominations Committee'.

2.  **Purpose**

    To ensure that there is a formal and transparent process for the appointment of new directors to the board and to make recommendations to the board on all new board appointments.

3.  **Members and chairman**

    (a)  The Committee shall comprise any three or more non-executive directors of the company, considered by the board to be independent for this purpose, appointed from time to time by Resolution of the board of whom one shall from time to time be appointed by the board to act as chairman.

    (b)  Notwithstanding paragraph 3(a) where a quorum would not otherwise be available for a meeting of the committee to take place the chairman and the senior non-executive director (or Deputy chairman) shall have the power to co-opt any appropriate non-executive director (including themselves) as an additional member of the committee.

**4. Quorum**

The quorum for the transaction of business by the committee shall be the chairman of the committee together with any one other member of the committee.

In the absence of the chairman of the committee the senior independent non-executive director or, in his absence the chairman of the board or any other non-executive director they co-opt to the committee in accordance with paragraph 3 (a) can take his place.

**5. Fees**

Additional remuneration at such a rate as the board may determine shall be payable to each member of the remuneration committee other than the chairman of the board or any other director co-opted to the committee in accordance with paragraph 3 (b).

**6. Conduct of Business**

(a) Meetings

The committee shall meet not less than once a year and at such other times as the chairman of the committee shall require. All meetings of the committee shall be convened by the company secretary on the instructions of the chairman of the committee or, in his absence, the member of the committee in accordance with paragraph 4 above.

(b) Consultation

The Committee shall consult with the chairman of the board (if not a member of the committee) and/or the Chief executive and may consult with the Human resources director, and shall have the power to employ the services of any external search consultant or other professional adviser as it thinks fit, and may invite any of such persons to attend such meetings of the committee as it considers appropriate. The budget for fees payable by the Committee to external advisers is to be agreed with the board at the beginning of each year.

(c) Support

The company secretary shall be the Secretary to the Committee and shall provide the Committee such support and advice as it may require and shall be entitled to independent access to the chairman of the Committee at all times.

(d) Voting

Each member of the committee shall have one vote. Note: there are three members of the Committee.

(e) Written Resolution

A resolution in writing signed by all members of the Committee entitled to receive notice of a meeting of the Committee shall be as valid and effective as if the same had been passed at a meeting of the committee duly convened and held.

**7. Duties of the Committee**

The Committee shall:

(a) regularly review the structure, size and composition of the board and make recommendations to the board with regard to any adjustments that are deemed necessary;

(b)    be responsible for identifying and nominating for the approval of the board, candidates to fill board vacancies as and when they arise;

(c)    keep under review the leadership needs of the organisation with a view to ensuring the continued ability to compete effectively in the organisation's market place; and

(d)    keep up to date and fully au fait with strategic issues and commercial changes affecting the company and the market in which it operates.

It shall also make recommendations to the board on:

(e)    plans for succession, in particular, of the chairman and the chief executive;

(f)    the re-appointment of any non-executive director at the conclusion of his or her specified term of office;

(g)    for the continuation (or not) in service of any director who has reached the age of [specify];

(h)    the re-election by shareholders of any director under the 'retirement by rotation' provisions in the company's articles of association;

(j)    any matters relating to the continuation in office as a director of any director at any time; and

(k)    the appointment of any director to executive or other office other than to the positions of chairman and chief executive, the recommendation for which would be considered at a meeting of all the non-executive directors regarding the position of chief executive and all the directors regarding the position of chairman.

**8.    Powers of the committee**

The committee is authorised to seek any information it requires from any employee of the company in order to perform its duties.

The committee is authorised to obtain, at the company's expense, outside legal or other professional advice on any matters within its terms of reference.

**9.    Additional duties of chairman**

The chairman of the Committee is authorised and requested to attend (or to arrange for another member of the Committee to attend each Annual General Meeting of the Company to deal with shareholders' questions about directors' remuneration.

## Draft letter from the chairman of the remuneration committee to a potential remuneration consultant

This letter should be sent by the chairman of the Remuneration Committee or signed on his behalf and not sent by the chief executive, finance director, company secretary or Human Resources director.

Dear Consultant

| EITHER |
|---|

Further to our meeting this morning it gives me great pleasure to invite you to attend the next meeting of the remuneration committee of ABC PLC at **[TIME]** on **[DATE]**dd/mm/yy. As chairman of the remuneration committee I am inviting you to attend to present your credentials and to quote for an assignment to help the committee review the following.

| OR: |
|---|

Further to your presentation to the remuneration committee of ABC PLC this morning I am delighted to confirm that we would like you to undertake an assignment to help the committee review the following.

- The salaries and benefits packages of the chairman, senior independent director and non executive directors.
- The short term cash bonus schemes for the executive directors and the chief executives of the operating divisions.
- The current long term incentive schemes which consist of a combination of share option schemes and long term incentive plans.

Our primary objective is to build shareholder value by being competitive in the remuneration marketplace without overcompensating our executive team. Your report needs to be specific to us at this stage in our growth and not simply a generalised statistical study.

As chairman of the remuneration committee, I will be your client for this assignment but the chief executive, finance director, company secretary and Human Resources director, know it (has been/will be) commissioned and you can ask them for any additional information you need.

We can arrange for you to meet individual executives if you need to.

Your draft report should be delivered to me and not discussed with others in advance and the final report needs to be ready for the remuneration committee meeting on 10th August.

I enclose the following information:

1. Job specifications, employment contracts and CVs for the directors to be included in the review.
2. Information on the make up of the current executive directors' packages which is of course published in our annual accounts.
3. Copies of the last five years' accounts with the full remuneration committee report.

4.    The legal documents setting up our share option and LTIP schemes.

We would like your review to include full details of other companies whose remuneration you consider to be relevant to ourselves, together with a recommendation on whether comparator group performance should become the criterion for full or partial encashment of our long-term incentive schemes. If you consider this a suitable mechanism would you please suggest what comparator companies should be included. If you need to check these with our principal institutional investors please give me a ring and I will arrange access for you.

We are naturally concerned to ensure that all parts of the remuneration package are as tax efficient for the company and the individuals as possible. We accept that you are not tax specialists but do expect that you have weighed up the issues of income and capital gains tax as well as national insurance in your recommendations.

If you need more information on executive directors' pension arrangements I am sure our company secretary XX would be delighted to provide you with it.

I look forward to receiving confirmation of your willingness to present on the dd/mm/yy.

---

**OR:**

---

I look forward to receiving confirmation of your willingness to accept this assignment on the following terms.

Terms as negotiated. and we look forward to receiving your draft report on dd/mm/yy.

Yours sincerely

Mr John Brown

Chairman of remuneration committee

ABC plc

## Draft letter from search firm to chairman with regard to appointing them to recruit a non-executive director

This letter is typically sent by the search firm to the chairman, who is typically also the chairman of the Nominations Committee. It is normally a summary of a meeting held to agree the points contained within and the chairman by signing his acceptence to it at the foot of the letter thereby appoints the search firm.

Dear Chairman

| **EITHER** |
| --- |

Thank you very much for giving us the opportunity to assist the selection process for your new non-executive director. X and I very much enjoyed our meeting with the nominations committee yesterday and delighted that you have chosen us for this very important assignment. Naturally we are disappointed that you have taken the decision not to use our comprehensive board audit process before proceeding with the search. However if you change your mind on this please just let us know.

As promised I am writing to summarise our discussions and cover the following.

- The background to the search.
- The specification and competencies we agreed that the ideal candidate should possess.
- Logistical considerations for candidates.
- Our process for conducting the search.
- Proposed remuneration for the new non-executive.
- Our fees, terms and conditions.

It is very important with regard to our description on the background to the company, the description of the role and the candidate specification, that you alert us to anything that you feel needs amendment. These will form the basis of the briefing notes to our researchers and when making our initial approaches to candidates.

---

### The background to the search

This part of the letter will cover around a page of description of the company, its products, markets, geographical spread, headline financial performance and so on. It will also contain a section on the situation of the company and a statement of the company's strategy.

It will then provide a brief profile of the current board and describe why a new non-executive is being sought. For example:

> 'The recent acquisition by the company of XYZ Inc in the United States has significantly increased the scale and geographical spread of the business and the board feels it is important to strengthen the board as a result.'

or

---

'The company's core institutional shareholders have expressed a desire to see someone on the board with a financial background.'

Or

'Following the announcement of the proposed retirement of X you are looking to succeed him with someone with similar experience but additionally the capability of becoming chairman of the Audit committee.'

## The specification and competencies required of the ideal candidate

We will be expecting all potential candidates to possess the generic characteristics and competencies of a good non-executive director for a company of your standing. At XYZ firm we believe these are the following:

(select from the list on page x)

However given the specific circumstances of the company at this stage in its development we would emphasise the following:

- strategic ability;
- city credibility; and
- international and organisational capability.

Before you see candidates, we will therefore have considered the following:

- Their track record of developing and implementing successful strategies relevant to the company and an appreciation of the key strategic variables facing you.
- Their track record and reputation with key institutional shareholders and advisers.
- Their appreciation of the issues currently facing the company with regard to investor relations.
- Their record in developing successful international operations and success in leading transformational acquisition integration.
- Their appreciation of the international challenges facing the company at the moment.

There then would be some additional specificity for example

'Given the background we will aim if possible to find someone who has lived and worked in Germany and built a successful German operation.'

> or
>
>> 'The acquisition in the US brings with it not just a US business but a collection of businesses in South America. We will therefore look for candidates with proven experience of successfully integrating acquisitions and operating experience of the US and Brazil etc.'

We understand that it is policy for all non-executives post their induction period to become members of either the Audit, remuneration or nominations committees. At this point you would like any candidates chosen for interview to be capable of serving on the X committee.

## Logistical considerations for candidates

We understand the following will need to be taken into account:

Formal board meetings are held nine times per annum. The locations and dates are set out in the attached appendix. There are also two additional board Away-days, one focussed on strategy, the other succession planning. The dates and locations for these are also in appendix X.

Meetings of the X committee are held in the late afternoon preceding the board dinner on the day before the board meeting.

Because of the rotation of board meetings around the company's key operating subsidiary locations there is typically a dinner held the night before the board. It is expected that the non executive will attend these dinners.

The company believes that physical presence is very important and so attendance of meetings by video or telephone is not acceptable.

You recognise that this is a significant time commitment and envisage it totalling thirty days per annum.

## Our process for conducting the search

The key stages in the process and likely timeframes once you have formally agreed the contents of this letter are as follows.

- Interviews with current board to give us a deeper understanding of the board and the special requirements of your situation (three weeks).
- Sourcing of potential candidates (four weeks).
- Presentation to the nominations committee of a shortlist of potential candidates( five or six) that we would like to approach (one week later).
- Approaching candidates and initial interviews conducted by ourselves(four weeks).
- Interviews with the chosen panel (four weeks).

- Agreement of terms in principle.
- Referencing and candidates' own due diligence.

Naturally some of these activities will run in parallel so we would expect that you should be able to have someone on board in time for your [Month] board meeting.

We would suggest that the presentation to the nominations committee takes place by conference call with a detailed report on each candidate supplied in advance.

Given our considerable experience of these selection processes we have produced several guidance notes for interviewing prospective non-executives. I have included these.

With regard to referencing we will provide a substantive referencing report to you and in addition provide you with contact details for you to make your own enquiries. If you would like and candidates are in agreement we can also undertake Psychometric testing. We can also suggest methods for successful induction if this would be helpful. The additional fees for these extra services and our complete board audit product are detailed below.

I will be taking personal responsibility for this assignment myself and will be supported by X and Y. In addition given our global reach and superb pool of talent in the USA I will be involving Z from our New York office.

## Remuneration for the chosen candidate

The basic components of remuneration will be the following.

- A fee of £25,000 per annum based on an assumed time commitment of thirty days.
- An additional fee of £3000 per annum payable for membership of board committees.
- An agreed basis of payment for circumstances where the director's time commitment is significantly greater than originally envisaged eg During a major transaction.
- A description of allowable expenses.
- Clarity over Directors and Officers liability insurance ie whether it is paid for by the company or the individual and the details of the cover provided. [See CHAPTER 13 for more information relating to Directors and Officers liability insurance.]
- A proposal regarding obtaining equity in the company where relevant, for example in venture capital or private equity backed businesses.
- Services provided by the company to enable the director to carry out his duties(eg access to legal advice).

## Our fees, terms and conditions

Our professional fees for this assignment will be £50,000, payable in four equal instalments. The first will be upon acceptance of this letter, the second upon offer of the position, the third upon appointment of the successful candidate and the fourth three months after appointment. We will also make an additional charge of ten per cent of the fee to cover other expenses excluding any international travel. VAT of course is chargeable on both on fees and expenses and invoices are payable within 14 days.

Should acceptable candidates not have been found within the next three months we will continue to search on your behalf for no additional cost.

If for any reason the search should be cancelled our fees will be adjusted to reflect the time commitment and expenses incurred up to that point.

In the event of potential candidates being hired by the company for positions other than the specific non-executive director appointment described above we would make an additional charge of £30,000.

A detailed copy of our firm's approach to doing business is attached.

I have to say I am very much looking forward to starting work and consider this a great assignment for our business. We are impressed with the thoroughness with which you have conducted the tendering process.

Kind regards

Yours sincerely

Joe Smooth

## Our approach to doing business

### Our general approach

Getting the right person is our mission. A rigorous approach to selection is therefore critical in achieving this aim. We believe that the track record of a candidate should be the starting point for understanding their capability in the proposed role, so place a great deal of emphasis on thorough research into candidates' backgrounds.

### Confidentiality and data protection

It is our policy not to divulge our client's identity without prior approval. We would not normally inform candidates of the client's identity in any event until we had established that they might be suitably qualified and interested in the role. We will do everything we can to avoid any speculation in the industry recognising that given the specification this may not be achievable in practice.

The client will also undertake to use material provided by our firm in connection with this search strictly for the purposes of assessing and selecting a candidate. The client will not disclose any material to anyone other than those in the client's organisation who are involved in the selection process. Any materials provided remain the property of our firm and should be returned if requested.

The client will not attempt to contact any candidate directly without our firm's prior knowledge and agreement.

The client undertakes to indemnify our firm against all losses, expenses and liabilities incurred by our firm and its directors or employees arising directly or indirectly as a result of the loss of unauthorised use or disclosure of any part of the material, or from breach of the terms of this engagement.

## Exclusivity

By accepting this assignment we undertake not to undertake non-executive assignments for any of the specified competitors in the list below.

## Sourcing candidates

We will develop through a combination of systematic research and the extensive database we have of potential candidates a comprehensive list. We always welcome suggestions from the board and will ask for them as part of our initial interviews. In addition we will need to know those individuals who may appear to be suitably qualified but who you deem not to be suitable candidates. It would also be helpful for you to provide us with candidates you have considered for non-executive positions with the company before.

## Reference information

Referencing information will contain third party opinion (as opposed to factual information) in relation to a candidate. The client should understand that such opinion is of the third party, and our firm makes no guarantee or endorsement as to its accuracy or reasonableness. Naturally all material is supplied in good faith, however we will not accept any responsibility for any errors or omissions in the material or for any loss or damage arising out of any reliance on the material.

## Client referrals

Given the impressive networks of current board members we would expect that the board may already have in mind suitable candidates to nominate for entry into the selection process. These candidates should be referred to us as soon as possible so we can add them to the pool generated by our systematic research. It is critical that they are treated on the same basis as other candidates and evaluated to the same high standards. For the sake of clarity there is no reduction in fee if the candidate chosen was originally suggested by the client.

## *Negotiating packages*

Our approach is to agree with the client the parameters of the package to be offered to the chosen candidate and then for us to agree this with the candidate in question. It is our policy for non-executive appointments to make this clear at earliest possible stage to avoid any embarrassment later.

## *Ensuring a successful appointment*

It is our policy to follow up all assignments ninety days following the appointment with a call to the chairman and to the new non-executive to evaluate the effectiveness of the appointment. We will then feed back to the nominations committee the results of this.

## ICSA Guidance note 011102
## Model board resolution on Independent Professional Advice

The London Stock Exchange's principles of good Governance and Code of Best Practice (The Combined Code) states in article A.1.3:

'There should be a procedure agreed by the board for directors, in the furtherance of their duties, to take independent professional advice if necessary, at the company's expense.'

**The following is suggested wording for a resolution of the board to give effect to the above principle.**

'It was resolved THAT

Subject to the following procedures and limitations, the directors of the company shall, both individually and collectively, have the right to consult the company's professional advisers [and, if necessary,] [or] [and if they are not satisfied with the advice received,] see independent professional advice at the company's expense in the furtherance of their duties as directors of the company.

1. A director shall give prior notice to [the chairman, the company secretary of the senior non-executive director] [the company secretary] [the chairman] of his or her intention to seek independent professional advice under this procedure and shall provide the name(s) of any professional advisers he proposes to instruct together with a brief summary of the subject matter.

2.    [the company secretary shall provide written acknowledgement of receipt of the notification which shall state whether
the fees for the professional advice sought are payable by
the company under these procedures.] A director shall
obtain the prior approval of [the chairman or in his absence
the Deputy chairman] [senior independent non-executive]
[where the fees of the independent professional adviser are
likely to exceed [a certain amount].

For the avoidance of doubt, the above restrictions shall not apply
to executive directors acting in the furtherance of their executive
responsibilities and within their delegated powers.

Independent professional advice for the purposes of this resolution shall include legal advice and the advice of accountants and
other professional advisers on matters of law, accounting and
other regulatory matters but shall exclude advice concerning the
personal interests of the director concerned (such as his service
contract with the company or his dealings in the company's securities or disputes with the company).

[Any advice obtained under this procedure shall be made available to the other members of the board, if the board so requests.]'

Paragraph 1 is intended to ensure that the company is aware that a director
intends to take independent advice.

Paragraph 2 is suggested for those companies who seek to place restrictions
on directors' freedom to consult professional advisers and who require prior
notification to be given. The company secretary's statement as to whether the
company would be liable to pay the fees could be guidance only.

## An alternative:

A much neater solution would be to authorise a member of the board (preferably the senior non-executive director) to commit the company to pay or
contribute [up to a fixed amount] to the costs of independent advice.
Whenever the director commits the company, he could be required to notify
the chairman or other director.

## ICSA Guidance note 011104
## Matters reserved for the Board

For latest updates visit ICSA website www.icsa.org.uk Guidance notes
section.

No matter how effective a board of directors may be it is not possible for
the directors to have hands on involvement in every area of the company's
business. An effective board controls the business but delegates day to day

responsibility to the executive management. That said there are a number of matters which are required, or that should be in the interests of the company, only to be decided by the board of directors as a whole. It is incumbent upon the board to make it clear what these Matters reserved for the board are.

The relative importance of some matters included in this Guidance Note will vary according to the size and nature of the company's business. For example all companies will have a different view on the establishment of financial limits for transactions which should be referred to the board. Equally, there may well be items not mentioned in the Guidance Note which some companies (eg those subject to additional forms of external regulation) would wish to include in their own schedule.

## Multiple Signatures

In drawing up a schedule of Matters reserved for the Board, companies should clarify which transactions require multiple board signatures on the relevant documentation.

## Delegation

Certain of the matters included in this Guidance Note should, under the recommendations of the Cadbury Committee and/or the Combined Code, be the responsibility of the audit, nomination or remuneration committee. However, full delegation is not permitted in these cases as the final decision on the matter is required to be taken by the whole board.

## Urgent Matters

In drawing up this schedule of Matters reserved for the Board it is important to establish procedures for dealing with matters that have to be dealt with urgently, often between board meetings. It is recommended that, where practical, the approval of all of the directors should be obtained by means of written resolution. In all cases however the procedures should balance the need for urgency with the overriding principle that each director should be given as much information as possible and have an opportunity to requisition an emergency meeting of the board to discuss the matter prior to commitment of the Company.

The following schedule has been produced to assist boards of directors and company secretaries in preparing a schedule of Matters reserved for the Board in accordance with good corporate governance.

Items marked * are not considered suitable for delegation to a committee of the board, eg because of Companies Act requirements or because, under the recommendations of the Cadbury Report or Combined Code, they are the responsibility of an audit, nomination or remuneration committee, with final decision required to be taken by the board as a whole.

# Companies Act Requirements.

1.* Approval of interim and final financial statements.
2.* Approval of the interim and final dividend and recommendation of the final dividend.
3.* Approval of any significant changes in accounting policies or practices.
4.* Appointment or removal of the company secretary.
5.* Remuneration of the auditors [where, as is usual, shareholders have delegated this power to the board] and recommendations for the appointment or removal of auditors [possibly following recommendations of the audit committee].
6. Resolutions and corresponding documentation to be put forward to the shareholders at a General Meeting.

## Stock Exchange/Financial Services Authority

7.* Approval of all circulars and listing particulars [approval of routine documents such as periodic circulars re scrip dividend procedures or exercise of conversion rights could be delegated to a committee.]
8.* Approval of press releases concerning matters decided by the board.

## Board Membership and board Committees

9. *Board appointments and removals and any special terms and conditions attached to the appointment [subject to recommendations of the remuneration committee].
10. *Terms of reference of chairman, chief executive and other executive directors.
11. *Terms of reference and membership of board committees.

## Management

12. Approval of the Group's long term objectives and commercial strategy.
13. Approval of the annual operating and capital expenditure budgets.
14. Changes relating to the Group's capital structure or its status as a plc.
15. Appointments to the boards of subsidiaries.
16. *Terms and conditions of directors and senior executives.
17. Changes to the Group's management and control structure.

## Cadbury/Combined Code recommendations

18. Major capital projects.
19. Material, either by reason of size or strategically, contracts of the company [or any subsidiary] in the ordinary course of business, eg bank borrowings [above a certain amount] and acquisition or disposal of fixed assets [above a certain amount].
20. Contracts of the company [or any subsidiary] not in the ordinary course of business, eg loans and repayments [above a certain amount]; foreign

currency transactions [above a certain amount]; major acquisitions or disposals [above a certain amount].
21. Major investments [including the acquisition or disposal of interests of more than [5] percent in the voting shares of any company or the making of any takeover bid.
22. Risk management strategy.
23. Treasury policies [including foreign currency exposure].

## Miscellaneous

24. Review of the company's overall corporate governance arrangements.
25. Major changes in the rules of the company's pension scheme, or changes of trustees or [when this subject is subject to the approval of the company] changes in the fund management arrangements.
26. Major changes in employee share schemes and the allocation of share options.
27. Formulation of policy regarding charitable donations.
28. Political donations.
29. Approval of the company's principal professional advisers.
30. Prosecution, defence or settlement of litigation [involving above [a certain amount] or being otherwise material to the interests of the company].
31. Internal control arrangements.
32. Health and Safety policy.
33. Environmental policy.
34. Directors and Officers liability insurance.
35. This schedule of matters reserved for board decisions.

## National Association of Pension Funds('NAPF') criteria for assessing the independence of directors

In assessing the independence of a non-executive director the assumption is that the individual is independent unless, in relation to the company, the director:

- was formerly an executive;
- is, or has been paid by the company in any other capacity than a non-executive;
- represents a trading partner or is connected to a company or partnership (or was prior to retirement) which does business with the company;
- has been a non-executive for nine years ie three 3-year terms;
- is closely related to an executive director;
- has been awarded share options, performance-related pay or is a member of the company's pension fund;
- represents a controlling or significant shareholder;
- is a new appointee selected other than by a formal process;
- has cross directorships with any executive director;
- for whatever reason is said by the company not to be independent.

They also add that there may be other circumstances which could cast doubt on the independence of a non-executive.

In their 2001 review the NAPF viewed 82% of the non-executives of the top 400 UK companies as independent.

## Terms of reference for the Higgs review of the role and effectiveness of non-executive directors

### Objective

Building on the work of the Company Law review and the Myners review, the Government has commissioned Derek Higgs to lead a short independent review of the role and effectiveness of non-executive directors in the UK.

### Background

Non-executive directors play a central role in UK corporate governance. The Company Law review noted 'a growing body of evidence from the US suggesting that companies with a strong contingent of non-executives produce superior performance.'

In the decade since the introduction of the Cadbury Code, the role of non-executives has undoubtedly strengthened.

From the point of view of UK productivity, performance, progressive strengthening of the quality and role of non-executives is strongly desirable.

### Proposal

Though the Government has an open mind, its preferred starting-point in this area is, if possible, an approach based on best practice, not regulation or legislation.

The Government believes it would be valuable for a senior figure from the business world, building on the work of the Company Law Review, of Myners, and of the Institute of Directors and others, to undertake a review to assess:

- the population of non-executive directors in the UK – who are they, how are they appointed, how the pool might be widened etc;
- their 'independence';
- their effectiveness;
- accountability: their relationship – actual and potential – with institutional investors;
- issues relating to non-executive directors' remuneration;
- the role of the Combined Code;
- what, if anything, could be done – by individual boards, by institutional investors, by Government or otherwise – to strengthen the quality, independence and effectiveness of non-executive directors.

This review will look at this in an international context.

The aim of the review is:

- to build and publish an accurate picture of the status quo;
- to lead a debate on these issues, especially in the business and financial worlds; and
- to make any recommendations – to Government and to others – which the reviewer thinks appropriate.

## Sample letter of non-executive director appointment

On [date], upon the recommendation of the nomination committee, the board of [company] ('the Company') has appointed you as non-executive director. I am writing to set out the terms of your appointment. It is agreed that this is a contract for services and is not a contract of employment.

## Appointment

Your appointment will be for an initial term of three years commencing on [date], unless otherwise terminated earlier by and at the discretion of either party upon [one month's] written notice. Continuation of your contract of appointment is contingent on satisfactory performance and re-election at forthcoming AGMs. Non-executive directors are typically expected to serve two three-year terms, although the board may invite you to serve for an additional period.

## Time commitment

Overall we anticipate a time commitment of [number] days per month after the induction phase. This will include attendance at [monthly] board meetings, the AGM, [one] annual board away day, and [at least one] site visit per year. In addition, you will be expected to devote appropriate preparation time ahead of each meeting.

By accepting this appointment, you have confirmed that you are able to allocate sufficient time to meet the expectations of your role. The agreement of the chairman should be sought before accepting additional commitments that might affect the time you are able to devote to your role as a non-executive director of the company.

## Role

Non-executive directors have the same general legal responsibilities to the company as any other director. The board as a whole is collectively responsible for promoting the success of the company by directing and supervising the company's affairs. The board:

- provides entrepreneurial leadership of the company within a framework

441

of prudent and effective controls which enable risk to be assessed and managed;
- sets the company's strategic aims, ensures that the necessary financial and human resources are in place for the company to meet its objectives, and reviews management performance; and
- sets the company's values and standards and ensures that its obligations to its shareholders and others are understood and met.

In addition to these requirements of all directors, the role of the non-executive has the following key elements:

- **Strategy**: Non-executive directors should constructively challenge and contribute to the development of strategy;
- **Performance**: Non-executive directors should scrutinise the performance of management in meeting agreed goals and objectives and monitor the reporting of performance;
- **Risk**: Non-executive directors should satisfy themselves that financial information is accurate and that financial controls and systems of risk management are robust and defensible; and
- **People**: Non-executive directors are responsible for determining appropriate levels of remuneration of executive directors and have a prime role in appointing, and where necessary removing, senior management and in succession planning.

## Fees

You will be paid a fee of £[amount] gross per annum which will be paid monthly in arrears, [plus [number] ordinary shares of the company per annum, both of] which will be subject to an annual review by the board. The company will reimburse you for all reasonable and properly documented expenses you incur in performing the duties of your office.

## Outside interests

It is accepted and acknowledged that you have business interests other than those of the company and have declared any conflicts that are apparent at present. In the event that you become aware of any potential conflicts of interest, these should be disclosed to the chairman and company secretary as soon as apparent.

[The board of the company have determined you to be independent according to the provision of the Combined Code.]

## Confidentiality

All information acquired during your appointment is confidential to the Company and should not be released, either during your appointment or following termination (by whatever means), to third parties without prior clearance from the chairman.

Your attention is also drawn to the requirements under both legislation and regulation as to the disclosure of price sensitive information. Consequently you should avoid making any statements that might risk a breach of these requirements without prior clearance from the chairman or company secretary.

## Induction

Immediately after appointment, the Company will provide a comprehensive, formal and tailored induction. This will include the information pack recommended by the Institute of Chartered Secretaries and Administrators, available at www.icsa.org.uk. We will also arrange for site visits and meetings with senior and middle management and the Company's auditors. We will also arrange for you to meet major investors in the first twelve months of your appointment.

## Review process

The performance of individual directors and the whole board and its committees is evaluated annually. If, in the interim, there are any matters which cause you concern about your role you should discuss them with the chairman as soon as is appropriate.

## Insurance

The Company has directors' and officers' liability insurance and it is intended to maintain such cover for the full term of your appointment. The current indemnity limit is £ [amount]; a copy of the policy document is attached.

## Independent professional advice

Occasions may arise when you consider that you need professional advice in the furtherance of your duties as a director. Circumstances may occur when it will be appropriate for you to seek advice from independent advisors at the company's expense. A copy of the board's agreed procedure under which directors may obtain such independent advice is attached. The Company will reimburse the full cost of expenditure incurred in accordance with the attached policy.

## Committees

This letter refers to your appointment as a non-executive director of the Company. In the event that you are also asked to serve on one or more of the board committees this will be covered in a separate communication setting out the committee(s)'s terms of reference, any specific responsibilities and any additional fees that may be involved.

This sample appointment letter has been compiled with the assistance of ICSA who have kindly agreed to produce updated guidance on their website www.icsa.org.uk in the future.

## Performance Evaluation Guidance

### Guidance on performance evaluation

This Review recommends that the Code is updated to reflect best practice that the performance of the board a whole, of its committees, and of its members, is evaluated at least once a year. Companies should disclose in their annual report whether such performance evaluation is taking place.

It is the responsibility of the chairman to select an effective process and to act on its outcome. The use of an external third party to conduct the evaluation will bring objectivity to the process.

The evaluation process will be used constructively as a mechanism to improve board effectiveness, maximise strengths and tackle weaknesses. The results of board evaluation should be shared with the board as a whole, while the results of individual assessments should remain confidential between the chairman and the non-executive director concerned.

The following are some of the questions that should be considered in a performance evaluation. They are, however, by no means definitive or exhaustive and companies will wish to tailor the questions to suit their own needs and circumstances.

The responses to these questions and others should enable boards to assess how they are performing and to identify how certain elements of their performance areas might be improved.

### Performance evaluation of the board

- How well has the board performed against any performance objectives that have been set?
- What has been the board's contribution to the testing and development of strategy?
- What has been the board's contribution to ensuring robust and effective risk management?
- Is the composition of the board and its committees appropriate, with the right mix of knowledge and skills to maximise performance in the light of future strategy? Are inside and outside the board relationships working effectively?
- How has the board responded to any problems or crises that have emerged and could or should these have been foreseen?
- Are the matters specifically reserved for the board the right ones?

- How well does the board communicate with the management team, company employees and others? How effectively does it use mechanisms such as the AGM and the annual report?
- Is the board as a whole up to date with latest developments in the regulatory environment and the market?
- How effective are the board's committees? (Specific questions on the performance of each committee should be included such as, for example, their role, their composition and their interaction with the board.)

The processes that help underpin the board's effectiveness should also be evaluated eg:

- Is appropriate, timely information of the right length and quality provided to the board and is management responsive to requests for clarification or amplification? Does the board provide helpful feedback to management on its requirements?
- Are sufficient board and committee meetings of appropriate length held to enable proper consideration of issues? Is time used effectively?
- Are board procedures conducive to effective performance and flexible enough to deal with all eventualities?

In addition, there are some specific issues relating to the chairman which should be included as part of an evaluation of the board's performance eg:

- Is the chairman demonstrating effective leadership of the board?
- Are relationships and communications with shareholders well managed?
- Are relationships and communications within the board constructive?
- Are the processes for setting the agenda working? Do they enable board members to raise issues and concerns?
- Is the company secretary being used appropriately and to maximum value?

## Performance evaluation of the non-executive director

The chairman and other board members should consider the following issues and the individual concerned should also be asked to assess themselves. For each non-executive director:

- How well prepared and informed are they for board meetings and is their meeting attendance satisfactory?
- Do they demonstrate a willingness to devote time and effort to understand the company and its business and a readiness to participate in events outside the boardroom, such as site visits?
- What has been the quality and value of their contributions at board meetings?
- What has been their contribution to development of strategy and to risk management?

445

- How successfully have they brought their knowledge and experience to bear in the consideration of strategy?
- How effectively have they probed to test information and assumptions? Where necessary, how resolute are they in maintaining their own views and resisting pressure from others?
- How effectively and proactively have they followed up their areas of concern?
- How effective and successful are their relationships with fellow board members, the company secretary and senior management? Does their performance and behaviour engender mutual trust and respect within the board?
- How actively and successfully do they refresh their knowledge and skills and are they up to date with:
  - the latest developments in areas such as corporate governance framework and financial reporting?
  - the industry and market conditions?
- How well do they communicate with fellow board members, senior management and others, for example shareholders. Are they able to present their views convincingly yet diplomatically and do they listen and take on board the views of others?

## Building CEO Capital – article from Burson Marsteller – October 25th 2001

NEW YORK, October 25, 2001 – Today's CEOs have little time to prove themselves, according to a new national study released by international communications consulting firm Burson-Marsteller. **Building CEO Capital™**, the 3rd study of influential business stakeholders since 1997, reveals that today's CEO has only five earnings quarters on average to prove him or herself..............

In addition, the Burson-Marsteller study of 1,155 US chief executives, senior managers, financial analysts, institutional investors, business media and government officials confirms that the reputation of the CEO contributes heavily to how companies are perceived today. Nearly half (48%) of a company's reputation is attributed to a CEO's reputation. This is a dramatic rise of 20% from 40% in 1997. This trend is not isolated to the United States. The companion survey among influential stakeholders in the United Kingdom confirms the US findings with 49% attributed to the CEO.

Christopher Komisarjevsky, President and CEO of Burson-Marsteller worldwide. 'Four years of research confirms that the CEO is arguably a company's most critical intangible asset driving the brand and the reputation of the company both internally and externally.'

There are significant returns on investment in CEO reputation. Nearly all business influentials reported that CEO reputation influences their decisions to invest in a company (95%), believe a company under pressure from the media (94%), recommend a company as a good alliance/merger partner (93%), and maintain confidence in a company when its share price is lagging (92%). Moreover, business influentials are more likely to recommend a company as a good place to work (88%) if the CEO is favorably regarded.

'The job of chief executive officer is exceedingly complex and increasingly short-lived,' said Dr. Leslie Gaines-Ross, chief knowledge and research officer of Burson-Marsteller. 'The study, conducted with RoperASW, also found that new CEOs are given, on average, eight months to develop a strategic vision, 19 months to increase share price and 21 months to turn a company around.'

What actions can a CEO take to build and better manage his or her reputation? The new study cited credibility, ethical standards and good internal communications as the leading three drivers of CEO reputation. Credibility has increased in importance since 1997. 'Delivering on promises made is an integral part of how CEOs build and sustain reputation today,' remarked Dr. Gaines-Ross. 'Furthermore, in light of the events of September 11, good CEO communications was put to the highest test as most Americans first heard the tragic news in the workplace. Many employees had a chance to re-evaluate the effectiveness of their CEO's ability to communicate clearly and sincerely.'

Overall, five factors are cited as critical in building CEO capital.

1. Being believable.
2. Demanding high ethical standards.
3. Communicating a clear vision inside the company.
4. Maintaining a high quality top management team.
5. Motivating and inspiring employees.

Surprising to some, increasing shareholder wealth was not among the top five drivers for building CEO reputation. 'Financial performance is often considered a given and a price of entry for CEO favorability,' says Gaines-Ross. 'It is necessary but clearly not all there is to building an admirable CEO reputation.'

## Useful websites

- www.icsa.org.uk
- www.dti.gov.uk/cld/non_exec_review/
- http://www.idpmultimedia.com.au
- www.iod.co.uk
- www.3i.com
- www.boardseat.com
- http://www.boardex.com/

- http://www.conference-board.org/
- http://www.calpers-governance.org/principles/international/
- ceogo.com
- http://www.dti.gov.uk/cld/non_exec_review/

# Table of Statutes

# Table of Statutory Instruments

# Index

453

461

# A complete range of reference works for Company Professionals

## Order Details

| (ty) | Title  ISBN | | Product Code | Unit Price | Total |
|---|---|---|---|---|---|
| | **New Books for 2003** | | | | |
| | Non-Executive Directors Handbook - pub March 03 | 0 7545 1759 4 | NEDH | £59.95 | |
| | Investor Relations Handbook - pub May 03 | 0 7545 1949 X | IRH | £75.00 | |
| | Listing Rules Transaction Processes - pub Sept 03 | 0 7545 2164 8 | LRT | £75.00 | |
| | Director's Remuneration - pub July 03 | 0 7545 2044 7 | TDR | £59.95 | |
| | Business Risk Management - pub Oct 03 | 0 7545 2163 X | BRM | £59.95 | |
| | Effective Credit Control and Debt Recovery - June 03 | 0 7545 2162 1 | ECCDR2 | £64.95 | |
| | **New editions** | | | | |
| | Company Law Handbook 10th edition - March 03+ | 0 7545 1738 1 | CH10 | £59.95 | |
| | Company Secretary's Handbook 13th edition - Nov 03+ | 0 7545 2339 X | CSH13 | £57.00 | |
| | Finance Director's Handbook 3rd edition - Oct 03 | 0 7545 2341 1 | FD3 | £59.95 | |
| | Director's Handbook 3rd edition - Oct 03 | 0 7545 0239 2 | DH3 | £59.95 | |
| | **Looseleafs** | | | | |
| | Business, the Internet and the Law* | 0 7545 1431 5 | BINLMW | £75.00 | |
| | Company Secretarial Procedures and Precedents | 0 406 99645 8 | CSPPMW | £225.00 | |
| | E-Contracts* | 0 7545 1504 4 | ECOMW | £80.00 | |
| | **Other (backlist)** | | | | |
| | Data Protection Handbook 2nd edition | 0 7545 1938 4 | DPH2 | £57.00 | |
| | Corporate Governance Handbook | 0 7545 1626 1 | CGH | £59.95 | |
| | Commercial Contracts | 0 7545 1948 1 | SPAPG | £59.95 | |
| | Company Secretary's Checklists | 0 7545 1897 3 | CSCK | £39.95 | |
| | Domain Names | 0 7545 1491 9 | DNPG | £39.95 | |
| | Start-Ups: Law and Business | 0 7545 1509 5 | SLBH | £59.95 | |
| | Company Acquisitions Handbook 6th edition | 0 7545 1262 2 | TPGCA6 | £52.00 | |
| | Personal Service Companies: A Practical Guide 2nd edition | 0 7545 1516 8 | PSCPG2 | £42.95 | |
| | Insurance Handbook 2nd edition | 0 7545 0744 0 | IH2 | £49.00 | |
| | SME Handbook | 0 7545 1275 4 | SME01 | £45.00 | |
| | Company Meetings Handbook | 0 7545 0211 2 | CMH01 | £49.95 | |
| | Data Protection Act | 0 7545 0135 3 | DPA | £40.00 | |
| | **Online package** | | | | |
| | www.companyserviceonline.com | | CSRB | £399.00 | |

Total amount due

## ❸ Confirm Delivery Details

-mail _____

ame _____

ob Title _____

iompany _____

iddress _____

_____

_____

ostcode _____ Tel _____

## ❸ Make Payment Choice

exisNexis Butterworths Tolley account, no. _____

r by credit card as follows: ☐ Mastercard ☐ Amex ☐ Visa

ly credit card no. is _____

nd its expiry date is _____

r with the attached cheque for £_____
(made payable to **LexisNexis Butterworths Tolley**)

ly VAT registration no. is _____

☐ Please supply the above product(s) with a 21 day money back guarantee (EU countries only)

ignature/Date _____

## ❹ Return Your Order

### Freepost
Nick King Marketing Department Butterworths Tolley
FREEPOST 6983, London WC2A 1BR

### Phone
Please phone Customer Services on: +44 (0)20 8662 2000

### Fax
Please fax your order to: +44 (0)20 8662 2012

### Online Bookshop
Visit our Online Catalogue and Bookshop at
www.lexisnexis.co.uk to order securely online.

### Bookshop
You can also order copies via our specialist bookshop which stocks a wide range of our titles. It is based at 35 Chancery Lane, London WC2A 1EL, nearest tubes are Chancery Lane and Temple.
www.lexisnexis.co.uk

☐ If you do NOT wish to be kept informed by mail of other LexisNexis products and services, please tick here.

☐ If you do NOT wish your mailing details to be passed on to companies approved by LexisNexis, to keep you Informed of their products and services, please tick here.

### * Pay As You Go (PAYG)
I understand that I will continue to receive, until countermanded, future updating material issued in connection with this work and will be invoiced for these issues when I receive them.

### 21 Day Money Back Guarantee
The book(s)/product(s) mentioned on this order form, are available in EU countries only with 21 days money back guarantee. This allows you to try it/them out and assess its/their usefulness before buying. If you should decide not to purchase the book(s) /product(s), simply return it/them to us in good condition and your invoice will be cancelled and any payment made refunded All orders placed with us are subject to our standard terms of trade, available on request and with the invoice. The book(s/product(s) detailed on this order form is/are intended to be (a) general reference guide(s) to the law and cannot be (a) substitute(s) for legal advice.

**+We are pleased to be able offer you these titles on an annual subscription basis. Simply tick the appropriate box below.**

☐ Please send me the above title(s). I understand that I will be sent all future editions automatically on publication, with a 10% discount. I am at liberty to cancel this arrangement at any time, or return the book if it does not meet with my requirements.

☐ Please send me the above title(s). I do not wish to participate in the subscription scheme, however, please advise me when a new edition becomes available.

# www.lexisnexis.co.uk
Thank you for your order, prices are subject to change without notice.

LexisNexis™ UK  35 Chancery Lane  London WC2A 1EL  A division of Reed Elsevier (UK) Ltd
Registered office  25 Victoria Street  London SW1H 0EX
Registered in England number 2746621 VAT Registered No. GB 730 8595 20